ALSO BY *Kate Moses*

Wintering: A Novel of Sylvia Plath

. . .

WITH *Camille Peri*

Mothers Who Think:
Tales of Real-Life Parenthood

Because I Said So:
33 Mothers Write About Children, Sex, Men,
Aging, Faith, Race & Themselves

CAKEWALK

CAKEWALK

a memoir

KATE MOSES

THE DIAL PRESS
New York

Copyright © 2010 by Kate Moses

Published in the United States by The Dial Press,
an imprint of The Random House Publishing Group,
a division of Random House, Inc., New York.

DIAL PRESS is a registered trademark of Random House, Inc.,
and the colophon is a trademark of Random House, Inc.

Grateful acknowledgment is made to the following for permission to
reprint previously published material:

HarperCollins Publishers: Excerpts from *A Birthday for Frances* by Russell Hoban,
copyright © 1968 by Russell C. Hoban; *Bread and Jam for Frances* by Russell
Hoban, copyright © 1964 by Russell C. Hoban and renewed 1992 by Russell C. Hoban;
and *A Baby Sister for Frances* by Russell Hoban, copyright © 1964 by Russell
Hoban and renewed 1992 by Russell Hoban. Reprinted by permission
of HarperCollins Publishers.

David Higham Associates: Excerpts from "Lorna Doone, Last Cookie
Song" in *Egg Thoughts and Other Frances Songs* by Russell Hoban
(HarperCollins Publishers), copyright © 1972 by Russell Hoban.
Reprinted by permission of David Higham Associates.

J. A. Zynczak, Inc.: "Love You," words and music by Sandra Dedrick and
Joe Zynczak, copyright © 1969 by Almitra Music. All rights reserved.
Reprinted by permission of J. A. Zynczak, Inc.

LIBRARY OF CONGRESS CATALOGING-IN-PUBLICATION DATA
Moses, Kate.
Cakewalk : a memoir / Kate Moses.
p.   cm.
ISBN 978-0-385-34298-8
EBOOK ISBN 978-0-440-33838-3
1. Moses, Kate. 2. Moses, Kate—Childhood and youth. 3. Women authors,
American—Biography. 4. Authors, American—Biography. 5. Desserts—
United States. 6. Cookery, American. I. Title.
PS3613.O779C35   2010
813'.6—dc22
[B]   2009033931

Printed in the United States of America on acid-free paper
www.dialpress.com
2 4 6 8 9 7 5 3 1
FIRST EDITION
Book design by Barbara M. Bachman

Give a little time for the child within you
Don't be afraid to be young and free.
Undo the locks and throw away the keys
and take off your shoes and socks, and run, you.

Run through the meadow and scare up the milking cows
Run down the beach kicking clouds of sand.
Walk a windy weather day, feel your face blow away
Stop and listen, love you.

Be like a circus clown, put away your circus frown;
Ride on a roller coaster upside down
Waltzing Mathilda, Carrie loves a kinkajoo,
Joey catch a kangaroo, hug you.

Dandelion, milkweed, silky on a sunny sky,
Reach out and hitch a ride and float on by;
Balloons down below blooming colors of the rainbow,
red, blue and yellow-green I love you.

Bicycles, tricycles, ice cream, candy
Lolly pops, popsicles, licorice sticks.
Solomon Grundy, Raggedy Andy
Tweedledum and Tweedledee, home free.

Cowboys and Indians, puppy dogs and sand pails,
Beach balls and baseballs and basketballs, too.
I love forget-me-nots, fluffernutter sugar pops
I'll hug you and kiss you and love you.

—*"LOVE YOU" BY THE FREE DESIGN, 1969*

CONTENTS

CAKEWALK

Let Them Eat Cake

I HELD MY ARMS UP HIGH, HONEY-COLORED HAIR TUMBLING TO my waist, eyes squinched shut against the scratchy fall of new fabric, and my mother pulled the dress she'd made for me all the way down over my head. I was not quite four, and I'd been invited over to play for the first time by a child who lived across the street.

It was 1965 in Palo Alto, California, a sleepy middle-class suburb of shiny modern Eichler homes and leaf-shaded cul-de-sacs like the one we'd just moved to, full of young hopeful families like ours. My dad was a brand-new lawyer working hard to prove himself at his first job; my mother, who'd dropped out of college to get married, was a housewife raising three children under the age of five. People told her she looked just like a young Elizabeth Taylor, she looked just like Jackie Kennedy, and she did, but even prettier. She had wanted to be an artist, her relentless creativity redirected into sewing curtains and clothes for our family, gardening, teaching herself to reupholster hand-me-down furniture, concocting elaborate birthday parties and messy art projects for my brothers and me. That day she was still unpacking boxes and, I suspect, as relieved to have one of us out of the house for an hour or two as she was anxious to make a good impression on our new neighbors.

She brushed my long hair and tied it with a bow to one side, princess-style, then crouched in front of me, curving her elegant hands on either side of my ribs, rocking me playfully and smoothing my dress, which matched the one she'd made for herself—mother-and-daughter dresses in red-and-black paisley, rickrack sewn along the hems. And before me, her face: eager, lovely, her wide green eyes coy and glittering, as if she knew some secret she'd share eventually, and if I was the lucky one, only with me. Her black hair was so soft and fine it felt like baby's hair, softer and far darker than mine or my brothers'. Her smile was both excited and encouraging.

"Ready, Cis?" she asked.

I was named after my mother, but nobody in my family ever called me Kathleen, not once; it is still a name I hardly recognize as my own. I was called Cissy, the sister, though my mother had other roles for me, other nicknames. "You're my Little Mommy," she declared when I brought a damp cloth for her head; she'd been crying on our sofa in graduate student housing, pregnant with the baby who became my younger brother, the third baby in three years. "You take good care of me," she said, accepting a bite of the cookie I held to her mouth, "you're my best friend." I was her best friend—I'd been chosen, I was important. "We're the only girls. We have to stick together."

Little Mommy, best friend, the only girl, the sister. Now I was the family ambassador. My mother took my hand and trotted me across our Palo Alto street, swinging my arm under the movie blue sky, the omniscient camera's wide-angle lens capturing the picture-perfect scene of our idyllic neighborhood, our charming family, the beautiful talented young mother and her compliant tidy daughter, the little mommy taking good care.

The neighbor girl's name is a blank to me, and I can't recall what we played. What I remember is the two of us lured to her kitchen by the intoxicating odor of caramelized sugar, and finding that her mother had vanished. What remained was a ceramic baking dish on the countertop breathing out hot, honeyed scent. There was a ring of burnt brown paper holding up a mound of what looked like burnished swirls of cloud. And that glorious smell! We leaned in from either side of the counter, perched on barstools on our bare knees, our noses almost touching the crisp edge of the paper.

We knew it would be wrong to eat whatever excelsior thing this was. But we leaned in farther, our toes flexed on the seats of the canting barstools, our elbows on the countertop of that spotless avocado-green kitchen, at first promising each other that we would only have a taste. A cloud of hesitation passed across the little girl's face. And this is where the story starts to become mine.

Just one taste, I assured her. Each.

I remember turning toward the sound of the little girl's mother pausing in the doorway to her kitchen, the sharp sound of her gasp: a laundry basket under her arm, her eyes as wide as mine must have been. The neighbor girl's hand and my own were wrist-deep in the dish, wiping out the last moist flecks with our fingertips. We had eaten the entire succulent, mellifluous thing with our hands, and we'd licked the paper clean, too.

What was that? I was thinking as I burst out the neighbor girl's front door and skittered across her lawn, her mother still on the phone shrieking to my mother, my sticky hair flying behind me and my stiff new dress flapping, my mother erupting out of our house across the street and running toward me, a look of abject mortification on her heart-shaped face.

I knew I had been very bad. I knew I was going to be punished, maybe even spanked. But I didn't care. Whatever it was, whatever that voluptuous thing was, it had been worth it. *What was it?* I was still wondering later, after my father had come home. That baked thing, that glazed and golden and sumptuous thing—I wanted it again. And again. And again. I lay on my bed, my bottom sore, sucking the last ambrosial flavor from my candied hair.

IT'S NOT THAT I'D never had cake or cookies or candy or ice cream before. Sugar was the mainstay of my diet as a child, present in some abundant form at virtually every meal. My family ate sugar morning, noon, and night: Apple butter oozed out of the omelets, Ding Dongs and soda cans rolled around in our lunchboxes, foil-sealed packets of honey were served alongside the Kentucky Fried Chicken we ate for dinner in front of the TV, before we proceeded inexorably to dessert. My mother stockpiled soft drinks by the case and Halloween-sized bags of candy year-round in our garage, regularly replenishing a freezer the dimensions of a Roman tomb with stacked boxes of packaged snack cakes, frozen pies, and gallon tubs of ice cream. Even my father, whose personal austerity rivaled that of any Buddhist monk, was a donut pusher who kept Baby Ruth bars under the rolled-up socks in his underwear drawer. At six I dreamt one night that I awoke in the bedroom I shared with my younger brother, and by the blue light of the moon shining through our window I opened every bureau drawer and found them overflowing with a pirate's booty of pink-frosted cupcakes and candy necklaces and pinwheel lolly pops and candy apples glittering like enormous red gemstones. I doubted I'd ever have a more rapturous dream.

As my childhood unfolded, sweetness of the less tangible variety was harder to come by. My parents were disastrously mismatched, too preoccupied by their individual misery and desperate compensations to recognize what havoc they were wreaking on our family. It was one thing to be surrounded by cataracts of sugar, day in, day out; it was quite another to think you had a right to enjoy it, or anything else. I looked for sweetness wherever I could find it.

All my life I've been teased for my cake obsession, my compulsive sweet tooth, my therapeutic baking, my repetitive and single-minded quests for the perfect pound cake or the perfect shortbread, my judgment of neighborhoods and vacation spots based on the quality of the local bakeries as much as the local bookstores. Here and there I've found allies, but mostly I've had to fight off a feeling of furtive criminality when it comes to cake: my baking of it, eating of it, wanting it.

And then I discovered Frances, the whimsical cake-loving heroine of Russell Hoban's sixties-era series of children's books about a family of badgers. I didn't find Frances until my son was too old for storybooks, but my daughter, then two, was ripe for hearing the same book read to her ad nauseam, and *Bedtime for Frances* was what she wanted. Why I never read Frances when I was a kid I don't know, but I sometimes think it could have saved me years of grief if I had. "Aren't you worried that maybe I will get sick and all my teeth will fall out from eating so much bread and jam?" Frances asks her mother after several meals of bread-and-jam on demand. "I don't think that will happen for quite a while," replies her mother. "So eat it all up and enjoy it."

I had been waiting almost forty years to hear those words. *Eat it all up and enjoy it*—that's what they do in the Frances stories, as I discovered when I brought home the other six books to read to my daughter. In every book, there was cake or custard or candy or some other sweet, always offered generously, even nonchalantly. No matter the story, no matter the dilemma Frances faces, a literal taste of sweetness is the grace note to life.

Frances, I realized, is an embodiment of the possibility that what seems excessive—a baby's first taste of ice cream, baking a cake for a friend for no reason, gingerbread houses, and taking pleasure in those things for their own sake—might actually be essential, like poetry and birdsong. And sweetness, she reminded me, is never more powerful than when we have known its absence. After the birth of a new sibling results in too little attention and a dearth of raisins for breakfast oatmeal, Mother Badger coaxes a disgruntled Frances out from under the dining table with the reassuring promise "You may be sure that there will always be plenty of chocolate cake around here."

At the heart of Frances's stories is the age-old challenge of childhood, and adulthood, too: joining the human race. To read about Frances is to watch her jostle her thwarted desires and conflicting feelings with all the awkwardness and yearning that I felt myself when I was small, and all too frequently when I got bigger. The title of *A Birthday for Frances* is itself a sly comment on the evolution of Frances's ego and superego against the tidal pull of her id, since the birthday in question is her little sister's. Frances's jealousy manifests itself in pitiful asides to her imaginary friend ("That is how it is, Alice . . . your birthday is always the one that is not now"), kicks under the table, and a long memory for past slights. An epic struggle ensues in Frances's tormented conscience when the cake is carried glowing to the party table. She can't bear to give up the coveted Chompo candy bar that is her present for little Gloria and sings under her breath, "Happy Chompo to me / is how it ought to be. . . ." It takes the entire party's encouragement to get her to relinquish the candy. Reading this scene, I could not help but think of the fateful moment in my neighbor's kitchen in Palo Alto, the other little girl and I poised to dig our fingers into the tawny, sugar-flecked crust of her mother's steaming confection. *Just one taste,* I told her, the battle already as lost as Thermopylae.

I almost couldn't bear reading the last Frances book, *Egg Thoughts and Other Frances Songs,* for the very reason that it was the last. There would be no more of her stories to lay alongside mine, offering me a chance to revisit the impetuous voluptuary I'd been, the curious little girl leaning over a warm cake in a stranger's kitchen, caught in a moment of heedless delight. Frances's impulsive, lustily belted-out songs, her free-flowing compositions on the puzzlements and wonders of life, are another way in which she has been my alter ego. My creations were not songs like hers, but poems and stories and memories I started shaping as soon as I could read and write, glimpses of lives I'd imagine myself into, glimpses of my own, the delicious taste of words the only thing I can compare to the incorruptible gratification of a stolen cake when I was three.

That melding of words and recollected sweetness is the impulse behind my favorite of Frances's songs, the one that to me sums up not just the gestalt of Frances but maybe life, too. Who else but pensive Frances would immortalize the humble appreciation of eating the final, plain cookie, the one left behind after all the good ones have been taken?

LORNA DOONE, LAST COOKIE SONG

All the sandwich cookies sweet
In their frilly paper neat
They are gone this afternoon,
They have left you, Lorna Doone . . .

You are plain and you are square
And your flavor's only fair.
Soon there'll be an empty place
Where we saw your smiling face.

Lorna Doone, Lorna Doone,
You were last but you weren't wasted.
Lorna Doone, Lorna Doone,
We'll remember how you tasted.

Life does not always reward us with the best cookie in the box, or the happiest family; sometimes you take what you get and make the best of it. In my case, that's where imagination came in as handily as learning how to bake. For both of those lifesavers, I have my confusing, painful, unforgettable childhood to thank. Which makes me wonder if my cake obsession, really, is not much more than my struggle to find a way to redeem with sweetness those moments that left, however bitter on occasion, such a lasting taste in my mouth.

Every child knows that you hang on to what makes you feel good. I just know that Frances is out there somewhere, and she's doing fine. She's got a son in college who will call just to tell her it's snowing. She still makes up little songs, and now her daughter sings along. Frances wishes she had a green thumb like her mother, but she'll settle for flowers on the table and a thick novel to read with her feet up, a sleepy dog resting his head on her lap. The spooks of her sleepless nights don't bother her anymore. And I know there's always plenty of cake at her house. Mine, too.

PLENTY OF CHOCOLATE CAKE WITH MOCHA FROSTING

∴

Small amount of unsweetened cocoa
6 ounces unsweetened chocolate (or bittersweet in a pinch)
3 cups light brown sugar
2¼ cups milk, at room temperature
3 cups unbleached all-purpose flour
1½ teaspoons baking soda
¾ teaspoon salt
¾ cup unsalted butter, at room temperature
5 large egg yolks, at room temperature
1½ tablespoons vanilla

• Preheat the oven to 350°. Butter three 8- or 9-inch round cake pans and dust with cocoa rather than flour, knocking out the excess.
• Melt the chocolate with 1½ cups of the brown sugar in ¾ cup of the milk over low heat or in a microwave, and let cool. Combine the flour, baking soda, and salt in the bowl of an electric mixer. Add the butter, yolks, vanilla, remaining 1½ cups brown sugar, and remaining 1½ cups milk. Beat on the lowest speed until blended, then beat at medium speed for 2 minutes, stopping to scrape the bowl and beaters a couple of times. Stir together the cooled chocolate mixture until uniform, then add it to the bowl and beat for 1 minute; the batter should become creamy and smooth. Divide the batter among the three pans and bake for about 25 to 30 minutes, or until the cake springs back when lightly touched and a toothpick inserted into the center comes out clean. Cool 10 minutes in the pans, then turn onto a rack to cool completely.

Makes one three-layer 8- or 9-inch cake, enough to serve 10 to 12.

MOCHA FROSTING

1½ cups unsalted butter, at room temperature
½ teaspoon salt
1½ pounds confectioners' sugar
½ cup heavy cream
3 tablespoons instant espresso
¼ cup unsweetened cocoa
2 teaspoons vanilla

• Beat the butter for a minute or two on medium speed, then add the salt and gradually add the confectioners' sugar, increasing the mixer speed to high when it is all added. Beat for another 5 minutes, until very creamy.

• Combine the cream, instant espresso, cocoa, and vanilla in a small bowl, stirring into a smooth paste. Add to the butter mixture and beat for 5 minutes more, adding small amounts of cream, a spoonful at a time, if the frosting is too thick.

Makes enough for a three-layer cake.

VARIATIONS

For cupcakes: Fill lined cupcake tins about two-thirds full and bake for about
   20 minutes. Makes about 36 cupcakes.

For a sheet cake: Butter a 10½-by-15½-inch baking pan and dust with cocoa,
   knocking out excess. Bake the cake for 35 to 40 minutes.

FROSTING VARIATIONS

For Light Chocolate Frosting, omit instant espresso from the recipe
   for Mocha Frosting.

For Simple Vanilla or Chocolate Buttercream, see pages 42 and 43.

For Fluffy White Frosting, see page 72.

For Almond Joy Cake with Fluffy White Frosting and Coconut Filling,
   see page 73.

For Creamy Chocolate Frosting, see page 210.

Treats and Threats

A CHOCOLATE BAR, SALTED PEANUTS, AND A BEER: THESE, MY MOTHER often told my brothers and me when we were kids, were the elements of a nutritionally perfect meal, the key to enduring any dire circumstance. No odyssey should be undertaken, no war should be waged, no suitcase should be packed without this emergency trinity. Individual packets of M&M's were essential for long rides in the car and other occasions of ordinary maternal bribery, but armed with chocolate bars, peanuts, and beer, you could survive anything. My mother drilled her recipe for extremis into our heads so authoritatively that I assumed it was part of the instructions given out in the glove compartment handbook that came with new cars.

On her seventieth birthday my mother stumbled over the memory that had planted this idea. We were in her kitchen in Las Vegas, preparing her birthday dinner with my two brothers and one of her sisters. My mom hadn't meant to illuminate any great mysteries; she's always been better at magic realism than logical explanations. She was just telling a story—she's spent her life telling stories—but now, at least one inexplicable leitmotif from my childhood began to make sense. Within days of the bombing of Pearl Harbor, her father's San Francisco business was requisitioned by the government. In return for the appropriation of his metallurgy lab, my grandfather, a chemical engineer, was made a civilian contractor to the navy. By mid-December of 1941 he was working in Pennsylvania, and my grandmother was packing up their house and preparing to take their two small children across country by train.

Up and down the Pacific coast people were jumpy, rumors flying about pending air attacks, enemy landings along remote California beaches, Japanese fishermen mining the waters. Neighborhood watches had been set up, and one night a man went door to door on my grand-parents' street in San Francisco's Ingleside District, telling everyone to lock themselves in their basements: Someone had seen a submarine periscope surfacing in San Francisco Bay.

By flashlight behind blackout curtains, my grandmother opened her suitcase in the basement and brought out Hershey bars and Planters roasted peanuts, and my three-year-old mother and her six-year-old brother and my grandmother had a party. Not until she was seventy did it occur to my mom that her mother had not kept a perpetual stash of chocolate and peanuts. "She was packed for the train to Pennsylvania. Frankie and I already had dog tags with our names on them. She must have had the chocolate and the peanuts for the trip."

"But what about the beer?" I asked my mother.

"Beer . . . ," my mom repeated, cocking her head and rapping a refrigerated canister of Pillsbury bread dough on the counter. We watched as the dough plumped over the split sides of the cardboard.

My family has been scattered since my brothers and I went away to college. The celebration of my mother's seventieth was the only time in the last fifteen years that Billy and John and I have all been together in the same room with her, and I can count the number of times I've seen her since I was twenty-two.

It suits her, Las Vegas, a fantasy playland blooming in the middle of a desert, a city of glitter and make-believe and outrageous hope against unbeatable odds, where she lives in a house with a garden view of the blinking neon sizzle of the Strip. I don't think she's painted or drawn or remade an old prom dress into a Martha Washington Halloween cos-tume in twenty-five years, but she's finally the artist of her own life, a postmodern assemblage of memory and possibilities. Her paintings, the ones she did when I was a child, cover the walls gallery-style, and the closets are full of Victorian velvet dresses that belonged to her grandmothers, and antique dolls wrapped in yellowed tissue. There's an entire room dedicated to arts and crafts supplies, everything pristine in their unopened packages—glue guns and gesso and paintbrushes, little packets of sequins and pompoms—and the rest of the cupboards in the house are packed with cartons of freebies from the casinos, mul-tiples of stuff she doesn't need but brings home anyway: dish sets, cof-feemakers, tool kits, his-and-hers bathrobes. Rice-a-Roni, Hamburger

Helper, Bisquick, canned cranberry sauce and potatoes, boxes of onion soup mix and cake mix and bottled lemon juice—despite being raised on a farm, or perhaps because of it, my mom has a deep and abiding loyalty to convenience foods, and all the flavors I grew up with still cram the shelves of her apocalyptic pantry.

Her memory of her childhood is just as astonishingly crowded. She remembers the addresses of every place she's ever lived, the names of all the nuns at her Catholic girls' school, her naughty boy cousins cutting off her hair while she sat on a potty chair in the yard and waved to passing motorists. She remembers everything she ever saw or heard or did or had. Her memory for my childhood, though, is more like the "lace dress" she made when she was a toddler: airy and full of holes. While my grandmother was in the bath one morning, my two-year-old mom took a pair of cuticle scissors to her mother's best silk slip, then floated it out the second-story window because she was sure it would be so pretty.

"You know, Mom," I prompted her, " 'chocolate bars, peanuts, and beer'—you told us that was the perfect meal."

"Your mother has always thought out of the box," my aunt said, nodding to my brothers and me. "Did she ever tell you how she accidentally turned off all the electricity in Bloomingdale's department store when she was five?"

"The perfect meal," my mom repeated absently. "I don't remember ever saying that. . . ."

THERE WAS THE STORY of my maternal grandmother being lifted from bed one night in childhood, waking to her father's shuddering embrace, her nightgown smeared with blood. My great-grandfather was a baseball player with the San Francisco Seals who drove an ambulance in the off-season, a job he hated. He'd just come from the morgue, his passenger a child who'd been struck by a cable car, a little girl the same age as his five-year-old daughter.

There was the story of my great-grandmother tying my three-year-old grandfather and his infant brother to a tree in Golden Gate Park after the 1906 earthquake. She was newly widowed, with no other way to keep her baby boys safe and save the belongings in their house; she took her sons across the street to the park and tied them to a tree trunk, then ran home to toss all of their things out of the windows, watching the roiling black smoke cloud of the Great Fire as it burned westward.

There were my mother's cousins, the notorious Reilly boys, who lit all the tree candles on Christmas morning to surprise their parents, but in the process set the drapes on fire. The family escaped with nothing but a single children's chair as their Victorian burned to the ground. There were other family stories about stepfathers assassinated in Death Valley, favorite dolls unwittingly named after baby sisters who'd died at birth, Russian princesses facing firing squads with jewels sewn into their skirts.

There were fairy tales of orphans expiring on the brink of rescue, disfigured one-eyed children, foolish boys drowning puppies accidentally; storybooks about virtuous girls contracting fatal diseases during acts of charity, leaving their toys to the poor. No matter how alarming or tragic, stories were my family's currency, our inheritance. I was greedy for stories, their insulin rush. I craved them like candy. My imagination's taste trained on their melancholy flavor, as familiar and inoculating as serum on a sugar cube, the sweet and the bitter so inseparable I could hardly tell the difference.

There was the little boy who broke his neck jumping off an ottoman while playing Superman, a dishtowel safety-pinned to his shoulders. We still lived in graduate student housing when my older brother, Billy, and I heard that story as we chased each other through the living room with dishtowels safety-pinned to our shoulders. My father was finishing law school at the time, my little brother, John, just a baby. There was John himself, deemed "accident prone" by my parents: two times breaking his collarbone while climbing out of his crib. Spurting blood from a nick on his ear when he turned his head as my mother trimmed his hair while he sat in the high chair. Later there would be emergency room visits after he repeatedly ate the snail poison our parents sprinkled under the cherry tree in the backyard of our Palo Alto house. And stitches and a blackened tooth from falling off a log pile during a Fourth of July picnic when we lived in Sonoma. We called him John-John. He was born three months after another little boy with that name had saluted his father's coffin at the slain president's funeral.

There was the missing baby that our father, only a child himself at the time, found floating at the bottom of a well in Australia. Billy's best friend in second grade, a little blond girl who went deaf from the measles. The youngest child in a neighbor's family, drowned in a riptide during a trip to the ocean. The Clutter teenagers, murdered in their beds in a book our mother left lying casually around, *In Cold Blood*. The children menaced by the Zodiac Killer, who, the newspaper said, had threatened to shoot out the tires of a school bus in a town only miles from our own.

"If the Zodiac Killer ever shot out the tires of your school bus," my ardent mother told us, spooning out bowls of molten chocolate pudding, cutting hot squares of apple cake with its streusel still sizzling, handing us just-baked sugar cookies straight from the spatula, "I'd say, 'Shoot me instead, don't hurt my children!' " We puffed our cheeks and blew, watched as steam rose off our spoons, tossed cookies back and forth in our fingers, but we were never patient enough; we burned our mouths so badly the skin peeled off our palates. "If a robber broke into our house and tied us all up," our mother would say as we fanned our cauterized tongues, "I'd tell him, 'Murder me instead, don't murder my children!' " Or if our house caught fire, or a boat we were on capsized, or a tsunami curled above our heads; if a blizzard or a plane crash or a meteor hurtled dispassionately toward us, she would be there, she reminded us often, standing between us and fateful calamity, senseless misfortune, strangers who meant us harm.

"Mom," my eleven-year-old daughter calls to me one idle summer Sunday, seeking me out in the kitchen, where I'm grating orange peel over a bowl of blueberries for a coffee cake, trying not to grate my knuckles as well as the orange. "Mom, did you know the words 'treat' and 'threat' are separated by just one letter?"

WHEN MY MOTHER met my father, he was about as exotic as anyone she'd ever come across. He was in law school at the same Jesuit college where she was a nineteen-year-old coed. The oldest daughter of an Irish Catholic family that lived on the outskirts of a small agricultural town south of San Francisco, she came from people who had made their way to the California territory five generations back, settling on the windswept coast of Northern California and then in what would become San Francisco around the time of the Gold Rush.

Educated from the age of eight at a no-nonsense convent school, my mother had always been whimsical, a capricious free spirit. How perplexing she must have been to her practical, absentminded mother and moody, disciplinarian father: my mother of the lace dress and the potty-chair haircut, who asked the butcher for an ox tail to tie to her waist so she could pretend to be a cow, who nailed alphabet blocks to the heels of her Mary Janes so she could tap-dance, who painted a pet chicken's toenails and taught it to march up and down on the piano keys before it ended up in a Sunday stew—much to her dismay. In high school my mom was the one caught smoking in the lavatory by the nuns; they rapped her knuckles with rulers and sent her to detention. They ripped up her fanciful drawings, admonishing her, "You must have copied that, Kathleen Hills."

I've never asked my mother what she studied during her two years of college, but I do not doubt that if she could have chosen a life for herself, it would have been bohemian, at least as seen through the narrow aperture of small-town California in the 1950s. Perhaps when she met my father, she thought that's what he could give her. He wasn't like the other boys she knew, the ones who lived pretty much the same life she did, under a judgmental parental thumb attached to the condemning hand of the church.

My father was a foreigner, he had minimal contact with his family, and he wasn't Catholic. He was born in Kobe, the son of a British family in the diplomatic service in Japan. He'd escaped with his parents and siblings to Australia when World War II broke out, returning alone to Yokohama for boarding school when the war ended. His parents had stayed in Melbourne, his father failing at running a potato chip factory, his mother an invalid with five children at the age of twenty-nine, after a stroke. My dad was raised mostly by proxy. He first sat down to dinner alone with his parents when he was seventeen and about to leave for Georgetown University in the States.

My parents' personalities and attitudes to the world were so at odds I can't imagine what else would have drawn them together but a colossal misapprehension. My father as a young man was serious, ambitious, and reserved, so desirous of fitting in and conforming to American culture that the first thing he did upon arriving in the U.S. was to work on losing his accent. But somehow my gregarious, optimistic mother must have convinced herself that my father was her ticket to an unpredictable life—he was even, it turned out, a little bit genuinely Japanese on his mother's side, fascinatingly but unthreateningly so, since you'd never know it to look at his pale blue eyes and blond crew cut. My introverted, repressed father, who longed for stability and routine, must have believed he'd found them in my mother, a well-brought-up farm girl who could sew and garden and use power tools and, as a bonus, had the looks of a matinee starlet.

My mother told the story, many times, of why they married: She'd apologized that she couldn't accept my future father's proposal unless he converted to Catholicism. When he did, she'd later tell her audience, which often included Billy and John and me, "He converted, so I had to marry him!" It seemed a funny story, the kind of teasingly self-mocking anecdote that married couples tell on themselves. When I was older—twelve or thirteen, by which time desperate unhappiness showed even on my mother's extraordinary face—she told me the rest of the story. Panicked on the night before her wedding, realizing she hardly knew her fiancé, my mother begged her parents to help her get out of the marriage. She was standing on a chair while my grandmother measured the hem of her going-away dress. She wanted to be an artist, my mother sobbed, she didn't want to get married; couldn't my grandparents call off the wedding and buy her a plane ticket to Paris? My grandmother had curlers in her hair and pins in her mouth. "Don't be ridiculous," my grandmother said through pursed lips, holding the pins steady. "The caterers will be arriving first thing in the morning, and the cake is already made."

SNIPPED THREAD AND BITS of eyelet and women's voices snowed down: At four I sat cross-legged beneath my grandmother's foot-pedal sewing machine, my lap filled with miniature candy bars, gathering fabric scraps as my mother sewed and she, her mother, and her sisters told stories to each other. We were at my grandparents' farm, upstairs in the sewing room, a converted tank house with sloping walls reached by a staircase through the kitchen pantry, where my retired-schoolteacher grandmother kept candy bars as rewards, she'd told me, for children who were learning to read and write. My redheaded grandmother's hair, ready for the beauty parlor, was flattened to her skull under a net, and my mother's fine dark hair was tied back under a scarf as she hemmed her sister's trousseau. My youngest aunt, a classic sixties bride-to-be, stood in the half-light of the doorway hugging herself in a creamy slip, pin curls slicked to her temples with beautician's tape.

Like De Chirico's disquieting muses, their heads nodded and nodded above me, their voices rising and falling in a harmony of family legend, each of them picking up the dramatic tension in turn, threads of stories left momentarily slack. Even the funny stories were inevitably dark: The gorilla who spit in the face of my lipsticked teenage mother during a high school field trip. The Mexican maid who tried to steal Aunt Patrice as a baby after burnishing her skin with walnut oil. The Reilly boys settling an argument by breaking a watermelon over the head of an elderly neighbor. The dead dog stuffed in a suitcase and ferried to the middle of the bay for burial at sea, but when the family lost their nerve on the crowded boat and toted the suitcase back home, inside they found somebody's pot roast.

I was the captive and anticipating audience, the listener and prompter, sitting at my mother's feet with scraps of dotted Swiss. *Tell the story about Pa's Dalmatians fighting the bears at the zoo. Tell the story about painting the chicken's toenails before it was cooked into stew.* I'll be a storyteller, too, I told myself, folding bits of limp fabric into pages, into books, chocolate and peanuts filling my mouth.

HILLS FAMILY SUGAR COOKIE CUTOUTS

∴

3½ cups unbleached all-purpose flour
1 teaspoon baking powder
¾ teaspoon salt
1 cup unsalted butter, at room temperature
1½ cups granulated sugar
2 large eggs, at room temperature
1½ teaspoons vanilla

• Sift the flour with baking powder and salt in a medium-sized bowl. Using an electric mixer, cream the butter for a full minute, then add the sugar and beat at medium speed until light, about 5 minutes. Beat in eggs and vanilla until fluffy and very light, another 2 to 4 minutes. With a wooden spoon gradually work the flour into the creamed mixture. Divide the dough into two portions and wrap in waxed paper or plastic wrap. Refrigerate until firm, at least several hours or overnight.

•   Heat the oven to 400°. On a floured surface, roll out the dough to ¼ inch thick, using more flour for the rolling pin, sprinkled on the dough, and additionally on the floured surface as needed to prevent sticking. Cut into desired shapes with cookie cutters and place on cookie sheets. This dough works beautifully if gathered and rerolled; if it gets too soft, chill for about 15 minutes.

•   Refrigerate or freeze the cut-out cookies on their baking sheets for 10 to15 minutes so they will retain their firm edges as they bake; if you're in a hurry, go ahead and bake the cookies immediately. Bake for 5 to 8 minutes or until cookies are puffed and only just barely starting to brown at the edges: Start with the shortest amount of time and watch carefully, especially with very small cookies. As the cookies are fragile right out of the oven, let cool slightly before moving to a wire rack to cool completely.

•   When cool, glaze and decorate as desired.

Makes up to 6 dozen cookies, depending on the size. This recipe can be easily doubled or tripled.

SUGAR COOKIE GLAZE

1 egg white
Pinch of salt
A few drops of vegetable oil
Up to 1 pound of confectioners' sugar
1 to 3 tablespoons of cream

•   Whisk the egg white and salt until loosened and beginning to foam. Add oil, confectioners' sugar, and cream gradually and whisk, adding more sugar and cream until the glaze is of spreading consistency: You want it to be thin enough to spread easily over the cookies to their edges, but not so thin it runs off the sides.

•   Using an offset spatula or a smooth table knife, spread the glaze over each cookie, filling in the shape to its edges. While the glaze is wet, you can decorate the cookies with colored sprinkles, or leave the glaze plain, let dry, and add more decoration with Royal Icing.

ROYAL ICING

If using egg whites: 3 large egg whites at room temperature
 and ½ teaspoon cream of tartar
If using meringue powder: 3 tablespoons meringue powder
 and 6 tablespoons warm water
3¾ cups confectioners' sugar
Optional: 1 to 2 drops of glycerin
Food coloring

Before you start, make sure that all utensils and containers are clean and grease-free. Have ready several small containers for dividing the icing and tinting it with different colors, if desired. You will need to keep the royal icing covered with a damp cloth, plastic wrap, or tight-fitting lid or it will dry out. Royal icing will keep, tightly covered, in the refrigerator for about one week. This recipe is proportioned for the firmest-textured icing; adjust the texture with the addition of water or sugar as explained below.

• If using egg whites, combine the egg whites, cream of tartar, and sugar and beat until the icing is thick and holds billowy peaks, about 6 to 8 minutes. Add glycerin for extra shine, if desired.

• If using meringue powder, whisk the meringue powder and sugar together in the bowl of an electric mixer. Add the water and beat on low speed for about 5 minutes, until icing is thick and holds billowy peaks. Don't overbeat or the icing texture will become hard to work with. Add glycerin for extra shine, if desired.

• To adjust the consistency of icing: To thicken, add sifted confectioners' sugar a spoonful at a time, whisking thoroughly until you reach the desired consistency. To thin, add warm water a few drops at a time, mixing with a spoon. Piped outlines and details require the thickest icing; flows of color over a whole cookie or in sections can be somewhat thinner.

• Royal icing hardens very quickly when exposed to air, so cover with a damp cloth, plastic wrap, or container lids when not in immediate use. Divide the icing into separate containers for each color to be used. Tint the icing with small amounts of food coloring until it reaches the color desired.

• To use, icing can be spread onto cookies with an offset spatula or table knife—even painted on with small, previously unused paintbrushes, such as the ones that come in a child's paint box—or it can be piped through a pastry bag and tips. For simple, plain outlines, use a zipper plastic bag with a tiny hole cut from one corner.

Makes about 3 cups of icing.

Family Fortune

"THERE'S YOUR SIGN——" MY GRANDFATHER WOULD MUTTER through clenched teeth, biting down on his cigar as we drove the Embarcadero Freeway into downtown San Francisco. My mother's father, Frank Fisher Hills, was pointing out the monumental HILLS BROS COFFEE sign you could see from the elevated overpass. Hills Brothers Coffee was one of the big local success stories after the Gold Rush, its founders striking it rich on their invention of the vacuum seal. The company sign stood atop its own brick coffee-roasting plant on prime waterfront real estate, proudly displaying our family name in blazing red neon for the entire city to admire. Except that ours, apparently, had been the branch of the family that thought it a dubious enterprise to supply coffee to the hungover denizens of the Barbary Coast, and refused to invest. The truth hardly mattered: We claimed the sign as our own. Its ten-foot-tall letters were a tangible reminder of a fortune we'd lost—one of several, apparently—and therefore irrefutable evidence of our family's elect status.

My maternal relatives indoctrinated their progeny early into the unassailable belief that we were the luckiest people on earth because we were Irish and Roman Catholic; being from San Francisco put us over the top, people whose patrimony could not be more enviable. Maybe the presidency of John Fitzgerald Kennedy, who spent his honeymoon with Jackie in California, had galvanized the family conviction, because otherwise, it was a bit of a head-scratcher. When I was old enough to know a little more history than the insular, self-congratulatory version I heard around the dinner table, I couldn't help but be skeptical. Weren't we the ambulance drivers, the washerwomen, and before that the despised and downtrodden huddled around peat fires in our rags, with a single rotting potato to feed the whole barefooted family?

"Oh, but we're *lace-curtain* Irish," my mother reassured me. Only someone who is lace-curtain Irish would fail to recognize that term as a snub.

This basic misunderstanding of a key concept related to our heritage, not to mention the heritage itself, with its magical transubstantiations and pots of leprechaun gold, may explain why my family thought itself imbued with innate luck, even if our luck happened to be mostly bad. We took inordinate pride in our crocheted fig leaves of social respectability, and clung to our legacy of colorful losses as further proof of our distinction.

The colorful losses were recounted with vigorous regularity, complicated tales of dashed hopes and missed chances, set pieces more elaborately furnished and tartly piquant with every retelling. My terse and brooding grandfather, whom we called Pa, was the primary figure in many of those stories. The episodes of his implausibly dramatic life read like the chapters of a Gothic novel. He was the three-year-old whose father had recently died of influenza and whose mother had tied him to a tree in Golden Gate Park after the 1906 earthquake. But there were whispers that Joel Hills the lumber mill operator wasn't really Pa's father—that it was really Rose's first love, the peripatetic nobleman Count Vladimir Baranov, an international entrepreneur and great-grandson of the first Russian governor of Alaska. Why Rose didn't marry the Count in the first place is as much a mystery as Pa's suspicious resemblance to him. The curtain of history has fallen over some of the details, but in any case the Count showed back up in San Francisco shortly after the earthquake, married the widowed Rose, and gave both of her young sons the name Baranov.

The Baranov family thenceforth lived in comfortable luxury in a grand Lyon Street Victorian right off Golden Gate Park. The charming, forward-thinking Count hobnobbed his way into San Francisco society and widening cultural and political circles with the striking six-foot-tall Rose on his arm, and traveled the world to keep an eye on his investments—mahogany forests and gold mines in South America, more gold and copper mines in Death Valley.

Sometime around the start of World War I, the Count was called to Russia by the advisors of Tsar Nicholas II, whose government was on increasingly precarious footing. Because of his own titled family's generations of loyalty to the tsars and his international connections, the

Count was entrusted with a shipload of Romanov treasures and domestic goods for use in the event that Nicholas, Empress Alexandra, and their five children would have to flee the country and live in exile. The Romanovs were thought to be the richest family in the world; though their wealth and privilege would prove the cause of their downfall, the family had hoped they would also be the means to save themselves. Packed with priceless heirlooms and jewels and gold and icons, furs and samovars and clothes and books, forty Romanov steamer trunks sailed back to San Francisco with the Count and were unloaded into the basement of the house on Lyon Street.

Everyone knows what happened to the ill-fated Romanovs after Nicholas was arrested and forced to abdicate in 1917, but most people don't realize that in the wake of the Bolshevik Revolution the tsarist White Russian resistance was organizing as far away as San Francisco. The house on Lyon Street became an undercover hotbed of counter-revolutionary intrigue. Pa was fourteen when the operatives and reconnaissance men started to arrive, diabolical black-caped characters who showed up under further cloak of darkness. Pa and his brother would watch through the upstairs banisters as their stepfather opened the door, the Count's two Russian wolfhound guard dogs straining at their collars as he held them back. Nobody was allowed into the padlocked basement, where the steamer trunks were kept and a secret escape passage, it was rumored, had been dug all the way across the park's panhandle. One night Pa walked into his parents' bedroom and saw the bed blanketed from headboard to footboard in thick stacks of thousand-dollar bills.

By the early twenties the Russian Civil War had ended. Lenin's ruthless thumb was on the scales of the new Soviet Union, and the Count, bowing to reality, retired his counterrevolutionary activities. That's when two final black-caped Russians showed up on Lyon Street, asking for a chat with the Count. His visitors wanted to see the Count's Death Valley mines, they said, and the accommodating Count agreed to drive them in his car.

He was never seen again. Neither were the two men or the car.

Was it a month later, a year? The police had already closed the case on the Count's disappearance when my great-grandmother received a letter in Russian, sent from Moscow. Unable to read it, she took the letter to the Bancroft Library at the University of California at Berkeley, where Pa was by now a chemical engineering student. Translated by the librarians, the letter claimed that the Count had died of sunstroke in Death Valley, and his body had been taken back to "the motherland" for burial. The motherland? The Count had been born in Alaska, lived most of his adult life in San Francisco, and had only occasionally visited Russia.

The Count had obviously been assassinated. Fearful that they would be killed, too, Rose and her sons changed their names back to Hills and laid low, moving in with Rose's sister temporarily. Once a week for almost a year, after nightfall, they snuck back into the basement of their house on Lyon Street, loaded their car with the Romanovs' steamer trunks—a lost family's ransom, the fortune they'd counted on to save them—and drove the trunks to the San Francisco dump, where Pa and his brother set them on fire and watched them burn.

HAVING DELIBERATELY DESTROYED a vast fortune and subsequently losing his metallurgy lab to the war effort, Pa became quite wealthy running a top-secret munitions factory in rural Pennsylvania during World War II. After the war, Pa gained control of his lucrative metallurgy patents and moved his growing family to Mexico City to start a new business. Again the black hand of dastardly luck intervened: Pa arrived at his office one morning to find that his business partner had drained the company accounts and fled the country. Wiped out financially and facing the threat of being thrown into a Mexican jail for defrauding his clients, Pa, too, fled with my pregnant grandmother and their three children, crossing over the border into California with the help of relatives.

Devastated by the betrayal and desperate to find a job, Pa left my grandmother with the kids at a borrowed cabin north of San Francisco while he looked for work that winter. With no heat, no phone, and such limited quarters that my thirteen-year-old uncle Frank had to sleep in a shed down the hill, the cabin is where my grandmother went into early labor alone, forced to pound on the floor with her shoe to wake my eight-year-old mother for help. My grandparents had already lost two newborn daughters, learning too late that they were Rh incompatible. The latest tiny baby—my youngest aunt—barely survived, and Pa couldn't be found for a week. When he did finally show up, collecting the older children from neighbors and taking them back to the cabin, he froze in the doorway of the bedroom where my grandmother had nearly hemorrhaged to death before the ambulance arrived, the untouched room a scene of horrific gore, blood everywhere, my broken grandfather too paralyzed with shock to tell his children to turn away.

Eventually Pa pulled himself and his finances together, purchasing a farm south of San Francisco that had been a nineteenth-century way station between Mission Dolores in San Francisco and Mission Santa Clara on the peninsula south of the bay. The early padres and their flocks could identify the house as they approached from a distance thanks to the gargantuan oak tree that spread its canopy horizontally behind it. By the time my grandfather bought the place, the farm had lost some of its missionary luster: The previous tenant had been Gypsy Rose Lee, the burlesque stripper, who'd holed up there after having a baby during her affair with Otto Preminger.

Surrounded by apricot orchards and flanked by its own plum and peach and avocado trees, with lemons the size of cats' heads growing by the front door, the farmhouse was still dominated by the mammoth oak when I was small. The tree gloomed darkly over the house and barn, dropping razor-sharp leaves all over the ground that were murder on tender little feet. In fact the whole farm seemed a little treacherous from a child's-eye view, unnervingly booby-trapped and imbued with an atmosphere of latent threat. As we turned in from the eucalyptus-lined main road half a mile from the house, my mother would point out the oversized mailbox where, if she or her siblings failed to make their beds in the morning—or worse, wet them!—their punishment was finding their dirty sheets balled up inside with the mail and having to carry the linens back up the long gravel drive in shame, to the catcalling delight of everyone else on the school bus.

My heart started racing with anxiety as soon as we could see the house. It was not exactly the welcoming over-the-river-and-through-the-woods kind of grandparents' house they sing about in kindergarten. Even though her eyes looked genial and confused behind her thick glasses and she always had that stash of candy bars in the pantry, I knew my dotty, fluffy-haired grandmother had been the one to cook my mom's piano-playing chicken, and she'd probably been the sheet monitor, too. Hanging behind her bed was a graphic portrait of Jesus Christ with a crown of bloody thorns caught in his wispy brown hair, his sad eyes following you as you backed out the door into the hall. But my grandma was too scatterbrained to be intimidating. It was Pa who scared me.

Tall and trim and dashing, with coal-black hair and a mustache, Pa looked like Clark Gable—a silent, brooding Clark Gable smoking an omnipresent cigar. Pa rarely looked up from whatever chore he was performing, let alone deigned to speak to us when we pitched out of the car after our parents and scattered across the farm as giddy as, well, children set loose on a farm. We could play freeze tag on the front lawn between the hydrangea bushes, we could dare ourselves to stand in front of the picture of Jesus and then shriek through the house, we could stir up pretend concoctions in the playhouse behind the kitchen or set up domino patterns in the front parlor or leaf through photo albums with pictures of dogs we knew all the names of though they were long dead by the time we were born, but we were not supposed to bother Pa.

It wasn't a difficult request. By the time my parents married, the producing farm was limited to Pa's orchard and his kitchen garden, and we weren't allowed over there. Out back, where the fallow fields had been taken over by brittle waist-high weeds, Pa stored his collection of army-surplus pontoon bridges, the pieces scattered around in a state of semi-assembly, as if the invading army had already been routed. We weren't allowed back there either, and we weren't allowed in the barn, where Pa kept wooden barrels filled with shards of broken glass and galvanized tubs of rusty metal and paint-peeling duck decoys and ammunition, the sinister raw materials of his homegrown experiments and distressing hobbies now that he was retired. He'd nailed up a bleached ox skull over the wide barn doors to keep us out, two staring white billiard balls glued into its eye sockets.

We weren't allowed in the little parlor off the dining room, a Victorian saloon with a sleek polished bar and a collection of shotguns hanging overhead, hundreds of tiny winking bottles of booze lined up against the mirrored walls. This was Pa's room, just as the barn and the garden and the fields were Pa's; the kitchen and the sewing room and the Jesus bedroom were my grandmother's. Late in the timeless afternoons of family gatherings, Pa retreated to his saloon with his cronies—elderly male relatives I could never tell apart—and sometimes a son-in-law or two, though never my straitlaced father, and they drank and smoked cigars and talked about duck hunting and pontoon bridges and the good dogs of yesteryear. I imagined my mom in there as a cowering eleven-year-old in pigtails, hands clapped to her neck and wide green eyes bugging out, her throat on fire from the Scotch Pa ordered her to drink in order to quell any nascent tendencies toward insurrection, while he stood behind the bar looking dispassionately on, handsome, terrifying Pa, the smoke from his cigar ribboning up in the mirrors' endless reflection.

You'd think that having grandparents who lived on a farm would mean I'd have a storehouse of sensory memories of the year-round cornucopia engendered by my grandfather's legendarily green thumb. What happened to all those apricots and peaches and plums and lemons? I've dragged the murky lake of memory and can dredge up only a single instance when I ate something grown by Pa. During a family dinner one autumn evening, he covered the kitchen floor with newspapers, and when all nine grandchildren were assembled in a circle on the linoleum, Pa presented us with one, exactly one, boiled artichoke that had come from his garden. We looked up at him, expectant—there were *nine* of us. But he straightened to his full height, chomped down on the end of his cigar, and stared back.

"Share it," he growled.

So how did this parsimonious old coot, my scary grandfather, end up being a fudge virtuoso? Peculiar as he was, nothing about Pa was as unaccountable as the fact that he was famous for his chocolate fudge, which he'd been making all his life.

I never saw Pa make it, but it appeared after holiday dinners, my grandmother bringing it out in a pink-and-gold-striped Joseph Magnin department store box lined with waxed paper. It was dense and dark and cut into generous, perfect squares that were at once succulent and richly formidable. It sheered off when you bit into it, like the heavily pressurized layers of metamorphic rock, and then it melted with voluptuous indolence on your tongue, filling your mouth with a lavalike flow of the most indescribably potent creamy chocolate. We were each allowed one piece, and then my grandmother ceremoniously and nonnegotiably settled the top back onto the box, the family treasure lost to us once more, its wonders only hearsay for another year.

"Don't get your hopes up too high," my mother would warn us when we asked her to make it, one of the rare instances when my mom displayed anything but unwavering faith in the ultimate triumphal success that was our family destiny. "I've tried many times. Nobody's ever been able to make it except Pa." She'd get out the candy thermometer and the heavy-bottomed Dutch oven, following the directions exactly, watching carefully—not stirring!—as the milk and cocoa and sugar boiled together on the stove, burbling and hissing ominously. We'd stare into the pot—not stirring!—as the fudge cooled on the counter to exactly 110° Fahrenheit before beating it and beating it and beating it until it proved its perfection by turning creamy and smooth and firm, rearing up against the wooden spoon like a chocolate tidal wave curling over in slow motion: *There's your sign.*

Except that part—the part where Pa's fudge turned out right— hardly ever happened, not for my mother and not for me when I took over the fudge-making reins in the family. The ingredients are simple and the method isn't complicated, but it requires precision and timing and assiduous care to attain the exact chemical reaction that turns everyday elements into something rhapsodic. Dozens—or dozens of dozens—of times I've attempted Pa's fudge, and I would estimate that a full ninety percent of the time the recipe has not worked. When it has, I've been jubilant. Most of the time, however, Pa's fudge ended up a potful of greasy chocolate sauce that separated and wouldn't set, or it scorched and had to be thrown out, or it came out crumbled and sandy, like parched dirt broken up by a hoe. Once when I set the cooked fudge out to cool on top of a crusty snowbank off our second-floor deck in Alaska, I came back to find the fudge pot simply gone—the pot had been so hot, it had plunged down its own perfectly cylindrical tunnel of melted snow.

Whatever Pa's secret was, his proprietary fudge alchemy, I don't think he'd have told me if I'd asked. But moth to the flame, I couldn't get enough of him. I'd find him hunched protectively over his shattered glass and rusted nails, intent on some intricate, unfathomable operation, twisting bits of broken mirror onto corroded wire, or pouring kerosene through a funnel into a jar filled with birdshot. Or he'd be out alone in the dry barren fields considering his pontoon bridges to nowhere, the lit cigar, held between his dirt-caked thumb and forefinger, breathing a red smolder by itself. If he looked up at me, if he saw me, he betrayed nothing.

I'd stand in the flammable weeds and inhale the scorched, sweet earth scent of my pa's cigars, the stories of his life replaying in my head. I didn't learn until I was in my forties that "Pa" was the name he'd called the Count, who may have been his biological father, the only father he ever knew. As a child I was too young myself to recognize my grandfather as having been young once also, a boy who liked fudge and called his dad "Pa"; to imagine him as a student of chemistry watching sparks spit and flare against the dark at the San Francisco dump, everything turning to ash but the silver samovars, the gold, the jewels; everything burning down to their elements but the diamonds, which were already pure carbon.

PA'S FUDGE

.·.

4 cups granulated sugar
⅔ cup cocoa
1½ cups whole milk
2 tablespoons corn syrup
½ teaspoon salt
6 tablespoons unsalted butter
2 teaspoons vanilla

• Mix sugar, cocoa, milk, corn syrup, and salt in a large, heavy saucepan or Dutch oven. Place over medium heat and stir faithfully until sugar is melted. Bring to boil and cook to soft-ball stage (234° Fahrenheit). Stir occasionally to prevent sticking and scorching. Remove from heat and add butter and vanilla. Let cool to 110° without stirring. While the fudge is cooling, butter the bottom and sides of an 8-inch square pan.
• Beat the fudge with a wooden spoon until it becomes very thick and loses its gloss. Quickly pour into the prepared pan. Score while warm into 1-inch squares, then allow to cool thoroughly for several hours or overnight. Cut with a sharp knife when cool, dipping the knife into hot water between cuts if necessary. Store the fudge between layers of waxed paper in a sealed container in a cool place.

Makes, or may not make, about 2 pounds of fudge.

FAUX PA'S FUDGE

∴

This recipe always works and tastes just like Pa's Fudge. Do not tell anyone that it isn't Pa's Fudge.

1¼ pounds high-quality milk chocolate

10 ounces high-quality dark or bittersweet chocolate

Optional: 1 heaping cup of walnut halves

4 cups granulated sugar

½ cup unsalted butter

1½ cups evaporated milk

½ teaspoon salt

2 cups marshmallow cream

1 tablespoon vanilla

• Butter the bottom and sides of a 10½-by-15½-inch pan. Chop or break the milk chocolate and dark chocolate into small pieces. Set aside. If using walnuts, toast them at 375° for 5 to 8 minutes, checking every few minutes until the nuts are fragrant and starting to lightly brown. Set aside.

• In a large, heavy saucepan or Dutch oven over low-medium heat, cook the sugar, butter, and evaporated milk, stirring constantly, until it comes to a full rolling boil. Boil, stirring constantly, for exactly 5 minutes. Remove from heat and allow the boiling to subside, then quickly add the chocolates and salt, stirring until the chocolate is thoroughly melted and the mixture is smooth. Add the marshmallow cream and vanilla, stirring until the fudge is thoroughly uniform and no traces of marshmallow can be seen. Add walnuts if using and stir in. Turn into the prepared pan and let cool for several hours or overnight, until completely firm. Score the top of the fudge into 1-inch squares and cut with a sharp knife, dipping the knife in hot water between cuts if necessary. Store the fudge between layers of waxed paper in a sealed container in a cool place. Can be refrigerated or frozen.

Makes about 5 pounds of fudge.

The Patron Saint of Lost Causes

WHEN MY BROTHERS AND I WERE SMALL, OUR HIGH-SPIRITED mother's unabashed enthusiasms and tireless ingenuity were as seductive as the come-hither tootling of the Pied Piper of Hamelin. She'd decided that the straightest route to being the best mother in the world was to be a friend and playmate to her kids, not an overbearing parent. Motherhood was a plum role in which she'd been cast, and she played it with gusto, the president and dazzling idol of her own homegrown fan club. Billy and John and I were her sidekicks and biggest fans, skipping after her to suck nectar out of honeysuckle blossoms in our backyard, rattle prizes from the bottom of Cracker Jack boxes, learn the dizzying elation of rolling down a grassy hill on a spring afternoon. She taught us to throw baseballs, do macramé, and dance the twist; we knew every line in every song in all the Disney movies and Rodgers and Hammerstein musicals. All she had to tell us was that Saint Jude was her favorite saint and he became our favorite, too—the patron saint of lost causes, the one we prayed to in unison when John-John stuffed both of his nostrils with raisins or the engine in our old woody station wagon wouldn't turn over.

"Okay, kids, it always works if we say the prayer and count to three. Ready? All together now: Holy Saint Jude, worker of miracles, patron of the hopeless, please make our car start. . . ."

My mom could figure out how to do anything. Mary Poppins and Maria from *The Sound of Music* had nothing on my mom, though if you throw in some *I Love Lucy* episodes you get a more accurate picture. She approached even the single-handed drudgery of being a sixties housewife as an adventure in breezy resourcefulness, her "Hey, kids! Let's put on a show!" attitude making everything seem fun even when we knew it wasn't.

Relentlessly adroit at getting by on little money in the early years of my father's career, my mother made Christmas angels out of Coke bottles and a nativity stable out of an avocado crate, piñatas and pirate treasure maps from grocery bags for our birthday parties. She talked the Avon lady out of all of her cunning miniature lipstick samples, and when they were used up, my mom unapologetically asked for more free samples. She saved plastic margarine tubs to use as unbreakable cereal bowls, stacking them next to the boxes of every conceivable sugary cereal known to mankind in a low kitchen cabinet so my brothers and I could help ourselves and let her sleep in. My mom was confident and handy, and if she didn't already know how to lay a brick fireplace hearth or rewire a light fixture, she made it up as she went along.

One of our Palo Alto neighbors was a breeder of prize-winning Shetland sheepdogs, and my mother cut a deal for a young female who had some invisible flaw that kept her out of the show ring, but wouldn't prevent her from having gorgeous puppies or making a loyal family companion. By taking in a pregnant dog, acting as midwife to her squirming brood, and returning all but one of the puppies, my shrewd mom got us two discount dogs for the price of one. Our sweet-natured, motherly Elaine and her son, Thor, were natural babysitters, an added boon for a woman with small active children and too many overambitious household projects. Their sheepdog instincts meant that our protective Shelties circled us constantly while we played outside, crouching and fixing us with the evil sheep-eye if we strayed too far from the house, nipping at our heels and forcing us back when we got close to the street.

Frugal as she could be when necessity dictated, my mother had a lot of stuff. She loved stuff. She had the acquisitive tendencies of a raccoon, collecting every glittery thing that fell into her path. There were artifacts galore from her life before she became our mother, mementos she'd drag out of closets and boxes to show us at the slightest hint of curiosity, or simply because she felt like revisiting the irrepressible exploits of her girlhood. My mom would instruct me to sit on her bed as she unveiled her dolls, slowly unwinding the crinkled layers of tissue they were wrapped in, telling me she'd saved them for the little girl she knew someday she'd have. I flushed with greed as she showed me the dolls that were meant for me alone, that I'd never have to share with Billy or John or anyone else: the famous Nancy and Susan, life-sized baby dolls named after her dead infant sisters, with pressed sawdust limbs and teeth that looked real, their painted faces crackling with age. Bisque ladies in buttoning kidskin boots and lace-trimmed pantaloons. A celluloid set of Mexican children from her eighth birthday, brown as chocolate, in striped serapes and bare flat feet. An ancient Chinese dancer with hands so long and delicate each finger was wrapped individually in cotton fleece.

Her sanctum sanctorum, the jewelry box, kept in the Danish modern dresser she shared with my father, held a Victorian emerald ring and gold wire eyeglasses that had been the Count's, and two gleaming platinum wristwatches given to Nana Rose and her sister when they were eleven years old—banded with black grosgrain ribbon, etched flowers and hand-painted numerals on their faces, sapphires flashing blue on their winding stems. There was the wedding gift from my Australian grandmother, a locket depicting Moses in the bulrushes: The minute cloisonné locket was crosshatched to look like a wicker basket, and inside was a gold baby no bigger than my fingernail. In a drawer that slid out from the bottom of the tufted satin box was a stack of black-and-white photographs of lanky young men resting their hands at my teenage mother's waist, my mother laughing in taffeta and dark lipstick. Most intriguing of all were the individually wrapped sugar cubes, keepsakes my mother had saved from parties and dances, the indelible details of which she'd recorded on every side of the crisp-edged paper wrappers in her florid Catholic-school hand. I looked over my mother's shoulder as she turned them in her fingers like tiny Rosetta stones, reading aloud and explaining the hieroglyphic notations.

This one is from the senior prom at Bellarmine. I went with Bob Durard—he's the one in the white jacket in that picture—yes, that's him—oh, he was so handsome! This must have been the time I got thrown into the Figinis' pool with all my clothes on. See how the ink bled down the wrapping? My best friend, Patty, lent me her blue satin strapless from I. Magnin's. . . .

The dolls and jewels and sugar cubes were just the tip of the iceberg. Our garage and our closets were bursting with boxes of ermine tails and old party-line telephones and hotel towels and wearable paper dresses that came folded inside Hershey's Cocoa tins, not to mention all the detritus of domestic life as well as the underpinnings of her avocation as a thwarted artist.

My mother lived in a fairly constant thrum of creative emergency, forever on the lookout for ways to put her itchy imagination to work. She amassed an extensive inventory of bargain-bin supplies—bolts of fabric and acrylic paints and lengths of balsa wood and styrofoam in different shapes and canvas stretcher bars and embroidery hoops and plastic flowers and sewing patterns and fifty-pound bags of clay and beading looms and colored pipe cleaners—because she never knew what she might need until inspiration struck.

Her convictions were as capricious as she was, entirely haphazard and dependent on what was reasonable in the moment, or convenient, or downright fantastical. *Dog spit is perfectly sanitary. A refrigerated egg will keep forever. Hotels expect you to take their towels home—it's not stealing, it's free advertising for the hotel.* Prompted by the chronically suicidal tendencies of Bonnie and Clyde, our pair of goldfish who repeatedly jumped out of their bowl and had to be scraped up off the kitchen floor with a spatula, gasping for oxygen and stuck to the linoleum, and the baby bunny that dropped dead only two days after it was given to Billy on Easter, my mom assured her worried children that she was going nowhere. "I'm never going to die!" she declared, her certainty incontestable. "I'm going to live forever!" When my brothers and I started pondering aloud the most insoluble details of the Christmas story as well as how babies are made, my mother insisted that, just like baby Jesus, we had been immaculately conceived.

When my mom was in charge of us, which was virtually always, though not infrequently in a somewhat passive supervisory capacity, Billy and John and I had few rules. There was no set bedtime, no bathtime, no assigned chores, no limit on how much television or how many sodas or bowls of Cap'n Crunch. The only thing required of us was that we fulfill her outsized expectations: that we be the brightest, most talented, most charged-with-potential children who'd ever lived. If she was the best mother in the world—a title to which she laid claim frequently, crowing with pleasure as Billy and John and I enthusiastically nodded our assent, burying our faces in her Pendleton skirts or her paper dresses, breathing in her intoxicating scent of Moon Drops lotion, cigarette smoke, and Chanel No. 5—then it followed that our superiority and specialness were not merely figments of her maternal indulgence, but ordained.

According to my mother we were practically royalty, the evidence of our elevation not just the family trait of having second toes longer than our big toes (an indicator that we descended from pointy-slipper-wearing nobles, another aggrandizing factoid from my mom) but because of the Count and those steamer trunks of Romanov goodies waiting for us to reclaim them from the effluvial depths of the San Francisco dump. We were the rightful heirs to greatness, prestige, and fantastic wealth in my mom's eyes. Judicious Billy would undoubtedly be president someday. I, my mother assured me, was going to be a famous artist. And John-John, if he ever stopped biting all the kids in the neighborhood, was going to be something really good, too.

Such exceptional children deserved appropriately spectacular acknowledgment on their birthdays, and my mother threw the full weight of her artistic skill behind our parties, especially our cakes. I'm sure my earliest birthday memory has stayed with me because of the three-dimensional bunny cake she made, cutting a sheet cake into strategically cantilevered pieces she glued together with lemon curd filling and creamy white buttercream. The little guy had a pink jelly-bean nose and black licorice whiskers; his ears were cut from white construction paper lined with pale pink felt. I sat in our metal high chair and watched the glowing coronas of light around the candles on the bunny's back as everyone sang to me at the table: I was two years old, which means my mother had a five-week-old infant and two toddlers in diapers when she made this cake.

For Billy's pirate birthday party, the whitecapped blue buttercream surf was thick with sharks circling a deserted island. Sunk deep on the sandy beach of coarse raw sugar was a treasure chest my mom had made of graham crackers stuck together with melted chocolate and filled with sparkling candies—silver dragées, Life Savers crushed with a hammer to look like chunks of semiprecious stone, rock candy diamonds, gold-foil coins. John's dinosaur cake was the sloping side of an erupting volcano (volcanoes being a popular recurring archetype in my family), with gushing chocolate-frosting lava carrying fallen plastic palm trees and candy rocks in its wake, and a choice contingent from our collection of dinosaurs locked in mortal combat in the valley below. For added realism my mom torched a plastic gazelle and an allosaurus with a butane lighter, then bloodied their melted wounds with red nail polish before adding them to the scene. My favorite cake of all was my own Noah's ark. My mom constructed the ark out of gingerbread and royal icing, and up the gangplank came a long line of dime-store chenille animals winding their way two by two over a sheetcake hillside of green coconut grass sprinkled with candied flowers, looking just like the illustration from the children's Bible stories book in our dentist's waiting room.

My gender-specific grant of special-teams status with my mom—*we're the only girls, we stick together*—was the cause of much private gloating on my part. I had the additional gratification of being the only one of my siblings to be born in San Francisco, the ne plus ultra of metropolitan origins according to the Hills family doctrine. I was the seventh generation of females in my mother's family to bear the rare honor of being a genuine San Franciscan, and my estimable birth had me convinced that not just the Hills Brothers Coffee sign but the entire city was mine. On trips to the zoo, I inspected the animals with the condescending hauteur of a visiting monarch: *Yes, Monkey Island appears to be well populated, and the flamingos are very pink today. My compliments.*

So when my mother and I happened to be at the Palo Alto dime store one afternoon shopping for more random bargains to clutter up our closets at home, and we saw that the store was sponsoring a Cinderella slipper contest, my mom knew right away that I was fated to win.

"*You . . . Could Be the Winner of a Fabulous Shopping Spree!*" announced the sign at the bottom of a tiered display on a skirted table, a tower of the most desirable items the store had to offer: linen tea towels and gold-plated demitasse spoons and ladies' kid gloves, but also Mr. Potato Heads and Easy-Bake Ovens and toy china tea sets, Whitman's chocolates and boxes of petits fours and skeins of embroidery floss and bouquets of crepe-paper flowers. At the very top of the pile, high above my head, Cinderella's glass slippers glinted on a velvet pillow. All you had to do to win was show up on the appointed day at the specified time a few weeks later and be the lucky little girl whose feet fit Cinderella's slippers.

My mom gazed up at the tower of five-and-dime splendor and those glistening Lucite slippers, squeezing my hand, her ecstatic face lit with beatific wonder. There could be no more perfect confluence of my mother's exuberant passions, no more unequivocal confirmation of our family's manifest destiny, than my foot fitting into those slippers and winning an entire store's worth of free loot we didn't need—unless it was *her* feet fitting the slippers.

"You can do it, Cis, I know it!" my mom whispered in my ear so we wouldn't tip our hand to the other mothers and daughters milling around the display. "That Cinderella slipper looks just perfect for your little foot!"

Except that my feet weren't little. Despite how pretty and slender and finely made my mother was as an adult, she'd told us that she was the same height she'd been since she was ten years old. She'd been a gargantuan child with enormous feet. Now her big feet looked lean and bony and elegant, like the rest of her, but when she was younger they'd been paddles. She told me all the time how much alike we were—*just like sisters, like best friends*—and I shivered with pleasure at the idea that I might be like my mom. But my feet, I thought, looking up at the Cinderella contest display and the tiny slippers, were just like hers, too.

As the contest approached, my mother drove the two of us back to the dime store to admire the desultory opulence that would soon, she was convinced, be ours. I followed her through the aisles as she reconnoitered in preparation for her free shopping spree, and I wondered if you were allowed to pray to Saint Jude to help you win a Mr. Potato Head and some felt squares.

"Isn't it thrilling, Cis!" she said, staring up at the glass slippers on their pillow. "The contest is almost here! Maybe they'll put our picture in the newspaper—"

I nodded, feeling forlorn. As much as I wanted to win, to be publically conferred with the specialness she insisted I possessed and that I fervently hoped I really did, it was my mom who seemed to me to be the real Cinderella. I'd seen what she looked like in ball gowns, satin gloves to her elbows and tall princes in white tuxedos standing erect and grinning beside her. Now her coach was an old woody station wagon that didn't start, and it was her job to clean up after the rest of us. I couldn't imagine my morose, inscrutable dad as the prince in my mom's fairy tale; he was more like the nagging stepmother. My mother was so pretty when she was excited, and I didn't want to let her down.

On the morning of the contest, I was so anxious that I threw up my Crispy Critters on the kitchen floor. I had to take another bath, and by the time my long hair was dried and brushed and bowed and I was dressed in my best party clothes—it was important to look the part, my mom said, buttoning our gloves and checking her lipstick in the mirror before turning around so I could tell her how beautiful she was, with her narrow waist and swishy flowered dress—we had to race downtown to make it to the store in time. We were already a few minutes late when my mother finally found a parking place and we ran inside the store, where a crowd was gathered around the Cinderella display. A flashbulb went off, and I saw that the slippers and the pillow were gone.

"That's all right," my mother said, pulling me forward, unfazed, "they've just started the fitting—"

And then the crowd erupted in applause. Another little girl was sitting in a plush armchair with both of Cinderella's slippers on her feet, and a man in a suit was placing a tiara on her head. Someone handed her a bouquet of real roses, and the photographer, on his knee, kept taking more pictures.

"Oh, no, we're too late!" my mom cried, her carefully made-up face falling. "Oh Cissy, I'm so sorry—"

I didn't know whether to cry with relief or disappointment or shame. I threw my arms around my mother and hid my face.

"It's all right, Cis, don't worry," she comforted me, patting my back, not understanding. "We don't need any of those things, anyway. We have plenty of goodies at home. Except . . . maybe these . . . ," she added, and I lifted my head to see.

She'd picked up a toy tea set and a box of petits fours off the contest display table. The tea set had pink roses on every cup. The petits fours were frosted in a rainbow of pastels, with piped decorations to make them look like miniature presents.

"What do you think, Cis? We're dressed for a party, and it would be a shame not to have one."

I nodded up and down.

"But I don't know . . . ," she said, narrowing her mascara'd eyes at the petit four box. "I wonder if these are really as good as they look. . . ."

"Your cakes are always better than anybody's," I assured her.

"You are so right," my mother said with happy certitude, setting down the box of petits fours and handing me the tea set. She squared her glamorous shoulders and tipped up her chin, revealing her long, shapely neck, then took me by the hand and flounced us down the aisles toward the cashier. "Everything I do," she said, "is *always* so much better."

VANILLA BIRTHDAY CAKE

∴

This versatile basic butter cake, moist and light and flavorful, is based on the classic 1-2-3-4 cake recipe. It works equally well in rounds, cupcakes, as sheet cake, or in shaped cake molds. For an even lighter cake, separate the eggs, adding the beaten egg whites as the last step.

2¾ cups unbleached all-purpose flour
1 tablespoon baking powder
½ teaspoon salt
1 cup unsalted butter, softened
2 cups sugar
4 large eggs, room temperature (separated if desired)
1 cup milk
1 teaspoon vanilla

•   Preheat oven to 350°. Butter and flour two or three 8- or 9-inch round cake pans. Whisk together the flour, baking powder, and salt in a small bowl and set aside.

•   Cream the butter on medium speed in the bowl of an electric mixer for a couple of minutes, then gradually add the sugar and beat until very fluffy and lightened in color, about 5 minutes. Add the eggs (or separated egg yolks) one at a time, beating for a couple of minutes after each addition and scraping down the bowl. Combine the milk and vanilla. On low speed and stopping the mixer for additions, add the flour mixture in three parts, alternating with the milk mixture; start and end with flour and beat just until fully combined after each addition. If you separated the eggs, beat the whites on medium speed in another bowl until soft peaks form; gently fold the beaten egg whites into the batter about a third at a time, just until they disappear.

•   Divide the batter among the prepared pans. Bake for 22 to 28 minutes, checking frequently until a cake tester inserted into center of cake comes out clean and the tops of the cakes spring back when lightly touched. Let the cakes cool in their pans on wire racks for 10 minutes, then turn out of the pans and allow to cool thoroughly on the wire racks before filling or frosting.

Makes two or three 8- or 9-inch layers.

For cupcakes: This recipe will make 24 to 36 cupcakes. Line standard muffin tins with paper liners. Fill the paper liners only two-thirds full, and bake for 18 to 22 minutes, until a cake tester comes out clean and the cakes spring back when touched lightly at the center. Frost when cool.

LEMON CURD

Great as a cake and tart filling, and also as a topping for scones or other baked goods.

> 12 large egg yolks, room temperature
> Pinch of salt
> 1¾ cups granulated sugar
> Grated zest from the lemons used to make . . .
> 1 cup lemon juice
> 1 cup unsalted butter, sliced into tablespoon-sized chips

• As lemon curd needs to cool completely before it is used, begin this recipe the night before or in the morning before use later in the day. Reserve the egg whites from the 12 eggs for another use (egg whites can be frozen).

• Place the egg yolks in a fine-mesh sieve set over a heavy, medium-sized noncorrosive saucepan. Push the yolks through the mesh with a spatula, discarding the white tails left behind after the yolks have passed through the mesh. Whisk the salt with the yolks, then gradually whisk in the sugar, then the zest and lemon juice, combining thoroughly. Turn up the heat to low-medium and whisk constantly with a timer set for 20 minutes. As the mixture begins to heat and grow frothy on the surface, switch to a wooden spoon and continue to stir constantly as the curd thickens. When it is very thick, on the verge of boiling, and will coat the back of the wooden spoon, it is done—it may take 12 minutes or up to

20, depending on your stove. Remove from the heat and begin whisking in 1 tablespoon of butter at a time until all the butter is incorporated and the curd is emulsified and smooth. Turn into a bowl, cover, and refrigerate overnight or all day to thoroughly chill and thicken before use. The curd will keep, covered and refrigerated, for up to two weeks.

Makes a generous 3 cups, enough to fill a two- or three-layer 8- or 9-inch cake, or a 9-inch tart.

For Lime, Orange, Tangerine, or other Citrus Curd: Substitute the equivalent amount of grated zest and juice for the lemon zest and juice.

SIMPLE VANILLA BUTTERCREAM

1 cup unsalted butter, at room temperature
½ teaspoon salt
8 cups confectioners' sugar, or possibly more
½ cup milk
2 teaspoons vanilla
Optional: food coloring

• Cream the butter for a couple of minutes in the bowl of an electric mixer on medium speed. Add the salt and about half of the sugar, then the milk and the vanilla, and beat, starting on the lowest speed and increasing speed as the mixture becomes uniform. Continue to beat until very creamy, about 3 to 5 minutes. Gradually add the remaining sugar about 1 cup at a time, beating until smooth; when all the sugar has been added, beat on medium speed until extremely creamy and light, about 5 minutes more. If frosting seems too creamy to hold its shape, add a bit more sugar, about ¼ cup at a time, and beat for another minute. Add a few drops of liquid or gel food coloring, if desired, and mix thoroughly.

Makes about 4 cups of frosting, enough for a three-layer 8- or 9-inch cake.

VARIATIONS

For Lemon Buttercream: Substitute ½ cup of lemon juice and the grated zest of the lemons for the milk. Decrease vanilla to 1 teaspoon and add 1 teaspoon of lemon extract.

For Almond Buttercream: Decrease vanilla to 1 teaspoon and add 1 teaspoon of almond extract.

For Chocolate Buttercream: Melt and cool 5 ounces of bittersweet chocolate. When all of the confectioners' sugar is incorporated, add the melted chocolate and continue to beat for about 5 minutes. If frosting is too thick, add a spoonful of milk at a time and mix thoroughly.

For an indescribably beautiful, memorably pink Blood Orange Cake: Rub the zest of a blood orange into the sugar before it is creamed with the butter for the cake. Substitute ¼ cup blood orange juice for ¼ cup of the milk, and lessen the vanilla to ½ teaspoon, adding ½ teaspoon lemon or orange extract and ½ teaspoon orange flower water with the vanilla. The cake may take 5 to 8 minutes longer to bake. Make a blood orange curd for the filling, and make the buttercream frosting with blood orange zest and juice, and orange flower water or orange extract substituting for the milk and vanilla.

Diamonds at the Dump, Redux

ASIDE FROM BEING EQUALLY CONFOUNDED BY MY MERCURIAL mother—though once they got married, she was solely my dad's problem—another thing my father and grandfather had in common was a significant relationship with the dump. Now you'd call it a municipal waste management center or a refuse collection site or a sanitary landfill, but when I was a kid it was the dump. As far as I could tell, going to the dump was my father's one consistent source of pleasure.

As often as possible my father loaded our station wagon with all the junk he could find, packing it in methodically over the blank expanse of a weekend morning. Before and after our many moves were always prime opportunities for this meditative exercise, but there was never a bad time for a dump run, about which there were wrong ways and right ways to proceed. You didn't just throw things into the back of the car. Cardboard boxes had to be flattened, soda cans stomped upon one by one and peeled off the sole of one's shoe and reexamined, newspapers gift-tied in multiple layers of twine. Household items were microscopically inspected for the flaws that had gotten them condemned, as if my dad required intimate understanding of every single thing that crapped out in our house before he could commit it to the dump's oblivion. Getting ready for the dump, he was not just attorney but the court of last appeal. Had the garden hose really split beyond repair? Were these batteries really dead? These shoes outgrown? This hand-me-down playpen too sprung and rusty for one more relative's kid?

My dad did not like waste or disorder, either in the things he was consigning to everlasting uselessness or in the way they fit together for their final journey. He was known to pause in his curbside preparations, car keys in his pocket, to rake the newly mowed lawn of grass cuttings or search the house for more expired toys, milk cartons, magazines, and dry-cleaning hangers to make sure he'd be traveling under full freight. Once he was satisfied that the car was packed to capacity, everything frayed or sloppy in our house accounted for and ready for permanent exile, he'd stand at the periphery of whatever my brothers and I were doing and mumble obliquely that he would be stopping by the ice cream parlor on the way back from the dump. Every child within a quarter-mile radius of our house would bolt to our car and hurl themselves bodily onto the front bench seat.

Despite the neighborhood popularity gained by such displays of adult largesse, what my father's dump-run briberies proved was that he didn't have a clue how to be a dad. His understanding of the job of family man was limited to fulfilling the responsibility of bringing home the bacon, as well as the ice cream and the donuts—and yelling at you if you smeared them on your clothes or attempted to eat more than the arbitrary amount he'd allotted. He didn't get that what children want most from their fathers is their father, in all his bumbling, couch-napping, bent-bicycle-tire-sorting humility.

Unlike my mother, who was an open book she thrust daily into our hands, eager to be known, reading over our shoulders and pointing out the exciting parts, my dad didn't reveal himself to us at all. He didn't tell stories about his life. He didn't offer opinions. He didn't share anything except his frequent but no less unpredictable flare-ups of anger. I understand now that my father's volatile furies were a function of his paralyzing fears—of failure, of waste, of being different, of standing out, of the messiness of life; ironically, of losing control—but children only know that they've been burned by a parent's caustic scorn. I sensed, very early, that my father was afraid of us. We could smell it on him, his fear, as he walked through the door of our house. We lifted our heads at the scent, swinging our faces in his direction, freezing like deer.

My father was quite literally the shadow I moved through in my earliest memory of him, following close behind me as I wheeled in parentally protected contentment around the graduate-student-housing parking lot on my tricycle at two, a Saf-T-Pop sucker dissolving on my tongue after a pediatrician's visit. My second distinct memory of my dad, though, is not so sanguine—it was the confrontation that alerted me to the brittle, isolated tyrant I would grow up with. This time he was chasing John-John through our Palo Alto house, intent on exacting corporal punishment for whatever nefarious misdeed a one-year-old was capable of. As John staggered past me, his pacifier in his mouth, I grabbed him and, covering him like Pocahontas protecting a pint-sized John Smith, growled at our father, "Don't you dare touch my little brother." Though I quickly grasped that I'd trespassed on my father's authority, I was nevertheless shocked by the spanking he gave me for defending my brother. My mother had told us that our family was a team. Now I realized that the team was really my mom, my brothers, and me, with my father on the opposing side. Perhaps my father was so threatened by my first open rebellion because he already sensed that he was an outsider in our eyes, and he didn't know how to break into our closed circle.

As much as he might have secretly wanted to, he could never approach us directly, and neither could we impose ourselves on him easily, as we did without thought with our porous mother. I think of the one time he played with us, one Sunday morning in Palo Alto, when by scooting shyly over to him on the carpet my brothers and I managed to squeeze ourselves under his arms, under his cleanly shaven chin, surrounding him, making it impossible for him to continue reading his morning paper. He began to crawl around on the floor, snarling and gnashing his teeth, making us laugh with crazed glee, letting us climb onto his back as he staggered theatrically under our weight on his hands and knees. One minute he was a fierce animal inviting us to tackle him, and the next he sat up, suddenly aware of himself, abruptly shrugging us off like Lainey had her weaned puppies, leaving us sprawled on the carpet gazing after him in confusion as he left the room.

The first time I visited my father's law office in Palo Alto, we had to wait outside while my dad completed some business at his desk. My mother, whose idea it was to take my father out for a picnic lunch to celebrate his first job as a real lawyer, held a picnic hamper in one hand and John-John by the other while Billy and I choreographed the ants pouring out of cracks in the sidewalk, building barricades with sickled eucalyptus leaves and smelling our camphorous hands as we waited for our dad to appear. Finally my father's secretary opened the door and spoke to my mother: My father would have to meet us later; he had important work to take care of. The secretary had brought out a bag of pink and white circus animal cookies freckled with colored sprinkles, and my mother let us eat our cookies as we walked alone to the park.

Every time I visited my father's first office, abashed and shuffling my feet, afraid I might be disturbing his important work, my dad's secretary pulled out a conciliatory bag of pink and white animal cookies from her desk drawer. So did the secretary at my dad's office when he opened a private practice in Sonoma, and at his office in Pennsylvania, and in Washington, D.C., and in Alaska. For years I thought my dad's greatest skill as a lawyer was his shrewd hiring of generous secretaries who bought those same cookies and kept them at the ready for my brothers and me. I was in college before I realized it had been my dad supplying the cookies all along. Maybe he'd remembered his homecoming that night in Palo Alto, after he never made it to his own celebratory picnic lunch with his family; how my brothers and I had covered for our own disappointment by telling him the thrilling news that his secretary had given us circus animal cookies with sprinkles.

He was a puzzle, my father. In the early years of our family, my mother spoke of his intellect with pride, his strange antipodean upbringing with fascinated awe. She remembered listening to a radio report when she was a little girl, a chilling news story about the search for a lost Australian toddler. When she met my dad years later, she learned he'd been the one to find that drowned child. But in keeping with my father's determination to be as American as possible and my Irish relatives' self-perpetuated mythos, not to mention my mom's cavalier confusion (even now, she refers to my husband's Nisei father, who spent World War II in a Japanese American relocation camp, as "Joe, who's a Chinese scientist"), my dad's Japanese contribution to our lineage went unexamined. There was no evidence of Japanese-ness in our family life aside from a fat porcelain Buddha my parents were given as a wedding present. It lived on the coffee table, and when I was little and my father had a bit of a potbelly, his fair hair shorn so habitually close to his scalp it looked transparent, I thought the bald Buddha was a portrait of him—though I couldn't account for the serene, toothy smile.

My dad was fluent in Japanese, my mother told us, and I wondered what that sounded like, since he refused every request for a demonstration. When I was learning to read and noticed his flowing cursive scribbles on a legal pad—not the distinct printed letters I knew—I thought, impressed, *So that's Japanese.* His ordinary speaking voice, too, I assumed was a function of his foreignness: so reticent and soft at its edges, almost a whisper, as if he were afraid his accent would slip in and embarrass him if he spoke any louder. As it was, he rarely said anything at home unless he was angry, and even then, aside from the soul-blistering diatribes he was prone to, he mostly sulked in pungent silence.

As our Australian relatives gradually made cameo appearances in our lives, my father's past took on a little more particularity, a few more scattered, isolated details. I squirreled away the presents of toy koala bears and aboriginal boomerangs painted with kangaroos, as well as random bits of information that passed by me at the dinner table along with the sukiyaki and other Japanese specialties cooked by my visiting aunts: There had been snakes hanging in the trees on the way to the outhouse in Melbourne, and my Australian grandmother had been riding a bicycle when she had her stroke. Once when he was a boy at the local lagoon, ready to go for a swim with his friends and brothers, my dad had yanked one of the other boys away from their diving spot—a shark was circling in the water below. My father hadn't realized his family was mixed race until he was an adult, on his last trip back to Australia, before marrying my mother: While looking through old photo albums with his siblings, finding a picture of himself as a little boy, he'd asked, "Who is that white-haired Japanese woman holding me?" "That's Grandma," his older sister told him.

The fleeting glimpses I was given into my dad's enigmatic origins only made it, and him, seem more inaccessible. Nothing explained his potent detachment, his parsimony and rigidity, how unmoved he seemed to be by us except when we made him mad. All I really knew about my dad was what was in front of me, and there wasn't much.

In stark contrast to my gleefully acquisitive mother, my father had almost no personal possessions. There were his black-framed eyeglasses, his white undershirts, his few dark suits. A barrister bookcase and a thick Oxford dictionary on its own stand. A suit valet that moved with us from house to house, mystifying in its uses, unused. On his thirtieth birthday my parents splurged on a console stereo phonograph in a smooth teak cabinet as big as the back seat of our car. We weren't allowed to touch my dad's new stereo or the handful of records that our mother picked out for him, but Billy and John and I were so excited about this conclusive manifestation of our father's importance in our family that we crouched on the floor in front of Herb Alpert and the Tijuana Brass and pretended to lick the whipped cream off the album cover.

At my father's office there was a wrinkled leather chair with a swiveling seat and wooden arms that curled under at the ends like cats' paws, and there were his diplomas and commendations on the wall behind his desk, rubricked and uncialed in their frames, but that, with the stereo, the dictionary, the meager wardrobe, was it. Except for the shoeshine kit.

My dad's shoeshine kit was kept in a galvanized metal box, and my father brought it out once a week from the floor of his nearly empty closet and set it on yesterday's newspaper in the kitchen, where he'd shine his shoes sitting cross-legged on the floor. If I sidled too near while he was performing his shoe-shining ritual, he'd jerk his arm out preemptively, his hand held up policeman-style to keep me back from the brushes, the flannel, the tattered rags of diaper, the cans of wax and pasty black he lifted out, one by one, and lined up in front of himself. I'd sit on my haunches, watching from a distance, as he wrapped a clean corner of rag around the tip of his finger and dipped it into the opened tub of polish, his other hand buried inside his shoe as he moved the rag over the leather in circles. He shined all of his shoes at one sitting, all two or three pairs, and then he sat back to wait as the polish dried. I waited, too, because there was always a moment at the end of his ceremony when he'd allow me, after he'd tested the polish to make sure it was completely dry, to cover my hand with a folded square of flannel and buff one of his shoes. I'd run my other hand into the toe, copying my dad, rubbing as carefully as he did. My father didn't talk to me as we worked, and I didn't try to talk to him—no different from most of the time I spent in his company. When we were finished, after he'd packed up his kit and stood, I reached up to hand him his polished shoes. I could see both of our faces on the convex surface of the shining leather, and as my dad curled his fingers under the tongues and lifted his shoes away, for a moment he took me with him, too.

SHINING HIS SHOES, going to the dump, cookies in his secretary's desk. My father needed those methodical preparations and carefully marshaled objects to protect himself as he worked up the nerve to approach the children whose dependence and trust so terrified him. Like every other kid on our block, I wanted ice cream, but the real reason I went to the dump with my dad was on the hunch, however vaguely, intuitively understood, that he was trying to find a way to reach us. He'd sit in remote silence behind the wheel as neighborhood children squealed and twirled the radio dials beside him; Billy and John and I would cringe, waiting for the explosion, finally joining in the general gaiety once we saw that our dad's horror of making a public scene kept him from yelling at the other kids to pipe down. He'd warn us in his dampered, muttering voice to stay in the car while he unloaded, and then as we slithered back and forth over the slick seats discussing what flavors we'd each choose, I'd see him pick his footing up a desultory mountain of trash, wiping his fingers on his starched handkerchief, to stand at the slippery summit against an untrammeled blue sky, gazing out at a vast smoking vista of domestic offal with his hands clasped behind his back. Seagulls wheeling and keening overhead, the air ripe with the poignant stink of decay, my father stood there for a while watching as bulldozers droned and scuttled over gutted appliances in the distance and dump trucks backed to the edge of the valley of junk, slanting their loads down the tumbling hillside of rotting debris. In the car behind him, his children watched through the windshield, waiting for the fulfillment of an ordinary promise. I wonder if he ever thought of the man he could have become, the father he might have been, if just once he'd risked joining us at the ice cream parlor, not merely standing at the cash register tallying up the charges, or opened his secretary's drawer to offer the bag of cookies to his bashful visiting kids, telling them, *I bought these just for you.*

My mother was unshakable in her faith that the Romanovs' lost fortune was still recoverable, even if it was buried at the dump under tons of garbage. All we had to do was find it. Swept out on the tide of her optimism, my brothers and I helped her map out the chimerical scenario—we'd bring our rakes and our shovels and our sandpails, and maybe the bulldozer guys would help us, once they saw my lovely mother in her sandals and her paper dress. Wouldn't anyone want to help us find the Romanov treasure, surely ours now by right? We'd have to dig far, far down, and it would be smelly, but once we'd gone deep enough there they'd be: the diamonds, the emeralds, the rubies, the silver and gold, probably smoke-smudged and slimy with gunk, but still the trove of riches that our family deserved.

My father could never have allowed himself to believe such a thing. But maybe he sensed that the dump made something precious available to him, something he could almost get his hands on for the cost of some sugar cones and a few scoops of mint chocolate chip.

PINK AND WHITE ANIMAL COOKIES

∴

You will need miniature animal cookie cutters to make these cookies, as well as at least two large, rimmed baking sheets and two wire racks that will fit inside the baking sheets. This basic shortbread recipe can also be cut into other shapes, rolled into balls, baked in wedges or squares, and flavored in various ways.

FOR THE COOKIES:

2 cups unbleached all-purpose flour
½ teaspoon salt
1 cup unsalted butter, at room temperature
1 teaspoon vanilla
⅔ cup confectioners' sugar
1 large egg yolk

• To make the cookies, whisk together the flour and salt and set aside. Cream the butter in the bowl of an electric mixer for several minutes, until fluffy and light, then add vanilla and gradually add the confectioners' sugar and continue to beat on medium speed until lightened in color and very fluffy, about 3 to 5 minutes more, scraping down the bowl occasionally. Add the egg yolk and again beat until very fluffy and light, a minute or two. Add the flour all at once, cautiously "pulsing" the mixer off and on at the lowest speed at first to keep the flour from flying out of the bowl, then beating on the lowest speed and scraping the bowl as necessary until the flour is just incorporated and the dough is uniform. Gather the dough into a ball, flatten into a disc and wrap in waxed paper or plastic wrap, and refrigerate until firm, at least several hours.
• Roll the chilled dough on a generously floured surface to ¼ inch thick (if making larger cookie cutouts with this recipe, roll ⅜ inch thick).

Cut with cookie cutters and place the cookies on a baking sheet. Because you are making so many tiny cookies that need chilling before they are baked, don't bother to place the cut cookies with enough space for expansion during baking—just load your baking sheets with as many cookies in one layer as they will hold (you will arrange them prior to baking). If the dough warms and softens while you are working, put it back in the refrigerator to chill before continuing. Refrigerate or freeze the cut, unbaked cookies for 15 to 20 minutes up to overnight to ensure that they'll keep their shape.

•   When ready to bake, preheat the oven to 325°. Spread the chilled cookies on the baking sheets, allowing an inch for expansion between each cookie, and leave the rest of the cookies in the refrigerator to wait their turn in the oven. Bake for 4 to 10 minutes or until cookies have lost their sheen and are only just barely starting to brown at the edges: Start with the shortest amount of time and watch carefully. Let cool slightly before moving to wire racks to cool completely. Glaze and decorate the cookies when cool.

PINK AND WHITE GLAZE

3 egg whites, at room temperature
⅛ teaspoon salt
3 cups confectioners' sugar, possibly more
1 tablespoon lemon juice, possibly more
Red or pink food coloring
Multicolored sprinkles, sometimes called "hundreds and
    thousands"

•   To make the glaze, whisk the egg whites and salt until a little foamy. Add the confectioners' sugar and 1 tablespoon of lemon juice and whisk until completely smooth, adding more lemon juice or sugar until you have an opaque, somewhat thick but drippy glaze that will coat a cookie and run down its sides, covering it completely—test a cookie if you're not sure. (This glaze can be used with other cookie recipes as well, thinned or thickened as desired.)

• Place a sheet of waxed paper or parchment paper on the bottom of two or more rimmed baking sheets to catch drips and stray sprinkles, then place a wire rack on top of each baking sheet. Divide the cookies in half—half will be white, half pink—and begin by glazing and decorating the white cookies: Drop a handful of cookies into the bowl of icing. Using a large fork, turn the cookies over in the icing until they are right side up, then fish them out one at a time with the fork. With your fingers, grasp the cookie by its edges and scrape off the excess icing from the back of the cookie, letting any additional icing drip back into the bowl. Place the cookies on the rack to dry, sprinkling with the multicolored sprinkles while they're still wet. Repeat with the pink half of the cookies: Add a tiny drop or two of red or pink food coloring to the remaining glaze and mix thoroughly to make a pale pink icing. Ice and decorate the pink cookies using the same method as the white cookies. Leave on the racks to dry for 2 to 4 hours.

Makes countless miniature cookies.

VARIATIONS

For shortbread wedges or squares: Preheat the oven to 325° while making the dough. After mixing the dough, pat it into a buttered 8-by-8-inch square pan or 8- or 9-inch round cake pan. Score the dough into squares or wedges with a knife, then prick the surface evenly with the tines of a fork. Bake until the shortbread has lost its sheen, is firm in the center, and just starting to color, about 40 to 50 minutes. Transfer the pan to a wire rack and allow to cool completely before cutting the cookies.

Makes 9 to 12 squares or 8 to 10 wedges.

For shortbread balls: Preheat the oven to 325° while making the dough. After mixing the dough, roll teaspoons of dough into balls and chill for 20 to 25 minutes before baking. Bake for 15 to 20 minutes, until the dough has lost its sheen and has just begun to color. Let cool on the cookie sheets for a few minutes before moving to a wire rack to cool completely. Or roll the cookies in confectioners' sugar while still warm and then place on a wire rack to cool.

Makes about 3 dozen balls.

Other shortbread flavors:

For brown sugar shortbread, substitute ½ cup packed light brown sugar for
the confectioners' sugar.

For vanilla bean shortbread, add ½ of a scraped vanilla bean to the butter.

For coffee or espresso shortbread, add 1 teaspoon very finely ground coffee
or espresso beans to the flour. For mocha shortbread, add 1 teaspoon
very finely ground coffee or espresso beans and 1 tablespoon cocoa to
the flour.

For lemon or orange shortbread, add the grated zest of 1 lemon or ½ orange
and ½ teaspoon lemon or orange extract to the butter.

For ginger shortbread, add 1 tablespoon finely minced candied ginger to the
butter and 2 teaspoons ground ginger to the flour.

For cardamom, cinnamon, nutmeg, clove, or black pepper shortbread, add
1 teaspoon finely ground spice to the flour.

Camp Meeker

OUTSIDE, HIGH IN THE CROWNS OF PRIMORDIAL REDWOODS, DUST
motes swirled through bars of early sun, dew-strung spider webs
trembled in glistening nets between the tallest branches of the trees.
You could see them from the bunk beds on the open porch where we
slept; you could hear woodpeckers hammering the tree trunks all
around as you huddled in your sleeping bag against the chill of the se-
quoia shade.

Soon even the unpaved lane that ran along one side of our summer-
house, a roadbed cushioned thick with the annual sheddings of the forest, would be too hot to walk on in bare feet. You'd want to walk,
because the steep meandering lane was lined with ripening blackberry
canes, and at the bottom of the hill, half falling into the ferny gully, was
a pine-board shack not much bigger than an outhouse but stocked with
every candy and gratuitous snack imaginable, its cash box presided
over by a succession of local teenagers. Beyond that was a redwood
stage where there were sing-alongs and talent shows on Saturday
nights. And beyond that, the reason my mother's family had headed
north of San Francisco every summer for five generations, was the
swimming hole.

Camp Meeker was a place to escape fogbound summers by the bay,
a rustic logging hamlet built up over a hillside in the redwood groves of
western Sonoma County, a few dozen turn-of-the-century cabins
overlooking a bend in a tributary of the Russian River left dammed
after the first-growth trees were logged out and the mill was closed.
Over the years, the swimming hole had gained a gritty beach softened
by pine needles at the slow-moving shallow pool where my brothers
and cousins and I were allowed to wade unwatched, separated from

a roped-off area with flags and floating orange buoys where the teenagers jumped each other's inner tubes and dunked heads.

Pa built our house when he was seventeen by knocking together the family's two original cabins on one narrow, plunging lot. He suspended the building on stilts over the steep hillside and wrapped a wide covered porch all around, with bunk beds lined up against the wall alongside the kitchen; outside the kitchen door, in perpetual shade, was a built-in icebox. The house was modest and uninsulated, the walls a single thickness of plastered lath or painted beadboard, with a cast-iron potbellied woodstove in the kitchen for cooking and heat. Eventually Pa enclosed the crawl space beneath the house for storage and added a third bedroom wedged in at the property line, right up against the lane. There was a whitewashed W.C. and a separate shower stall out on the porch. When you yanked the porcelain-knobbed chains for the toilet or the shower, you could hear water flushing through the pipes all the way down the ivy-covered slope below.

Most of my childhood cleaves along the planes of my family's many moves: seven different households and five schools before I turned ten. Camp Meeker was the one constant. Recollection frames summers there as unbroken time, weeks spent running down the hot lane to the water, my grandmother calling to us from the front porch to hold hands. Plotting contributions to the next talent show while eating sandy peanut butter lunches on the beach. Spending whatever change the adults gave us, clammy in our pockets, on candy we chose ourselves at the snack shack. Picking blackberries, warm and bursting on our fingers, from the canes growing wild right outside our door, and bringing whatever we didn't eat to my grandmother, who cooked them into jam.

In the kitchen with my grandmother, I sat on a bench at the oilcloth-covered table, picking seeds from quartered lemons as she measured the berries and turned them into the cast-iron kettle with cups of sugar.

"The lemon seeds are full of pectin," she told me, a teacher to her core. "Pectin is what thickens the jam." She tied the seeds into a square of muslin and dropped the bundle into the kettle. "Here, you juice the berries before we put the pot on the stove," she said, handing me the potato masher.

When the blackberry jam came to a rolling boil, she'd skim the mauve-pink froth from the surface with a wooden spoon and knock it onto a plate, the syrupy jam bleeding into a carmine pool beneath. Helpers got to taste: I scraped the effervescent foam from its tea saucer with a soup spoon, a musk like roses, dark and sweet, perfuming the cabin and my mouth.

Come night all the kids but the babies were put to bed in the bunks on the porch, and as long as we could keep our eyes open we watched the ochre flicker of light from the kerosene lamps inside, the adults pounding the round oak table in the front room and roaring over their games of poker and hearts, the soft wings of giant moths beating the glass at the kitchen windows, stars blinking into place between the towering, shadowed branches of the trees. Muttering deep in their throats, Lainey and Thor patrolled the closed circuit of the railed porch, protecting us from the groaning sequoias.

It seemed endless, our summers at Camp Meeker. It may have been only a week or two here and there, over years; maybe it was less than that, weekends when my father could get away from his work. The vividness of Camp Meeker overmatches the slide of relative time in my child's memory of being there: the scorching intensity and glazed golden light wherever the sun broke out in brief angled swatches between the Olympian trees, the cool relief of Victorian crystal doorknobs as they turned in my hand, the small lacquered game cabinet housing Yahtzee and felted dice cups and neatly arranged decks of Bicycle brand playing cards. In one of the bedrooms was the dresser that my mother, a July baby, had slept in as a newborn, its turned wooden drawer pulls carved to look like tassels, a shelf on either side of the vanity mirror for candles.

Over the deep porcelain sink in the kitchen were the stacks of my grandmother's "Denmark Blue" dishes, a set of English transferware that had been her own mother's. Though it had only a rudimentary kitchen where cooking was largely confined to assembly lines of sandwiches, burning toast on the woodstove, and making jam, Camp Meeker possessed this authoritative artillery of specialized Edwardian tableware, each piece fluted at the rim, its creamy white surface embellished with five-petaled flowers in indigo blue, surrounded by a delicate tracery of stylized flourishes. Of course there were dinner and luncheon and bread plates and wide shallow soup bowls, a coffeepot and cups and saucers, but there were also pie plates and fruit coupés and tiny condiment dishes, lidded tureens and platters of various shapes and sizes (for chops, for turkeys, for molded salads), a gravy boat that looked like Napoleon's hat, a lidded jelly compote, a covered cheese plate with holes for ventilation, and hourglass-shaped eggcups: shallow side up for hard-boiled eggs, deep side up for soft. At the beginning of each summer's stay, my grandmother would wash every dish, spreading them out to dry across the kitchen table and its benches. While she stood at the sink, her rubber-gloved hands deep in soapy water, I used the eggcups and the endearing little jelly dish with the acorn-shaped knob on its lid as a shell game to hide the ceramic animal figurines that came in boxes of Red Rose tea.

No matter how dramatically hot it had been when we were put to bed, so hot my grandmother would wring out our pillowcases in cool water to help us sleep, by morning when the previous day's convected warmth had sunk deep into the loam of the forest, leaving the air stripped and stark and cold, we were curled in the flannel linings of our sleeping bags, clinging to a sibling or a cousin if you were lucky enough to share a bunk. When my grandmother's frothy red head appeared between the checked gingham curtains hanging in the kitchen windows—my grandmother always the first one up, lighting the woodstove while our parents slept off bourbon-sluiced poker games and wakeful babies—my brothers and cousins and I would stumble in through the kitchen door, dragging our bags and blankies to climb back into bed with her and hear thrillingly grisly stories before the customary Camp Meeker breakfast of charred toast and blackberry jam.

Pa made only rare appearances at Camp Meeker when the whole family was there; the back bedroom where my grandmother usually slept by herself had two narrow iron bedsteads pushed to either side of the small room, so whoever was littlest that year among the current crop of cousins got tucked in beside her, rubbing a cheek against her satiny quilted bed jacket. The rest of us dog-piled under the covers in the other bed, elbowing for pillows and space, a tufted chenille bedspread pulled up to our chins.

In her hairnet and bifocals, cautioning us not to open the bedroom curtains because the neighbors might see her undressed, my modest, abstracted grandmother was hard to imagine as the audacious flapper we'd been told she once was, a party girl who hid in the dunes from the police during gin raids on Ocean Beach. But I've since seen a newspaper photograph of her from 1927, taken for an article on appropriate dress for schoolteachers. Next to her is another teacher, an older experienced woman in thick humorless stockings and a skirt to her ankles. And there is my twenty-three-year-old grandmother, mistress of the first grade, her skirt hiked almost to her knees, her hair fashionably bobbed, smiling coyly at the camera. You can almost picture her with a flask hidden under her dress, swinging from a chain between her breasts.

She may have had a wild streak in her youth, but when it came to children her impulse was always toward character development and moral uprightness. Even the Madame Alexander dolls she gave me for every birthday and Christmas were virtuous figures from history or literature—Martha Washington, Betsy Ross, Marmee and the March girls from *Little Women*. Gleaned from her long years of teaching, my grandmother's stories and fairy tales were always meant to instruct, although they were about as far from Dick and Jane as you could get, as casually harrowing as any other storyteller's in the family. There was the song she sang to us about a grandfather clock that stood ninety years on the floor, ticking reliably for its owner, only to stop . . . short . . . never to run again when the old . . . man . . . died. At least when the grandfather clock stopped dead, it was only a clock, unlike most of the victims in my grandmother's tales, which skewed overwhelmingly toward selfless children and cute animals. Even Solomon Grundy went from baby to aged corpse in a week.

Have common sense was the obvious moral of the tale of Epaminondas, a dense little boy sent by his mother to market with a cake he held so tightly in his fists it was ground to crumbs by the time he arrived. The way to carry cake, his mother corrected him, was to tuck it under his hat. So when she gave him a pound of sweet butter to take to market, Epaminondas put it under his hat, and it melted down his face. The way to carry butter, Epaminondas's mother told him, was to wrap it in leaves and walk by a stream, dipping the butter in the cool water over and over. So when his mother gave him a puppy to take to market, Epaminondas wrapped it in leaves and dipped it and dipped it and dipped it in the cool water of the stream. . . .

While my grandmother outlined the horrific stupidity of Epaminondas, placidly unaware that every child in the room was on the verge of wailing hysteria, I privately contemplated what kind of cake his mom had given him to take to market—I was sure it was yellow cake, tall and light and moist, with drooping swirls of chocolate frosting just like the one on Duncan Hines boxes. The cake was a lot more pleasant to think about than the poor drowned puppy, though I thought about the puppy, too, Lainey's recent motherhood and the leisurely currents of cold moving beneath the hospitable surface of our fern-banked river making its fate all too graphically available for contemplation.

Even more vividly tragic was the story of the Little Match Girl, which in my grandmother's version seemed purpose-built for Camp Meeker: There was a potbellied stove, a kindly grandma, tall trees and a starry night, piles of treats on pretty plates, the solace of religion, and lots of matches, a cornerstone of Camp Meeker life. Years later when I read a translation of Hans Christian Andersen's fairy tale, I saw that the only significant detail my grandmother had imported was a church, where the wretched little waif froze to death on the icy steps; in the original it had been a nameless alley. We didn't have a church at Camp Meeker either, but we had the snack shack, which was close to religion in some circles.

Heart-wrenching and hideous as her story was, I was more than a little envious of the Little Match Girl and her swooning confectionery visions, her catapulting straight to heaven on the strength of innocent faith, the glory of being recognized as unquestionably noble and good. I convinced myself that we had a lot in common. She was barefoot, I was barefoot. She was cold, I was cold—in the morning, anyway. She was good, and I wanted to be.

My hairnetted grandmother needed only to strike a match to the woodstove, a momentary spit and flare, and in its brief halo of light I'd see her, the barefoot girl with the honey-colored hair, her reflection flashing back to me in the slumping glass of the kitchen window. It was the Little Match Girl looking in from the cold, balanced on the rusting springs of my bunk on the sleeping porch, the feathered fallings of the trees scattered around her over the wide painted floorboards. Before the flame sputtered blue and reduced to its cooling heart, I saw through her eyes as she huddled over the small heat of her match: the kitchen with its woodstove glowing red against the shimmering wall, the stacks of dishes blue and white, the row of jam jars on the shelf, their milky coatings of paraffin illuminated in a second's flaring light.

In my mind I light another match and it's just as I remember: the oilcloth-covered table, blackberries sparkling with sugar, charred sour-dough toast and warm pink foam—the Little Match Girl's feast, so close I can almost touch it. And outside, behind her, there are the trees, the sequoias: manifest sentinels of time, night after night their crowns catching stars wheeling in patterns above my bunk, stars yielding long enough for me to pin them to memory's map. The Little Match Girl lifts her face to a vision of warmth—a woodstove, a bittersweet feast, a presentiment of heaven. Night and time resume their evolutions. Each star goes out like a match.

BLACKBERRY JAM AND VARIATIONS

.·.

This recipe is a basic formula that can be used not just for blackberries but for many of the fruits you'd want to make into jam. You don't need packaged pectin or paraffin—just fruit, sugar, and lemon seeds. The lemon seeds contribute natural pectin, which assists the jelling and thickening process in low-pectin fruits, such as most berries, peaches and nectarines, grapes, apricots, cherries, figs, pineapple, and rhubarb. High-pectin fruits, such as currants, plums, cranberries, and quince, probably don't need the boost of lemon seeds. Either way, use fruit that is at its peak (even just *slightly* underripe, which is when pectin content is highest), and follow the same rule as for blackberry jam: 1 cup pre-pared fruit to ¾ cup sugar.

Small batches of preserves are easiest to control in cooking. I prefer to work with 4 cups of fruit and 3 cups of sugar, yielding 4 or 5 cups of jam, an average batch. You can double or triple this amount without problems, though you have to consider whether your largest kettle can hold all the jars you'll need without having them clank together and per-haps break during the sterilization process.

Though it might be enticing to use pretty jars and crocks you've saved, the glass jars made specially for canning are designed to prevent spoilage and they're reusable. So are the screw-top rings, though the flat gummed lids can deteriorate in storage and should not be used a second time. The only other special equipment I recommend buying is a canning funnel and jar-lifting tongs; everything else you need is probably already in your kitchen. If you become a therapeutic jam maker, you might want to invest in a canning kettle with a removable rack for holding jars.

Once you've mastered the basic technique, you can adjust it to your own taste. You might try a combination of fruits, such as strawberries and rhubarb, or mixed berries. Or you can add strips of lemon or orange peel or spices. Cinnamon sticks are lovely with blackberries or figs, as is cardamom with plum jam or star anise with apricots; fresh ginger, tied into the muslin with the lemon seeds, is wonderful with peaches. Just be sure not to reduce the amount of sugar: It's necessary for jelling and preservation.

INGREDIENTS:

4 cups blackberries, gently packed into the measuring cup
3 cups granulated sugar
Seeds of 2 or 3 lemons

EQUIPMENT NEEDED:

Glass canning jars with screw-on lids and caps
Large kettle with lid, such as a spaghetti pot, for sterilizing
    jars before and after filling
Clean dishtowels
Heavy-bottomed cooking pot, such as a Dutch oven or
    large saucepan
Small saucepan
Ladle
Jar-lifting tongs
Wide-mouthed canning funnel
Muslin or double-thickness cheesecloth
Kitchen twine
Saucer or small plate
Optional: candy thermometer

•   Combine the blackberries and sugar in a heavy-bottomed cooking pot and mash the berries lightly with a potato masher. (If making jam with a fruit that browns easily, add a few tablespoons of lemon juice.) Tie the lemon seeds into the muslin with the kitchen twine and add them to the pot. Allow the berries and sugar to macerate while you prepare your equipment.

•   First inspect the canning jars for nicks or cracks and the rings and lids for rust or other imperfections. Wash the jars, rings, and lids well in hot soapy water; dampen a clean dishtowel and place it in the bottom of the large kettle. (If you have a canning kettle, use that and skip the dishtowel.) Arrange the jars on top, making sure they don't touch each other or the sides of the kettle. Prepare one or two jars more than you think you'll need in case of breakage or if you end up with more jam than you expect. Fill the jars with water, then fill the kettle so the jars are completely covered by a good 2 inches. Bring the kettle to a boil, then reduce the heat to low while the jam cooks. Place the clean jars and lids in a saucepan, bring to a boil, then remove from heat and set aside. Place a saucer in the freezer—you will use this for testing whether the jam is cooked.

•   Bring the fruit mixture to a boil over medium heat, stirring occasionally. Skim the foam that rises to the surface (and eat it as a treat). Continue to cook the jam at a gentle boil, stirring often, until the mixture just begins to thicken, usually about 15 to 20 minutes. You will notice that the foaming has subsided and the thickened jam has darkened slightly and burbles rather than boils. Begin to test for jelling, removing the jam from the heat during the test and keeping in mind that most jams (blackberry and raspberry in particular) continue to cook and thicken after they've been removed from the stove. If using a candy thermometer, the jam will be ready at 221° Fahrenheit, the jell point, but it may be ready several degrees before that, so start testing earlier to avoid overcooking the jam. (I've had jam finish cooking 10 minutes after it reached a boil, jam that was ready when the thermometer read 215°, and jam that was gummy and overcooked at 221°, so it pays to be attentive.)

•   To do a freezer test, take the pot off the heat. Drop a teaspoonful of jam onto the saucer you put in the freezer, then return it to the freezer for

2 minutes. Remove the saucer and check the jam: If it has a surface film that wrinkles when the plate is tipped or the jam is nudged, the jam is ready. If not, return the saucer to the freezer and the pot to the flame, and test again in 5 minutes. Most jams from soft fruits such as blackberries will jell in 15 to 30 minutes; firmer fruits may take 45 minutes to an hour.

• When the jam is ready, remove it from the heat. Remove the lemon seeds, which can be rinsed, dried, and used again for another batch of jam.

• To pack and seal the jam, use the jar-lifting tongs to lift out each hot jar, dumping the water back into the pot and draining the jar thoroughly. Set the canning funnel inside a hot jar and ladle hot preserves into the jar to within ½ inch of the rim. When all the jars are filled, use a clean dishtowel dampened with water to wipe the jar rims clean. Top each jar with a lid and a ring, screwing on the ring but not too tightly.

Using the jar-lifting tongs, replace the filled canning jars in the kettle. Make sure the water covers the jars by a good inch. Cover the pot and bring to a boil, then reduce the heat and boil gently for 10 minutes. Turn off the heat and again lift out the jars, keeping them upright. Place them on a dry dishtowel, making sure none of the jars are touching. The lids are designed to seal themselves and you will hear them ping as a vacuum forms in each jar. Let cool completely. Check the seal of the lids: They should be concave, with no give when you press on them; if any jars have not sealed, place them in the refrigerator and use the jam immediately. Otherwise, store the preserves in a cool dry spot for up to a year.

Makes 4 to 5 cups of jam.

Alligator Toes

Disneyland! It was the mecca of childhood, only the words "Christmas" and "birthday" more evocative of carefree innocence and unfettered gluttonous glee to an American kid in the 1960s. In our house the sainted genius Walt Disney had exalted status on par with President Kennedy, Santa Claus, and the Beatles. Billy and John and I had watched *The Mickey Mouse Club* five days a week since we were old enough to sit up by ourselves, and every Sunday night we warbled soulfully along with Jiminy Cricket as he sang "When You Wish upon a Star" on *The Wonderful World of Disney*. My mother had regaled us from time immemorial about her trip to Disneyland the first summer it opened, driving with a friend in a convertible down the palm-dotted California coast when she was eighteen. She described the miniature train chugging through history into dinosaur days, at first the peaceful brontosauri blissfully chewing their prehistoric cud among the giant ferns and dragonflies, then the ferocious tyrannosaur and razor-teethed flying lizard battling it out against a backdrop of fiery volcanic destruction. She told us about the Jungle Cruise and the waggling ears of surfacing hippos, Tom Sawyer's island with its swaggering rope bridges and hidden caves. She said there was a candy kitchen on Main Street where you could press your face to the window as they poured out copper vats of molten chocolate fudge.

"Not as good as Pa's," I said, loyal acolyte of the family faith.

"No, not as good as Pa's," my mother confirmed, her eyes dark and serious before they shimmered with anticipation, "but almost!"

My parents had decided that we were ready for our first trip to the Magic Kingdom, and to make things even more unbearably exciting, we were going to Disneyland on the same weekend I was turning five. My mother packed our car the night before we left, flattening the back seat and loading it with our suitcases and books and games and a cooler full of baloney sandwiches for the daylong drive to Southern California. In the morning my brothers and I were carried out of the house in our pajamas while the dawn sky was still bruised and dreamlike, and for breakfast my mom handed around miniature boxes of our favorite cereals that you ate right from the cardboard containers, cutting through the top with the picnic knife and pouring in about a teaspoon of milk before it overflowed and Sugar Pops slopped all over the back seat. Lainey and Thor were conveniently available to lick the car upholstery clean because Walt Disney had thought of everything—there was a dog kennel right next to the park's entrance, so everyone's mutts could bark at each other to their hearts' content while their owners spent great moments with Mr. Lincoln and marveled at Monsanto's House of the Future.

That evening I had my birthday dinner across from Disneyland at Howard Johnson's, instantaneously proclaimed by Billy and John and me as our family's favorite motel chain, a bar already set low since we'd never stayed in a hotel before, or eaten in a restaurant that didn't have a drive-through window. But just like McDonald's, HoJo's had french fries, served alongside our other new favorite thing, fried clams, in greasy paper-lined orange baskets matching the rest of the turquoise-and-orange décor.

I was busy scribbling on my paper placemat after eating my fried clams, bickering with my brothers over the crayons the waitress had given to us, when she came back carrying a cake lit by the nimbus of a single candle. Not just a piece of cake, but a whole, petite cake, a snowy coconut dome just the right size for a little girl turning five, and the entire restaurant full of Disney-frantic children and their parents sang to me before I made my wish and blew. Inside, the cake had a filling that tasted like an Almond Joy candy bar, and outside it was covered in fluffy marshmallow frosting flecked all over with shredded coconut flakes. I didn't have to share; Billy and John grimaced at the coconut and ate ice cream from frosty silver bowls instead. The leftover cake was even better the next morning, when the frosting had seized up into a sugary crust along the edges.

Everything was blissfully sweet, in fact, right up until my family of five walked hand in swinging hand through the Main Street gates.

That's when the difference between my mother's childlike relish of the world and my father's glum despotism became as glaring as the strong Orange County sun beating down on our mouse-eared heads.

My father was constitutionally incapable of having fun. He didn't know how to relax, let alone surrender to the make-believe world of blithe amusement and wholesome indulgence that was Disneyland's ethos. We were going to put out an eye at the shooting gallery or see something inappropriately salacious at the Horseshoe Review. We were going to ruin our teeth on frozen lemonade, our appetites for lunch on Frito-Lay. We were going to lose John-John in the crowds, or he'd fall through the elevated walkways at the Swiss Family Robinson Treehouse—we'd better keep him on that leash we brought! We were the Swiss Family Robinson as far as my father was concerned, washed ashore to a threatening land of weird animals and pirates and palm trees, but our chances for survival were slim.

While my mother scurried with us from Main Street to Frontierland to Sleeping Beauty's Castle and back again, squealing beside us on every ride, singing along to the glitter-sparkled dolls in "It's a Small World" and gullibly convinced by the simulated tropical rainstorm at the end of the Tiki Room's animatronic show, my dad stood by the turnstiles in the unforgiving sun, holding John-John's limp leash between his hands, glancing at his watch and counting the minutes until our family fun, our Disneyland, our childhood was over.

"C'mon, Daddy, ride the Matterhorn with us!" we cried, wanting him to be with us, to let us know that our pleasure was allowable by having some himself.

"I'll wait here," he'd answer every time, setting his jaw. As we whirled in the teacups and watched our mother's fine Black Irish hair fly out from her head, I saw my dad standing alone under the miserly shade of some spindly tree, dizzying multiples of my unsmiling, re-fusenik, not-having-a-good-time dad repeating back to me again and again as we turned.

By lunchtime on Sunday it was legitimately time for us to head toward the gates for the long afternoon of driving back to Northern California, but my father had also long before hit the limit of his limited patience for frivolity. My mother had promised we could each choose some trinket to take home with us, prompting an apoplexy of indecision and the necessity of racing once again from land to land in search of the perfect Disney souvenirs, or risk the despair of making a wrong and irredeemable choice. We were loitering indecisively at the Jungle Cruise's souvenir stand, listening to the ride operators broadcast the same hokey jokes we'd heard during our ride the day before, my brothers and I fingering giant conch shells and coconuts carved into monkey faces, when amenable John settled on the trinket right in front of him: a rubber alligator as long as his arm.

"Okay, but the rest of you kids, hurry up," my dad ordered, stony-faced and glancing again at his watch.

Then Billy, the responsible eldest child, decided he would be satisfied with an alligator, too.

"Fine, give it to me," my dad said, pulling out his wallet. "Cissy, you've got one minute, we have to leave."

Nearly vibrating with the panic of having to make an instantaneous choice, my eyes darted over the stuff in the bins. This wasn't just my first-Disneyland-trip trinket, it was my birthday-at-Disneyland trinket, too. It had to be good. We'd looked at Tinkerbell necklaces, Minnie Mouse dolls, Cinderella jewelry boxes, and I couldn't decide—it was too much pressure, and I felt like I was going to wet my pants. Compulsively squeezing the squishy belly of one of the rubber alligators my brothers were getting, I realized that a rubber alligator was the one thing I couldn't live without.

"You can't have one of those. Those are for boys," my father said, turning back to the cash register clerk and cutting off further discussion.

But I knew: I wanted an alligator. It was the only thing I wanted.

"*NO,*" my father barked conclusively, handing Billy and John their yellow Disneyland bags with Mickey Mouse's face stamped all over. "Alligators are for boys. Besides, you already had a treat—you got your own cake."

I was far from being any kind of precocious feminist. Though my mother was unequivocal in telling my brothers and me that we could be anything we wanted, her marriage and our family spun its wheels in the deeply rutted trench of the traditional gender divide: Men got to be president and the breadwinners, women got to be mommies and, as a bonus, keep the house clean. I was as girly a girl as you could find, convinced early by my unashamedly feminista mother that it was the luckiest thing in the world to be a girl, with all its arabesques of lipstick samples and nail polish and hair ribbons and Kool-Aid tea parties with dolls. I was a girl who would ask for a toy vacuum cleaner when I was in kindergarten and refuse to even try on a pair of pants until we moved to Alaska when I was eleven.

Still, I knew it was grossly, perversely unfair that my dad was refusing to let me have an alligator like my brothers, let alone that he was citing my birthday cake as a secondary justification for his arbitrary tyranny. I could tell that Billy and John knew it, too—they hadn't even wanted any of my birthday cake, and it was my *birthday*! I watched them shuffle uncomfortably, heads down, kneading their crinkling Disney bags at their chests. We were not children who risked tantrums, but I was on the verge of a major meltdown of powerless, weeping frustration, as furious at the hot tears I could feel springing to my eyes as I was at my unjust father.

My mother went into a fluster of last-ditch diplomacy, pulling my dad aside and trying to reason with him as he scowled with his arms knotted across his chest, her wispy hair flying out of her bun, just like it had in the Mad Hatter's teacups, as she cajoled and pacified. My father stood glowering by the Dole pineapple juice concession as my mother scurried back to my brothers and me, gathering us like a flock of wayward chicks before a tornado and telling us we had to hurry to the car, it would all be okay, Daddy said it was all right if I chose a souvenir from somewhere along Main Street as we headed for the exit.

Running alongside my scrambling mother, holding her hand and swinging my head right and left as she pointed out possibilities in the store windows of Main Street, I couldn't imagine what we might find that would be as good as a rubber alligator.

"How about a Donald Duck pencil? How about a Snow White locket?" My mom ticked off items hopefully as we darted through the crowds, trying to keep up with my dad, who was far ahead tugging Billy and John by the hands. There were Mickey Mouse balloons—too ephemeral; autograph books with Bambi on them—no time to find any characters to get their signatures; and splotches of fake dog vomit in the magic shop—something I had plenty of, for real, at home. I was still fighting back tears when my mom jerked to a halt in front of the hat shop. There, in the window, was a Mary Poppins hat with three glossy fake cherries adorning the polka-dot-ribboned brim. It wasn't an alligator, but it wasn't dog vomit, either.

We raced inside, my mom babbling to the hat store lady that we wanted a Mary Poppins hat with cherries. The lady smiled and turned her back to us, sorting through her stock, and presented us with a Mary Poppins hat—but instead of cherries it had a fake flower, a limp daisy that looked like a fried egg. All of the Mary Poppins hats behind the counter had fried eggs.

"What about the one in the window?" my mom asked, a whinge of desperation in her voice. The one in the window, we were graciously informed, was glued to the hat stand. And I'd run completely out of time.

The Mary Poppins hat's elastic was so tight under my chin that it cut off the circulation under my ears. I rubbed under my jaw and stomped to our car with the fried egg on my head, my mother shooting me encouraging looks, my brothers oblivious to my outraged, disappointed sulk as they peeked at the good souvenirs inside their bags.

When we got to our car out in the frying parking lot, my brothers threw their alligator bags into the way back of the car with all of our other stuff, and I climbed in there, too, dumping my hat into the corner by the empty cooler. I didn't want to sit with my brothers, even if it wasn't their fault. I sat with the dogs and the dirty laundry and pouted as my father steered us toward the freeway.

I sighed as loudly as I dared. I tossed my hair and harrumphed, crossing my arms violently over my chest. I turned my head and glared at my father just long enough to feel brave and righteous but not so long that he'd see me in the rearview mirror. My dad, for no good reason at all, had ruined the perfect happiness of my birthday trip to Disneyland, but nobody was paying any attention. Billy and John were poring over the Disneyland map in the middle seat; my parents were busy not speaking to each other up front. I kicked out my feet at my dumb fried-egg hat, and that's when I heard the crinkle of my brothers' yellow Disney bags by the wheelwell.

Very, very quietly I pulled the alligators from their bags. *It isn't fair!* I kept thinking as I kneaded the green rubber, the dogs panting on either side of me. The alligators I'd been denied had the same satisfying texture as a gumdrop. I squeezed their faces so their jaws opened and closed. I thought about how much fun I could have had if I'd gotten one, too: When my brothers got tired of theirs, I could dress all three in dolls' clothes and play family, with a mommy alligator, a daddy alligator, and a little girl.

I already knew it was going to be a long, long ride home. I turned my head to the front of the car one last time to make sure no one was watching me. And then like a cowboy who shoots his horse to take cover behind its body during a gun battle, I held the rubber alligators to my mouth and one by one bit off all their toes.

COCONUT LAYER CAKE

∴

FOR THE CAKE:

2¾ cups unbleached all-purpose flour

1 tablespoon baking powder

½ teaspoon salt

½ teaspoon freshly grated nutmeg

1 cup unsalted butter, at room temperature

2 cups granulated sugar

4 large eggs, at room temperature, separated

1 cup light coconut milk, well stirred before measuring

2 teaspoons vanilla extract

1 cup sweetened, shredded coconut for garnish

FOR THE FILLING:

¾ cup granulated sugar

¼ cup unbleached all-purpose flour

¾ cup light coconut milk, well stirred before measuring

¾ cup milk

2 teaspoons vanilla extract

¼ teaspoon salt

14 ounces sweetened, shredded coconut

FOR THE FLUFFY WHITE FROSTING:

3 egg whites, at room temperature
Pinch of salt
2 teaspoons vanilla extract
½ cup cold water
1½ cups granulated sugar
Rounded ¼ teaspoon cream of tartar

• Heat oven to 350°. Butter and flour three 8- or 9-inch round cake pans.

• For the cake: Whisk together the flour, baking powder, salt, and nutmeg and set aside. Beat the butter for a full minute, then gradually add the sugar and beat until very creamy on medium speed, about 3 to 5 minutes. Add the egg yolks, one at a time, beating for another full minute after each addition. Add the vanilla to the milk. On low speed, add the flour mixture in three parts alternately with the milk mixture in two parts, beginning and ending with flour; beat just until smooth after each addition, scraping the bowl after each addition as well.

• Beat the reserved egg whites in a separate bowl on medium speed until they form soft peaks but are still glossy and not dry. Fold half of the whites gently into the batter, then the rest, just until they disappear.

• Divide the batter among the cake pans and bake for 20 to 25 minutes, or until a toothpick inserted in the center comes out clean. Let cakes cool in pans for about 10 minutes, then turn out onto wire racks to cool completely.

• While the cakes cool, toast the 1 cup of coconut reserved for the garnish. Spread it on a cookie sheet and toast for about 10 minutes, stirring and watching carefully—every 3 minutes or so, until it is evenly golden brown—it will burn easily, so keep watch! Cool thoroughly.

• For the filling, whisk together the sugar and flour, then add the milks and thoroughly combine. Cook over medium-high heat, whisking continually, until thickened and bubbly but still pale in color, about 5 minutes. Remove from the heat and stir in the vanilla extract, salt, and coconut. Cool to room temperature before filling the cake.

• When the cake and the filling have cooled completely, place the bottom layer of the cake on a serving plate. Spread half the filling on top. Center the middle layer of cake over the bottom layer and spread with remaining filling. Add the top layer of cake. Now make the frosting.

• For the frosting, combine the egg whites, salt, and vanilla extract in the bowl of an electric mixer fitted with the whip attachment. In a medium saucepan over high heat, combine the water, sugar, and cream of tartar. Stir to dissolve the sugar but do not stir again after the mixture begins to bubble at the edges. Let the mixture come to a full rolling boil, then remove immediately from heat.

• With the mixer on medium-high speed, beat the egg white mixture until foamy, about one minute. Without turning off the mixer, pour the hot sugar syrup into the egg whites in a thin, steady stream. Continue beating constantly on medium-high for 5 to 7 minutes, until the frosting is creamy, voluminous, and holds stiff peaks.

• Frost the top and sides of the cake immediately. Generously sprinkle the top with toasted coconut. Best served the day it is made.

Makes one 3-layer cake.

VARIATIONS

For a completely snowy-white cake:
Do not toast the shredded coconut for the garnish.

For 36 cupcakes:
Line cupcake tins with paper liners and divide cake batter evenly among them. Bake at 350° for 18 to 20 minutes, until cupcakes spring back when lightly touched and a toothpick comes out clean when inserted into the center of a cupcake. When cupcakes are cool, spread a layer of filling ¼ inch thick over the top of each cake, then frost.

For Almond Joy Cake:
Use the recipe for Plenty of Chocolate Cake (page 9), baking three layers. For the filling, substitute ½ teaspoon almond extract for ½ teaspoon vanilla, and toast 1 cup roughly chopped almonds at 350° for

about 10 minutes, stirring every few minutes until the almonds become fragrant and lightly brown; let cool before adding to the coconut filling. Frost with the Fluffy White Frosting and garnish the cake with un-toasted coconut. This also makes great cupcakes: Fill the cupcake cups a scant two-thirds full and bake for 18 to 20 minutes. When cool, top with a ¼-inch layer of the coconut-almond filling, then frost with Fluffy White Frosting.

Petaluma Means Pets

IN THE SPRING OF MY KINDERGARTEN YEAR, MY PARENTS PACKED up our house in Palo Alto and moved us north of the Golden Gate to Sonoma County's picturesque landscape of rolling oak-studded hills patchworked with vineyards and farmland. My dad had opened a private practice with a classmate from law school on the idyllic main square in Sonoma, the county seat of the valley, on the cusp of becoming world famous for its wine. Sonoma was still a small town then, and the closest place my parents could find to live was on the other side of the valley in the agricultural sticks of Petaluma, which was famous for being either the arm-wrestling capital of the world or the poultry capital of the world, depending on whether you were upwind or down from the turkey and chicken ranches. They hurriedly rented a vacant farmhouse at the edge of town, part of a defunct dairy farm located on a tract of land slated for the imminent development of a subdivision. Across a pasture mined with cow pies was the historic Petaluma adobe, a leftover from the days of the early Californios, and the appropriately named Adobe Elementary, where Billy finished first grade and I spent the last six weeks of kindergarten answering to the name "Kenneth."

All the grazing land surrounding our farmhouse had been leased to an industrial dairy down the road, leaving us just the defeated house, the gravel barnyard where my parents parked the car, and a fenced weedlot in the back with a rusting swing set and some desperate leggy geraniums that hadn't been watered in years. There was a weathered empty barn and a concrete cattle trough the size of a kiddie pool full of sharp-eyed goldfish, the fish originally put there to eat the algae and keep the water clean for the cows, my mother told us, but they'd lived there so long undisturbed each fish was at least a foot long, glossy, muscular leviathans that were both a little menacing and uncatchable.

In a small square paddock between the barn and the road was some-one's swaybacked, aged white horse.

"Look, Cis, we have our own horse!" my mother cried on the day we arrived. I'd been bitten by a horse at one of her high school re-unions when I was two and subsequently felt a little cool toward horses, but I had my mother's sense of the romantic and I wanted to be enchanted by this sad decrepit nag. We climbed up the rungs of the fence like they did in *National Velvet* and gazed at the mangy old horse standing impassive in its yard of muck, its knees and elbows scarred, its dingy coat threadbare in patches like an old teddy bear.

"Isn't it wonderful to have a horse!" my mother sighed, to which I nodded in agreement. I knew it must be wonderful to have a horse, al-though not, as even a six-year-old could plainly see, this particular horse.

The industrial dairy's soporific cattle stood at masticating ease all day in the pastures on three sides of us, occasionally mustering out of their wall-eyed lassitude to swish their tails at flies. They didn't belong to us, but no one had told that to Lainey and Thor. Twice a day the cowboys arrived with their horses and long white cattle trucks to round up the cows and take them down the road for milking, and our vigilant little dogs would bolt through the dry-rotted fencing to defend their herd against the cowboys, biting the cows' ankles and stampeding them into the most inconvenient corners of the fields. They worked in relay, one holding the cowboys and their horses at bay while the other stared down hundreds of terrified bovines, the passive thousand-pound dairy cows incapable of defying two tiny sheepdogs.

After a week or so of this routine, the exasperated cowboys asked my mom to keep Lainey and Thor inside while the cows were moved, and sometimes she'd remember to keep the door shut. When she did, the dogs would leap at the farmhouse windows, whining with urgency as the trucks rolled up into the barnyard, their compression brakes re-leasing with a loud flatulent squeak. Later, when it was safe to let the dogs out, they'd tear across the empty pastures trailing the scent of their departed herd, heads down in the close-cropped weeds, their shoulders sliding under their woolly coats.

"A real working dairy ranch with our own cows!" my mom an-nounced. "You know what *that* means, kids!" You bet we did: It meant chocolate milk and pudding and custard and ice cream. Now that we lived so far out in the boonies, where the Good Humor man ventured not, it was imperative that we supply our own ice cream. John-John liked rainbow sherbet push-ups, Billy was an ice cream sandwich loyalist, and my dad was not averse to a soothing after-dinner Fudgsicle to go with the hidden sock-drawer Baby Ruth he'd eat when we were in bed. I'd take a Nutty Buddy if I could get it, but what I really craved were It's-Its: a San Francisco invention of vanilla ice cream slathered between two oatmeal cookies, the whole thing dipped in chocolate and frozen. My mom took our orders, and suddenly, as if straight from our mouths to the cows' ears, our freezer was jammed with boxes of ice cream novelties.

"This ice cream in my It's-It is from our cows, right, Mommy?" I asked one night during dessert, just to confirm what I already knew to be true. My brothers swiveled their faces over toward our mom's; at the end of the table, my dad snorted heavily through his nose and kept sucking his Fudgsicle. Behind her stalling sphinxlike smile, my mother's green eyes skittered like the ball on a roulette table, her mind hoping to bounce onto a semi-truthful answer. "Well, it *might just be*," she said, her voice heavy with innuendo, "it *definitely* came from a cow."

Technically *petaluma* means something like "wrong side of the hill." According to my mother, Petaluma meant pets. A horse, two dogs, rented cows, and a trough full of wily goldfish: All we needed was a cat. My mom had started taking art classes at the local community college, bringing home semi-abstract paintings that we never identified correctly. My brothers and I could see the disappointment on her face when we thought the bird's-eye-view of our Palo Alto house was an upright vacuum cleaner, or a Madonna and Child portrait looked to us like George Washington with a cantaloupe. So when my mom squealed to a halt next to the goldfish trough one afternoon and put down the station wagon's tailgate, Billy and John-John and I came running with our bamboo fishing poles baited with diaper pins, ready to dutifully admire another of her artworks. Instead there was a cardboard box lined with tea towels in the trunk of the car—a makeshift nest for three tiny kittens. She'd only planned to surprise us with one kitten from the litter born to my Palo Alto kindergarten teacher's cat, but once she saw them she couldn't decide, and took all three. How could she resist? There were two boys and a girl, one for each of us.

"I always wanted a pet cat when I was a little girl—" she began, and we knew the story so well she didn't need to finish. Grandma had dismissed the idea, telling our mom that if she wanted to grow up and have cats licking the butter on her dining room table for heaven's sake, she could go right ahead. So these were the kittens that would turn into cats that would live on our dining room table and lick the butter! This prospect was just as exciting as our recent discovery that dogs would clean the inside of your mouth if you let them.

Pets were educational, my mother liked to tell us. You could learn kindness and responsibility, and, most convenient for parents who would rather approach the topic of sex education from an oblique angle, you could learn all about the miracle of birth through your instinctively compliant animals, especially if you didn't bother to have them neutered or spayed. A genius at instigating, my mother wasn't known for her follow-through; besides, she liked the idea of growing your own. We'd already experienced the miracle of a litter of three Sheltie puppies, and in addition to the backup babysitting and general pleasure of loyal canine company, the permanently stained chenille bedspread that resulted and had been relegated to the back of our station wagon meant that long trips were made thus forevermore comfortable. With the acquisition of Musette, Jean-Tom, and Robespierre—we named our kittens after our current favorite cartoon movie, *Gay Purr-ee*, arguably a step up in sophistication from the lame names John and I had given Thor's two siblings, Brownie for the brown puppy and Blackie for the black one—we experienced the miracle of incestuous, six-toed feline birth over and over, our house becoming a veritable kitten factory for the next five years.

It was much more fun being at home on our crummy little farm than being at school. It was more fun walking to school, for that matter, than being at school. Every morning, Billy and I carried our cartoon-character lunchboxes out to the picketed gate leading to the cattle pastures, empty because the cows were away being milked, and high-stepped our way across the fields over crisp-edged yellow pancakes of cow dung. If we got across the fields early enough, we had time to explore the deserted Petaluma adobe, where you could see bits of straw sticking out of the mud bricks it had been built of more than a hundred years before. High up in the dark corners, bats hung by their toes from the ceiling, their wings wrapped around themselves like silent movie stars.

Billy didn't like to be late, so he'd stand in the middle of the adobe's courtyard, shouting for me to hurry. If the bell rang while I was still wandering around, he'd leave me behind, running fast toward the crowd of kids and teachers siphoning in through the classroom doors. I trudged toward the school alone, yanking up my kneesocks, knowing it would be another harrowing day of kindergarten.

I'd loved kindergarten in Palo Alto. I loved it so much that after the first day, when I realized that as soon as my classmates and I left with our mothers at lunchtime a second class of kindergartners came into our room and got to do the same things for the rest of the afternoon, I asked if I could stay all day for a double dose of kindergarten. And they let me! Every day I got two graham cracker snacks, two nap times, two story circles, two sharing times on the rug, two celery feedings of Marshmallow, the classroom bunny, all at exactly the same time as the day before and the day before that. Twice I got to demonstrate how to dance the twist accompanied by the Beatles' "I Want to Hold Your Hand" on my Close 'n Play, twice shake a jar of cream until it turned into butter. Nothing in my life had the routine and predictability of kindergarten. There was even a kid who projectile-vomited every week during story circle.

And then I got to Adobe Elementary, where they thought kids wanted freedom to explore and independent discovery, the chance to make up their own rules and feel their growing autonomy in the world. I didn't want that—I had enough freedom and autonomy and no-rules at home with my mom, and she had better art supplies. What I wanted from school was someone to tell me when to take a nap.

Kindergarten in Petaluma was a daily free-for-all, and all anyone in my class wanted to do, when left to their own devices, was dress up or stack the blocks. I thought blocks were mind-numbingly dull, and the dress-up closet was mediocre by any standard. There were a couple of stained housedresses and a grimy naked doll. There wasn't a single velvet cape or pair of white gloves or a tutu, no Mardi Gras beads or pirate eye patches or wigs. At my house I had a shirt box full of real fox stoles with dangling clawed feet, taffeta prom dresses, a rabbit fur muff, and a hoop skirt, and that was just in my room—don't get me started on what my mom had. When I asked the teacher if I could fingerpaint, she said the class had already completed their "unit" on fingerpainting and now we were "exploring blocks." Blocks!

Compounding my disenchantment was the fact that nobody knew

my name, not even me. Three-quarters of the way through a school year, when I heard the name "Kathleen" I didn't realize I was the one being spoken to. There was a kid named Kenneth in the Petaluma class, and in the protoliterate culture that is kindergarten he and I became interchangeable, receiving each other's drawings and alphabet exercises when the helper of the day handed out our papers. I never learned any of the other kids' names, either, so if they wanted to call me Kenneth at least it was fair. I gritted my teeth and spitwashed the dirty baby doll's face, looking wistfully out the window at the peaceful evocative adobe, cool and quiet and lasting, with its damp bat-infested walls smelling of earth and straw, and beyond to our house, where at least I could count on a Dr Pepper, Fluffernutter, and astronaut food sticks for my after-school snack.

My parents only planned to live in Petaluma for a few months before finding something more permanent in Sonoma. Nevertheless, my mother decided to turn the farmhouse's desolate, sunbaked backyard into a full-blown garden. Her father's daughter, she had a particularly green thumb and spent afternoons and weekends hacking away at the hardscrabble Petaluma dirt, my father sometimes joining us outside when he was home from long hours at his office, my mother giving him detailed instructions and dragging hoses and tools around while my brothers and I played on the rusting swing set.

One weekend Billy and John were rocking back and forth in the two-sided swing, seeing how high they could go. My mother had just retreated to the kitchen to collect cold drinks for us as my dad continued to break up topsoil for another planting bed, turning the earth with a pitchfork as my mother had instructed. I was sitting barefoot near my father, fiddling with the grass, pulling up blades straight between my toes while keeping the garden hose wedged under my instep—one of those purposeless tasks that little children concentrate their whole attention on. My dad was no handyman, and he was never good at looking casual. It was a Sunday afternoon, and he was wearing khaki slacks and a white V-neck T-shirt, but he still appeared as if he'd just come from court.

I was dimly aware as I played that my dad was having trouble with a big clod of dirt. He had been leaning into his pitchfork, driving it down, then raising a fork full of dark earth and twisting it over, back into the bed. Now he couldn't get the pitchfork to sink. He pushed it down, elbows bent, a couple of times, stepping onto it lightly in his good shined shoes for leverage. The screen door slammed open; my mother appeared out of the shadowed kitchen with three Frescas held tight to her ribs and a cold beer in each hand, the tinted brown glass of the beer bottles already beading. My father stomped his foot onto the metal shoulders of the pitchfork, leaned his full weight on the handle, and lifted. Released suddenly with the force of his effort, up came a heavy ball of crumbling black earth carried on the tines, matted grains of it tumbling off and falling onto me.

I looked up. From where I sat on the grass, the clod of dirt rose high into the sky, lifting toward the full sun that seemed centered over our yard. Dirt was showering down. The soil on the pitchfork appeared to be moving independently of its skyward lift, and as more dirt fell away and time slowed to a clicking of frames, I saw wrinkled pink feet churning desperately in the air, the raw starry nose of a mole waving like a sea anemone. Impaled on my father's pitchfork, the mole was framed in a halo of white sunlight against the perfect, impassive blue. Beyond it, the swing set's rusty squeak; the far echo of my mother's voice shouting my father's name in horror. The dying mole was falling, my father having yanked his hands away from the fork, recoiling from what he'd done.

I was already running. I heard the thud behind me as I headed for the gate, and the punch and rip of my mother's pitchfork, left upright in the grass, as it punctured my foot, going all the way through. I kept on running. The name they called me dissolved into air as my parents shouted it over and over, fading into the space expanding between us.

IT'S-ITS FROM YOUR OWN COWS

∴

If you don't have a cow, you'll have to go to the store. To give everything enough time to freeze properly, make the ice cream custard two days before serving and allow the churned ice cream to freeze overnight before assembling the It's-Its.

FOR THE VANILLA ICE CREAM:

2 cups heavy cream
2 cups half-and-half
1 vanilla bean
6 large egg yolks
Pinch of salt
¾ cup granulated sugar

• In a medium-sized heavy saucepan, combine the cream and half-and-half and bring to just under a boil over medium heat, then remove from the flame. Split the vanilla bean and scrape the seeds from the pod; add both the seeds and the pod to the cream mixture and let steep for about 20 minutes.

• Bring the cream mixture to just under a second boil over medium heat; meanwhile whisk the egg yolks and salt in a medium bowl until combined, then add the sugar and continue to whisk until the egg mixture begins to thicken and lighten in color. When the cream is just under a boil, slowly pour about a cup of the hot liquid over the egg mixture while whisking steadily (a soup ladle is convenient for pouring the first cup of hot cream into the eggs). Slowly pour the rest of the cream mixture into the eggs, whisking steadily until it is fully combined. Pour the custard back into the saucepan and cook over medium heat, stirring constantly with a wooden spoon, until the custard has thickened enough to coat the back of the spoon, and your finger run across the back of the spoon leaves a trail in the custard. This will take about 5 to 10 minutes; if checking with a candy thermometer, the custard will reach 170°.

• Strain the custard into a heatproof bowl, discarding the vanilla bean pod. Allow the custard to cool to room temperature, then chill thoroughly, overnight if possible, before churning according to your ice cream maker's directions.

• When the ice cream is churned, spoon it into a freezer-friendly container and freeze until very hard, preferably overnight, before proceeding.

Makes a generous quart of ice cream, enough for about 8 or 10 It's-Its.

FOR THE OATMEAL COOKIES:

3 cups rolled oats, quick or old-fashioned

1½ cups unbleached all-purpose flour

1 teaspoon cinnamon

1 teaspoon ground ginger

½ teaspoon freshly grated nutmeg

¼ teaspoon ground cloves

1 teaspoon baking soda

1 teaspoon baking powder

1 teaspoon salt

1¼ cups unsalted butter, at room temperature

1¼ cups firmly packed light brown sugar

¾ cup granulated sugar

2 large eggs, at room temperature

1½ teaspoons vanilla

Optional: grated zest of an orange

• Process 1 cup of the rolled oats in a blender or food processor until it is a powder; combine the powderized oats, the rest of the oats, the flour, spices, baking soda, baking powder, and salt in a medium bowl. Set aside.

• In the bowl of an electric mixer, beat the butter on medium speed for a full minute, then add the sugars and beat until very light, about 5 minutes. Add the eggs and vanilla and beat again until very light and fluffy. If using the orange zest, beat in until combined. Add the flour-oat mixture, a heaping cup at a time, and mix in on low speed just until the flour disappears, scraping the sides of the bowl. Chill the cookie dough until firm before baking, at least an hour.

• When ready to bake, preheat the oven to 375° and lightly grease a baking sheet or two. Scoop even, rounded spoonfuls of dough, about 2 tablespoons each, and roll briefly between your palms into balls. Place the balls on the cookie sheets with plenty of room for expansion—the cookies will spread to be about 3 inches across. Bake for 8 to 10 minutes, until the cookies are puffed and starting to brown at the edges. Remove from the oven and allow to cool for a minute or two before removing to wire racks to cool completely.

Makes about 3 dozen cookies.

TO ASSEMBLE THE IT'S-ITS FOR EACH SANDWICH:

2 oatmeal cookies
Approximately ½ to ⅔ cup vanilla ice cream
Approximately 2 ounces high-quality dark, semisweet, or
   milk chocolate, roughly chopped or broken up

• Have ready a baking sheet lined with parchment that will fit in your freezer to hold the assembled It's-Its. For each It's-It, place a cookie wrong side up on the baking sheet, top with a scoop or slab of vanilla ice cream, then add the second cookie right side up, gently pressing the cookies together until the ice cream oozes to the edges of the cookies. You want about ½ inch of ice cream in each sandwich. Immediately place the assembled sandwiches in the freezer while you melt the chocolate.

• Over simmering water in a double boiler, or in the microwave, heat the chocolate just until melted. Allow to cool a bit—you do not want the chocolate to be too hot, just fully liquid, or it will melt the ice cream. Transfer the melted chocolate to a bowl small and deep enough to dip half an It's-It at a time, then dip the sandwiches halfway and return to the freezer immediately. When the chocolate has hardened, dip the other half of the cookie and return to the freezer to firm up completely before serving.

CHAPTER
9

Valley of the Moon

Sonoma smelled of cinnamon and donuts and root beer floats, popped corn and hot sour bread, grapes fermenting in cool subterranean cellars. From the first summer day when my family drove into the valley through the blonded hills, down shaded lanes lined with titanic eucalyptus trees, past vineyards heavy with dusty grapes and Carpenter's Gothic farmhouses with wraparound verandas, finally arriving at a town at the center of which was a leafy green plaza complete with bandstand and duck pond, Sonoma looked like a picture from a storybook.

So far as I could tell, it seemed to be a village made for children. Just beyond the high school was a miniature steam-powered railroad, and frescoed on a wall across from city hall was a map of the valley to tell you where you were and how to get home if you got lost. My dad drove us slowly around the Plaza: On one side was the movie theater, its art deco marquee lit up that afternoon with the double feature of *Yellow Submarine* and *The Love Bug;* next door was the bakery where they sold cinnamon pull-apart coffee cakes; and next to that, we could see, was my dad's office in a small square adobe with his name inscribed on a brass plaque on the door. His law office was right across from the Plaza's bandstand, the playground, and the red-brick library.

The duck pond was on the corner. I saw at least a dozen kids at its reedy banks, and two or three self-satisfied mother ducks leading families of bobbing ducklings in their wake. No matter where you lived in Sonoma, you were only a bike ride away from the duck pond, and the donut shop where you were hit by the aroma of hot sugar before you opened the wooden screen door, and the A&W drive-in with its root beer floats, and the Sprouse-Reitz Five & Dime's bins of cheap toys and candy, and our church, appealingly named after Saint Francis, the patron saint of animals. It only got better as we approached our new house, a one-story ranch on the corner lot of a street that ended in a double cul-de-sac. One of the neighbors' yards was a folly of plaster trolls, statues of baby deer, and long-tongued giant toads set up on diamond-patterned beds of red-and-white volcanic rock; plastic pinwheels stuck in the dirt spun gaily in the slightest breeze. Later I'd hear my mother and her friends whisper that the yard was an eyesore and the lady who lived there a crackpot, but I felt like I was moving to the precincts of Hansel and Gretel.

Never during the rest of my childhood did I feel such safety and belonging as I did for the two years we lived in Sonoma, surrounded by families we saw every week at church or met under the charitable shade of hundred-year-old trees, riding bikes with my brothers and the neighbor kids to the Plaza or the movie theater, flowing easily from one house to another for impromptu spaghetti dinners where we children would all sit together trading stories from the schoolyard, listening to the nearby laughter of our parents over their bottles of wine. In Sonoma it seemed that behind every screen door was an adult who knew my name, and yet only rarely do I glimpse my mother during that chapter of my memories, even more rarely my father. My mom receded to the periphery of our lives, sewing and making things and gardening, handing us bags of stale bread to take to the duck pond, plotting practical jokes on the sidewalk with her new friends—I had a sense then that she had her own life beyond us, people who sought out her company, and I felt proud: Everyone loved my beautiful, exuberant mother.

I was proud of my father, too, with his office on the Plaza, his name known to all who passed by, how serious and smart he was behind his desk, his starched white sleeves rolled up at the cuffs, dusty light angling in through the windows as he glanced up from a pile of papers when I arrived to walk home with him after the library across the street closed for the day. I carried my latest stack of library books and my father stopped at the bakery, tucking his folded newspaper under his arm so he could carry his briefcase and the pink bakery box, its strings taut under his fingers. My mother, my father, their friends: Even when they were offstage I had a sense of their constancy, as reliable as the kindly face of the moon I saw hovering each night at the window of the room I shared with John, bathing my pillow in her benevolent blue light. The

Valley of the Moon, the adults called our home, every child I knew awash in the luxurious glow of living in a small town, held steady and protected in the cupped palm of our valley.

My rampantly social mom joined the Junior Women's Club, whose purpose seemed mainly to have costume parties for the adults, but they also assembled the kids to ride their decorated bikes in the Fourth of July parade around the Plaza, and they sewed stuffed animals for prizes at the carnival games during the town ox roast each spring and for the festival when the grapes were harvested every fall. When school started, my mom threw herself into the PTA, another platform for social and artistic enterprise. She went into full-blown production of macramé fern hangers to sell at the school fair, and earned kudos for the matching Tweedledum and Tweedledee suits she made for Billy and his cohort Mark to wear in the Sassarini Elementary production of *Alice in Wonderland*. A year later when John began kindergarten, she outfitted him as a lion and turned the interior of the kindergarten building into a three-ring big-top tent for the class circus.

By then our house was a three-ring circus, too—if you wanted a kitten, you need look no further. Musette had matured from surprised teenage mother to blasé serial matriarch, and any kittens we didn't find homes for stayed on with us and had more kittens of their own. When my mom's cantankerous Aunt Helen invited herself over one Saturday, she was aghast to find a litter of mewling kittens in every drawer and cupboard she snooped through. It happened to be our high-water mark of feline ownership. Counting the adults, for a brief but memorable time we had seventeen cats. The butter on the table was licked down to a hummock, rasped all over with feathery tongue marks. Aunt Helen kept her gloves on through lunch and never asked to come back.

In Sonoma my mother's new best pal was Mary Anne, the sole single woman among a coterie of young moms. Mary Anne had just graduated from college and started working for the family business—she was the only daughter of the Sebastianis, one of the town's prosperous winemaking families, local nobility who'd paid for the town's streetlights and built the bus depot, the hospital, and the movie theater—but she didn't seem to mind taking Billy and John and me for a swim at her parents' house while our mom buried our family room in the makings of crepe-paper flowers. "When I have kids, I hope I'm as fun as your mom," Mary Anne would tell us, the four of us waving goodbye as my mother, dressed in her white vinyl go-go boots and Jackie Kennedy sunglasses, drove off in the station wagon loaded with supplies to festoon the veterans' hall in advance of some gala.

On our way to the Sebastianis' pool, we'd stop by their winery, a pleasantly dank stone warehouse where the old walls and the moist closed air and the carved wooden barrels stacked to the beams of the ceiling all held the dark tang of yeast and fruit and alcohol, a heady odor emblematic of the town, both pungent and spicily sweet. Up in the wooded foothills above the town, overlooking the original vineyard of century-old rootstock, the Sebastianis' house was an Italian villa built of the same rough local stone as the winery. Bougainvillea exploded in red and orange up the sides of shady verandas enclosed in stone arches, and peacocks perched on the gnarled branches of a giant valley oak at the end of the circular driveway, shrieking bloody murder at anyone who parked below. With a waterside view of the whole valley, the pool was off the back veranda that led into the kitchen, where Mary Anne's mother, Sylvia, was always in the midst of some fascinatingly archaic cooking project.

Delicious as it was to splash around as peacocks strutted past on their patrol of the property, I didn't stay in the pool for long. Though I was invariably wrapped in a towel and dripping all over her tile floor, Sylvia let me follow her around the kitchen, giving me jobs like running the rolling pin over the wooden mold filled with homemade raviolis so that the crimped edges would seal, or sliding cannoli shells off the end of a broomstick after they'd cooled into shape. It was like hands-on day at a living history museum—no such thing as Chef Boyardee and canned cheese here. I've hesitated to replicate Sylvia's cannolis as an adult, fearful they just wouldn't taste the same without the added zest from the bloodcurdling screams of resident peacocks.

My mother wasn't the only one who made friends in Sonoma. First grade had just begun when I noticed a girl from my class hanging upside down by her knees on the monkey bars while I stood in the redwood chips, a library book clasped to my chest, my feet in their Mary Janes firmly on the ground. The girl reached up her hands to grip the bar and swung her legs over her head, flipping forward and landing on her feet. She turned around brushing her hands on her rust-colored corduroys, lean and relaxed, an unflappable expression on her inquisitive face. Her brown hair was cut in a pixie. My long hair had never been cut, and I hadn't worn anything but dresses since I was in diapers. Fiddling with the placket of my sailor dress to make sure it was still covering my undershirt, I watched the girl approach.

"I have better monkey bars at my house," she said. "Want to come over?"

Eve's mom picked us up after school on Friday afternoons in an old green Porsche that looked like a frog and matched my sleepover bag, a frog-shaped pillow with a zipper mouth I could put my nightgown inside. That was about the extent of what Eve and I had in common. I was prudish, girly, clumsy, and frequently pricked by free-floating anxieties, my musical taste running to "How Much Is That Doggie in the Window?" and the indecipherable but soothingly melodic "Norwegian Wood," compared to Eve's tomboy fearlessness and her passion for doo-wop ballads in which drag-racing teenagers perished in fiery car crashes. We both liked to make believe under the weeping willow outside her front door, but I wanted to pretend that we were a family living within the green-walled chamber created by the tree's languorous sweeping branches, and Eve thought playing house was boring—she wanted us to be Robin Hood and his merry men hiding in the forest, or scuba divers caught by a monster octopus, or bandits planning a jail break. On the whole we were an unlikely pair, Eve and I, but it didn't seem to matter—as I'd read in a Joan Walsh Anglund book from the children's section of the library, a friend is someone who likes you, and Eve kept inviting me over.

Her mom had a full-time job and most days after school Eve went to something called day care, which I imagined as a kind of juvenile police detention, a bunch of kids crowded into a dirt-packed yard surrounded by barbed wire, akin to the set of *Hogan's Heroes*. She was an only child, another state of outlandish exoticism in my six-year-old experience. Her dad *cooked*—on Saturday mornings he made us a real breakfast: link sausages he sautéed in white wine until they were savory and crisp, and silver-dollar pancakes from scratch with genuine maple syrup. Hanging in the hallway of Eve's house was her parents' marriage certificate, hand lettered and ornamented with painted bluebirds and vines and twisting ribbons; just seeing it on my way to brush my teeth, I flushed with a reassurance I didn't understand, a confirmation of security that extended beyond my playmate's small family.

At school Eve was effortlessly, unselfconsciously popular, envied for her crocheted granny-square poncho and prowess with a Hula-hoop, the girl even boys competed to play with: I can see her with her head thrown back, joyous, so nimble and light she was almost flying through the air at the tail of a game of Crack the Whip. I clapped erasers by the lunchroom doors, afraid I'd skin my knees if I ran in a dress, but it was okay. I basked by association in the godhead of the chosen.

> *350*
> *1 egg*
> *1 cp. sugar*
> *1 cp. penut butter*

That's the recipe, written in pencil on the inside front cover of my copy of *Betty Crocker's New Boys and Girls Cookbook*, circa 1969, that made me a hero on the last day of first grade.

I arrived at the schoolyard that morning with Billy to find that the teachers had a surprise for us. Our schoolwork was finished, and we'd spend the last day of the year playing games and running relay races and doing special projects in the classrooms, where the desks were all pushed to the walls and covered with butcher paper for painting and papier-mâché and making pinhole cameras and beaded friendship bracelets. We were allowed to choose whichever activity we most wanted to try, and if you wanted to do more than one, you could switch at recess.

In the first-grade room, across from the cafeteria kitchen, a teacher had set up mixing bowls and measuring cups and ingredients for making cookies, which would be given out to everyone at the games on the yard after lunch. I didn't have to look any further. I tied on an apron and asked the teacher what I could do to help.

"Oh, you're not just going to help," she said. "You're going to bake the cookies yourself."

This was revelatory news—I'd never cooked anything completely by myself except bowls of cereal, which hardly counted. But I'd been helping in the kitchen for as long as I could remember, and I knew what it meant to beat an egg and how to measure by leveling the top of a cup with the side of a table knife. The recipe for peanut butter cookies that the teacher had written on the chalkboard was simple, with only those three ingredients: egg, sugar, and peanut butter. Actually, it seemed like something must be missing. Where was the flour and the butter and the baking powder?

"Trust me," the teacher said, "it's all there. This recipe works like magic."

My fellow bakers and I were going to have to make a lot of cookies to feed all the kids in the school, so the teacher helped us add up how much of each ingredient we'd need and we got to work, picking errant bits of eggshell out of our bowls and slopping the eggs around with mountains of sugar, stirring in the peanut butter until the batter congealed into a gritty brown mass. We rolled balls of dough between our palms and arranged them in orderly rows on the baking sheets, flattening the tops with crisscrosses made by fork tines. When our bowls were empty and the baking sheets full, we started over again.

It was recess by the time we were ready to bake the cookies in the cafeteria's oven. Most of the other kids wanted to move on to the fourth-grade room, where they were building a huge papier-mâché dragon on a framework of chicken wire, but I'd caught the baking bug, and I wasn't going anywhere. While the cookies baked, we lined cafeteria trays with colored construction paper, and when the cookies were done, the teacher instructed us how to take them out of the oven without burning ourselves, and we waited, our faces just above the hot pans, gulping drafts of peanutty perfume, while they cooled enough to slip them off with a metal spatula.

I was the first one out the lunchroom door, and the whole school, assembled by the kindergarten building for a brown-bag picnic, cheered when they saw us coming with our decorated trays piled with warm cookies. Sitting in the grass with Eve, who'd made me a bracelet of braided yarn to match the one she made for herself, I slowly nibbled my peanut butter cookie, my maiden effort as a baker and a hands-down success. They were gone in minutes, all the kids begging for seconds. Intense and chewy on the inside, crumbly at the edges, the cookie was so good I had to save half of mine to share with my mother and John-John when they arrived to take us home. It was the strangest thing: Making the cookies was just as satisfying as eating them. I loved the orderliness of it, the rules and precision, how masterful and generous I felt at the same time. Knowing that other people liked what I had made for them, that I'd made them happy, was the best part.

My mother and my brothers and I were planning to walk to the Plaza together to meet my dad, and my mom had promised that we could each pick out a treat to celebrate the end of the school year. For once I didn't want a root beer float or a cinnamon cake or a donut. I wanted to make my own, and I thought maybe the bookstore might have a cookbook for kids my age. Before I left school, though, I ran back to my old classroom to ask the teacher if I could keep her cookie recipe.

"Of course," she said. "Do you want me to give you a piece of paper so you can write it down?"

"No," I answered. "I'll remember."

PEANUT BUTTER COOKIES

.·.

These are great peanut butter cookies just as they are. Even so, I sometimes succumb to adding vanilla to bring out even more of their flavor, and you might want to try the addition of roasted salted peanuts for more crunch, or chopped milk chocolate, or both chocolate and peanuts, or for peanut-butter-and-jelly lovers, a dollop of strawberry jam.

> 1 large egg, at room temperature
> 1 cup granulated sugar
> 1 cup natural-style, salted peanut butter, crunchy or smooth
> Optional:
> > 1 teaspoon vanilla
> > About ½ cup roasted salted peanuts
> > Or about ½ cup (2 to 3 ounces) high-quality milk
> > > chocolate, coarsely chopped
> > Or both salted peanuts and milk chocolate,
> > > about ⅔ cup in all
> > About ½ cup strawberry jam or jelly

- Preheat the oven to 350° and lightly grease a cookie sheet.
- In a medium-sized bowl, beat the egg well with a whisk, fork, or wooden spoon. Add the sugar and beat just until mixed, then add the

nt butter (and vanilla if using), stirring just until the dough is uni-

ng the peanuts and/or chocolate, stir them into the dough.

ball-sized portions of dough into balls with your hands

ds if the dough is too sticky). Place the balls several

he cookie sheet, about 8 cookies to a pan. Use a floured
fork to flatten the balls of dough, leaving a crisscross mark from the fork
tines, or if you are making peanut butter and jelly cookies, press the back
of a floured spoon into the dough balls to make an indentation, then fill
with a teaspoon of strawberry jam or jelly.

• Bake for 8 to 12 minutes, until the cookies are puffed, set, and beginning to brown on the edges. Watch carefully in the last minutes: The bottoms burn quickly once they start to brown. Remove from the oven and
allow the cookies to cool for several minutes—they are fragile when
warm—before transferring to a wire rack to cool completely.

Makes 12 to 15 cookies.

Centrifugal Force

THE VERBOTENS HAD MOVED FROM KANSAS TO THE BACK OF OUR double cul-de-sac right after I completed first grade, and I spent the first month of the summer lugging my Barbie Dream House up the sidewalk to play with Ursula and Heidi Verboten, who were a year older and a year younger than me. Mrs. Verboten liked her five kids to play where she could keep an eye on them and make sure they did their chores and ate only snacks she approved of, like cubed cheese or apple slices. But some mornings Ursula and Heidi would get permission from their mother to walk together to my house to help me carry my Barbie stuff.

"Did you remember?" Ursula would ask me after I called goodbye to my mom and closed our front door. I'd open the snapping roof of the Dream House, pull out a double packet of Pop-Tarts, and hand one each to Ursula and Heidi.

"They're better if you put them in the toaster," I'd tell them.

"That's okay," Ursula would answer, her mouth full. They scarfed the Pop-Tarts down, showering crumbs on the sidewalk while I carried the Barbies the whole way. The Verboten sisters always finished eating just before we reached their end of the cul-de-sac, where Mrs. Verboten was waiting on the driveway, watching for us and hammering her newest baby's back, a cigarette hanging out of her mouth.

For lunch at the Verbotens', there might be cottage cheese, though it was plain, not made into a bunny's tail with a canned pear-half body and cinnamon Red Hots for eyes, like at my house. Or there were sandwiches of dry tuna on dark chewy bread baked by Mrs. Verboten, which I choked down while trying not to see Mrs. Verboten across the table from me nursing her baby, who would let go once in a while and look around at us, grinning and drooling milky spit from his toothless mouth, green goo crusting at his nose. We drank water: no Kool-Aid, no Tang, no chocolate milk. There was never any dessert for lunch, not even a vanilla wafer, though there was usually something better sitting out on the kitchen counter, Coffee Nips or After Dinner Mints or, once, a whole chocolate cake with lumpy icing oozing from between the layers.

"What a big cake," I said to Mrs. Verboten, swallowing my dry tuna.

"Yes, it is," she said, blowing smoke out her nose. "Mr. Verboten's boss is coming over for dinner. It's German chocolate. There are nuts and coconut in the icing, children wouldn't like it."

I knew I liked coconut and nuts despite being a child, but there was something disturbing about that cake, even though I wanted it. The frosting looked kind of hairy and clumped. Cakes were supposed to have frosting covering themselves completely up. This cake's secrets were all out in the open. It was like a cake without its pants on.

"What did that cake taste like?" I asked Ursula and Heidi as we sat cross-legged on their bedroom floor the next day, setting up the Dream House.

Ursula and Heidi looked at each other, their expressions blank. "I dunno," one of them said, shrugging her shoulders, "we had cantaloupe."

Happy as I was that girls my age had moved into our neighborhood, I didn't actually like Barbies. Something about Barbie's naked body made me deeply uncomfortable, as did Ken's undifferentiated pubic lump. I wore undershirts and shorts beneath my dresses every day, and rubber-banded my knee socks so they'd stay up. If I had to play Barbie, I played with Skipper, the flat-chested little girl doll with long blond hair who was supposed to be Barbie's kid sister.

The opposite was true of the Verboten sisters. They wanted to play Barbie every day, and they couldn't wait to strip the clothes off all the dolls, including Skipper, for the purposes of examination and discussion.

"Barbie and Ken are married, so let's put them in bed together," Ursula suggested, but the bed that came with my Dream House was a hard plastic single with a pillow molded onto it, so the dolls kept falling off.

"We'll pretend," said Heidi, the younger sister, running to the bathroom for a facecloth. When she returned, she handed it to me. "You put them in bed together," she said to me, and though her urging had the ring of genuine playtime to it, Ursula's seconding did not.

"Yeah, you do it," Ursula said darkly, "but make sure Ken is on top."

My knees were sweating under the rubber bands. I leaned over the dolls, picked up the facecloth, and took naked Ken in my hand. I was just tenting the facecloth over Barbie's and Ken's stiff limbs when all the air sucked out of the room.

"What the hell is going on here?" Mrs. Verboten yelled, a cloth diaper draped over her shoulder, her big aproned belly round and threatening. Her mouth tightened around her cigarette as she tossed all the Barbie stuff back into the Dream House and snapped it shut. "You're a bad influence, Cissy Moses," she hissed into my stunned face. "You're not a nice girl, and I won't let you play with my children anymore."

It was all right if I was banished from the Verbotens', I thought on the way home. In fact I was sort of relieved, though the not-nice-girl and bad-inflence part bothered me. I worried that I was a not-nice girl and a bad influence, too. I'd been hoping nobody else would notice.

Eve had gone on a trip to Europe with her parents that summer, and the Verboten sisters weren't even allowed to talk to me. I had my Betty Crocker cookbook, but I wasn't supposed to use the stove when my mother wasn't around, which was frequently, so when Billy and John and I ran out of the peanut butter cookies and Rice Krispy Treats I'd made under supervision, Billy came up with a recipe that required no adult input: Wonder Bread slathered with margarine and all the granulated sugar that the butter would absorb. If you froze it, the margarine hardened and made it easier to eat without the bread drooping and the sugar sliding off into the grass. My improvement was to use powdered sugar instead of granulated and mix the sugar into the margarine, not unlike frosting. Frosting bread was an unqualified hit with the neighborhood kids, but our snack largesse encountered an unexpected roadblock when my father tried to fix himself a baloney sandwich and found that we had consumed all the bread in the house just a day after our mother had done the weekly grocery shopping.

Who needed bread? It was the frosting that everyone wanted. Billy's shrewd friend Mark had the brainstorm that we could charge, so we went into production. We used the plastic margarine tubs my mother saved for our cereal bowls and divided full tubs of margarine among them, industriously stirring in boxes of powdered sugar and setting up our frosting stand in John-John's Radio Flyer wagon on the corner in front of our house. Our original idea was that the frosting stand would be mobile, like an ice cream truck, but as soon as word got out our customers started coming to us in droves from the streets all around. Billy and Mark rode their bikes to the Plaza and drummed up additional clientele at the playground. Our product line featured frosting on a saltine, frosting on a spoon, or to-go hits of frosting in Dixie cups from the dispenser we'd emptied in our bathroom. We charged if the kids brought money, but we never turned anyone away and only shut down the stand at the height of the afternoon when the metal wagon got so hot the frosting melted faster than we could dole it out.

After a couple of weeks, we'd turned enough profit to buy four tickets to a matinee of *Pippi Longstocking* at the Sebastiani Theatre, and who knows what kind of market share our frosting monopoly could have enjoyed if it hadn't been for our parish priest, that killjoy, who happened by one day with a patronizing grin and a glinting nickel held up between his fingers, thinking we were selling something wholesome, like lemonade. When he saw our Dixie cups of melted frosting, his smile vanished.

"Don't you know there are starving children in Africa who would give anything for the healthy food your mother buys for you?" our priest scolded, shaking his head. "Does she know that you're out here wasting your parents' money on frivolous junk?"

Billy and I stared at each other. Which was worse: to lie to a priest and say our blameless, perfectly respectable mother had no idea what we were doing, or to tell him that she thought our frosting stand was a stroke of genius and had been keeping us supplied with margarine tubs and powdered sugar? At least the truth wouldn't land us in hell.

"She's not here," I said, which was also true. The Sonoma Junior Women's Club was having a Wild West–themed fundraiser, and my mom, as usual, was in charge of decorations. "She's at the bar at the Sonoma Hotel," I explained, "looking for a spittoon."

MUSETTE HAD PRODUCED ANOTHER litter of kittens, but after back-to-back litters every four months for more than a year, she'd grown weary of the whole thing and one day decided she was done, at least with the ones who were currently suckling her to skin and bones. She stood up from the shady spot under the juniper bush where they'd been kneading her belly and began to saunter away, kittens still dangling from her nipples. The kittens dragged through the grass of the front lawn, dropping off Musette's teats one by one. In a few deft leaps Musette had made it up onto the flat roof, where Robespierre was already napping in the sun; all we could see were the ends of their tails twitching over the gutter above the front door. They wouldn't come down, and my mother left a stepladder leaning against the house so she could carry bowls of cat food and water up to the roof every morning.

Billy and John and I, with help from the neighborhood gang, took over the care of Musette's abandoned kittens for the rest of the summer and into the fall. Every day, we brought them out to the lawn in their basket and settled them in the shade, taking turns giving them *Apollo 11* rides in a plastic laundry hamper, the kittens blinking and subdued no matter how fast we scooted the hamper over the grass.

A few weeks into second grade, I was returning from the Sprouse-Reitz one afternoon after spending the last of my share of the frosting-stand profits on a Sugar Daddy candy bar, a thick slab of hard caramel on a stick. Though I had my bike I was walking, because I'd forgotten to wear shorts beneath my skirt to cover my underpants while I rode. I was not the only one in my family whose modesty bordered on the pathological. My brothers and I had never seen our parents in their underwear let alone undressed except once, a story I didn't hear until I was an adult. One morning John had woken with a fever, and my mom kept him home from kindergarten. She didn't know that he'd crawled into her bed to watch cartoons while she was bathing. After stepping out of the tub, she walked into her bedroom naked and dripping wet. When John saw her, he clapped his hands over his eyes and wailed, "Make it go away! Make it go away!"

Walking home from Sprouse-Reitz with my Sugar Daddy, I happened to notice an intriguing new word in big spray-painted letters on a wall at my school. Right about then I had become irritatingly smug about my growing vocabulary. During first grade my teacher had told us that the secret to learning a new word was to use it in a sentence, and I'd taken her advice to heart, sounding out every new word I saw and not just writing a sentence but an entire limerick based on the word. I'd collected so many of my original limericks over the summer that I'd made them into a book with my own illustrations, and my second-grade teacher was so impressed she ran copies on the mimeograph machine and stapled them together with craft paper covers to make it look like a real book. She gave one to every student in the class, and one to the principal, too. I couldn't help but swell with pride—while aping an expression of ingenuous humility—when my teacher read my masterpiece aloud, the limerick that I knew was really good because of how my mom had covered her mouth with her hand when she'd read it. It began:

My Grandfather Frank of the Hills
Has four children and has to take pills. . . .

A month into second grade—sure to be a yearlong spectacle of my burgeoning intelligence and artistry!—I was still wallowing in my teacher's praise, and here, right in front of me, was another opportunity to suck up.

I stood on the embankment in front of the school while I memorized the letters of my new word and sounded it out, leaning down now and then to pick thistle barbs out of my rubber-banded kneesocks. It was such an unfamiliar word I had no idea what it meant, so I made a guess. I thought it might be the rubbery flesh between the webbed toes of an aquatic bird, and that made a perfect rhyme, so I tried it out to myself:

A goose has a fuck
But not as wet as a duck.

That was almost as good as the one about Pa, and I recited it all the way home, where I found Billy and John and the other kids testing centrifugal force on the kittens. Billy and Mark had tied a rope around the handle of a wicker basket and put the kittens inside, and then one of them would get the rope swinging in high, fast arcs, finally circling the kittens up into a full orbit over his head. The kittens didn't seem to mind. They only blinked at us from the bottom of the basket after they'd made their splashdown.

This was pretty impressive. Maybe a little too impressive, since I was in danger of losing what I'd imagined to be a captive audience for my newest rhyme. As Billy and Mark continued to spin the basket of kittens at high speed over their heads, dismissing the rest of our whining for turns, I trod the front yard like a second-rate Shakespearean actor, declaiming my X-rated doggerel over and over while taking loud slurpy licks of my Sugar Daddy. Just in case the other kids hadn't picked up on the fact that I had expanded my prodigious vocabulary yet again, I started using my new word in a few other choice sentences as well. That's when my mother's voice came warbling through the window, calling me inside.

I knew from her fake falsetto of unconcern that something had gone wrong. I poked my Sugar Daddy deep into my mouth and trudged like the doomed into the laundry room, where my mother was sitting at her sewing machine, making herself a leather miniskirt. The leather was thick, and she was using the fingers of both hands to force it along under the foot of the needle. She had a counterfeit expression of motherly calm on her face as she began to question me about the word she'd just heard me trumpet to every kid in our neighborhood.

"And do you know what that word means?" she asked me in the singsong register that mothers use when they're about to tell you something you really don't want to know. She kept her foot on the sewing machine pedal, moving the pattern pieces forward as the needle flashed up and down, making a rasping sound on the leather. Her speech began with the phrase "When a man and a woman love each other very, very much . . ." and proceeded through an all-too-vivid description of distended body parts and biological scenarios more nightmarish than anything I could have thought up for another ten years. She kept glancing over at me with a fractured look of mortified, forced serenity on her face, the sewing machine needle clattering faster and faster on either side of her hands as she saw from my expression that her birds-and-bees speech was not going well and she got more and more nervous. If John had been there, he would have been clapping his hands to his ears and wailing, *Make it go away!*

The pieces started to come together: the Verbotens, Barbie and Ken, my intriguing new word, the needle pumping between my mother's fingers. "Ith tha wha you do with Thaththy?" I asked, horrified, the Sugar Daddy's caramel blob stuck to the roof of my mouth.

"It's a beautiful, beautiful thing!" my mother cried, sounding like she didn't believe it for a minute herself. Dots of perspiration were popping out on her forehead, and I'd started to back away—I couldn't help myself—and that's when two of her fingers slipped under the sewing machine needle. My mother gasped, speechless with pain, and blood spurted like an exploding fountain pen. In the long awful seconds while my mother stared at her bloody sewn fingers and I tried to get the Sugar Daddy out of my mouth so I could scream for my brothers, I thought to myself, *That is the worst story I ever heard.*

VERBOTEN GERMAN CHOCOLATE CAKE

∴

4 ounces semisweet chocolate

2 cups unbleached all-purpose flour

1 teaspoon baking soda

½ teaspoon salt

1 cup unsalted butter, at room temperature

2 cups granulated sugar

4 large eggs, separated, at room temperature

1 teaspoon vanilla

1 cup buttermilk

•   Preheat oven to 350°. Butter three 8- or 9-inch cake pans and fit the bottoms with waxed or parchment paper. Melt the chocolate over a double boiler or in a bowl covered with a paper towel in a microwave for 1 to 2 minutes, and let cool. Whisk together the flour, baking soda, and salt in a small bowl and set aside.

•   Beat the butter in the bowl of an electric mixer on medium speed for a couple of minutes, then gradually add the sugar, beating until light, about 3 to 5 minutes. Add the egg yolks one at a time, beating well after each addition, about 1 minute each. Mix in the cooled, melted chocolate and the vanilla until thoroughly blended.

•   Add the flour mixture in three portions, alternating with the buttermilk in two portions, beginning and ending with flour and beating on low speed just until combined.

• In a separate bowl, with clean beaters, beat the egg whites on medium speed just until they hold stiff peaks but are not dry; gently fold half of the beaten whites into the batter, then the other half, just until they disappear. Divide the batter among the three cake pans and bake for about 25 to 30 minutes, until the cakes spring back when touched lightly at the center. Remove from the oven and immediately run a heatproof spatula or smooth table knife around the sides of each pan to loosen the cakes, then let the cakes cool in the pans for 15 minutes. Remove the cakes from the pans, peel off the paper, and cool completely on wire racks.

COCONUT PECAN ICING

2½ cups chopped pecans
2¼ cups evaporated milk (one 12-ounce can plus half of
    one 12-ounce can)
2¼ cups granulated sugar
6 egg yolks, slightly beaten
1 cup plus 2 tablespoons unsalted butter
1 tablespoon vanilla
¼ teaspoon salt
3½ cups flaked coconut

• Toast the pecans in a 375° oven until fragrant and just starting to brown, about 8 to 10 minutes, stirring every couple of minutes to keep them from burning. Allow to cool slightly as you proceed with making the rest of the icing.

• Combine the evaporated milk, sugar, egg yolks, and butter in a heavy, medium-sized saucepan. Cook over medium heat, stirring constantly, until the mixture is thickened and uniform and is a pale tawny color, about 12 minutes. It will begin to boil, but do not let it scorch. Remove from heat and add the vanilla, salt, coconut, and chopped pecans. Beat well and allow to cool a bit before using—it thickens as it cools. (If it cools too much and becomes too thick, thin with a little milk.) Generously frost the tops of each layer with a third of the icing, leaving the sides unfrosted. Allow to cool thoroughly and set before serving.

Makes one 8- or 9-inch three-layer cake.

Twilight

ONE EARLY JUNE NIGHT, ONE LAST NIGHT BEFORE SUMMER overtook spring in one leaf-lit, green-swelled, birdsonged heave, my parents carried us half-asleep to our station wagon, my mother tucking M&M's bags into our hands as they settled us wrapped in blankets in the flattened back of the car. The engine came to vibrating life, and my parents drove us in silence through our town, the whole valley curling with grapevines in a long lingering twilight, a blue bowl of night holding us in place, new stars flecked above us. We had been told that we were going to move again, we were leaving Sonoma. My father was about to go to Pennsylvania to start his new job, but before he left there was one last thing he had to do.

The motion of the car, the turns down familiar streets lulled us back to sleep, and I didn't wake again until the warmth of the car's heater had begun to dissipate, the engine's steady hum become an absence. Billy was sitting up beside me, still clutching his bag of tiny candies. *Look,* he said, not pointing but staring out the windshield of our car.

Outside, in the shadowed front yard of a house we knew, our parents were running across the lawn, stringing rolls of toilet paper between the dark trees. They crisscrossed in front of each other, trailing swags of paper behind them, winding it around branches and across the unlit windows of the house, hanging it over the rain gutters and spooling it long and unbroken across the grass. My father unwound his roll up to the parked car in the driveway and wrapped toilet paper over the windshield wipers and the radio antenna, then ran back across the yard toward my mother, who was stopped under the trees, watching him, bent over with laughter.

Wake up, John, my brother Billy and I whispered, shaking John under the blanket. *Wake up, look!*

John's eyes opened and he sat up, blinking, M&M's slipping loose off his pajama top, making a clacking sound as they spilled to the blanket on his lap.

Our father was running to our mother, dropping his roll of toilet paper in the grass on the way. When he reached her, he grabbed her by the shoulders and she reached for him, too, holding him by one shoulder and raising her other hand to her mouth. They were both laughing so hard they could hardly stand, leaning into each other for support. We couldn't hear them through the closed windows of our car, but we knew they were making no sound, they were trying to be quiet, they didn't want to be caught. It was a game, it was a joke.

The yard and the house and the car in the driveway seemed lit up by all the long crossing streams of white toilet paper, luminous against the dark. Our parents looked at what they'd done, and they collapsed into laughter again under one of the trees, holding each other, their hands clasping each other's elbows, their foreheads touching. In our car, my brothers and I were laughing, too, giddy with our parents' silliness, their joke, our father reaching for the roll of paper he'd dropped in the grass, our mother's face bright and thrown back, pulling on his arm, pulling him back to her.

We threw our own heads back and roared, hugging our arms to our skinny ribs, watching them together—our beautiful thwarted mother, our lonely frightened father—shivering with happiness in our thin pajamas, our breath scented with chocolate, our laughter rising in the cool air of the closed car, fragile as tissue.

Strawberry Milkshake

THE BEER, I THOUGHT, MUST BE IN THE COMPARTMENT UNDER THE trunk with the tire jack, or in the cooler with the baloney sandwiches and cartons of milk packed in ice, but otherwise I was puzzled. "Where are the Hershey bars and peanuts?" I asked.

"Huh?" my mom replied, distracted, her arms stretched over the roof of the station wagon, adjusting bungee cords. It was the morning we were leaving Sonoma, and all the neighbor kids and their mothers were crowded around our fully loaded car, which my mom had strategically packed inside and on top with everything we'd need for the week it would take us to drive across the country.

For days on end as Billy and John and I had raced our bikes in the cul-de-sac with the neighbor kids or gone swimming with Mary Anne or to movie matinees chaperoned by one of the other moms, my mother had been packing up in preparation for the moving van and driving us across the country by herself. When we reached Ohio, she would leave us for a couple of weeks with relatives we knew only by name, my father's younger brother Don and his family, while she and our dad found us a new place to live in Pennsylvania.

My father had already taken an airplane to Philadelphia, where he had a new job working for the government in the Department of Interior's Bureau of Indian Affairs. He'd sent us presents made by the tribes he was working for: I got a beaded doll without a face, which was hard to love though I tried. I'd asked my mother why he didn't want his little adobe office on the Plaza anymore, with its crackly leather chair and the enticing hot cinnamon from the bakery wafting through the open windows. She'd answered in terms that she must have thought were appropriately concrete but free of confusing details: His job in

Sonoma made him sad. Years later I learned that most of his private practice work had been filing divorces.

Shortly before my dad's departure, Pa, like a cigar-chomping King Lear, had called a poker game with his children to decide how to divide their inheritance of his estate. In a halo of cigar smoke, my parents and aunts and uncles sat around my grandmother's kitchen table at the farmhouse with Pa, jelly glasses of Scotch set in front of each player. My mother surprised everyone by winning the game, and she got the big prize—Camp Meeker, though we were about to leave California, perhaps forever. But it came in handy for storing all of our baby clothes and outgrown toys and my dad's books from law school, which my mother sealed in huge barrels and left in the musty cobwebbed crawl space under the porch, with a promise from her sisters that they'd keep an eye on the place and sweep the roof of redwood sheddings once in a while.

MY MOM HAD BEEN promoting our trip across America as a great adventure. Since she was about to drive three thousand miles by herself with three children, two dogs, and three cats, one of whom was going to give birth again any day, her only hope for survival was to whip us into an enthusiastic frenzy and pray the spirit of fun would carry us through.

I couldn't wait. Seven solid days of McDonald's, A&W, Kentucky Fried, Shakey's Pizza, International House of Pancakes, Arby's, Foster's Freeze—nothing could be better. And every night in a new motel: My mother, I knew, had left room in her suitcase for all the hotel towels we would be collecting for our new house in Pennsylvania. Holiday Inn's bath linens had a better color scheme, but by dint of some carefully timed wheedling I'd extracted the promise that we'd stay at a Howard Johnson's whenever we had the chance. If there was anything that could beat McDonald's Filet-o-Fish it was HoJo's crispy fried clams, and I saw the entire cross-country trip as an opportunity for reunion with Howard Johnson's coconut cake. I'd clung to the blissful, candlelit memory of my very own coconut cake in the wake of the unfortunate rubber alligator incident, when I'd sunk from the exalted heights of birthday girldom to being the bad one everybody was mad at.

In those innocent days before car seats and seat belt laws, kids could roll all over a car unrestricted, so my mother put the back seat down in the station wagon and made our car into a big playroom. She padded the floor with the stained chenille bedspread Lainey had given birth on, and she lined the edges with board games and coloring books and pillows and the camping cooler. Jean-Tom and Robespierre yowled in one mesh-sided cat carrier and pregnant Musette had a second to her preoccupied self, but the dogs were free to wander the interior, on the lookout for unattended sandwiches, ready to press their damp noses against my mom's neck as she drove. Our suitcases and an enormous bag of dog food were strapped onto the luggage rack under a canvas dropcloth.

"Your tail is riding kind of low," one of the teenage Verboten boys snickered from the curb when we'd gotten into the car. My mom sat in front by herself in her red bandana, the Triple A Triptiks sharing the passenger seat with her purse and files of important papers and boxes of breakables she hadn't trusted to the movers. She checked her lipstick in the rearview mirror and beamed at us over her shoulder.

"This is going to be *fun!*" she cried, and we all hooted and waved as she laid on the horn and pulled away, the younger neighborhood kids racing after us on their bikes, handlebar tassels flying, to the end of the street.

That first day out, somewhere near the high-desert town of Winnemucca, Nevada, a freak flash flood washed out the highway. We turned back to the only motel we could reach; the proprietor put us in an upstairs room, as the creek we were on was expected to keep rising. We sat on the lumpy beds and ate the rest of the baloney for dinner, listening to the endless surge of water pouring down the creek, the bar's neon sign throbbing red all night through the curtains.

"A flash flood—now, that's exciting!" my mom said, peering out the motel's window at the churning creek. "This'll be something you can write on a postcard to your friends. I bet they've never been in a flash flood before!"

On the second day, a salt storm kicked up while we were crossing the Great Salt Lake Desert. We waited it out for hours, pulled to the shoulder of the highway like every other vehicle on the road, visibility nil as the storm continued to hiss at the windows, sandblasting the paint off our car. The wind blew so hard it knocked a livestock truck on its side, and giant hogs came bursting out of the opacity, lifting their pink snouts and squealing in panic as they trotted past us on either side of the station wagon, men chasing after them wearing their shirts tied over their faces.

"A salt storm!" my mother marveled, gazing out the blind white windshield as Billy and John and I played checkers in the back. "What are the chances we'd be lucky enough to see something like this?"

On the third day, after arriving in Denver long after dark, too late and too tired to look for a Howard Johnson's or any other cheap motel, my mother awoke in the middle of the night in our expensive downtown hotel room to discover that Musette was having her kittens inside my mom's open suitcase—on top of all of her clothes, except for the grubby outfit she'd dropped on the carpet after wearing it for two days straight. Two kittens, three kittens, a fourth; then the fifth kitten started to be born breech. My mother went into veterinary midwife action. She tried to help Musette ease that kitten out, but it was stuck.

"What's going to happen, Mommy?" we asked, creeping out from under the covers to lean across the end of the bed, where our mother was hunched in front of her suitcase, muttering "geez louise, geez louise" over and over, telling us to stay back, the hotel's towels bloody all around her.

"I don't know—" she said, her response unusually curt, then softening, as if she suddenly remembered us. "But it's going to be okay, don't you worry . . ."

Throwing on her dirty clothes, a smear of blood across her cheek from pushing her hair off her face, my mother loaded us back into the car with Musette and the kittens. She drove up and down Denver's deserted streets in a futile search for a veterinarian's office, enlisting us all in a joint prayer to Saint Jude. Finally she was able to flag down a policeman, who escorted us to the only emergency vet in the city. We got back to our hotel and the other animals as the sun was rising behind the bright sharp edges of the downtown buildings. Musette survived, and the first four kittens. My mom's hands trembled as she packed us all into the station wagon to head for Kansas.

"That was the worst of it," she said, shooting us a weak smile in the rearview mirror and starting the engine.

After we'd passed through Topeka, the midday sky closed up and went black. As the local radio station we were listening to announced the tornado warning, the cars in the opposite lane of the highway pulled squealing onto the shoulder, the entire lane of traffic turning around and merging into ours, all of us heading east at increasing speed. Behind us, we could see the tornado's funnel sucking all the blackness toward itself.

"Put the leashes on the dogs now, Billy," my mom said, her voice brittle with false calm as she outlined detailed instructions for each of us in case she decided to pull into a ditch. The speedometer was showing ninety miles per hour, both lanes of the highway bumper-to-bumper with vehicles racing eastward, some cars and trucks passing us neatly by along the shoulders. "Not until I tell you to, okay? But here's the plan—Billy, you take the dogs. Cissy, you take the boy cats in their carrier. John-John, you sit right by the door, Mommy will hold your hand and bring Musette. If I stop, we'll all crawl under the car, got it? Billy, tell me what it looks like now."

"It's closer, Mommy. It looks bigger." The radio had stopped working, broadcasting only a deafening spray of static.

My mom gunned the engine and drove. One hundred miles an hour, one hundred ten.

"That's fast, isn't it, Mommy?" John piped up. "Yeah, that's *fast*," Billy and I confirmed, nodding our heads up and down.

When we rattled to a halt in Lawrence, Kansas, a couple of hours later, our engine was blowing billows of smoke almost as black as the tornado, which my mother had outrun at a sustained 115 miles an hour. We spent the next day splashing in the pool of a motel in Lawrence while the station wagon was being serviced, my mother lying prone on a lounge chair in the shade, a wet washcloth draped over her face. "Don't talk to me," she said when we came over and poked her shoulder to see if she was still breathing, "I just outran a tornado. Wait until Sally Verboten hears about this."

We reached St. Louis on the sixth day, but we seemed unable to get past it. My mom was hopelessly lost, driving in circles on the bewildering loop of elevated freeways ringing the city, Billy and John and I offering moral support by pointing out the soaring Gateway Arch every time it came back into view. "It's coming up on the right now, Mommy." "I see it, Mommy! It's on the left, over there." My mother stared straight ahead, tears dribbling down the graceful line of her jaw, more confused every time she pulled off the road to ask directions.

On the last day of our trip, we were finally closing in on our cousins in Dayton. Inspired by the St. Louis Arch, my brothers and I campaigned heavily for McDonald's. Again. There'd been exactly one HoJo's on our entire route, and pancakes with blueberry syrup at IHOP had launched us every morning; otherwise we'd stayed in whatever motels we could find and eaten every meal courtesy of McDonald's. Not again, my mother said, but finally we wore her down. It didn't hurt that she realized we would reach Dayton well after dinnertime and a McDonald's sign appeared up the highway, beckoning in the distance like a mirage oasis in the desert, as we'd all begun to whine.

"Okay," she said wearily, flicking on her turn signal for the exit ramp, "but we're not sitting inside. We'll go to the drive-through."

If you had a strawberry milkshake and a packet of fresh french fries, the best way to eat them, to my eight-year-old mind, was to munch a few fries, drink a bit of the milkshake, and dip the rest of the fries into the milkshake to taste the thick icy sweetness of the shake against the hot salt of the fries. The straw and the plastic lid on the shake, therefore, were impediments to complete satisfaction.

I was enjoying my first handful of fries and just prying the lid off my strawberry shake, humming noisily and perched cross-legged right behind the driver's seat, when my mother swung around to face me, her unwashed hair flying out from under her sweaty bandana, which she'd worn every day since my dad left for his new job.

"DON'T—" she started to threaten through clenched teeth, her face contorted with menace, too exhausted and ground down to pretend anymore, this close to the finish line. "Don'tyoudare," she warned me, pointing a long, skinny finger at me, "takethetopoffthatmilkshakeit'll-spillallover."

Chastened, I snapped the milkshake lid back onto the waxed cup. I sucked demurely on the straw. But after a while I just sort of forgot. As I started to pry the lid off my milkshake a second time, the cup somehow exploded in my hand, sending a pink tsunami of milkshake toward the back of my mother's head. In the rearview mirror I watched her eyes grow wide and black when the cold sting of milkshake splashed over her neck and started dripping down her dirty, five-days-worn collar, down her back between her shoulder blades.

For an hour she raved. "I hate this goddamned family—nobody helps me—I have to do everything myself—I wish I could run away—" She wept and swore, her hands shaking with rage on the steering wheel. We were blown back by the force of her fury and frustration, huddled together at the tailgate of the station wagon, hugging the dogs. We escaped the car as if it were on fire as soon as we pulled to a stop in front of Uncle Don and Aunt Virginia's house, and I peeped through a window curtain in their living room and watched my mother continue to stammer and weep as she stood on the driveway rinsing herself off with the garden hose, holding the gushing end down the back of her filthy shirt.

"C'mon, kids," my aunt Virginia said cheerfully, luring me away from the window, rounding my brothers up from the couch where they sat next to each other, mute and paralyzed and white-faced. Her own two toddlers were already asleep in their bedrooms. She'd started running a bath for our mom; we could hear the water pounding into the tub. "Let's go in the kitchen," she said. "We can make popcorn balls."

OHIO RAINED. Except for the Fourth of July, when we had a barbecue on Uncle Don's damp squeaking lawn and a bee stung me on the neck, Billy and John and I stared out the windows at green dripping Ohio.

The only thing for us to do in the inclement weather was to sit in the living room while our little cousins took their endless naps, eating popcorn and watching soap operas with Aunt Virginia as she ironed her clean laundry. Aunt Virginia seemed like a teenager, her teeth flashing silver from braces as she told us stories of her single days before she met Uncle Don. She wore white lipstick and boldly patterned go-go dresses when we occasionally left the house to drive to a market or some other errand. Limitless stands of green cornfields lined up on either side of the road. It wasn't Oklahoma, but just like the Rodgers and Hammerstein musical, along every road in Ohio the corn stood as high as an elephant's eye, the stalks stiff and straight even as the rainstorms bucketed down so hard that they threatened to wash it all away, leaving us to starve.

But we were far from starving. Aunt Virginia also seemed like a teenager, and not unlike our mother, in her blasé, profligate attitude toward snacking. Uncle Don didn't mind; we didn't have to sneak anything. We could eat all day long. Sure, we could make popcorn balls again. We could make them every day if we wanted. Some days we made popcorn balls with corn syrup that seeped at its own slow pace out of the bottle, and I paid attention as Aunt Virginia buttered the inside of the saucepan so the boiling sugar concoction wouldn't stick.

Sometimes we colored them red or green or blue. Sometimes we made caramel corn with brown sugar and salted nuts and it was better than Cracker Jack. Other times we made popcorn à la Rice Krispie Treats, glued together with marshmallows and margarine melted into a stretchy goo. We buttered our hands, too, when we helped shape the popcorn into balls big enough to last through an entire episode of *General Hospital* or *Guiding Light*.

If we weren't eating popcorn balls and watching TV, we were eating chocolate-covered peanuts, or bottled pimento cheese smeared on crackers, or grilled Velveeta-and-bacon sandwiches. At dinner, with the ham steaks or the meatloaf or the chicken-fried steak, there were little potatoes baked in rock salt until they were crispy and wrinkled or potatoes fried in leftover bacon grease or our favorite, twice-baked potatoes, the potatoes cut in half and their insides scooped out after they were baked the first time, then mashed with butter and cream and spooned back into their skins with a little paprika sprinkled on top for decoration before they were baked again. Aunt Virginia and Uncle Don didn't seem to spend much time in line at McDonald's or KFC.

"Maybe tomorrow we'll go outside," Aunt Virginia would say hopefully, gazing out the kitchen window at the perpetually unpromising sky, even-tempered and patient though she undoubtedly had not anticipated being stuck inside with five bored children for two weeks when she agreed to watch us while my mom and dad house-hunted.

At last we were escorted to our new house in Chester County, Pennsylvania, in a rural township of gently sloping fields and Amish dairy farms that was the last stop on the Main Line. What had my mother done without us? Though my father had disappeared every day for as long as I could remember, doing his job or going to the dump with carloads of grass clippings, my mother had always been close by. This was the first time my brothers and I had ever been truly away from her. She'd found us a place to live, Uncle Don and Aunt Virginia had told us, but how long could that take? I pictured her with my dad driving up to unknown but comfortingly familiar motel rooms with Hojos towels on the bathroom rack, eating fried clams in the restaurant with no one to share them with, packing the Hojos towels into her suitcase all by herself, with no one to help her squeeze them down while she zipped the suitcase shut. Beyond that I had no idea how she might have spent her time.

Now I wonder if she might have taken a walk alone, or an uninterrupted bath. Maybe she read a book. Maybe she finished the thoughts in her head, or lost track of where she was altogether. Maybe she spent every minute going from bank to phone booth to hardware store, unpacking, organizing, cleaning a kitchen and bathrooms that weren't left quite clean enough by the people who'd lived there before. Maybe she found herself sitting in the middle of a wide green lawn in Pennsylvania, watching shadows bend the fading light under a vast old black walnut tree, and in the distance her three children were shambling out of a car and approaching her, shyly, and she didn't look back to how beleaguered she felt the last time she saw them but, instead, without thinking, she swung her arms out to hold her sweet bumbling kids, her skinny blond boys and her newly tubby, graceless little girl—who made her feel lucky to wake up every morning, who were running toward her across a vast space, relying on her to show them what it felt like to be home.

CARAMEL CORN

∴

6 cups freshly popped corn

2 cups roasted, salted mixed nuts: a combination of peanuts, almonds, pecans, cashews, macadamias, and/or walnuts, to your taste

½ cup unsalted butter

1 cup firmly packed light brown sugar

¼ cup light corn syrup

½ teaspoon salt

1 teaspoon baking soda

1 teaspoon vanilla

• Generously butter a baking sheet and set aside. Combine the popcorn and nuts, spread them on the baking sheet, and place in a low oven (200°) to warm while you make the caramel.

• In a heavy-bottomed, medium saucepan, melt the butter over low heat, then stir in the brown sugar, corn syrup, and salt. Turn the heat to medium and bring to a boil, stirring, then clip on a candy thermometer. Continue to cook, stirring frequently, until the temperature reaches hard-ball stage, or 250° to 260°. Turn off the heat, stir in the baking soda and vanilla, and quickly pour over the popcorn, tossing with wooden spoons to coat evenly. Return the caramel corn to the oven to further crisp the caramel, about 30 to 45 minutes (it will still feel soft when warm, but it will become crisp as it cools). Remove from the oven and allow to cool completely before eating. The caramel corn will keep, stored in an airtight container, for about a week.

Makes about 8 cups of caramel corn. The recipe can easily be doubled for a crowd.

Sugartown

Iᴛ sᴏᴜɴᴅᴇᴅ ʟɪᴋᴇ ᴀ ᴊᴏᴋᴇ—ᴛᴏᴏ ʟᴜᴅɪᴄʀᴏᴜsʟʏ ɢᴏᴏᴅ ᴛᴏ ʙᴇ ᴛʀᴜᴇ— but it wasn't: Our new address in Pennsylvania was Sugartown Road, our new school, the one we'd attend in the fall, Sugartown Elementary. The house had been built at a crossroads sometime around the Revolutionary War, bordered on one side by acres of unfenced lawn fixed at its roadside corner by a giant, gnarled black walnut tree, a smaller yard in back enclosed by weathered basket-woven fencing overgrown with dusty Concord grape vines. Between our house and the school was an abandoned pear orchard alive with humming bees, dandelions and tall Queen Anne's lace growing between the trees, and pears hanging heavy-bottomed and green on the laden branches.

The previous owners of our quirky aged house had left behind bits and pieces of furniture that my mother scrubbed and repaired and put to use: hooked wool rugs and darkly stained antiques and one of those old-fashioned washing machines that looked like a squat enamel barrel with a minatory device called a mangle on top. There was hot water in the kitchen, but my mother had to boil water in all of her biggest pots when it was time for us to take baths. By some stroke of completely unexpected luck, I'd been given my own room, all pink and white. When my mother led me through the door, Musette was nursing her kittens on my bed in a soft blade of sunlight coming through the window's gingham curtains. In the corner, beside my very own bookshelf, there was a wooden rocking chair with ladylike spindles and goosefeather cushions in a pattern of blowsy cabbage roses. All sorts of old-fashioned girls' books with gilded lettering on the spines were lined up on the shelf, which my mother had painted white to match the rocker and its little footstool. The boys were sharing a cavernous bedroom with checkerboard linoleum on the floor, a room so large they could have all of their Tinkertoys and Legos erected at once and there was still space to run past without knocking anything over.

Our vast front yard was perfect, my mother said, for games of Kick the Can, and she promised to teach us. Those first couple of days, thunderstorms gathered in the afternoons, and the distant snapping and tympanic rumbling of the sky grew increasingly portentous as our dad flattened boxes on the gravel driveway, prepping for a satisfying run to the local landfill, and Billy and John and I ran screaming to beat our mother to an empty coffee can set upright in the middle of the lawn, then past it to the front porch, which we'd named our home base. Lainey and Thor chased after us in wide circles, their bushy tails propelling. My mother was "it" when the clouds opened up during our first game, and we watched her run toward us from the black walnut tree as the rain began to fall. From under the awning of the front porch where we stood heaving for breath, our hands at our aching sides, we saw the rain sway like a curtain across the lawn. My mother ran through it, one minute dry, the next soaking wet, laughing with her mouth open, shouting "Home free!" as she reached us, her hair stuck in dark tendrils to her head and shoulders.

The next afternoon, it was long after my mother had said she should've gone inside to start dinner, but we were still out on the front lawn playing Kick the Can, all five of us now. Something had gotten into our dad. He'd sidled over from where he'd been picking up fallen walnut husks the wind had knocked off the tree prematurely, and amazingly, now he was playing, too. He ran just as hard as we did toward the can, all of us bolting from wherever we'd been hiding in the shadows, Billy and John and I never wanting to stop, giddy and exhilarated as we shouted to both our parents. We didn't question our father's participation. It seemed a bubble that would burst into nothingness if you touched it.

The condensed, roiling thunderclouds had inked in the night even faster than the previous evening, and we raced and shrieked across the grass until we could hardly see each other, tripping over the dogs, our breath catching in the gusty electric air. We shouted as we ran toward the safety of our base on the front porch, our new old house outlined darker in the deepening twilight, when suddenly everything flared. I didn't see the lightning strike by the back door but my mother did; what I saw, what we all saw, was a ball of exploding light blazing through my parents' bedroom at one end of the house and shooting through to the kitchen, illuminating all the rooms one by one for a split second. Then it was blindingly dark, and at first all I could make out were my mother's arms spread wide on either side of her, pale and blue as milk, holding all of us back. Our parents made us wait outside while they checked the house, turning on the lights in every room. There was no damage, just a smell that was scorched and sulphuric, like someone had lit the fuse of the world but at the last minute changed their mind.

ADDING TO HIS ASCETIC'S inventory of worldly possessions—his shoeshine kit, his suit valet, his dictionary on its dictionary stand—with measured consideration and solemnity my father purchased a brand new pale yellow hardtop Volkswagen Beetle. We'd never had two cars before, but we'd never needed to; now that my father commuted to Philadelphia and we lived in the middle of nowhere, with no neighbors or stores or libraries within walking distance, my mother needed a way to get around during the week. We admired our gleaming new Beetle on the gravel driveway, proud that we were a Volkswagen family endowed with the flower power grooviness such ownership implied. My dad buffed invisible specks of dust from the rounded wheel covers with a chamois cloth that was strictly off-limits to my brothers and me, as was touching any part of the car without explicit permission. Instead we argued over the replica toy VW bug given to us by the sideburned car salesman, an exact miniature of our car that flashed its headlights and pottered a few feet before its batteries ran out.

During the week my dad only drove his bug back and forth to the Malvern train depot, taking the commuter train the rest of the way to Philadelphia's majestic Thirtieth Street Station, so on weekends he liked to go for drives. We wandered the back roads of Pennsylvania with no particular destination, mandatory family outings that soon wore the new-car thrill off the VW for Billy and John and me, as we bickered and elbowed each other and complained of car sickness in the Beetle's narrow back seat. Sometimes we pulled over at historic landmark signs to read who had done what to whom and when, my dad idling the puttering engine as my mother squinted at the bronze citations and recited them to us. Sometimes we didn't stop at all, simply turning around and heading home when my dad's sanguine Sunday driving mood had soured because of our squabbles. My mom stared out the window of the front passenger door as if we were passing something she knew she'd never see again, her body angled away from us, her eyes hidden behind her sunglasses. After my brothers and I shoved each other out of the car, my dad would sit in the driver's seat by himself, making notes on mileage and gas prices in a little leather-bound book he kept in the glove compartment.

The tense atmosphere of our family car trips eased when we started adding actual destinations and picnic lunches. My brothers wanted to see the tangible manifestations of history: real battlefields and cannons and rooms where Revolutionary heroes had made their shrewd decisions wearing powdered wigs and velvet waistcoats. I wanted to see those things, too, sort of, at least the wigs and velvet parts, but more than that I wanted to see Amish people driving horse-drawn buggies through covered bridges, then follow them straight to the parking lots of their dairy stores, which Aunt Virginia had told me about. The Amish dairies sold homemade ice cream and pies and cakes as well as milk and butter. After I heard their tasty-sounding names, my mouth watered for shoofly pie and friendship bread and funnel cakes. While I waited for the Amish dairies to reach the top of our tourist agenda, I settled for getting into the picnic hamper, where I knew I could find at least a Hoho or a Twinkie.

From my father's point of view, it was probably a disappointingly brief drive from our house to nearby Valley Forge, where George Washington had wintered his ragtag amateur army while he waited for the weather to turn and a chance to chase the British out of Philadelphia. We wandered through dense stands of maples and oaks, inspecting tiny log cabins where the Continental soldiers had sheltered through miserable months of waist-high snow and bitter cold. Many of them died of exposure and disease, the park signs told us, the army too famished and weak to give the bodies proper burial; there were no blankets, no boots, there was no dry wood for fires. I refused to leave the marked walking path though my brothers ran up and down the forested slopes, kicking up peat and leaves between the trees, imagining themselves minutemen tamping powder into their muskets. My imagination was more vividly macabre. I was sure if I left the path I'd trip on some dead soldier's shallowly covered thigh bone, or worse, come face-to-face with a skull, its tattered tricorner hat moldering on top at a grisly angle.

Another sign told us that things finally got better for the Revolutionary troops when the best gingerbread baker in Philadelphia showed up and fed them some decent food. "Nah," my father said in answer to my question, using the casually dismissive, scornful tone we'd all grown used to. "They didn't eat gingerbread men. They were starving and there were thousands of them. They needed bread."

I pictured it anyway: the red-cheeked baker, a German-born patriot appointed Supervisor of Baking by George Washington himself, standing with his helpers in the snow, all of them in their puffy chef hats passing out trays of hot gingerbread men to the grateful bedraggled soldiers. Who wouldn't want gingerbread if they could have it? A loaf of bread would feed you, but a gingerbread man would make you glad to be alive.

One day, dressed in our nicest ironed clothes, we all drove with my father in the Beetle to the Malvern train depot, and then we took the train to Philadelphia to see the Liberty Bell and my father's office, which was next door to Independence Hall. If Valley Forge made me as uneasy as my father's volatile temper, the Liberty Bell proved to be a source of almost pathological anxiety. At first it was thrilling that we could walk through the halls of my dad's office building and right smack into the room where the Liberty Bell hung, the walls swagged with red, white, and blue bunting. It was still housed in Independence Hall then, where, we were told, it had cracked the first time it was rung, then rung again to call the people of Philadelphia to the first reading of the Declaration of Independence.

It was the crack that worried me. It was a big crack. If something made of such thick, strong metal could break apart like that, what did that mean for our country? For my family? At night my parents watched newsreels of the war in Vietnam, where one of my uncles was a lieutenant colonel in the navy. Sometimes they remembered to tell us to leave the room, but other times we saw the troops jumping out of helicopters, people running through rice fields with babies on their backs, forests of palm trees exploding.

Back in California, my mother had cried as we drove through a pounding spring rain listening to the car radio on the day Martin Luther King, Jr., was killed; we were on our way to pick up John-John from his integrated preschool in East Palo Alto, where people were rioting in the streets and the teachers had locked themselves inside the

building with the children. Later I'd seen the photograph of men pointing, Reverend King lying on a balcony in Memphis. The photograph
of Robert Kennedy lying on the floor of a hotel kitchen in Los Angeles.
The college girl screaming over her friend sprawled on the ground in
Ohio; my mother winced and turned away when she told me the friend
had only tripped during the rioting. There were riots and police with
tear gas in Chicago, Berkeley, New York, half a million people marching against the war in Washington, D.C.

Every afternoon at our house on Sugartown Road, just before my
father came back in the Beetle from the train depot, my mother led us
through the drill of chores we needed to accomplish to keep him from
being angry when he got home: "Billy, you put the newspaper together
so it looks like no one has touched it. Cissy, get the dogs outside and
make your bed. John and I will put all the toys away. Quick, everyone,
he's almost here!" It was just like racing the tornado, or like the soldiers jumping out of helicopters in Vietnam, their commander shouting "Go! Go! Go!"

I stared at the Liberty Bell, wondering why someone didn't fix it. If
the *Apollo 13* astronauts could figure out how to save themselves and
return to earth using duct tape, couldn't someone in Philadelphia fix
the crack in that bell? My dad came up behind me, impatient in his suit.
He had to get to work, he said; the look on his face made me think he
was glad to leave us.

AT LAST, ON THE WAY back from some other excursion, we stopped at
an Amish dairy down the road from our house. Alongside the milk and
cream and freshly churned butter were trays of cookies covered with
wire domes, a tin bucket of molasses taffy, just-baked pies and cakes
lined up on the whitewashed shelves along the walls: brown sugar pie,
sugar cream pie, angel food cookies, whoopie pies. The Amish dairy
became a regular stop on my mother's weekly round of errands, but
she wouldn't buy anything but milk no matter how politely I asked.
"Next time . . . ," she'd say, staring vaguely in another direction as I
pointed out the shoofly pie, the Amish specialty I most coveted, but
next time she'd come up with some other excuse. She told me once
when we were well out of earshot of the white-capped Amish dairy
ladies that she didn't think I'd like the flavor of shoofly pie, but I knew

from its rich molasses smell and the browned crumbs sprinkled over its surface that she was wrong. Most often she said we had plenty of sweets at home. Shortly before the new school year started, Billy and John and I discovered that this was a monumental understatement.

We'd sunk to new lows in our efforts to stave off the boredom of being the only kids we knew, the only kids within miles. Frosting stands didn't work on Sugartown Road: Our intersection was a place that people passed through on their way somewhere else. We were crabby and lethargic in the sticky heat of the East Coast, which was curiously devoid of swimming pools. We made a few halfhearted stabs at running through sprinklers, and if forced we'd trudge like convicts in a chain gang to the school's deserted playground, where the tetherball poles were useless, the balls locked away in the building for the summer. After thirty seconds on the swings, we'd slide off the hot rubber seats and stagger home, grousing all the way.

I was mostly content to sit in my rocker in my girly pink bedroom, reading *Stuart Little* or *Mrs. Wiggs of the Cabbage Patch* with a kitten kneading my lap; alone in my room, it was easier to pretend that I was an only child, which topped the list of things I liked to pretend to be. The détente among my brothers and me had been uneasy from our babyhoods, the result, I now understand, of being so close in age that we were forever in competition for the same sustenance, the same toys, the same attention from our young inexperienced parents. Without the buffer of relatives, neighbors, and playmates, and with our mother preoccupied by the daily effort to keep our ancient dispirited house from falling apart around us, in Pennsylvania our sibling rivalry was swiftly evolving along Darwinian models, the gender separation enforced by our new sleeping arrangements underscoring the idea that we were neighboring but enemy camps.

I don't know where our mother was the day Billy, John, and I first explored the dank basement, sniping in our torpor as we descended the groaning stairs. The molecules of air in that basement hadn't moved since 1776, and everything was crusted with dimness. The freezer we'd inherited from the previous occupants beckoned us eerily forward with its electric hum and promise of cool relief. When we lifted the lid, we found it was stocked with a staggering array of frozen, individually packaged baked goods, a selection to rival the shelves of the A&P: regional delicacies such as Little Debbie Oatmeal Pies and Tastykake

Krimpets as well as the entire product lines of Hostess, Dolly Madison, and Pepperidge Farm, from cupcakes to Devil Dogs to poundcake to pink marshmallow Sno Balls.

We gaped at each other in astonishment. It was a treasure trove of cake, an unprecedented bounty of frosted and crème-filled delectation, bathed in the arctic blue glow of the open freezer. Perhaps, we suggested to each other in lowered voices, our mother was planning ahead, ensuring that she wouldn't run out of junk food to load into our lunchboxes if there were a huge snowstorm in six months and all the roads were closed. . . . Years later, when she began hoarding multiple cases of Top Ramen noodles, canned cranberry jelly, and discounted meatballs in gravy ("You don't like them? That's okay, the dogs will") not to mention fur coats, Lee Press-On Nails, and grocery bags of unopened mail in addition to the lipsticks, bottles of Moon Drops lotion, and art supplies she'd always collected, I realized that my mother's stockpiling tendency stemmed from different unfilled needs.

But in August 1970 my brothers and I were innocent of the concept of compensatory behavior, and we were alone in a promised land of frozen snack cakes. For the last few days of summer and on into the deflated afternoons of the first weeks of school, while our mom was otherwise occupied doing who knows what, Billy and John and I were down in the stifled cool of our basement living a sugar-fueled shadow life around the freezer. A Ding Dong here, a Butterscotch Krimpet there—she'd never know the difference, we thought, and I don't think she ever did. We balled up the foil and cellophane evidence and hid it under the staircase. For once there was nothing to fight over. There was plenty of everything for each of us.

WHEN SCHOOL STARTED in September, I walked with my brothers every morning through the pear orchard, lifting my face to the honeyed scent of anticipation. I'd been waiting for the pears since we moved in. Small and hard and secret at first, with the coming of fall the pears were turning yellow and fragrant on the undisturbed branches. The grapes in our backyard were puckeringly sour and full of tiny bitter seeds we spit on the ground, and my mom had tried to harvest the black walnuts but they turned out to be disgusting, literally black inside and oily and acidic, like something you'd use to tan leather. I was sure the pears would be luscious. I'd practically grown them myself.

I was just as excited about entering third grade. They didn't give out candy at the door of Sugartown Elementary as I'd hoped, but the first week had gone really well even so. When my new teacher, Miss Hyde, announced she would be reading *Ramona the Pest* to us, I raised my hand and informed her that I'd already read *Ramona the Pest* and *Beezus and Ramona,* too. The next day, Miss Hyde called me to her desk to give me a copy of *Henry Huggins* checked out from the school library. When I was finished reading the book, Miss Hyde wanted me to tell her all about it, she said, though I still had to listen quietly while she read *Ramona the Pest* to the rest of the class and not spoil the surprise for the other children. I sat at my desk as quiet as a mouse while Miss Hyde read aloud, my hands clapped ostentatiously over my mouth the whole time so she'd see how good I was at following directions.

I wasn't just the smartypants new third grader gunning for teacher's pet. I was cashing in my social currency, too. My classmates had heard that I was from California—yes, I'd seen actual hippies and Disneyland—and they seemed suitably impressed that I lived right next to the school. I made sure that they knew we had a Love Bug and a litter of kittens and a freezer full of Twinkies, and I grinned right back when I saw some of the other third-grade girls smiling at me and pointing from another table in the cafeteria when I opened my *Josie and the Pussycats* lunchbox. Everything was working out just fine at Sugartown Elementary, and in the afternoons Billy and John and I sprawled companionably in front of the television together, watching *Dark Shadows* and taking turns sneaking down to the basement for Ding Dongs.

So I was shocked at Billy's reaction when I threatened to beat up the kid who was bullying him on the playground one day during recess. As soon as I heard that one of the big boys was picking on my brother, I rushed to the scene. Encircled by heckling onlookers, some cross-eyed galoot was menacing Billy by the tetherball courts, and my skinny cerebral older brother, trying to reason with the guy, was about to be pummeled into the asphalt. My familial loyalty aroused, I muscled my way to the front of the peanut gallery.

"Sit on him! Sit on him!" the hecklers brayed when they saw me.

"You bet I'll sit on you if you touch my brother!" I warned the bully. I lunged forward with my fists balled.

He took one look at me and fled.

That afternoon as we headed home after school, Billy ran far ahead across the playing fields, yelling at me to leave him alone. Bewildered, I trudged alone up the steep embankment into the orchard. Billy was really mad at me, and I didn't know why. We were a team, our mom always said; wasn't it my responsibility to stick up for my brother? More than my responsibility—it was my instinct. I thought I'd be greeted as a hero by my family. I breathed in the pear smell hovering under the trees, trying to comfort myself.

Back at home, Billy had flung himself facedown on his bed and refused to talk to anyone except our mom.

"He's embarrassed," she explained after she left the boys' bedroom, shutting the door behind herself. She seemed embarrassed, too. "It's just . . ." She hesitated. "Well, he's the big brother and you're the, uh, sister. Boys don't like girls to defend them."

Billy was slow to forgive, and he didn't talk to me at school or walk home with me anymore. The other kids at school relished the story of my threat to sit on a fifth grader, which only made things worse. It's not like they thought I was a hero, either. The kids thought it was hilarious, and they ran shrieking from me across the playground, shouting to each other, "She'll sit on you! She'll sit on you!"

Confused, wretched, and lonely, at school I stood in line for the tetherball games during recess, though pointlessly, because as soon as it was my turn everyone else ran away. From then on I started every schoolday morning with a clutching stomachache as I thought about the other kids. At home in the afternoons, I would sneak a box of Lucky Charms into my parents' bedroom and eat all the marshmallow charms while crouched down on the far side of the bed, out of sight. "Mom, she did it again!" Billy would yell at breakfast as he poured his Lucky Charms and found nothing but the boring cereal bits.

Life in Sugartown reached the nadir of bitterness on the autumn Saturday when I was outside with my family collecting black walnut husks in a wheelbarrow so they wouldn't break the lawn mower again. I sucked deep draughts of crisp fall air and surveyed the golden glory of my pear orchard. It was time to pick the pears, I announced, they were finally deliciously ripe!

"That orchard doesn't belong to us," my dad said, raking leaves into a garbage bag. "We can't pick the pears."

But—but—I'd been waiting for months! And the orchard didn't seem to have another owner. We'd never seen anyone else. No one walked through the trees but our family. No one loved those pears but me.

"We can't pick any pears, not even one," my scrupulous lawyer father said with the unequivocal finality of a prosecutor delivering his final argument to the jury. "It would be stealing." Case closed.

At least there was Miss Hyde. Miss Hyde, who had frosted blond hair and a soothing voice she never raised. When she started to speak, enunciating the word "children" as if it were something you'd say in church, the entire class would hush and lean forward over their desks, listening. She was beautiful in a way totally different from my mother. Miss Hyde reminded me of the Japanese tea garden in Golden Gate Park, a trickle of water that made my heart slow down. She let me stay in the classroom during lunch and recess, reading or eating my lunch alone, working on my stories about dolls who came to life when no one could see them.

My mom was lonely, too. She missed her friends in Sonoma and our relatives, and we were so far out in the sticks she had few of the usual outlets for her copious creativity except keeping one step ahead of our tumbledown house.

"You feel a little warm," she suggested one weekday morning as I held my stomach and groaned with dread over school. "Maybe you should stay home and rest today."

We watched old movies on television, and I helped fold my father's handkerchiefs into neat squares as my mom ironed them. After lunch she taught me how to waltz in the front room. While we cleaned the kitchen together, she turned the radio up and we sang all the words to "Close to You" with Karen Carpenter.

TV Guide listed all the movies on television for the week, and I scanned the daytime listings for musicals, and anything with Elizabeth Taylor or Gene Tierney. In the morning as my mother packed our lunchboxes, I'd moan about my stomach, though it didn't feel too bad. In fact it felt pretty good. My mother would survey me with a concerned, motherly look and a faint gleam in her green eyes.

"Well, maybe you should stay home again," she'd say. "I can help you practice your times tables so you can keep up, and then we could work on your diorama . . ." Working on my diorama was something we could do while sitting in front of the TV singing along to *Show Boat* or watching *The Ghost and Mrs. Muir.*

My beloved Miss Hyde had assigned our class to make dioramas to illustrate our first book reports, due at the end of the fall semester, and we got to choose whichever book we wanted. I had picked *Charlotte's Web,* not least because of something Wilbur the pig says in the book: "It is not often that someone comes along who is a true friend and a good writer." Wilbur was referring to Charlotte the spider, but I hoped Miss Hyde might recognize me as both of those things, too.

The diorama my mother and I designed together depicted the farm-yard with Charlotte and her famous web in the corner of the big barn door and all the animal characters gathered around, Wilbur looking up admiringly at the ingenuity that saved him. It was my mom's idea to make Wilbur out of a spool of thread covered with pink felt, but I made him myself, using pink pipe cleaners for his legs and corkscrew tail, and tiny black beads sewn on for eyes.

Charlotte was a black sequin carefully cut into eight legs with cuti-cle scissors, a black bead in the middle for her head. Our plan was to dangle her from a web made of thread dipped in glue and arranged on waxed paper while it dried to keep its shape—again, my mom's idea. I, however, had the responsibility for coming up with the word spelled out in Charlotte's web. I consulted the book and told my mother the word—actually a phrase—that would let Miss Hyde know immedi-ately the literary inspiration for my diorama, and my shrewd insight as a reader.

" 'Some pig,' " I announced to my mother.

My mom's smile faltered a little, but she shored it up. "Boy, Cis, that's a lot to write in such a tiny web. Is there maybe a shorter word we could use?"

"There's 'Terrific,' " I said, "but that has even more letters than 'Some pig.' "

"Oh, no," my mom said, " 'Terrific' is fine. 'Terrific' will fit."

"But if 'Terrific' will fit," I argued, puzzled, "why won't 'Some pig'? 'Some pig' is more important. That's the first thing Charlotte writes to save Wilbur."

"Well, uh," my mom stalled, "well then, how about other words? Maybe we're overlooking something . . ."

"Charlotte writes 'Humble' in the web at the county fair, but if we use 'Humble' we have to change the whole diorama and make it the fairgrounds," I told her. "And Templeton the rat finds 'Crunchy' on a piece of paper at the dump, but Charlotte thinks 'Crunchy' will remind people of crunchy bacon." If I'd learned anything from *Charlotte's Web*, it was that words were powerful, and the right word—or the wrong one—could change your life.

"Yes, that's a good point, I don't think we should use 'Crunchy,'" my mom said quickly. "But, honey," she continued, "I don't think 'Some pig' is the best choice." She was still smiling, but there was a tremble of concern in her eyes.

And that's when I got it. That's when I realized I was fat. F-A-T. Suddenly everything made sense: That was why my mom wouldn't buy me a pie at the Amish dairy. Why Billy was so lastingly humiliated and wouldn't talk to me at school or walk home with me. Why the other kids thought my threat to sit on the bully was so hilarious.

I was too heartsick and mortified to write any word at all in my web. Now all I wanted was for winter vacation to begin so I could drown my sorrows in hard sauce and store-bought eggnog while watching *How the Grinch Stole Christmas*. On the Friday of the last week of school, I tromped home through the pear orchard by myself under a dense gray sky, trying to hold my too-tight California coat closed, feeling stunningly cold and miserable. We'd had a few flurries and now meager clots of snow lay dirty and forlorn around the trunks of the trees. I slipped and slid in my inadequate rain boots over flattened yellowed grass and ooze, the orchard floor everywhere smeared with rotting pears. My face, my hands, and my feet were freezing. I heard ahead of me the creak and slam of our back screen door as Billy and John reached our house and went inside, and then I heard my brothers yelling.

"Cissy! Come and see what Mom's made!"

I looked up. There was soft pale smoke chugging out of the chimney on the roof of our house. Handfuls of snowflakes were spinning downward through the sky. When I opened the back door, the warmth and spicy odor of our kitchen wafted over me. Gingerbread—my mother was making gingerbread people, boys and girls. She'd turned on the lights of our Christmas tree so we'd see them glittering in every color as we walked in. Our furnace had gone out, but my mom had started a fire in the big stone fireplace, and the whole house was cozy and inviting.

Billy and John and I sat on stools at the kitchen counter, warming our hands around mugs of hot lemonade our mother had ready for us when we arrived, and the four of us decorated gingerbread people as my mom took them out of the oven, giving them buttons of raisins and chocolate chips. We ate them warm and sipping our lemonade, listening to Johnny Mathis and Andy Williams singing Christmas carols. We sang along, my brothers and my mom and I, watching the snow fall harder outside the kitchen windows, the pure tranquil snow sifting down to blanket our world, covering everything cracked and broken and lost.

HILLS FAMILY CHRISTMAS GINGERBREAD COOKIES
.·.

3½ to 4 cups unbleached all-purpose flour

1 teaspoon baking soda

½ teaspoon salt

3 tablespoons ground ginger

1 tablespoon cinnamon

1 teaspoon ground cloves

1 teaspoon freshly ground white pepper

½ teaspoon freshly grated nutmeg

1 heaping tablespoon unsweetened cocoa

1 cup unsalted butter, at room temperature

1 cup granulated sugar

1 large egg, at room temperature

½ cup unsulfured dark molasses (not mild and not
    blackstrap)

• Combine 3½ cups of the flour, the baking soda, salt, spices, and cocoa and sift. Set aside.

• In the bowl of an electric mixer, beat the butter at medium speed for a couple of minutes, then gradually add the granulated sugar, creaming until light and very fluffy, about 5 minutes. Add the egg, beating until very creamy and light, then the molasses, again beating until the mixture is creamy and light. With the mixer on low speed or by hand, mix in the dry ingredients by halves just until all the flour has disappeared. The dough will be soft, but it should have body and stick to itself rather than your fingers when you press it lightly—if it seems too sticky and soft, sprinkle ¼ cup of the remaining flour over the dough and mix it in until it disappears. If the dough is still too soft, add the last ¼ cup of flour. Divide the dough into one or two portions and wrap in waxed paper. Chill until firm, at least 3 hours or overnight. The dough can be made up to three days ahead and kept refrigerated, well wrapped and airtight.

• When ready to bake, preheat the oven to 350°. Roll the dough thickly—⅜ inch for large cookies, ¼ inch for small—on a generously floured surface, using more flour on the rolling pin and sprinkled on the dough as needed to prevent sticking. Cut the dough into shapes and place on baking sheets. Refrigerate or freeze the cookies for at least 20 minutes before baking. Bake for 5 to 10 minutes, until the cookies have puffed and the dough looks smooth, not shiny, and evenly cooked (a gingerbread-man-sized cookie will take about 7 to 9 minutes). Let the cookies cool for a few minutes on the sheets before removing to wire racks to cool completely.

• Glaze with the opaque, slightly lemony glaze used for Pink and White Animal Cookies (page 52) or the thin translucent glaze recipe below. If desired, add raisins or cinnamon candies as decorations.

Makes about 18 large, thick gingerbread cookies, more if the cookies are smaller.

GINGERBREAD GLAZE

2 cups confectioners' sugar
2 tablespoons water
Dash of vanilla

• Whisk together all the ingredients until smooth. If the glaze is too thin, add more sugar by the spoonful; if too thick, add drops of water. Glaze cookies with a pastry brush, adding decorations if desired while the glaze is wet.

Can This Marriage Be Saved?

B Y THE END OF THE SCHOOL YEAR AT SUGARTOWN ELEMENTARY, WE were moving again. My dad had been promoted and asked to come to Washington, D.C. We would live nearby in Virginia, where my parents had bought a house still under construction in a subdivision that was spanking new: new houses, new streets, new schools, even a pool for the whole neighborhood to use. Our new house was being built just for us, with bedrooms for both of my brothers and me. My mother was going to get to choose everything, from the faucets in the bathrooms to the carpets and the kitchen cabinets, and decorate all the rooms however she liked.

First, though, we went to Atlantic City for a beach vacation with Uncle Don, Aunt Virginia, and the little Ohio cousins. My mom packed a stack of ladies' magazines to read while she baked herself to a tawny Californian crisp in the sand, and I read them in the car on the drive to the Jersey shore, titillated by the information they contained that was clearly not meant for me.

"Cancer"—that was a new word. I pored over the pages describing this disease, something horrible and deadly, with lumps. In every issue of the magazine was an article called "Can This Marriage Be Saved?" in which some married couple with ordinary-enough-sounding names and kids and relatives and car payments started telling about the rotten things they'd done to each other. Then a marriage counselor would say what they could do to make up for it, finally passing judgment on whether there was any hope. If I were Hazel, and Stan had gambled away all of the money we were going to use to send our son to military school or started bringing flowers to his secretary, I don't know if I'd want to keep being married. But I was nine and I wanted everything to work out.

I looked up from the back of the station wagon. My parents sat in the front seat like strangers on a bus as the bridges and blueberry fields of New Jersey rushed by outside the windows. Our car was packed with beach towels and blow-up toys my mother had hunted down in the variety stores of Chester County because it would be highway robbery to buy them in Atlantic City, my dad said, and we were going to build sandcastles and walk on the boardwalk and see them pull long ropes of saltwater taffy—and still my parents looked just like they did in the Beetle during our grim Sunday drives. The humming voltage of our father's silence as he stared down the road resonated to the back seat where my brothers and I sat. Our mother hugged her side of the seat, her sunglasses hiding her eyes, her bony shoulders pulled into herself. The space between them seemed as impassible as a wall of solid brick.

I went back to reading my mom's magazines and flipped forward to the ends of the articles, wanting to make sure Hazel and Stan or Joanna and Bob ended up happy and in love. Sometimes I read the marriage counselor's conclusions over and over, trying to break their equivocatingly adult code, and still I couldn't tell what happened to Joanna and Bob.

My mother called the musty vacation rental we were all staying in together a beach bungalow, but it wasn't anywhere near the beach. Every day, my mom and Aunt Virginia loaded up our lunch hampers and we piled into the cars and drove to the ocean. The mothers set up housekeeping under umbrellas, and while they lay prone on their towels, the straps of their bathing suit tops dangling loose over their arms so they wouldn't have tan lines on their shoulders, my brothers and cousins and I played in the shallow surf, constructing moated fortresses and burying each other to our necks in the sand, digging after the telltale bubbles of creatures that escaped too quickly for us to catch them.

In California we swam in pools and slow-moving rivers, but we'd rarely gone to the beach and never into the water of the Pacific, which was always cold and forbiddingly dramatic. The warm sandy surf at Atlantic City seemed friendlier. I jumped around in the water for hours, letting the waves smash foaming at my back and feeling the suck of the sand as the tide pulled the sea out from under my feet. Late in the afternoons we'd ride tired and damp in our gritty swimsuits back to the bungalow, but that's when the vacation really started.

Maybe the salty breezes had cleared the tension in the air between my parents. Maybe they, like me, were relieved by the presence of our relatives, people who knew us and liked us anyway, showing my mother and father a wider horizon than the fraught, narrow vista they saw each other from every day. As we witnessed the mind-boggling spectacle of our parents making dinner together in the little kitchen— all of our parents, my dad, too, talking and laughing—Billy and John and I made up dance routines and belted out "Stop! In the Name of Love" along with the Supremes on the hi-fi. The big kids, we taught our little cousins the words to the songs as my dad and uncle blackened hot dogs on the hibachi outside. Every night, my mom and Aunt Virginia made dessert from fruit they picked up at produce stands on the drive back from the beach, and we'd wolf down slices of peach pie made without a pie pan because there wasn't one in the bungalow, or slurp up vanilla ice cream melting over blueberry crisp before collapsing, sunburnt and content, onto our pillows.

On our way home to the bungalow one hot blue afternoon, we stopped by the fruit stand so my mother could buy apples for that night's pie. I was rereading one of her magazines while we waited in the car with all the windows rolled down, and I'd noticed ever since we left the beach that my bottom felt numb. It was starting to bother me. I picked at the elastic on my bathing suit, and I ground around on the seat, but I still couldn't feel anything down there. Billy and John shoved me from either side as I bumped into them. My dad called, "Hey, you kids, what's going on back there?" eyeing us in the rearview mirror, though his voice sounded uncharacteristically easy and relaxed.

"Nothing," I said, and sat as still as I could, feeling the discomfiting sensation of . . . nothingness . . . no matter how hard I sank my weight into the seat of the car. I certainly couldn't tell my father—I couldn't tell anybody—about something as embarrassing as my private parts going numb, but I couldn't forget about it, either. By holding a magazine over my lap, I was able to scrabble my fingers around unseen at the crotch of my swimsuit, and the repeated prodding and poking confirmed the fear that had already been spreading with dire blackness in my imagination. There was something there—big, inert, and lumpy. I knew immediately what it was.

Back at the bungalow, I observed my family's carefree dinner preparations from the poignant distance of someone certain to never again know such casual happiness. I listened to Diana Ross's clear voice lift the notes of "I Hear a Symphony" and fought back tears, thinking how terrible it was, this cancer I'd caught in my bottom, picturing my mother so exquisitely sad at my funeral, her shoulders flawlessly tan in a sleeveless black dress.

I could do little more than move my charred hamburger around on my paper plate during dinner, or pick at the apple pie my proud mother brought to the table, its crust luxuriously pleated and browned.

There was no fooling my mom. If I was crying Atlantic City–salty tears into my uneaten pie, there was something wrong. She led me by the hand into a bedroom and closed the door. I could hardly bear to tell her. Just thinking about how sad she was going to be made me blubber. Finally I got it out: I had cancer.

"What makes you think you have cancer?" she asked, her words slow and deliberate, the way adults talk when they're trying to be respectful of your feelings but they know you don't know what you're talking about.

It was humiliating, but at least we were both girls. I told her about my numb bottom and the firm, nerveless lump I'd been feeling all afternoon inside my bathing suit.

"I think you better show me," she said, and she slipped her fingers under the shoulder straps of my suit and started helping me peel it off inside out. When our hands got to my hips, I pushed the suit down to my knees, and as the damp material went slack over my thighs a silvery fish the length of a hot dog bun went flopping, rubbery and dead, to the floor between my feet.

She promised me she wouldn't tell Billy or John. She promised she wouldn't tell anyone. She wrapped the fish in several layers of Kleenex and flushed it down the toilet, then she helped me pull my nightgown over my head and we held hands as we walked back to the table, where everyone was still eating their pie.

Later that night, breathing in the mothball scent of my pillow, I heard my mom with my dad and my aunt and uncle still sitting at the table by themselves, talking late into the night. I heard my mother's high, amused voice turn down low, and the sibilant sound of my name, and then the pause before they all started laughing. I could feel my face grow hot, but really I didn't mind. I turned my pillow over to the cool side. I was going to be okay, we were all going to be okay, and without even trying I'd given my parents something they would always be able to talk about.

FREE-FORM CROSTATAS WITH CRUMBLE TOPPING

.·.

PASTRY FOR 2 CROSTATAS:

2 cups unbleached all-purpose flour
¼ cup granulated sugar
½ teaspoon salt
1 cup (8 ounces) unsalted butter, very cold or frozen,
    cut into slices
¼ cup ice water

It's important that the butter in this dough stays cold, so work quickly and touch the dough with your hands as little as possible.

• Whisk together the flour, sugar, and salt in a bowl. Add the butter slices and quickly cut in with a pastry cutter or two table knives until the particles are the size of small peas. Stirring with a fork, add the ice water and continue to mix until the dough begins to come together. Turn the dough out onto a sheet of waxed paper and press the dough together into a solid mass. Generously flour your work surface and a rolling pin, and quickly roll the dough into a thick rectangle. Fold it in thirds like a letter, lightly roll it just to get the layers of dough to adhere, then cut the dough into two equal portions. Wrap them in waxed paper or plastic wrap and chill for at least an hour or up to two days. (If you won't be making both crostatas immediately, one of the portions of dough can be frozen for up to two weeks.)

CRUMBLE TOPPING FOR 1 CROSTATA:

⅓ cup unbleached all-purpose flour
⅓ cup firmly packed light brown sugar
¼ teaspoon salt

½ teaspoon cinnamon

Additional spices (see Variations)

6 tablespoons unsalted butter, cold and cut into slices

• Combine the flour, sugar, salt, cinnamon, and additional spices depending on the kind of fruit you're using. Add the butter slices, tossing them with the dry ingredients and rubbing everything together between your fingers until the mixture is crumbly. Chill while you prepare the fruit.

FRUIT FILLING FOR 1 CROSTATA:

2 cups of prepared fresh fruit (see Variations)

Zest of 1 orange

• To assemble the crostata, preheat the oven to 450°. Toss the prepared fruit with the orange zest.

• Roll one portion of the pastry into a free-form shape about 11 inches across. Transfer to a sheet of parchment on a baking sheet, gently folding the rolled pastry in half to move it, if necessary. Cover the pastry with the fruit, leaving a border of 1½ to 2 inches all around the edge of the dough. Sprinkle the crumble topping over the fruit. Gently fold the border over the fruit, pleating as necessary and making sure the fruit is completely enclosed at the edges of the pastry.

• Bake for 20 to 25 minutes, until the crust is golden and the fruit is tender and juicy. Let cool on the baking sheet for 5 to 10 minutes, then serve warm, transferring to a large serving dish with wide spatulas and sliding the crostata off the parchment, or allow to cool completely on the parchment on a wire rack.

Makes one 9-inch pie.

VARIATIONS

Apple: To the Crumble Topping, add ¼ teaspoon of nutmeg, allspice, or ground cloves, or a combination. Peel, core, and slice firm, juicy apples into eighths or 1-inch chunks.

Peach, Nectarine, or Pear: To the Crumble Topping, add ½ teaspoon of ground ginger. Peel, seed, and slice the fruit, adding 1 tablespoon finely diced candied ginger with the orange zest, if desired.

Apricot: To the Crumble Topping, add ½ teaspoon almond flavoring and ½ cup of sliced almonds. Seed the apricots and cut them into quarters or sixths, depending on their size. If you like, you can arrange them in an overlapping pattern, starting at the center of the crostata and working outward.

Fig: To the Crumble Topping, add ¼ teaspoon cardamom. Stem the figs, and either quarter them or slice them, in which case you can arrange them in an overlapping pattern, starting at the center of the crostata and working outward.

Plum: Plum is good with just cinnamon in the Crumble Topping, or you can add ¼ teaspoon cardamom. Core and slice the plums.

Berry: For raspberry or blueberry, substitute the zest of 1 lemon for the orange zest. Blackberry or boysenberry is good with the addition of ¼ teaspoon clove to the Crumble Topping. Strawberries can be sliced and arranged in an overlapping pattern, or mixed with chopped rhubarb, with an additional 2 tablespoons granulated sugar and 2 tablespoons flour mixed together and added to the fruit with the orange zest. Cranberries can be mixed with ½ cup of toasted, roughly chopped walnuts and ⅓ cup dark brown sugar in addition to the orange zest.

Bugged by Nixon

IN SONOMA MY FAMILY HAD LIVED IN A TOWN FULL OF RELATIONS AND friends, a place where everyone knew each other, voices calling out your name and asking if your mom was aware you were eating Jolly Ranchers an hour before dinnertime, or threatening to call the home of the fifth-grade boy who'd pelted you in the shins with gravel from his slingshot while you were feeding the ducks at the Plaza. In Pennsylvania we'd had no one at all, no neighbors or onlookers, no one to keep watch on us as we flailed, only one meager outpost of relatives who, though they lived in the next state over, were still so far from us we saw them only as we arrived and as we moved away.

In Fairfax, Virginia, in a brand new house in a brand new subdivision on the very last, newest street, where behind us was nothing but a weedy field strewn with giant wooden spools of electrical wire left behind by the construction company, we were surrounded by families like us: all new, all from somewhere distant. All the fathers worked in the government, like mine, though on our street most of the fathers worked in the U.S. Secret Service, the drapes of their houses kept closed all day long, every day. We rarely saw the fathers, but when we did, they were dressed in dark suits and sunglasses, their shoulders hiked up straight, marching in their front doors and shutting them.

There was a rumor that a contingent of the Von Trapp family of *Sound of Music* fame lived at the end of our circular street. In the early evenings right after we moved in, before my father arrived home from his office in Washington, my mother would take a break from sewing Roman shades or assembling our new furniture to pour herself a beer into a plastic tumbler, and she and Billy and John and I would stroll down our block, one or two of our cats skulking along behind us on the sidewalk trying to seem nonchalant, as if they weren't really following us at all, as if they were Secret Service cats trying to look like anyone else in the crowd.

"Don't act like we're looking," my mom whispered to us, rolling her sweating tumbler over her forehead in the sticky heat as we approached the house rumored to belong to the Von Trapps. "Pretend we're just new neighbors taking a walk." We were hoping to catch the Von Trapps in dirndl skirts or lederhosen, maybe singing as one by one they trooped up the stairs to bed, but the Von Trapps were elusive. Even when we waited until sunset, when the sky banded in mauve and purple over the tops of the shadowed trees beyond the empty field, the dark shapes of bats jerking through the air in the halos of the streetlights, and the drapes in the Von Trapp house went translucent as they turned on their lamps inside, we never saw them.

"AFFIRMATIVE ON THAT, and hey, Mac, take my order, too—how 'bout a Reuben sandwich, easy on the mustard, and a cream soda."

My mom had spent the day showing all the other mothers on our street how to découpage, or maybe it was sculpting with paper that day, or wallpapering a neighbor's laundry room. She hadn't had time to prepare dinner, which had lately been hamburgers, or hamburger patties, or Hamburger Helper. Now she was squeezing the phone receiver to her ear with her shoulder, flipping through the phone book for the number of the local fried fish place to order dinner for my dad to pick up on the way home, when she heard a man's voice. He was ordering his dinner, too.

At first she thought the man's voice on the line was another issue to bring up with the land developer that had built our subdivision. Maybe our phone lines had been crossed with someone else's when the wires were installed. But it was 1971, and there'd been a lot of talk in the news about wiretapping. My mother listened with mounting hand-over-the-receiver interest as the man on our phone line breathed and occasionally said something pitifully ordinary to one of his colleagues.

We were being bugged! Our phones had been tapped! It made sense, sort of: There we were, surrounded by Secret Service agents, and my father was climbing the ranks of the civil service. He was working for a government agency that didn't have a name yet but would eventually become the Department of Energy. He'd become an expert in mineral law, called upon to write speeches for the president after the Bretton Woods Accord ended and the cost of oil started to rise. Obviously, according to my mother, the United States government had big plans for my father.

After listening with rapt attention to the phone for a while, my mother silently set the receiver down. She ran across the street to check in with the neighbor who'd admitted her husband was a Secret Service agent while my mom was decorating their son's room to look like a barnyard, painting a mural of cows and sheep behind the bunk bed and stapling hay and chicken wire to the wall. The neighbor called her husband, and the husband called his contacts in the FBI, and by the time my father came home, late from work as usual, my mother had it all confirmed and was bursting with her news.

My father shook his head with a patronizing little smile, put down his briefcase—by now a leather box six inches thick with a coded lock—and handed my mother the greasy bags of battered shrimp and hush puppies. There was no reason, our father said, sighing with pained sufferage, for anyone to want to bug our phone line. Our mother, he suggested, was imagining the whole thing.

Actually, what he said was, "Lackey, you're crazy." "Lackey" had been my mother's nickname since childhood, when one of her younger sisters had been unable to pronounce Kathleen. Her nickname had been cute and memorable when my mother was a girl, but after her marriage it had become increasingly unfortunate, not to mention fitting, that my father addressed her by a word that meant a servant of low rank.

"I heard it clear as day!" my mother countered, her certainty unshakable. "He ordered a Reuben sandwich and a cream soda!"

"What's a cream soda?" I asked, suddenly interested.

A COUPLE OF WEEKS LATER, my mother got a package from the White House, with a letter on White House stationery. The letter thanked her for her good citizenship and her ongoing support of the president, and it was signed by Richard Milhous Nixon. It came with a pen that was engraved *The White House*, nestled on satin inside a flocked blue box.

"I was right! I was right!" my mother chortled, waving her White House pen. "Here's the proof!"

"That signature doesn't look real," I said, peering closely at the letter. "It looks like a rubber stamp."

"They can't come right out and admit it, but this is the proof," my mom gloated to herself, ignoring me and trying out the pen on the cover of *TV Guide*. "Wait until your father sees *this*." Then she got serious. "Maybe you better not tell the kids about this," she said, meaning, I gathered, my new friends in Virginia, of which there were, let's see, none. "Remember, this is a matter of national security. And you don't want to make anyone feel left out. Not everyone has a father important enough to be bugged by Nixon."

MY FATHER'S ONLY response to my mother's letter from the president was to raise his eyebrows and shrug. He didn't do much more when, shortly before Easter, we received another letter from the White House, this time an engraved invitation to attend the White House tour and annual Easter egg roll on the Monday after the holiday.

"It's a public event," my dad said, snapping his *Washington Post* and not taking his eyes off the article he was reading. "Maybe they're sending invitations to government employees with families. But it's open to everyone. Anyone can go."

"How many people work for the government in Washington— thousands?" my mom said, directing her argument to my brothers and me, since my father pretended not to listen. "They're not going to send thousands of invitations! No, we have obviously been specially picked. The White House wants *our* family at the Easter egg roll. Games and contests and prizes, and a tour of the White House! And boy, wait until they get a load of our eggs!" My mother was firing up; you could practically see the wheels of exuberant grandiosity turning behind her glittering green eyes. "Kids, we are going to make the most special eggs anyone ever saw!" my mom vowed over my dad's sighs and eye-rolling from the couch. "We are going to win that Easter egg roll!"

THOUGH SHE'D STARTED collecting a new assortment of friends in our neighborhood, other government-work widows who gave her kudos for her originality, marveling at her artistic talent and her youthful beauty, my mother, like me, still missed California. She kept up her subscription to the weekly *Sonoma Index-Tribune* and to *Sunset* magazine, which is where she found the recipe for molded sugar Easter eggs.

"This is it! This is it!" she announced, holding up the page of the magazine so I could see. "These are the eggs we're going to make for the White House! Oh boy, nobody will have eggs like these—c'mon!" I ran after her upstairs and watched as she started rummaging through the deep closet between the bathroom and my bedroom, probably meant by the subdivision's architect to be a linen closet. In our house, it was "the supply closet": There was nothing inside but art supplies.

My mom had recently started buying a new kind of pantyhose, L'eggs, sold at the grocery store and packaged in two-part plastic eggs, which we pressed into service as the mold for our panoramic eggs. We mixed sugar with egg whites and packed it into the L'eggs container halves, scooping out the soft sugar in the middle of each one when the outer layer was dry.

When the eggs were completely hard, my mother went to work on their décor. The finished eggs wore fabulists' swags of royal icing and headpieces of millinery flowers and piped frosting roses. Inside the eggs, seen through a round cut-out window framed by frills of icing, were idyllic Easter pastorals with tiny porcelain or papier-mâché animals bedded on shredded coconut she'd dyed green, or on moss or snips of real grass. One had a duck and ducklings swimming on a pond that had been a lipstick mirror, a blue frosting waterfall splashing down into it; another had a family of tiny china bunnies carrying minute baskets of colored eggs made out of candy sprinkles. One had a speckled fawn sleeping beneath a waving forest of crepe-paper ferns dripping with "raindrops" made by a glue gun. Even Billy and John and I were impressed; she'd really outdone herself.

"But, Mom," Billy said gently, "it's an Easter egg *roll*. . . ."

"You're right!" she said, smacking her forehead. "Okay, we better get busy."

We boiled and dyed a basketful of eggs, assuming the eggs for the roll didn't have to be so ornate since they'd be lolling around in the grass of the South Lawn. On the morning of Easter Monday, my mother called our school to tell them we'd be absent—we'd been *invited* to the White House—and we drove into Washington with my father, who dropped us off at the public entrance to the White House and continued to his office a few blocks away.

The South Lawn looked like a carnival, with thousands of kids in their Easter finery and military bands in dress uniform and people in bunny suits handing out Nixon eggs. We found the table for entering our sugar eggs in the "most beautiful egg" contest, and my mother turned on our Super-8 movie camera to film us playing egg croquet and tossing eggs back and forth and running across the lawn with eggs on spoons.

"Oh my gosh, we *won! We WON!*" my mother squealed when the people in bunny suits started distributing ribbons. She motioned for Billy and John and I to stand closer together, holding our eggs and our ribbons in front of us, as she kept her eye on the viewfinder of the camera, backing away to get us all in the picture because we were jumping up and down.

My brothers and I weren't ready to leave. There was still the egg roll to do, and there was a hunt with candy, not that we needed it, since we had our usual over-the-top Easter baskets waiting for us at home, and our grandmother had sent each of us a See's Candy egg the size of a grenade, solid with chocolate buttercream filling. But our mother wanted to take the White House tour, so we promised not to leave the South Lawn, and she'd come back to find us when the tour was over.

LATER THAT AFTERNOON, I sat with my brothers and our mom on cold plastic chairs in a basement-level hallway painted the color of a bad day, hanging my head as White House guards watched closed-circuit televisions and us. We were waiting for my father to come from his office to bail us out.

My mother hadn't exactly been arrested. She'd been caught fingering the guest towels in the First Lady's private powder room. When my father arrived, his face looked like it was going to explode. My mother's face looked more like Mr. Toad's in *The Wind in the Willows* after he'd seen his first motorcar. When she'd realized that the president's private quarters were not on the White House tour, she had gone looking for them herself.

"It's really a beautiful room," my mother whispered to me while we waited. "Pat Nixon has done a nice job. Probably not as elegant as Jackie's, though . . ."

"It's not like a hotel, Mom," Billy hissed at her, mortified. "You can't steal the towels."

"I wasn't going to *steal* them," she said, then paused, indignant. "It's the White House, Billy. They have whole warehouses full of nothing but guest towels. They never would have missed them. Besides, we won the Easter egg roll. It was going to be a great souvenir. Don't be a party pooper."

Later that evening, after my father had finished ranting all the way home to Fairfax and my mother had finished trying to jolly him down, punctuating his diatribes with jokily exasperated repetitions of the phrase "Oh, Bill . . . ," but ultimately giving up and staring out the window of our car, the glum silence in our house was broken by a newscaster reporting that the White House had held its annual Easter egg roll.

"Quick! Turn it up, John!" my mother shouted, running in from the kitchen where she'd been slapping our hamburger patties together. "I bet we'll be on the news!"

By God, she was right. The film clip showed the network cameraman backing up on the South Lawn to get a shot of a woman in a Pendleton skirt and knee-high black boots backing up to get a shot of three dressed-up children jumping up and down, grinning and holding their winning Easter eggs and ribbons.

"It's us! It's us! We're on the news!" my mother cried. "See, I told you!"

Billy and John and I were jumping up and down again. We weren't disgraced—we were famous! We were on the news! We couldn't wait to get back to school on Tuesday.

"Just stay with the tour next time, okay?" my dad groused, somewhat mollified since the news had not reported that there had been a crook in the White House, and she was his wife.

"*Next* time—" my mother said, her voice charged with elated distraction. "*Next year!*—we should start planning right away. I can hardly wait till next year! They didn't know what they were in for when they started bugging *me*."

PANORAMIC EASTER EGGS

∴

MATERIALS NEEDED:

Egg-shaped mold in 2 halves, clean and dry
Pieces of cardboard larger than the molds
Aluminum foil
Pastry bags and tips
Food coloring
Shredded coconut dyed green
Other decorations: imitation or dried flowers, candy such as
    tiny jelly beans, tiny toy animals or creatures

TO MAKE THE SUGAR EGGS:

1 egg white
3½ cups granulated sugar
½ cup confectioners' sugar

• In a medium bowl, beat the egg white until it is completely loosened and beginning to get frothy. Mix the sugars together, then add to the egg white and mix until evenly moistened and the texture of damp sand. If you'd like to color your eggs, you can add food coloring now, mixing thoroughly before proceeding.

• Firmly pack the sugar mixture into both halves of the mold, making sure there are no air bubbles. Level the edge of the molds with a knife. Cover one half with a piece of aluminum foil and then a piece of cardboard, then invert onto a flat level surface. Remove the mold and repeat with the other half. Cover any remaining sugar mixture to keep it from drying out before you're ready to use it again.

• With a straight, sharp knife, cleanly cut off the narrowest end of one of the molded sugar eggs, reserving the sugar mixture you've cut off to use on another egg. Check the diameter of the semicircle you've made to see if it's the size you want—this will be half of the window—then cut off an identical piece of the narrow end of the second egg, also reserving the cut-off sugar mixture and returning it to the bowl. To keep the window edge moist so that it can be scooped out later, fold the aluminum foil up over the flat edge.

• Let the eggs dry for two or three hours, depending on heat and humidity, checking occasionally and gently to see how thick the outside shell has become: Feel the surface, but also pull back the foil to gauge the thickness of the drying shell at the window end. (You will be scooping out the moist interior, leaving a sugar shell ½ to ¼ inch thick.) When the outside feels sufficiently dry, using the cardboard as support turn the molded egg halves over, remove the foil, and scoop out the molds' interiors with a spoon, leaving walls ½ to ¼ inch thick. Save the excess sugar mixture for another egg.

• Set the shells back on the cardboard and let dry completely, several hours or overnight.

Makes two or more eggs, depending on the size of your mold.

TO ASSEMBLE:

1 recipe Royal Icing (see page 20)

• To decorate, decide first how you would like to arrange the interior scene. If you want to use colored icing on the egg's interior, put small portions of icing in little bowls and color them as desired. Then apply a coating of icing to the bottom half of the molded egg shell so the coconut "grass" will adhere, and arrange your creatures as you like, using icing to glue them into place. You may have to hold your decorations in place for a few minutes while the icing begins to harden, and remember to leave headroom for the top half of the egg when arranging any tall elements in your scene.

• When the interior is decorated to your liking, let it set long enough for the creatures inside to stand firmly on their own. Color the remaining icing as you like for the exterior decorations (if you know how to pipe flowers, this would be the time to do it). Affix a decorative tip to the pastry bag and fill the bag one-half to two-thirds full, then pipe a ribbon of icing along the elliptical edge of the bottom half of the egg; this will cement the two halves together. (Not too much icing here, or it will squeeze into the interior when you put the halves together and mar your scene.) Carefully fit the two halves edge-to-edge and hold them together on your work surface, applying light pressure for a minute or two while the frosting hardens. Now you can decorate the egg's exterior, piping icing over the seam where the halves meet, around the window, and however else you like, crowning the top of the egg with a showy display of icing and flowers.

• When you're satisfied with your egg, let it dry thoroughly on its cardboard before tucking it into someone's Easter basket. If you can manage to keep children from trying to eat them, these eggs will keep for years, gently wrapped and out of the damp.

Apart from That, How Was the Play?

IF I HADN'T FALLEN DEEPLY, MOURNFULLY IN LOVE WITH ABRAHAM
Lincoln at the end of fourth grade, it's not inconceivable that I might
have had someone my age to stay with when Pa died and my parents
rushed back to California for the funeral. Instead, while Billy and John
camped out with kids from their classes, there was nowhere for me to
go but the home of some neighbors willing to take me, a couple with a
three-year-old son—the Stuckpiles.

Like all the fathers in our neighborhood, Mr. Stuckpile was never
around, easing his car into the garage just in time for dinner each night,
disappearing into some remote corner of the house afterward, leaving
only the trace of a rinsed coffee cup and a cereal bowl in the kitchen
sink as evidence of his existence every morning. Mrs. Stuckpile,
though, seemed proud to be my temporary guardian, even grateful for
my company for a week. I saw the look of pleased relief on her face
when she swung open the door every afternoon after I'd hunched
across the school playground by myself and shown up at her house instead of my own next door.

"Are those your friends?" she asked me, peering curiously past my
head at the kids milling down our street.

"No," I answered. Since I had none, I didn't need to turn around to
look. If I did, I'd see the kids from my grade slowing at the bottom of
the Stuckpiles' driveway to make kissy faces at me, or oink, or huddle
and then laugh uproariously before they moved on, shoving each other
forward.

My initial mistake, no doubt, was developing my first crush on a
homely president who'd been dead for over a hundred years. I might
have gotten away with it if it weren't for the involuntary blushing and
stammering during the oral presentation of my history report and the

triplets who, with Darwinian efficiency, cut me out for disembowelment by the entire fourth grade.

"Cripes, listen to her—she's *in love with Abraham Lincoln!*"

I can still see their leering towheaded faces as they brayed my secret to the class: the identical Mitchell brothers from South Carolina, Mark, Michael, and Matthew, one of them always in a faded Led Zeppelin T-shirt. They looked more like Huey, Dewey, and Louie, with their matching white hair, ski-jump noses, and orange stippling of freckles, but they were my three Fates, mercilessly snipping the thread of my friendship potential. I wasn't just fat, I was also an eggheaded dork, and they let everybody know it. I didn't figure out what Led Zeppelin was until I was in college.

What was so wrong with a passion for Abraham Lincoln, anyway? Motherless, with an indifferent father, all told he only went to school for about a year because his hardscrabble family kept moving, and still he taught himself to read and write, memorizing words and phrases he wrote on the floorboards with charcoal cinders. He walked miles barefoot in the rain to borrow a book and walked miles back to return it. Running for president, he received a letter from an eleven-year-old girl who suggested he'd look less gaunt if he grew whiskers; when the train that took him to Washington for his inauguration stopped in the little girl's hometown, the newly bearded president-elect called out to her and said, "What do you think? I took your advice." He was a tender parent and a kind husband to his nutty wife, poor Mary Todd, driven to the brink of insanity by grief for their dead sons. Abraham Lincoln cared. You could see it in the grainy old photographs. You could see it in his troubled face: the toll taken by years of bloody civil war, by the force and burden of his convictions. It was his duty, his charge, to awaken in his countrymen the better angels of their nature. Just thinking about him made me feel calm and protected and even hopeful, less like I was living under perpetual siege, any moment to be crushed out like one of my mother's cigarettes.

Had I figured out already, at ten, that my family was totally screwed up? Not exactly. I thought the problem was the murderers—the murderers who came to my bedroom every night and stood over me, breathing heavily, as I lay still and quiet under the sheet I'd pulled over my head, trying to work up the nerve to open my eyes. The murderers had begun to appear around the time my father started taking lots of business trips for his work. On one of the nights when my dad was away and my mother had gone to bed, leaving Billy and John and me to watch television all night long if we felt like it, I'd seen a scary news show about burglars and a homeowner's botched attempt at self-defense with the pistol he kept in his bedside table. The show ended with a gunfight at the front door. Though it almost stopped my heart with terror, I couldn't force myself to stop replaying the scene in my head, the homeowner slumped dead in his pajamas on the porch steps, his body riddled with bullets.

After that I slept each night with the top sheet yanked up over my head, but it didn't help much since I'd wake in the pitiless dark knowing the murderers were right there, watching for me to move so they could gun me down. For hours I'd lay awake, paralyzed with fear. Or I tried not to sleep at all, waiting in my room until my parents went to bed. If my dad was home, my mother would let me curl up on the floor in their room, countering my father's grumbling complaints by saying I needed reassurance and I'd eventually grow out of it, just like she thought I'd eventually grow out of my terrible chronic stomachaches. But if my dad was gone on a business trip, she locked their door, the next morning apologizing that she hadn't heard me as I knocked and whispered in the hall on the other side.

I wonder now if my decision to join the elementary school safety patrol was a subconscious attempt to circumvent the murderers problem, though at the time I believed my mom: It was an honor to be on the safety patrol, she told me. Other kids would look up to me and be impressed. It showed you were trustworthy and responsible and helpful. I wanted to be seen as trustworthy and responsible and helpful— Lincoln-like in my character. The kindergartners and the parents who walked their kids to school did seem impressed by my thick orange plastic belt and its shiny silver badge as I stood in the crosswalk at my post each morning and afternoon. The reaction of the older kids, however, made it clear that my being on the safety patrol was no less lame than loving Honest Abe. Maybe five-year-olds and adults whose livelihood depended on service to the government thought it was cool to be on the safety patrol, but my peers had locked arms with the rest of the country in its Question Authority phase. "It's the Fuzz! It's the Man!" was my classmates' battle cry as they stampeded across the street before I could raise my arms and escort them. "Off the Pigs!" they'd shout over their shoulders as they charged through the school's landscaping, trampling the flowers, using outside voices as they ran through the open doors, thumbing their noses at me and at every safety rule.

Mrs. Stuckpile didn't have a clue about any of this. She didn't know that I was an elementary school outcast. All she saw was a trustworthy, responsible, helpful girl who liked to read and was willing to play with her drooling, testosterone-charged toddler and give her a break from the tedium of banging Tonka trucks into each other for a few hours a day.

"I'm sorry about your grandfather," Mrs. Stuckpile apologized as we watched my mom and dad drive off in the station wagon, heading for the airport. I was sorry, too, mostly because I was having trouble working up some sadness for Pa, and because I'd begged my mother to take me with her back to California, but she hadn't. The whole thing was a mess of confusing emotions. I was still scared of Pa, and I was scared of Pa dead, and I was absolutely terrified of the idea of seeing a dead anything, especially a person, so much so that I couldn't even ask my mother if that was what was going to happen at Pa's funeral. I wanted to go back to California anyway, which made me feel selfish, especially as I witnessed my mother's shocked grief over her father while she lined up every suitcase we owned and packed them with clothes sorted into separate piles: one for me, one for John, one for Billy, one for my parents.

"No," my mother told me, her face puffy and distorted from crying, "your dad and I need to do this alone."

What did that mean? It wasn't a vacation, I knew, but part of me was relieved and hopeful: They were doing something together. That, too, was a cause for guilt: My grandfather was *dead*, I should be sad, I should be crying. Guilt-inducing, too, once I got over the disappointment of not going back to California and remaining in Fairfax where I was a fat, stomachache-y, dead-president-loving, safety-rule-enforcing, murderer-pursued loser, was my curiosity about staying in someone else's house and looking out the window toward my own—empty, dark, unpeopled—and liking the feeling of that distance. Our house without us seemed suddenly detached from any personal history or expectation, full of possibility you couldn't anticipate, like turning to the first page of a book whose story was completely unknown to you. Maybe I, while I was away from there, could be different, too.

Mrs. Stuckpile, for one, seemed to think so. Though their house was smaller than ours and I had to sleep on a pallet of folded blankets in her little boy's room, Mrs. Stuckpile treated me like a visiting dignitary. Her three-year-old was napping when I got home from school the first day, and she'd set the table with china teacups and saucers, and she'd baked jam tarts for the two of us to have as an after-school snack. Nobody prepared snacks for us at home. My brothers and I just opened the refrigerator and the cupboards and ate whatever we found while sitting in front of the television.

"You know how to cook?" Mrs. Stuckpile said, incredulous, when I asked her for the recipe for the jam tarts, which were right out of Alice in Wonderland, crimped as crinolines and sparkling with a sugary glaze.

"I'm still learning," I said with a shrug, but I could tell she was impressed.

"Do you want coffee, too?" she asked uncertainly, but willing.

I had a splash of coffee in my teacup filled with milk. Despite the august legacy of Hills Brothers, it was my first taste of real coffee aside from Coffee Nips candies. Mrs. Stuckpile interviewed me, asking about my hobbies and what was going on in the chapter of *On the Banks of Plum Creek* I was reading that day. Later, when I was a new mother, I recognized her somewhat awestruck fascination with me. When you are fully immersed in the daily care and quirks and habits of a small dependent child, an older kid who is articulate, civilized, and capable of moving around in the world without getting itself killed can seem as supernatural as a wizard.

Every school day while I was at the Stuckpiles', Mrs. Stuckpile baked something for my snack and wrote out the recipe for me on a three-by-five card with "Here's What's Cookin' " printed at the top and a little picture of a sliced apple. She talked to me like I was grown up and capable. Later in the afternoons, Mrs. Stuckpile paid me a quarter to sit on the floor with her little boy while he bashed his toys around so she could prepare dinner.

I got the feeling Mr. Stuckpile wasn't as excited to have me around for a week as his wife was. The Stuckpiles' kid was fed, bathed, and in bed, out of sight, by the time Mr. Stuckpile got home. On the first night at their house, I could see Mr. Stuckpile hadn't expected to have me join them at the dinner table, or to keep his tie on as Mrs. Stuckpile asked him to do though he'd been loosening the knot on the way in from the garage. The next night, as I helped Mrs. Stuckpile set the dinner table, she handed me two plates and two sets of silverware.

"It's just us tonight," she said. "Maybe tomorrow, too. Mr. Stuckpile is going to be working late. Too bad for him," she said, a flavor of righteousness in her voice. After dinner we had more milky coffee and slices of minty grasshopper pie while we played hearts at the table.

The murderers hadn't followed me next door. When I ran into one of my brothers in the school cafeteria, we compared exacting data on our respective placements.

"How is it at your house?" Billy asked me.

"Great," I said. "How is it at yours?"

"It's great, too." Then we carried our trays to separate tables.

One afternoon while we were sitting with our teacups and cookies, waiting for her little boy to wake up, Mrs. Stuckpile said, "Hey. I have an idea. Want to play Ouija board?" The Ouija board, she explained, was psychic. It spelled out answers to questions when you placed your fingers on a planchette that moved around the board on its own. "It's fun," she said, pulling the box out of a stack of games in a closet, "it's like a séance. Did you know Lincoln's wife believed in psychics? She even held séances at the White House."

I'd told Mrs. Stuckpile that Abraham Lincoln was my favorite president, and I'd given her the highlights of my history report, but I'd purposely skipped the rest of the miserable story.

"Oh—" Mrs. Stuckpile said, suddenly doubtful, pausing with the Ouija board box held to her chest. "Maybe your mom wouldn't like me doing this with you. I guess it's kind of adult."

I knew without thinking that my mom wouldn't care, but more than that, I wanted to do something adult. I couldn't wait to be an adult. I yearned for it. I'd said so to my mom one Saturday when I brought her the icy cold beer she asked for as she was mowing the lawn, pushing the hand mower hard, over and over, against the rough weedy edges of the big vegetable garden she'd planted at the back of the yard she'd landscaped herself.

"Don't be in a hurry to grow up," she'd advised me, wiping her sweaty palm on her shirt as she took the beading glass from my hand. "Childhood is much better. Did you put ice in this?" She smiled as if what I'd done would be charming if I hadn't ruined a perfectly good beer.

If I'd been grown up, I'd have known you don't put ice in beer. If I were grown up, I'd have a screen door at the top of a flight of wooden steps, and inside the screen door, a typewriter. And a window to look out of.

"Okay," Mrs. Stuckpile said eagerly, "if you're sure." She set up the board between us, with its arching alphabet in old-fashioned lettering and an eerie GOOD BYE written across the bottom. The heart-shaped planchette rested in the center of the board as we placed our fingers on either side of the little window with its pointing pin.

"Don't push down," she told me. "It has to be able to move on its own. Let's ask some simple questions first so you can see how it feels. And when one of us asks a question, concentrate so the Ouija spirit will know we're serious and want him to answer."

Mrs. Stuckpile started, asking a question with an easy answer. I barely touched my fingertips to the surface of the wooden planchette and thought hard about the question. Slowly the planchette started moving. I lifted my fingers and it stopped.

"Seriously, I'm not moving it," Mrs. Stuckpile laughed. "I'm playing, too." We put our fingers back on the planchette and she asked the question again.

Were my parents in California? *YES*. Were Lainey and Thor okay at the neighbors on the other side of our house? *YES*. Was Mrs. Stuckpile making ham steaks for dinner? *NO*.

"So you want to ask something really big?" Mrs. Stuckpile asked me.

I had lots of questions I wanted answers to, but none I wanted to say out loud in front of Mrs. Stuckpile in case it might diminish my standing in her eyes. "What should I ask?" I said, hitting the ball back to her.

"How about . . . will you get married? I always asked that one," she answered.

We rested our fingers on the planchette and I asked my question. The little felt feet of the planchette made a squeaking sound across the board as they moved the pointing pin over the word *YES*.

So I was going to get married. Funny, when I thought about my screen door and my typewriter and my window, I hadn't noticed anyone else.

"Who?" Mrs. Stuckpile urged me. "Now ask, who?"

"Who am I going to marry?" I asked the Ouija spirit, suddenly hoping it would tell me. The planchette started to move over the letters of the alphabet. *G*, it said, coming to a squeaky halt, then slowly moved again. *A. R. Y.*

"Gary?" I said.

"*Gary!*" Mrs. Stuckpile yelped. "You're going to marry someone named Gary!"

Gary? My heart sank. That was the stupidest, most banal, boring name I could imagine. Why not Abraham? This was not the future I wanted, even if I hadn't imagined it yet.

"Believe me, I know," Mrs. Stuckpile said, slowly nodding her head. "How do you think I feel about the name Stuckpile?"

JAM TARTS

∴

Jam tarts à la Alice in Wonderland tend to be round and open-faced, but I first had them folded over into half-moon turnovers. You can use this recipe either way and with any type of jam, though tart fillings (blackberry, plum, sour cherry, lemon) are particularly good with the short, tender pastry and lemony glaze.

½ cup unsalted butter, at room temperature

¼ cup granulated sugar

½ teaspoon salt

1 large egg yolk

½ teaspoon vanilla

1½ cups unbleached all-purpose flour

About ¾ cup jam or citrus curd, preferably homemade

• Cream the butter on medium speed for a minute, then add the sugar and salt and beat until creamy and light, about 3 to 5 minutes. Add the egg yolk and vanilla and again beat until very fluffy and light. Add the flour all at once and "pulse" the mixer on low speed until the flour just disappears, scraping the bowl and beaters a couple of times to help it along. Turn the dough onto a sheet of waxed paper and gather together, flattening into a disc. Chill thoroughly, about 3 hours.

• When ready to make the tarts, preheat the oven to 350°. If the dough is too hard to roll, let it sit on the counter for about 15 to 20 minutes. Roll out to a thickness of ⅛ inch. If the dough develops cracks, it patches easily—pinch it together, or add a scrap of dough.

• To make the tarts turnover style, cut 3- to 4-inch circles of dough with a cookie cutter, tart ring, or rim of a tea cup or jar dipped in flour. Arrange them on a cookie sheet and place a teaspoonful of your filling of choice in the center of each circle. Gently fold the circle in half, enclosing the filling and pressing the edges together gently but firmly. Crimp the edges with the tines of a fork, but don't cut through the dough or the filling will leak out during baking. Bake the tarts until they are golden brown along the edges and look set and just beginning to brown on their domed centers, about 12 to 18 minutes, turning the pans halfway through the baking time to make sure they all color evenly.

• If making round miniature tarts, use a muffin pan or tartlet pan. Butter the pan and cut circles of dough ½ inch in diameter larger than your pan's indentations. Fit the dough circles into the indentations and prick the bottom of the dough just once with a fork. Bake the tart bottoms for 5 to 8 minutes, until starting to turn golden on the edges, then take out of the oven and fill with a spoonful of jam. If you like, you can place strips of dough crosswise over the top, or cut out hearts or diamonds as decorative top crusts, though open tarts are traditional. Bake for an additional 6 to 8 minutes, until the edges (and tops, if you've made them) of the tarts are golden brown.

• Either way, while the tarts bake, make the glaze.

1½ cups confectioners' sugar
3 tablespoons lemon juice

• Whisk the confectioners' sugar and lemon juice in a small bowl. When the tarts are ready, remove from the oven and allow to cool on the baking pans for 5 minutes before gently transferring them to a wire rack with a piece of waxed or parchment paper placed beneath to catch drips.

Brush the tops of the tarts with the glaze while still warm and let cool completely. If you absolutely can't wait to eat a warm tart, be careful, as the filling will be scaldingly hot at first.

Makes about eighteen 3–inch tarts.

For Blackberry Jam and Variations, see page 61.
For Lemon Curd, see page 41.

Pretend I'm the Babysitter

W E'D NEVER BEEN ON AN AIRPLANE OURSELVES, SO BILLY AND
John and I watched, agog, from the cushy bench seats in the departure
lounge as every last one of the business-suited men and dressed-up families shuffled to the front of the line and handed their tickets to the uni-
formed attendant, and we waved frantically as our father turned around
to give us a cursory raise of a hand in return before he descended the
stairs to the tarmac, where the jet engines were already roaring. We ran
to the observation windows and tried to make out faces through the
shadowy portholes of the plane, pressing our foreheads to the glass until
the jumbo jet was inched backward out of the gate and maneuvered
around and trundled toward the runway. Every time we went to the airport, we'd plead to stay until we saw our dad's airplane angling up into
the sky and away, spewing a billowing trail of white exhaust. It strained
credulity that something so bulky and awkward and lumbering could
actually get off the ground, let alone stay aloft.

Sometimes we'd get to watch it take off. Usually, though, my mom
had already turned to leave as soon as the back of my dad's crewcutted
head disappeared through the door of the gate. We filed behind her,
scurrying to keep up, as she took long hip-forward strides through the
crowds at Dulles Airport or Washington National, coolly extracting
her keys and trademark Jackie O sunglasses from the purse dangling at
her elbow, tossing her hair back and sliding the dark frames up her
aquiline nose, looking far too young and pretty to have a gaggle of
half-grown children and a morose husband.

Pretend I'm the babysitter. She only had to tell us once. After the first
time, it was a given. My brothers and I clomped after her through the
gauntlet of airline ticket counters, weaving around stalled clumps of
confused foreign tourists and saffron brigades of chanting Hare Krish-

nas, and one of us would ask in a voice meant to be overheard as we shot giddy looks at each other, "When are our parents coming back?"

"Oh . . . I don't know," our mother would respond in a tone of studied nonchalance, slowly gazing from side to side to see if anyone was looking our way as we descended the escalator to the parking lot.

In Virginia, time in our family had divided. There was the time when my father was home, and the time when he was not. As the demands and ramifications of his job expanded, my dad worked increasingly longer hours in D.C., arriving back at our house in the evenings so late and leaving for his commute so early that sometimes we didn't see him for days on end. Even so, the knowledge of his proximity loomed over us like the rain cloud that hovered above Charlie Brown's head in the comic strip. When my dad was technically "home," my mother and my brothers and I braced ourselves for the relentless tirade of hectoring and complaint he subjected us to if he wasn't in the midst of a baleful black sulk. After fifteen years of unhappy marriage, my mother's reliable, defensive buoyancy had begun to ebb, and she shocked us with episodes of brittle weeping and furious maternal reproach. You could skip the flash floods, tornadoes, and veterinary emergencies and proceed directly to the strawberry milkshake if you wanted to break her down.

When my father was away on business—which occurred so frequently that Billy and John and I were surprised when he stomped down the stairs as we were watching Saturday morning cartoons—it was as if someone had hooked up a hose to our house and started pumping oxygen in. It was breakfast for dinner every night and dogs on the couch. We didn't want to go to school? Okay, come up with a flimsy excuse: The babysitter didn't like to get up early, anyway. "Sick," we dragged the blankets off the beds and watched reruns of old television shows all day in our pajamas under a tent in the family room. There was no clean laundry and the dishes piled up in the sink. Our babysitter, she told us, had not been hired as a maid but as a companion to the children. We ate French toast for days on end.

Thrilling as it was to be enlisted in our mother's recurring conceit of rebellious independence, referring to her within that context was a puzzler. No child of our acquaintance had ever called a parent by first name, and I didn't meet anyone who did until I was nineteen. Calling our mom "Kathleen" or "Lackey" felt a little alarmingly true-to-life, a tiny hole ripped in the gauzy curtain of make-believe none of us wanted to put our eyes to. Billy and John and I solved the problem obliquely, calling her "the babysitter" to each other and avoiding nomenclature entirely when speaking to her directly, the way you do when you run into an acquaintance whose name you've forgotten.

We knew instinctively not to promote our mother's imaginary status around anyone we knew, but in the company of strangers we laid it on thick. "You're the prettiest babysitter we've ever had!" we'd bellow at the Green Stamps store. "It's our babysitter's birthday," we told the straw-hatted waiter at Farrell's Ice Cream Parlour as our mother mugged and twittered, "and our parents told us to buy her the biggest sundae on the menu." We whooped and cheered as four waiters paraded something called "The Trough" through the restaurant on a stretcher to the sound of sirens and clanging bells. After we laid waste to a dozen flavors of ice cream, five sauces, nuts, bananas, and cherries and collected all the little plastic piggies that had been stuck into the whipped cream, the babysitter picked up the check.

The one doggedly troubling aspect of my mom playing babysitter was that I could never picture her as simultaneously the babysitter and my parent in the way that my father in absentia was still ineluctably my father. In the mental picture I carried of my family, I saw my brothers and myself in our customary places, and I saw my dad in a suit on a business trip, and in the place where my mom had been there was a blank spot. Where had she gone? From a flesh-and-blood perspective, she was right there in front of me, steering the car, or under the blanket tent eating popcorn and watching the Three Stooges with us, but in some ineffable way the construct of parental certitude had collapsed, a house of cards I couldn't reassemble until someone told me I was a slob or I smelled hamburger frying in the kitchen.

In addition to all of its other miseries, my fifth-grade *annus horribilis* had encompassed the flooding of our neighborhood during Hurricane Agnes, vomiting raspberry-flavored barium in a failed effort to discover the cause of my mysterious stomachaches, and breaking a foot and five of my toes at the beginning of winter, the result of chasing one of the cats down our staircase as it tried to eat my parakeet. It culminated with a tonsillectomy. My dad was away on a business trip during my operation, and when I surfaced from the general anaesthesia, groggy and flat as a cutlet, my throat so sore and swollen it felt like someone had jammed a fist with the skin peeled off in there, I wasn't sure if it was my mom or the babysitter who was taking care of me.

"It's not so bad," whoever she was announced cheerfully, fluffing up pillows for me on the couch in front of the TV. "You have an excuse to stay home from school for a few days, and you can have all the French toast you want!"

I gagged on the ice chips. The mashed baby aspirin felt like gravel going down my throat. The shivering cubes of Jell-O were too dense and pointy. And I really, really couldn't stand the bitter metallic taste of the penicillin I was supposed to take every eight hours, a lingering nasty flavor I couldn't wash away because even ice water was too painful.

"How about that French toast?" my babysitter/mom cajoled after two days of my refusal to swallow anything. "You have to eat something. I'll make it just the way you like it."

I didn't want the French toast. I knew it would hurt. But she made it anyway, and she sat on the couch next to me, holding the plate and offering me a bite saturated with melted butter and powdered sugar *and* maple syrup to make it more likely to slide down my raw wounded throat.

I could tell as the fork reached my mouth that something was wrong. The French toast smelled weird. After forcing down one bite, tears springing to my eyes, I shook my head. No more.

"C'mon, Cis, it's really good! You know it's your favorite—"

I did love French toast, but this French toast was awful. It was downright disgusting. It wasn't just my sore throat: This French toast tasted genuinely bad. There was something wrong with it. It tasted like earwax drowning in maple syrup. The babysitter must have made it, because my mom's French toast was excellent.

"Oh, no, it's perfectly fine," argued the babysitter. "It's the same as always. It's really good!"

I cried and gagged as she insisted I eat everything on the plate.

Hours later, I woke to someone gently shaking my shoulder. Somehow I knew it was my mother this time, kneeling beside the couch with the brown penicillin bottle and a big spoon. I could still taste the putrid flavor of the French toast in my mouth.

"Cis, I am *really* sorry," she said. "You were right. I put the penicillin in your French toast, and I pretended it was fine when you said it tasted bad. But I just talked to the doctor's office, and they told me that cooking destroys the medicine. So I forced you to eat that awful stuff for nothing. And now I have to make you take the penicillin again, anyway."

The medicine tasted just as horrible as before, but it didn't matter. My mom had come back. Only a real mother would make you eat something she knew was that vile.

FRENCH TOAST, WITHOUT THE PENICILLIN

∴

FOR EACH SERVING:

1 large egg
⅔ cup whole milk
A pinch each of salt, cinnamon, cloves, nutmeg, and ginger
A dash of vanilla
Two 1-inch-thick slices of brioche, challah, or cinnamon
    bread, preferably a day or two old
Unsalted butter
Confectioners' sugar or maple syrup

• In a shallow pan large enough to hold all the bread slices in a single layer, whisk the egg well and add the milk, spices, and vanilla. (If making four servings or more, add an extra egg and an extra ½ cup of milk "for the pan.") Place each slice of bread in the egg mixture, turning to coat both sides completely, and leave in the pan until all of the egg mixture has been absorbed by the bread.

• Heat a frying pan until a drop of water sizzles, then add a pat of butter (the pan should not be so hot that the butter burns), swirl it over the bottom of the pan, and add as many slices as will fit comfortably without crowding. Cook until the bottom of the French toast is crusty and browning, then turn, adding more butter to prevent sticking as necessary. Cook until the second side is crusty and brown and the toast is puffed and cooked through; adjust heat as necessary to prevent too much browning.

• Serve immediately with additional butter and confectioners' sugar or maple syrup.

Anna Karenina

ONE OPPRESSIVELY HUMID, NARCOLEPTIC SUNDAY AFTERNOON during our last summer in Fairfax, my brothers and I were rounded up from in front of the television and forcibly conducted to the garage by our fed-up mother, who wanted us to help her tidy it up. My father must have been at his office; he was forever at his office if he wasn't away on a business trip. My mom paused in the midst of what had become by then a familiar jeremiad about chronic cleaning issues, ungrateful children, and subsequent maternal escape fantasies ("You never . . . you always . . . I wish I could just leave!"). Even pretending, her particular area of expertise, was no longer a viable safeguard against three children who were growing too old and cynical to fully believe in their role as her band of merry followers, kids who could jump into any chalk pavement picture she drew for us; it was easier to turn into zombies in front of the TV. And convenient as it was to shape a pipe dream of blithe liberation around the frequent absences of a rigid, bullying husband, sooner or later he always came back.

As she paused to stand disheartened amid the repository of banal suburban squalor that was our disorderly garage, the three of us children fingered the handlebar fringe on our dusty unused bicycles and eyed the covers of heaped-up *National Geographic*s nobody ever bothered to read, the cases of cream soda and Fresca and Tab stacked by the door, the metal cabinet where we knew she hid the candy bars, and we tuned her out. Only my mother's uncharacteristic moment of silence caught my attention, followed by her genuinely pained sigh—the sound of having your breath knocked out of you. I glanced up to see her staring at a row of old books lined up on shelves she'd built into the wall above the freezer.

"Oh," she gasped to herself, her hair sweaty under that red bandana. She was gazing at the title on the faded spine of a copy of *Anna Karenina*.

I don't remember the titles of any of the other books on those garage shelves, her books from high school and college, before she got married. *Anna Karenina* was the only one that mattered.

"This was my favorite, my *favorite* book—" she said, leaning over the freezer on tiptoe and reaching as high as she could to pull *Anna Karenina* down from the shelf. The cover was black, with a green vine lined in silver running up to the title; she placed her hand on the cloth, feeling its texture, then opened the book. "Oh, it was so romantic!" she sighed. It was a story of doomed romance, she told us, of irresistible desire, and of a beautiful, passionate heroine who had thrown herself under a train.

"There's a scene I absolutely loved," my mother said, running her fingertips over the yellowed pages, scanning the lines, "when Anna makes raspberry jam with all the women in her family. While they cooked, they were sewing and telling stories. . . . As they make the jam, they skim the foam with a spoon and put it on a plate to save for the children to eat with their tea. It was the best part of the jam, Anna said. I remember every word—it sounded so delicious! I wanted to taste it so badly, that pink foam skimmed from the top of the jam. . . ."

"Grandma did that," I said, eager for the unexpected opportunity to align myself with my mom and her beloved book. "She skimmed the blackberry jam at Camp Meeker. It *was* the best part." I could see it: my grandmother tapping the wooden spoon against the edge of a saucer, the foam a deep mauve, and pooling below, dark purple-red syrup running over the blue-and-white pattern of the china.

"She did?" my mother asked, coming out of her revery, staring at me.

I was confused. Didn't my mom know everything that I knew? Hadn't she been there? "When she made jam," I said. "You know, Mom. She burned the toast and let us eat the foam with melted butter. Don't you remember?"

"No," my mother said, shaking her head. "No," she said, bereft.

I WAS MUCH OLDER, a mother, married twice, when I finally read the book that had become my mother's favorite when she was a teenager. And I realized she'd been wrong. It wasn't Anna who made jam with the women in her family. It was Kitty, Anna's alter ego, whose awkward courtship and bewildering, mortifying early years of marriage to Levin are the counterpoint to Anna's passionate, tortured affair with Count Vronsky. But what's more important, *Anna Karenina* isn't a book about romance. It's a mirror held up to the real, grimy, quotidian interactions of married life, of which romance is little more than a passing mood: marriage, that slippery social contract that, if it works at all, depends more on indulgent disconnection than on some kind of sacred accord. The book I read wasn't about thrilling, heedless passion. It was about apprehending, or not, the mystery of other people.

LATER THAT LAST humid Virginia summer, in the garage where I learned about *Anna Karenina,* our cheerful but arthritic Shetland sheepdog, Lainey, lay stiff and lifeless on a collapsed cardboard box after being run over by a dry-cleaning delivery van. My mother was devastated. Sweaty and crying in her red bandana, her black hair curling in wisps around her face, she crouched on the garage floor, leaning over our poor good dog, our fair Elaine. My mother sat on the floor and sobbed, blood drying to a crust on her bare forearms, the tragic heroine of her own frustrated life.

Every person in the house felt that there was no sense in their living together, and that the stray people brought together by chance in any inn had more in common with one another than they, the members of the family and household. . . .

Anna Karenina by Count Leo Tolstoy, translated by Constance Garnett (New York: Grosset & Dunlap, 1931), p. 1.

The Last Frontier

"Look, kids, here's a recipe for making ice cream out of seal blubber! Here's a recipe for making fake candy out of moose droppings!"

We were sprawled out over the double beds in a room at the Captain Cook Hotel in downtown Anchorage, Alaska, where we were staying for a week while we waited for our newest new house to be ready for us. My mom was reading to my brothers and me from a guidebook for recent arrivals to the Last Frontier, the title something like *Everything You Always Wanted to Know About Living in Anchorage, but Were Afraid to Ask.* She was trying to get us excited about moving to Alaska, the exotic novelty of which had worn off about a day after we arrived. Billy and John were mildly intrigued by the idea that it would be light all night during the summer and we'd get to cross-country ski to school in the winter, but the question I was afraid to ask was, how long do we have to stay here?

We were in Alaska because my dad was now the government's attorney in Anchorage, his job to work with the consortium of companies that was building a new oil pipeline. In 1974, when we arrived, Anchorage was as random as it was ugly, its haphazard stabs at culture reliant on a boom-and-bust economy and a tenacious make-do, pioneering spirit. Another boom time was coming, and people were flooding to the state hoping to get rich because of the pipeline. *Time* ran an article on the oil rush, calling Anchorage, with its unattractive skyline of cinderblock malls and sprawling subdivisions seemingly devoid of any semblance of city planning, "the San Jose of the North." Being born-and-bred Californians, we knew a comparison to a homely backwater like San Jose was no compliment, though it didn't stop proud shopkeepers and business owners all over Anchorage from taping the article to their storefront windows.

There were only two movie theaters in town, and they played the same films for six months at a time. There was a library and a bookstore, but there were no museums, no children's theater, no theme parks except for Alaskaland up north in Fairbanks, where you could see the wreckage of the plane that Will Rogers had died in when it crashed—now, that's a good time. There was the "Pioneer Cabin," a log hut left over from the Alaskan gold rush days; you could stand on your toes and peer into the cobwebbed windows, but there was nothing inside to see. Oh, and there was a mangy, depressed lion chained up in a rusty cage behind the Hamburger Haven. When we visited our new school, peeking in the windows of the locked-up building and walking around the deserted playground, the one kid we saw there knocking a flaccid ball against the wall sized us up as newcomers and told us, "See that swing set? They say a third grader hung himself from it a few years ago, he was so bored."

Back at the Captain Cook, we'd already discovered one of the idiosyncracies of Alaskan life described in my mom's guidebook. There were only three television channels and they played cartoons most of the time, as bad weather tended to disrupt the long-range radio signals for television broadcasts. You might turn on the TV expecting to see Huntley and Brinkley, but instead you got Rocky and Bullwinkle, or Boris and Natasha.

Outside, dripping icicles hung from our hotel windows, and the salted sidewalks were heaped up with banks of exhaust-blackened snow, drilled through here and there by hot yellow streams of dog pee. This was the first week of April—meaning we'd moved not just in the middle of the school year but almost at the end, when everyone else had already figured out who they wanted to hang around with and the friendship opportunities were basically nil. Just to ensure that everything about me would be as socially handicapped as possible, true to my maternal genes I'd shot up in height during the last few months so that I was as tall as my mom, taller than any of the boys in my sixth-grade class in Fairfax. I was starting to develop, too, which I vehemently denied whenever my mother slid her eyes over me and eagerly suggested we go shopping for my first bra. None of my clothes fit me anymore—they'd been demoralizingly tight before I'd gotten taller, anyway—and

I braced myself for spending the next few years hunched over with my arms folded across my chest. At least it was still frigid in Alaska despite its being spring break, and I prayed my new school would be cold enough that I'd have an excuse to keep my coat on. I was turning twelve right after we moved into our new house, a couple of days before I'd start school, and my secret birthday wish that year was to not be a complete pariah. Failing that, a puppy would do. I got the puppy, but a hackneyed Alaskan prank put the nail in my social coffin.

After a week in the hotel waiting for our kitchen cabinets and carpets to be installed, the weather too dismally cold to go outside, watching the same cartoons every day and rereading our library books until we could recite them by heart, swimming in the Captain Cook's overchlorinated indoor pool until my brothers' hair turned green, trying out the recipes from my mother's book didn't seem so bad.

It wasn't likely that we'd find any seal blubber for the Eskimo ice cream. Fake candy made out of moose droppings seemed more plausible, since finding moose turds was as easy as walking out the door of the hotel. There were moose everywhere, all year round, the equivalent of deer in California. Notoriously nearsighted and clumsy, they stomped long-legged and a little flustered down the center of the streets of downtown, like joggers in a city marathon who'd lost their way. My brothers and I equipped ourselves with the plastic bag put in the rooms for laundry service, and within a block or two we found several fresh, steamy piles of moose excrement, looking just like the giant droppings of a mutant rabbit.

The problem was not finding the ingredients, and it was certainly not our execution, which was flawless thanks to my mother. She cleared the shelves of the local hobby store of paintbrushes and gold enamel and paper candy cups. We had a box of See's Candy left from our detour to California on the way to Anchorage, and after she instructed Billy and John and me to finish up the candy, she embellished the empty box with lace and felt doodads and gilded lettering so it looked like the gaudiest, most enticing box of chocolates that ever graced the age of man.

No, our problem was that everyone in Anchorage had read the same guidebook. Even the Captain Cook Hotel sold spray-painted moose nuggets attached to key chains in the gift shop. We were like Dylan Thomas in *A Child's Christmas in Wales,* standing on a snowy street corner with a candy cigarette hanging out of his mouth, waiting for a stranger to come by and scold him so he could pop the cigarette into his mouth and chew it up—except that he'd see another kid right across the street, also with a candy cigarette between his lips, waiting for his own chance to prank a stranger. No matter if we tried it out on the contractor who was finishing our house ("Oh no, kids, you can't fool me with that old trick") or a waitress at the hotel restaurant ("Aww, you must be new in town!"), it was a gag that was long past its prime.

So if you were turning twelve and you'd just moved to Alaska in the middle—no, the end—of the school year, and you really wanted the kids in your class to like you, it probably wouldn't have been advisable to bring moose nuggets as a sort of joke happy-to-meet-you gift, even if your mom hadn't taken you to the Sears Mall for your birthday and bought you a mustard yellow pantsuit in the juniors Lemon Frog department so you could wear it on your first day at your new school, feeling stylish and camouflaged—elastic-waist pants and a matching jacket roomy enough to wear several layers of body-concealing T-shirts underneath—as you presented your overblown valentine of moose roca while the teacher introduced you to the other sixth graders.

And it would be an even worse idea to wear your birthday pantsuit again the second day, believing it had made such a good impression the day before, because you would soon be disabused of that notion when you heard one of your fellow students whisper as you walked in the classroom, "Uh-oh, the new fat girl is back, and she's wearing that ugly yellow pantsuit again. It looks like she's got boobs." To which another kid would answer, "Yeah, but at least she didn't bring more moose poo."

MOOSE NUGGET CANDY

∴

Firm, dry moose droppings
Newspaper
Gold spray paint
Candy box with little pleated candy cups

- Lay the moose droppings on sheets of newspaper. Spray them with gold paint, rolling them over during coats to cover completely. When dry, pack into candy box with little pleated cups and close the box. Or don't. If you must, offer it to someone well over the age of twelve from a moose-free area, like Florida or Brazil.

Rhubarb

It MIGHT BE ALASKA, BUT MY MOTHER WAS GOING TO HAVE A GARden just the same. When the weather finally turned from arctic spring to brisk nordic summer, my mom turned her attention from unpacking and decorating and buying state-of-the-art household gadgets—a trash compactor, a microwave oven, Water Pik massaging showerheads for the bathrooms—to making a garden out of the bare rocky embankment on which our house perched at the top of a hillside. She asked around and figured out what would grow during Alaska's short summer, then commenced planting rhubarb under the stands of birch trees out back that the construction guys hadn't cut down.

Anchorage: Dogged optimist that she was, my mother had actually been excited about moving there. Maybe it had sounded solid to her, a place where a marriage buffeted on rough seas could reach a safe harbor, going straight into dry dock and having all of its barnacled misery scraped off. But Alaska turned out to be the site of our shipwreck. The next six years left us all at sea, clinging to the floating debris of our family.

Rhubarb was an appropriate emblem for the start of our Alaskan life. Its large, lumpy green leaves are poisonous, the long red stalks acidic and inedible unless doused with lots of sugar. That's how I learned to cook it that first summer when my mother's crop came in, chopping the ruby stalks into tiny bits I mixed with granulated sugar, then topping it with a brown sugar crumble. But "rhubarb" is also slang for a bitter, heated argument, and that's what I heard each night while I lay with the sheet pulled over my head in the latest rendition of my girly pink bedroom: the ominous, indistinct rise and fall and rise of anger and blame that filtered through the walls of our house from my parents' bedroom upstairs.

I don't know specifically what my parents were fighting about—my mother's new Alaskan friends, who were mostly male; my father's chronic antisocial behavior and negativity; or the fact that they'd made this dramatic move so far away from everything and everyone familiar, anything that might have given them some safety net of support for their misguided union. Left with nothing but each other, they seemed to be discovering afresh that they had nothing in common, and the marriage they'd been patching together was finally foundering. Maybe it was that my father's unhappiness drove him to berate the rest of us day in, day out. Or maybe it was that my mother's standard response to my father's fury and belittling, after a requisite stab at clownish deflection that never worked, was to retreat. Whatever it was, you could feel it in the air, like earthquake weather or thunderstorms: an ionic charge that filled your lungs with every breath.

My brothers and I responded to the heightening cold war between our parents by upping the volume on our own petty jealousies. Our mother's habit of rewarding our talents and slightest achievements with extravagant praise had devolved with her growing distraction and desperation into the dubious parenting tactic of comparing us unfavorably to each other—*why can't you save your allowance like your brother, why can't you take better care of your things like your sister*—which didn't make us aspire to each other's good qualities but only to resent our siblings all the more. No more the occasional jab or tattling: We were downright vicious, frequently out for deep humiliation if not blood. Even the split-level layout of our new house conspired to intensify the embattled atmosphere, with Billy and John and I each occupying a bedroom at one of the three corners of the house on the lower basement level, rival armies holed up in their separate bunkers during a period of trench warfare.

My mother, meanwhile, escaped the hostile atmosphere in the house by withdrawing to the garden she was determined to create. She was out on the steep slope of our front yard day after long midnight-sun day, attacking the hillside bare-armed, her hair tied back, pulling up deep-rooted weeds and levering out boulders. My brothers and I hardly paused in our heated arguments and throttling fistfights to notice until one afternoon when we saw her shoveling carloads of topsoil onto the plunging slope. She'd rented a manual soil compactor with a heavy sand-filled metal barrel, which she began rolling down the embankment, then pulling up again with a rope, over and over, leaving her hands raw and blistered. We wandered over, curious, rubbing our own bruises.

"Strawberries," she said, her mouth an implacable line. She pushed a damp wisp of hair off her dirty face with the back of her hand. Inside the open trunk of our station wagon were dozens of flats of strawberry plants. "I'm going to plant this hillside with strawberries, and every summer, we're going to sit in the sunshine at the top of this hill and gorge ourselves."

The scene rose up before me: the thin Alaskan sun on our faces as we sat together, all of us, even my dad, the birch trees flickering their leaves behind us at the crest of our hill as we picked our ripe berries and shared them, like people in a movie of what a family is supposed to be, the juice of the strawberries staining our mouths and our fingers, marking us with its indelible sweetness.

We helped our mother for a while, our fingernails becoming as black and caked with dirt as hers as we set the plants, tamping them into the slope in rows and sprinkling each delicate seedling with a watering can. But when the initial planting was done and what the strawberries needed was regular watering and weeding, my brothers and I went back to our arguing and beating each other up and sitting in the dim basement family room, reluctantly together, watching television and waiting for our dad's angry bellow from the top of the stairs: his yelling at us that we hadn't done something that no one had told us to do, or that we'd done something that no one had told us not to.

When we plodded upstairs to clean up the mess in the kitchen or fold the newspaper back together, our glaring dad standing by, his arms knotted across his suit jacket, I'd walk past the cathedral windows in our living room and look out to our front yard. My mother always seemed to be out there alone, slowly moving the sprayer of the hose along the rows, showering the leaves, leaning down now and then to carefully pluck a weed from between the runners, gazing over the hillside she'd planted and imagining what it would be like when her plan came to fruition.

ONCE WE MOVED to Alaska, my dad no longer traveled so frequently for his work. He was home every weekend and walked in the door by

dinnertime on weeknights, distracted and dissatisfied and randomly ir-
ritable, an oppressive presence who could rarely be appeased. He
stalked my mother through the house and the yard, keeping up a sneer-
ing harangue of whispered accusations and provocative attacks, intent
on having the final, blistering word in an argument that never finished.
He was withering in his condemnations of the character of his children:
Our rooms were messy or we hadn't finished our homework or we'd
forgotten to set the table. We were lazy, we were pigs, we were waste-
ful and ingrates; we were all going to end up juvenile delinquents,
working at McDonald's if we were lucky.

After my brothers and I had fled into our bedrooms at night, my
mother used housework as her own excuse to elude my dad. Other than
taking out the trash and occasionally loading the dishwasher, my father
rarely did anything that could be considered a household chore.
Knowing that my mom was doing laundry and that we were all supposedly asleep was enough to keep him from following her downstairs. He
would stand at the top of the staircase and call down to her, surly and
impatient, asking repeatedly when she'd be through. Eventually he'd
give up on her vague demurring responses and go to bed himself, and
that's when my mother would come to get me so that I could keep her
company as we folded towels and watched McLean Stevenson guest-
host for Johnny Carson on *The Tonight Show*. I'd come awake to my
mom shaking my shoulder, standing barefoot beside my bed in my
dark room and leaning down to whisper, excited and urgent, "Wake up,
Cis. He's on—"

Our nights folding laundry in front of the TV were the only peaceful moments in the house for either of us. For my brothers and me, no
grievance was too minor to fight over, and the escalating brutality of
our retaliations had hardened us. We rarely communicated except to
tell each other to shut up or get out of the way.

Every school-day morning, I woke to three violent pounds on my
bedroom door—*bam bam bam*—followed by Billy's growled order,
devoid of pleasantries: "*Get up.*" The two of us trudged separately to
the bus stop at the bottom of the hill—until he caught up with us in
ninth grade, John attended a different school—and through junior
high and high school, I followed Billy's explicit instructions never to
speak to him in public or even acknowledge that he was my brother. In
response I felt smugly justified in not telling the afternoon bus driver to

wait if Billy was late getting out of a student council meeting or swim team practice at the end of the school day. If I saw my brother burst through the gymnasium doors and run for the bus as it pulled away from the parking lot, knowing that for much of the school year Billy's wet hair would be frozen to his head by the time he'd walked the three miles home through our subdivision, I'd hunch down on the bus seat so he couldn't see me, assuring myself it was his own fault. When I was the one who missed the afternoon bus and was the last to arrive home from school, sometimes I'd find my little dog—a yappy incontinent Maltese disliked by everyone else in the family, for good reason, I have to admit—shut inside the microwave oven, barking silently behind the tempered glass.

We knew better than to bicker at the dining room table during dinner, a nightly command performance tense with the potential for tripping my father's hair-trigger castigations. Even during meals when no arguments had broken out and no one had trespassed any rules of etiquette—no spilling, no slurping, no elbows on the table or reaching, and for me, no seconds—my dad sat eyeing us from his chair at the end of the table, sullenly silent though sighing now and then as he ate, as if to let us know what a trial it was for him, being the head of such a disappointing family.

We fought a lot, and we were as uninterested in helping around the house as the average children, but my brothers and I were far from bad. By any standard other than our cynical dad's, Billy and John and I were good kids. My brothers' only real vice was harassing their sister. Otherwise they were both Boy Scouts in practice and temperament—our father, unlikely as it seemed even then, was their troop leader—the kind of boys liked by their friends' parents, model students with perfect grades, the ones who end up in the honor society and lettering in sports and drinking nothing more potent than sparkling cider at their high school graduation parties. Even as we tormented each other, I knew my brothers were nice boys, and I was secretly proud of them, though I'd have rather shaved my head than tell them so: responsible, circumspect Billy, who was concerned for the world and captain of the swim team; and generous, sanguine John, quick to forgive at the slightest kindness.

I wasn't as confident of the intrinsic soundness of my own character, but until I was almost fifteen my preoccupations remained naïvely childish. I collected tiny tchotchkes and primped my doll collection and wrote stories about them that I copied in microscopic handwriting into miniature notebooks. I unashamedly embroidered my homemade clothes, my head bursting with trivia about dogs, which absolutely nobody of my immediate acquaintance cared to know. I spent every cent I was given on candy and pink Hostess Sno Balls, which I scarfed down immediately and in private, incapable of even contemplating the possibility of delayed gratification. By the start of seventh grade, I was as tall as I am now, but I was at the fat, friendless bottom of the adolescent food chain, along with the kids with glasses or buck teeth or divorced parents or families with weird beliefs, like not being able to jump on a trampoline on Sunday or eating no meat. What I craved more than anything was my parents' approval, and when my mother started seeking me out at night to sit with her, I was almost breathless with pleasure and relief. I was still the chosen one, her best friend, and she told me so.

"We're the girls, we have to stick together," she'd whisper, sitting next to me on the couch downstairs, the two of us nodding in agreement as she loaded my lap with a pile of clean clothes still warm from the dryer. Our late laundry nights became routine, seemingly just the two of us alone in the still house, united in female solidarity and in our fascination with McLean Stevenson.

My mom and I couldn't get enough of McLean Stevenson. He filled in regularly on *The Tonight Show* whenever Johnny Carson went on vacation, and before that he'd been the actor who played droll, bumbling Colonel Henry Blake on the television sitcom *M*A*S*H*. He was awkward and self-effacing, tall and lean and gangly as one of the long-ago boys in my mother's prom pictures. McLean Stevenson was perfect for us. Everything we knew about him from *M*A*S*H* episodes and *The Tonight Show* confirmed that he was a softhearted gentleman with a good sense of humor. He liked kids: On *M*A*S*H* he had three, including a daughter he called from Korea on her birthday, getting teary-eyed as he hung up the phone.

"You write the letter, Cis," my mother urged. "You're the writer. That'll be your job. You tell him about us. He'll pay attention to a letter from a little girl."

I thought about the letter I would write, and how McLean Stevenson would fall for us: a twelve-year-old girl and her beautiful stranded mother, both of them harboring the secret heartbreak of their unappreciative, unhappy family. McLean Stevenson would save us. McLean Stevenson would take us away from my angry, sullen father and my mean brothers, and we would live happily ever after, somewhere—anywhere—else, away from the misery and disappointment of our house.

"HAVE YOU WRITTEN the letter yet?" my mother would whisper in passing, like an undercover agent offering the secret code, as we ran around the house with my brothers in the late afternoon, furiously cleaning up before my dad got home.

I hadn't written the letter yet. My hesitation troubled me as much as the letter itself. In my bed at night, I worried about my letter and about the person who was supposed to write it: a fat selfish twelve-year-old willing to save herself and sacrifice her brothers, her family. Being the girls together had been thrilling but benign when I was small, an invitation to try out lipstick samples and wear matching dresses. Now something far more serious was at stake. We weren't a team any longer, my mother, my brothers, and me. It was just me and my mom alone, plotting our escape. No one else counted in our equation.

But what if I let my mother down? What if it was my fault she was stuck in our wretched family forever? I was her best friend. I was still her Little Mommy; it was still my job to take good care of her. She was counting on me. Of this unequivocal fact I was certain.

I would have done anything for my mother, for her love and her praise and her companionship. For her happiness, which felt like mine. It was the same year we started waiting for McLean Stevenson, the year we moved to Alaska, that she took me aside one afternoon and cut me a deal. She would give me a dollar, she promised, for every pound I lost. She peered over my shoulder as I stood on the scale in her bathroom, and in the mirror I saw how different we appeared: my mother lovely and delicate and slim, her model's cheekbones almost sculpted, her small breasts high on her evident rib cage. Even her feet and hands, her wrists and ankles were thin, as elegantly fine-boned and graceful as the rest of her. I wanted to look like her—who wouldn't want to look like her?

I really tried to control what I put in my mouth, which was easiest during our family dinners, so chronically unpleasant that I rarely had much appetite, anyway. Every day I weighed myself, just as my mom told me to do, just as she had done for years herself, and when by some miracle I saw that the needle on the bathroom scale had dropped even slightly, my mother crooned with delight and lavished me with a dollar. Soon we'd be able to share clothes, she told me; we would go shopping together and buy things we could both wear, like the best friends we were. I imagined us in the front seat of a shiny convertible driving the bright manicured streets of Los Angeles, the letters of the HOLLY-WOOD sign beneficent on the hills above us; my glamorous raven-haired mother at the wheel in her Jackie O sunglasses, her lacquered nails perfect and a gossamer scarf billowing out from where it was tied at her swanlike neck, crisp department store bags lined up on the upholstery of the back seat, the two of us driving to *The Tonight Show* studios to pick up McLean. But somehow, inevitably, I'd find myself walking alone through our characterless Alaskan subdivision toward the Safeway at the main intersection, a dollar or two in my pocket. I'd tell myself I was only going to look as I stood before the candy display at the front of the store. I took the long route home as I ate my Sno Balls or Nestlé's $100,000 bar, hurrying past the elementary school playground, toeing the balled-up candy wrappers into the storm drain at the curb before someone saw me.

The dollar deal didn't really work. My brothers still called me "sumo wrestler," and I'd heard a friend of Billy's ask him, as they passed me on the staircase of the junior high, "Hey, isn't that fat girl your sister?" My mom bought me a box of Ayds, a diet candy I'd seen advertised in the back of Archie comic books. Ayds looked like caramels individually wrapped in waxed paper, and you were supposed to eat one before meals to make you feel full. They tasted metallic and vegetal, but they were still a little too close to candy for me. After I emptied the box of a month's supply in a quick few days, my mother again called me into her bathroom.

"I'm going to share some tricks with you," she said conspiratorially, digging back in the linen closet behind the Holiday Inn hand towels. "We have to stick together, right?"

She showed me her stash of over-the-counter diet pills and diuretics, and prescription bottles for some thyroid problem that I didn't understand but apparently could make you fat. She pressed one of the little blue diuretics out of its foil packet and one of the diet pills, a red-and-yellow capsule, and placed them on my palm.

"You don't want to take these all the time," she warned me, "just when you need a little extra help. Some people take laxatives, too, but I don't think that's very healthy. Just ask me when you want one of these, and I'll get them out for you. You know I'm your friend, and best friends help each other."

Later, after I regularly wiped out my mother's supply of diet pills and diuretics and thyroid medication, she would hide the replacements in a different place. But she was never any good at keeping secrets, and I'd always find the new stash.

One Saturday afternoon at the end of our second Alaskan summer, a time when the long mild days seemed to come to a precipitous halt overnight, all the leaves curling inward and yellowing, our breath suddenly clouding in front of us in the chill air, I was making rhubarb crisp as an excuse to eat clumps of brown sugar out of the box. Hunched over the kitchen counter with my back to the room so no one could see what I was doing, I was furiously spooning sugar into my mouth when my father stormed by asking for my mom. She was outside in the yard, preparing her garden for winter.

Through the open window over the sink, I heard them arguing out back, my father's voice low and accusatory, my mother's breezily pacifying over the hissing spray of the garden hose. Then there was a metallic clank, and my mother cried out. I stood frozen at the sink, listening to the hard chugging spray of the hose, my mom pleading with my dad to stop, her throaty cry. A moment later there was stomping up the stairs to the back deck, and my mom lunged for the sliding glass door, yanking it open. She was completely covered in dirt and water. It was in her hair, in her ears, caked on her soaking wet clothes and running down her arms and legs. She was dripping with cold muddy water from her head to her feet. It looked like my father had dumped a bucket of potting soil over my mother's head and then turned the hose on her.

I ran after her, squeezing in through my parents' bedroom door just before she slammed it shut and turned the lock. She paced the room, shaking violently. "I hate him—I hate him—I hate him—" she muttered again and again, frantic with rage, rubbing the mud back and forth on her arms. I stood with my back against the door, afraid to move. "I hate him, Cis, I hate him," she repeated, and then she stopped in front of me, searching my face. "Cis, you have to help me," she pleaded, tears streaking down her filthy cheeks. "You have to help me get out of this."

RHUBARB CRISP
∴

1 cup walnuts, coarsely chopped
3 or 4 ribs of rhubarb (enough to make 4 cups when
    chopped)
1 cup granulated sugar
2 tablespoons cornstarch
1 teaspoon vanilla
1 cup unbleached all-purpose flour
1 cup firmly packed light brown sugar
1 teaspoon cinnamon
½ teaspoon salt
1 cup rolled oats
½ cup melted butter

• Preheat the oven to 350°. Generously butter an 8-inch square or round baking pan. Spread the walnuts on a cookie sheet and toast for 8 to 10 minutes until fragrant and lightly browned, stirring every few minutes to prevent burning.
• Slice the rhubarb into 1-inch chunks and roughly chop. In a medium-sized bowl, mix with the granulated sugar and cornstarch, then the vanilla.
• In a separate bowl, mix the flour, brown sugar, cinnamon, salt, and rolled oats. Add the melted butter and the walnuts, mixing with a fork or with your fingers into moist crumbs. Press half of the crumble mixture into the bottom of the prepared pan. Distribute the rhubarb mixture over the bottom crumble crust, then sprinkle the rest of the crumble mixture over the top. Bake for 40 to 50 minutes, until the rhubarb is juicy, bubbling, and tender. Serve warm or cool.

Makes 4 to 6 servings.

VARIATIONS

For Strawberry-Rhubarb Crisp: Substitute 2 cups of sliced strawberries for half of the rhubarb.

For Apple, Pear, Peach, Plum, Apricot, or Berry Crisp: Substitute 4 cups of prepared chosen fruit (peeled, seeded, and sliced or chunked as necessary) for the rhubarb. Omit the granulated sugar and cornstarch. Substitute 1 cup chopped toasted almonds for the walnuts if desired.

For Cranberry or Cranberry-Apple Crisp: Substitute 4 cups cranberries or 2 cups cranberries and 2 cups chunked or sliced apples for the rhubarb, roughly chopping half the cranberries. Omit the cornstarch, and for Cranberry-Apple, use only ½ cup granulated sugar.

Chocolate Chips for Weirdos

T HE CHINLESS GIRL IN ROUND-THE-CLOCK HEADGEAR. THE TEARY elfin boy who wore puka shells or an ascot every day. The obese adopted sisters who fought more viciously than even Billy, John, and me. The beanpole girl with the only divorced parents in the neighborhood. The girl whose mother had died when she was a baby, who had a step-mother she called "Aunt" and a smelly Chesapeake Bay retriever with a scrofulous skin condition. The math genius Native Alaskan boy who boarded with a foster family and wore his pants hiked to his armpits. The half-Japanese girl with the disastrous perm and an obsession with Peter Frampton.

I wouldn't exactly have called them my friends. They were more like my relegation in the imperial Roman sense, the kids so lame and halt and strange that they abided in a state of exile even in the freakish halls of junior high.

And then there was Lynn. What was she doing with the rest of us, I sometimes wondered. She had no obvious abnormalities, except for showing up from Tennessee halfway through seventh grade and a low, elongated twang in her voice, but not the sort of blatant accent that would have automatically banished her to the pariah crowd. She looked and behaved like any ordinary person, in fact better than ordinary. At a time when most adolescents were going through individualized horror-show mutations of physical awkwardness, Lynn was actually quite lovely. She was tall and poised and calm, her skin unblemished and her thick auburn hair falling in soft even waves down her back like a model's in a Breck shampoo commercial. Who knows what pubescent trauma she'd clawed her way through before she got to Anchorage, but by the time I met her she already had a woman's body and confidence, with just enough stupid sense of humor and craving for junk food to let us know she was still one of us. Maybe it was simply the fact that she hung around with the weirdos that gave her weirdo status.

I fit right in with this group. Long, greasy hair, a bushy dark unibrow Frida Kahlo would have envied, clothed in the approximately sixteen layers I believed would disguise my bulk, my favorite sweater giving off an odor of damp sheep whenever it rained. These were the years when I confided in the motley crew of losers who deigned to know me that I wanted my own name. I still couldn't get the hang of being called by my mother's name, and it was too embarrassing to be called Cissy in junior high. I soon regretted asking for suggestions from a bunch of kids with names like Doris and Norman and Sue, who threw themselves at the task of finding me a new identity with all the compensatory passion of people whose own boring or humiliating selves made them cringe. *How about Kitty, Kathy, Katinka? How about Desiree? How about Mo?* I pretended to go deaf when classmates with bad haircuts and hand-me-down unicorn sweatshirts leapt gracelessly through their hallway games of Chinese jumprope to the thumping rhythm of "Kung Fu Fighting," shouting "Kitty! Oh, Kitty!" at me as I slumped by during lunch hour.

Junior high was also when I hit on the brilliant idea to embroider my one pair of jeans with every breed of dog recognized by the American Kennel Club, all hundred and twenty-two of them. It was an ambitious project, one that kept me head down needling French knots to mimic a standard poodle's coat during countless hours on the couch in front of *Love, American Style*. While the seventh-grade history teacher with the Nazi concentration camp numbers tattooed on her arm lectured us about Haile Selassie, I was sketching dogs at my desk, congratulating myself for my cleverness in realizing that I could finish the greyhound, the whippet, and the Italian greyhound with the same template pattern applied in different sizes. I demurred at invitations to play weekend cribbage tournaments with the hate-each-other sisters across the street, even if it meant I'd miss seeing Tina chase Terrie around the house with the fireplace poker. I needed time to ponder my ethical stance on the weighty issue of illustrating all three color varieties of American cocker spaniels with a single representative, a decision that caused me some deep soul-searching since I feared my scorn for the overbred stupidity of American cockers was tainting the objectivity of my otherwise noble endeavor.

Every few weeks I wore my work-in-progress to school, convinced in my monomaniacal dorkdom that all the pubescents I knew were as fascinated by my dedicated effort to impart purebred dog culture to the world as I was. As I sat through science class, pretending to listen to the teacher with the hair growing out of his ears explain Darwin's law of survival of the fittest, I stretched my denim-clad legs under the desk so everyone could marvel at the progress of my needlework, sure that all the kids were whispering about me in their heads in the most awestruck, envious terms.

—*Wow, would you look at that, she's almost completed the entire hound group!*

—*I can't wait to see what she does with the bichon frise!*

—*Boy, I wish I had the vision and selfless maturity to achieve something as startlingly unique and beneficial to dog lovers everywhere as this masterwork of artistry that Kath . . . Cis . . . Kitty . . . what is her name again?*

I might have been a founding member of the junior high geek squad, but I felt sure I was destined for bigger and better things, and thanks to the insurmountable evidence of my embroidered jeans, everyone else was going to know it, too. In the dank unfinished basement of Mariko Stevenson's house, which smelled always of unclean gerbil cage and perpetually steaming rice cooker, I thumbed through the Lip Smacker ads in a soy-sauce-stained stack of *Tiger Beat* magazines and knew that Peter Frampton was singing only for me: "*I want you-ooh-ooh . . . to show me the way . . .*"

I had one other outlet for pride and agency in those grotesque outcast years of early adolescence, and that was baking. I had the kitchen almost totally to myself. Seventh grade, eighth grade—somewhere along that timeline of rampant misery and familial disgust, my mother went on what she called "general strike," shrugging off all housewifely duties. No more laundry, no more cleaning up after us, no more cooking. One day she called me into the kitchen for a hand-off demonstration. "This is how you make a roux," she said, and showed me how to whisk a few spoonfuls of flour into an equal amount of melted butter, cook it briskly for a few minutes, then gradually add milk or broth to create a sauce. "This is how you roast a chicken," she said next, shaking a canister of Lawry's Seasoned Salt into a thick orange crust all over the flaccid body of a chicken prior to shoving it into the oven.

"Okay, you're in charge," she concluded, and I don't know if it's my memory's embellishment or if she really smacked her palms across each other in a final flourish, dismissing once and for all the burden of being the family drudge.

My father ate nothing but Campbell's alphabet soup and toast for about a year. Billy saved his allowance and started buying his own food. John lived on milk and Raisin Bran until he left for college. My mother hadn't eaten in years, subsisting on Tab, cigarettes, thyroid medication, and over-the-counter diet pills. I baked.

I rarely made a cake from scratch. My trusty *Betty Crocker's New Boys and Girls Cookbook* relied predictably on Bisquick and cake mixes, so I did, too, though I ventured beyond strict brand loyalty in my nascent connoisseurship, testing the same flavors across different brands and haughtily assessing the results with what I thought was a keenly discerning palate.

Cookies, though, were another matter. I prided myself on my expanding international repertoire, of which shortbread and Mexican wedding cookies were the sole exotics. I was dying to try Florentines, which I'd seen in a photograph in my mother's encyclopedia of world cooking—a series of books that lived, never used, in a lint-blanketed bookcase at the door to the laundry room—but I could never find preserved ginger or candied lemon peel in the Anchorage Safeway. I didn't taste a Florentine until my first trip to Italy when I was twenty-five, hauling up short in front of the window of a genuine Florentine *pasticceria* at the remembered sight, now real and before me, of chocolate rippled with the tines of a fork across the back of a disk of caramelized lace.

Oatmeal cookies, snickerdoodles, gingersnaps, lemon bars, sugar cookies, brownies—my cookies were on the whole standard and unsurprising, baked goods with a hearty whiff of American middle-class suburbia. I didn't know anything different, but I worked hard to make them as good as they could be, conscientious about following recipes exactly and employing the methods for measuring, beating, chilling, and preheating that I'd learned from my mother back in the day when playing mommy had been entertainingly novel. Baking was something I seemed to have a knack for, and I hoarded not just the rare sense of competence I felt when I was in the kitchen, but the enticing results of my efforts as well. I was a flagrantly territorial, menacing despot ruling over the fiefdom of the Mixmaster and the cooling racks, denying permission to anyone who asked for a taste of creamed butter-and-sugar, hiding the finished cookies in places like the piano bench, or the closet where my mom kept her grandmothers' velvet dresses in dry cleaner bags. It wasn't that I wanted to eat all those cookies myself—although I usually did—it was that I wanted undiminished physical evidence of my ability to wield control even if it was ephemeral, every single cookie accounted for and proving by its very existence that in some real, albeit pathetic and petty way, I held power in the world.

My mother, as I said, didn't eat anything that couldn't be purchased in a pharmacy or a 7-Eleven, and my dad refused to be party to a hobby that was keeping me fat and thereby underwriting my permanent membership in the adolescent losers' club; he turned away with self-righteous disapproval, especially after he dropped thirty pounds on the Campbell Soup Diet. That left only my brothers as potential consumers of my cookies, so desperate for their own fleeting taste of sweetness that they risked my volcanic wrath and the sharp tines of the meat fork in the backs of their hands for snatching hot cookies from the racks when they thought I wasn't looking, or overwhelming me, two against one, when I tried to slip past them into my bedroom with a Tupperware container of millionaire slices disguised in a bath towel. Billy even volunteered to buy all the ingredients if I'd make him a batch of cookies, and sometimes I'd grudgingly take him up on the offer, trying not to feel bad about myself when I'd see him count out half a batch of snickerdoodles and give them to John.

Chocolate chip cookies were, in my self-aggrandizing mind, my *chef d'oeuvre*, and they were the enticement for the sleepover party I decided to throw for the girls in my misfit cabal. *Mmm, homemade cookies,* the freaky girls crowed, *we can hardly wait!*

My brothers made sure to dematerialize from the house for the night of my party, happy to absent themselves and shaking their heads in derision at my undeniably lame guest list. What choice did I have? It was these girls—my self-selecting sorority of weirdos—or nobody. As soon as Billy and John were gone, I took over the kitchen, setting up an unthreatened assembly line of chocolate chip varietals: semisweet, semisweet with walnuts, and—get ready for this!—M&M's. In those days, Nestlé Toll House Semi-Sweet Chocolate Morsels held an unchallenged monopoly. I thought I was a savant of culinary originality.

When my compatriots arrived with their sleeping bags and dental equipment, I met them at the door resplendent in my canine-themed jeans and hurriedly shuffled them downstairs to the family room, more commonly known as the TV room. Since there was a television in every room of our house, including the bedrooms, the kitchen, and my parents' bathroom, the title of TV room was justified by virtue of its having our *biggest* TV. I'd already popped the corn, dumped six-packs of soda into the bar sink, and arranged my still-warm cookies on top of the console so no one would have to go upstairs and cope with the unspeakable prospect of encountering my parents.

We watched TV. We gossiped knowingly about popular kids who would never have any idea who we were. We played records from my family's cutting-edge collection of John Denver, Olivia Newton-John, and the Captain and Tennille. I gave a curatorial tour of my bedroom and its décor of dog pictures snipped from bags of Ken-L-Ration kibble. By two a.m. my father had stopped warning us from the top of the stairs to turn off the lights and pipe down. We were collapsed on a patchwork of crumb-strewn sleeping bags on the shag carpeting, passing around the hard salty nibs at the bottom of the empty popcorn bowl and the final broken scraps of cold cookies while whispering Truth or Dare challenges at each other when Sue, the girl with the single mom and a body like a fourth-grade boy, piped up into the darkness.

"I'll tell you something true, you don't even have to dare me. These cookies have no flavor."

"Yeah," chinless Doris concurred, her mouth full. "They're not very good."

I bolted upright from my sleeping bag, hugging my pillow to my chest in dismay.

"Yeah, they're sort of bland," Terrie said. "There's the chocolate, but otherwise they're flavorless."

"My mom's are much better," Sue continued. "How'd you make these, anyway?"

"It's the best recipe," I sputtered. "It's the official, original Toll House recipe. A cup of white sugar, a cup of brown sugar, a cup of shortening, a teaspoon of vanilla . . ."

"Ugh, it's the shortening," Sue said. "Shortening is gross."

"Yup. Good cookies have real butter in them."

"Yeah, butter. Definitely."

"I think this popcorn is stale, too."

Butter? I used margarine for frosting, but my mother and grand-mother had always used Crisco for everything else. I began to shrivel with shame—my cookies were inferior. My bow was broken in my hands. And then my wounded pride was suddenly countermanded by rearing indignation: How dare this bunch of freeloading geeks eat all my cookies and then criticize them? Who else but me had thought to host a party for them, to bake for them, to provide the same opportunity for adolescent fun that all the normal kids had all the time, at least in our downtrodden, underdog imaginations?

It was as if Lynn read my mind. She reclined on the couch cushions like a Manet odalisque in the oversized T-shirt she wore for a night-gown, resting her head on one long, graceful arm, her breasts high and weighty beneath the faded jersey, her glossy hair cascading over her shoulders in waves.

"I dunno," she drawled, "they're a lot better than no cookies. My mama says, you better appreciate whatever good comes to y'all." No-body had anything to say after that, not even me, and the dark and the night pulled in around us.

BY THE START of ninth grade, the junior high freak show had folded its tent, all the performers going their separate ways. Doris and Mariko had begun lurking at the periphery of the high schoolers' smoking lounge, a dire concrete courtyard between the junior high and the high school where kids with hair hanging in their bloodshot eyes and frayed elephant-leg jeans hunkered around in circles sucking down nicotine until the bell rang, then tossed their cigarettes into clots of dirty snow. Sue joined the student council with the other smart kids, Norman the debate team. Lynn and her family had moved back to Tennessee right after school got out at the end of eighth grade.

I stopped talking to the rest of them for good after Doris announced to everyone in the library that I had a flabby ass, but I'd already ripped up my membership card on the last day of junior high, when I wore my embroidered jeans to school for the final time. I'd slid sideways down the aisle of social studies class, sucking in my gut and holding my stack of books over my chest to hide my breasts, and as I lowered myself into the narrow seat, breathlessly waiting for someone to acknowledge that the nineteen breeds of the nonsporting group were now displayed in toto over the seam on my right leg (notice the meticulous satin-stitching of the dalmatian's spots, the pale pink floss I used for the inside of the French bulldog's batlike ears), the popular boy who sat in front of me stopped throwing bits of spitty paper out toward the rest of the class. He stared hard at my jeans. Then he smacked both hands to his blond forehead.

"For the love of God," Brian Porter groaned, holding his head as if he was in pain, "she's wearing her *dog pants* again!"

When I got home from school that day, I ripped all the dog-food-bag pictures off my bedroom walls. I changed clothes and shoved my dog pants deep into the garbage can at the bottom of our steep driveway, my face still burning from the remembered humiliation of my classmates pointing at me, their heads thrown back in laughter—everyone, including my fellow freaks, except Lynn. Lynn had met my gaze, shrugging her shoulders, and slowly shook her head from side to side.

During my ninth-grade year I talked to no one except the art teacher, Mrs. Evans, refusing to answer to anyone unless they called me by the new name I'd chosen for myself, "Kate." That spring I took a break from perfecting my chocolate chip recipe to go on a diet during which I allowed myself only ice water and raw carrots. After six weeks my fingernails and skin had turned orange from an acute overdose of vitamin A, and a hank of hair the diameter of a tangerine had fallen out of my scalp, which I hid by wearing a ponytail all summer high on the crown of my head. I had a tonsure, but at least I was skinny. By the start of tenth grade, I would look so normal that a senior boy with mutton-chop sideburns would ask me out on my first date. One night when I accompanied my father to pick up the pizza the rest of my family was eating for dinner, some leering pipeline worker collecting his pitcher of beer at the counter handed me a dime and slurred, "Give me a call after you dump this old guy."

My mother had always been the swan, but maybe I wasn't such an ugly duckling after all—though I would be the last one to recognize it. At school I still avoided my classmates and stayed in the art room with Ruby Evans. She'd signed off on so many bogus "independent study" periods and "teacher assistant" periods for me that I rarely had to attend any other classes. I mainly sat in the back of her class, reading novels and writing stories and drawing, or forging hall passes for other students with Mrs. Evans's calligraphic signature, which she'd shown me how to duplicate.

At home, my family continued its interminable disintegration. I divided my time between reading behind the locked door of my bedroom and baking late at night, when everyone else was either asleep or gone or behind their own locked doors. In the solitary refuge of our kitchen, I gradually gained the confidence in my basic skill as a baker to start improvising, playing with proportions and ingredients until what I made tasted the way I imagined it could.

The chocolate chip cookies I bake these days only remotely resemble the cookies I baked when I was in junior high and high school. Still, when I make them, I sometimes think about those weirdo kids from junior high, friends for as long as we needed each other, learning to appreciate what good came to us—or not—and about Lynn in particular, who perished with her entire family in a terrible car crash on a highway somewhere in Tennessee shortly before her fifteenth birthday.

She wouldn't recognize me now, and I still see her as I saw her last, on the final day of eighth grade. It was a tiny gesture of solidarity she offered me, her pretty hair swaying at her shoulders as she shook her head no: *No, you don't have to be who they think you are.* A generous act of kindness and maturity—it would have been so easy, in the cruel arena of adolescence, to do the opposite—by a girl who would never get the chance to be anything but fourteen years old.

ABSOLUTELY BEST CHOCOLATE CHIP COOKIES

∴

4 cups unbleached all-purpose flour

2 teaspoons baking soda

1 teaspoon baking powder

½ teaspoon salt

1 tablespoon instant espresso powder

1½ cups salted butter, at room temperature

1 cup granulated sugar

1½ cups firmly packed light brown sugar

1 tablespoon vanilla

2 large eggs, at room temperature

1½ pounds high-quality chocolate, coarsely chopped: milk,
 semisweet, bittersweet, or dark

Optional: 2 cups coarsely chopped, toasted, and cooled
 walnuts

• Stir together the flour, baking soda, baking powder, salt, and espresso powder and set aside.

• In the bowl of an electric mixer, beat the butter on medium speed for a couple of minutes, then add the sugars, beating until very light, about 5 minutes. Add the vanilla and the eggs and beat again until very light and fluffy. With only minimal strokes of the mixer blade or by hand, stir in the flour mixture in three or four parts, mixing just until it disappears. Stir in the chopped chocolate and nuts, if using. The cookie dough can be used immediately, but it is better if chilled, covered, at least overnight or up to 2 days.

• Preheat the oven to 350°. On an ungreased cookie sheet, place balls of dough the size of golf balls at least 2 inches apart. Bake for 10 to 13 minutes, checking after 10 minutes, until the edges are light brown and the surface is crackly and set but the centers are still soft. Let cool for about 5 minutes on the cookie sheet, then transfer to a wire rack to finish cooling completely.

Makes 4 to 5 dozen cookies.

The German Club Picnic

"SHOULD I WEAR THE ELEPHANT BELT BUCKLE, OR THE DONKEY?" my mother asked me. She was standing in front of the mirrored doors to her closet, holding first one and then the other red-white-and-blue belt to her narrow waist.

"Suit yourself," I said from where I sat on her bed, turning the pages of my book.

"You are just no fun anymore," she said, pouting. I glanced up, shooting her an incredulous look. But she didn't see me: She was studying her own face in the mirror, scraping a smear of lipstick off one tooth.

It was the weekend of the Fourth of July, 1976, the year of America's Bicentennial, and liberty smelled like the bright red polish my mom used to paint her toenails before she put on her strappy new sandals. She was thirty-seven, married for nearly eighteen oppressive, demoralizing years, and she was giddy with the thought of having not just two weeks free of the open rancor between herself and my dad, but also an invitation to the German Club picnic: a weekend party with people who felt no shame for their appreciation of imported beer. She was getting dolled up, ripping off sales tags, deciding between politico-commercialized belt buckles to wear with her new denim miniskirt, lacing the gathers of her dirndl blouse to show off her delicate collarbones and her small breasts. "All you need is enough to fill a champagne glass," she advised me, adjusting the white eyelet. Lately she'd repeated this bit of maternal wisdom so often you'd think I'd have become immune to the embarrassment it caused me, but I had not.

I did not want to go to the German Club picnic. I did not want to watch drunken, red-faced fathers hand lit sparklers to their small children. I was fourteen, and I wanted to stay home reading in my bedroom with the door closed, if not locked. I was not even sure I wanted to be with my mom.

Though it had come to seem that my mother kept me briefed on every detail of her life with my father however wretched or private, apparently there were still occasional negotiations between them that were conducted without my input, and the decision that my father would take my brothers on vacation to Hawaii, leaving me at home alone with her thousands of miles away, was one of them. I was her deputy, her liberator: the one who knew her secrets, or thought I did, and whose responsibility it was to help free her from the stranglehold of her marriage and my father's brutalizing domination, increasingly directed at me as he sensed my role as her proxy.

"You should be the one to tell him, Cis," my mother would say to me. "How can he argue if his children tell him to leave?" But it wasn't going to be his "children"; it was going to be me. "I'll be right behind you," she promised, "we have to stick together."

For so much of my life I would have relished having my gregarious, seductive mother to myself, and after we moved to Anchorage I mostly did, except that since ending up on Alaska's last traumatic frontier my mother had somehow turned herself into a card-carrying affiliate of the Anchorage German Club, wearing dirndl skirts, sitting on committees planning the next Oktoberfest, and trading recipes for salmon schnitzel.

Only my mother liked the German Club. My father's opinion hardly mattered—so far as we knew, he had no friends and no desire for any. Perhaps Billy and John and I would have found the German Club more appealing if we had been younger. Instead we sat, bored almost to the point of stupor, through slide shows of other families' vacations in the Tyrol, appalled at the sight of grown men in embroidered lederhosen. In a rare instance of sibling solidarity, together the three of us made fun of the clichéd, oom-pah-pah names of the club members—the Hansels and Gretels and Friedrichs and Liselottes, the children named Wolfie and Brunhilde and Heidi.

Our mother didn't care. This fun-loving Arctic-Teutonic subculture had taken her in. They called her *liebchen* and Katarina. They drank and they smoked and they told bawdy jokes, even when children—disapproving, frowning, teenage children—were in the room. They—well, one of them—slapped her on the bottom when she was passing a bowl of spaetzle around the table, then they—all of them—laughed heartily. Their tears fell into their beer steins as they listened to her play a ham-handed rendition of "Eidelweiss" on her dusty guitar. After putting up with our whining for a while—we didn't want to sit around in someone's basement rumpus room singing folk songs, or eating caribou bratwurst, or babysitting any more blond children whose favorite storybooks were written in a language we couldn't read—she mostly stopped dragging us to the German Club's events.

SO. I DID NOT want to go to the German Club picnic. At all. It was a weekend-long affair with the German Club families and couples and hangers-on camping along a stream somewhere in the mosquito-ridden greenery "just outside of Anchorage," my mother assured me. The possibility was never broached that my mother might leave me behind. I had to go, or she could not. She pleaded; I resisted. There were no other kids my age; there would be nothing, by virtue of her own rules of etiquette, for me to do. "You can't bring a book," she told me. "It would be rude."

Finally we arrived at a compromise: We would go, but only for an afternoon. We drove off in the station wagon with nothing but the clothes on our backs—my mom wore the donkey belt because it was cuter—a spray can of insect repellent, and a German potato salad with lots of vinegar and soggy bacon.

Three hours later, we rattled to the end of a rough dirt road and parked in a painfully green meadow under a drippy overcast sky. Winnebagos and Airstreams marked the periphery of the campsite on the bank of a trickling glacial stream at the edge of a birch forest.

"Katarina, you've made it!" bellowed the president of the German Club—let's call him Uncle Drosselmeyer. "Now the party can begin!" My mother was surrounded by her lederhosened and dirndled friends, who were eager to herd her away to play cards or accordion or yodel or whatever. I stood by the car as my mom was bustled off, sliding through the long, neon grass in her slick new sandals, held by her manicured hands—an enchanted, red-toenailed Clara being led into the misty Sugar Plum forest by the fairies.

Sullen and instantaneously bored, I walked toward the stream, bookless, to watch with apathetic interest what the little kids were doing at the water's edge. They had been catching tadpoles, dozens of them, and dumping them into buckets with water and silt. The kids were all shoeless and businesslike. They paid no attention to me, too busy assessing and maintaining their captives, who squirmed away from your fingers when you tried to touch them, burying their blunt gelid heads in the mud while their tails continued to twitch: children hiding their faces in their mothers' skirts.

After a while, who knows how long, a huge man staggered over. He was enormous, broad shouldered and tall like a giant, a stereotypical Aryan giant but with longish seventies hair and Tom Jones sideburns. The German giant—let's call him the Nutcracker—swayed in place as he contemplated the children and their tadpoles, his meaty fist curled around the handle of a pewter beer stein. Even without the stein I would have known he was drunk. He lurched to the edge of the stream and asked the children if he could see their frogs. One little boy lifted a plastic measuring cup full to the brim with tadpoles and murky water. The Nutcracker took it, looked into it for a moment, then turned his back. Only I could see that he was pouring the contents of the cup back into the stream. From where the children stood, it looked as if he was pouring the tadpoles into his beer.

The kids were too stunned to cry or shout, all of them imagining the tadpoles tumbling through the foam, flagellating upward through the amber liquid. Then the Nutcracker turned back around, facing the kids. He lifted his stein to his mouth, took a big swig, and tossed it into the grass. Two or three of the kids broke into sobs. They all ran to find their mothers, shrieking. I watched the Nutcracker lunge away into the trees.

I stalked off through the drizzle to find my mother, who was sitting under the awning of one of the Winnebagos playing poker with the men, someone else's sweater draped over her shoulders. She was studying her cards, a cigarette displayed between her perfectly polished fingers.

I hissed in her ear, loudly so everyone at the card table could hear. "Your drunken friends are drinking live tadpoles in their beer," I lied. "I saw it. There's a giant man torturing the little kids."

"The Nutcracker," Uncle Drosselmeyer said, raising his eyebrows meaningfully at my mother. "It was just a joke, don't worry," he said, now to me, launching his bleary face into a big smile. "He's a bachelor. He doesn't understand kids. Go back and play now, he won't bother you." He picked up his gaudy ceramic beer stein and poured some of it into my mother's plastic cup. "*Prost,*" he said to her, touching his beer to hers. "*Prost!*" all the poker players responded, raising their dorky ceramic steins and taking swigs of beer.

"Let's *go,*" I breathed at my mother, now more quietly; getting everyone's attention had backfired. She kept playing her hand and smoking. She took sips of her beer, leaving lipstick on the rim of the cup. I stood gloomily behind her camp chair. Finally she whispered back. We would stay through dinner, then leave.

I didn't want their disgusting sausages. I didn't want the potato salad. There was nothing to drink but beer or Hi-C. I was absolutely unaccommodated. I paced in the long sopping grass, slapping mosquitoes, my damp hair molded to my skull. The barbecue had to be moved indoors, their caribou short ribs and mooseburgers cooked in the kitchen of a recreational vehicle.

Time and the evening dragged on—Alaska, remember: land of the midnight sun. The card game, interrupted while the little kids were fed and put to bed, had migrated inside Uncle Drosselmeyer's Winnebago. I sat, furious, my arms crossed, in our station wagon, willing my mother to appear. I gave up twirling the car's radio dial, hunting for a viable station, out of fear that I'd wear down the battery and we would never leave. I waited until the trees started to blacken and the sky turned a moody Technicolor blue (was it nine o'clock? ten? eleven?), then I pounded across the meadow in my soggy shirtsleeves to bang on Uncle Drosselmeyer's door.

Where were all the other mothers? My mother sat like a queen among courtiers, the only woman surrounded by bearded men in leather suspenders, the thick air acrid with cigarette smoke. I couldn't get anywhere near her. They were crowded around the RV's built-in dining nook. The Nutcracker was there, nodding semiconsciously over the poker chips, slamming a plastic cup on the linoleum dinette after every swig.

"Every party needs a pooper," my mother singsonged when she saw my accusatory face at the door. "That's why we invited you. Party pooper!"

"*Prost!*" said Uncle Drosselmeyer, raising his stein.

Hours after I'd figured it out—but was still trying to forestall the truth with poisonous looks from my perch on the shag-carpeted steps

of the Winnebago—my mother admitted the bad news. We were staying. She cited the long bumpy drive in the dark, that she'd left plenty
of food and water for the dogs, et cetera, et cetera. We would sleep in
the car. We would leave first thing in the morning.

There was nothing for me to do. Even if I made a scene, no one was
on my side. Someone offered me a jacket, which I refused. I got tired of
staring my mother down as she played poker, and I went to bed in the
back of the station wagon. It adjusted to a nearly flat position, though
the surface was hard corrugated plastic, and all I had to cover myself
was Lainey's threadbare puppy-birth blanket. It was impossible to get
comfortable, and I was explosively angry at my mother.

Somehow I fell asleep. I only know this to be true because I woke to
darkness and the ripe scent of sour beer on skin, and my mother's shrill
whisper: "What? Wait a minute, shhh—you'll—"

The drunken, giant Nutcracker was in our station wagon, my
mother between us. I pretended to be asleep. My mother kept whispering for him to stop, and he was slurring and cajoling. The blanket kept
pulling around, and the voices quieted, replaced by the textured sound
of bodies and clothing. I couldn't stand it. It had to end. I grabbed the
edge of the blanket and yanked it violently over myself, rolling as far as
I could to the edge of the car. There was a sudden drawn-out silence.
Then the click of the door opening, and the grass-cushioned thump of
the Nutcracker's expulsion from the car.

"Cis," my mother whispered to me. "Cis . . ."

I refused to answer.

The next day when I awoke, my mother was already up and out of
the station wagon. I was hungry. The German Club mothers were
serving breakfast at the picnic tables. I could smell eggs and bacon and
German pancakes, the only good thing about the German Club, when
I opened the car door.

Paper plates were tumbling over the wet grass as I walked across
the meadow to breakfast. Uncle Drosselmeyer's wife served me at the
kids' table. All the women were wearing kerchiefs over their hair except my mother, who was sitting with the men at another table. She was
smoking, not eating. She had her sunglasses on though it was still completely gray and muggy. She didn't look in my direction. Uncle
Drosselmeyer, who had been sitting next to her, got up and lumbered
over to me.

My mother must have asked him to talk to me—Uncle Drossel-meyer, the president of the German Club, the patriarch, the figure of authority, oom-pah-pah. I wanted to roll my eyes, but I kept them fixed on my plate. Uncle Drosselmeyer made his awkward speech, mutter-ing something about my parents, about something breaking, some-thing else about the stupid behavior of drunken men. Already my appetite was gone. Whatever happened, Uncle Drosselmeyer assured me, the one thing I could count on was my mother.

My heart sank. Anything, I thought, but that, staring at my deflated pancake—all hot air, like Uncle Drosselmeyer. "I'm not hungry," I called over my shoulder to the assembled Anchorage German Club, and even if I had been any longer, I wouldn't have admitted it. I bushwacked back down to the edge of the stream and planted myself on the gritty bank, its moist cold seeping up through the seat of my un-embroidered jeans. The Nutcracker's pewter stein was still there, half full of stale beer, and the wreckage of the kids' water games—pie tins filled with silt, wet socks, tadpoles arrested overnight in an inch of muddy water.

I was hoping my mother would be sufficiently shamefaced that she'd want to leave soon. Until then I didn't want to talk to anyone, and I especially didn't want to talk to her. I didn't know what she would say to me, how she could possibly explain herself. Whatever it was, I didn't want to hear it. I didn't care about her excuses or her rea-sons or our sticking together. That in itself—that I didn't care, I didn't want to hear *any more*—chilled me far more than the wet stream bank.

I heard a rustling in the bushes downstream. When I looked over, there was the Nutcracker's colossal back. He was hugging a tree on the bank with one arm, pissing in the stream. His beer stein was beside me. He would have to walk right by where I sat to get back to the campsite.

I did it quickly, unthinking—as if I'd been primed for such an ac-tion. I knocked back the lid of the stein, reached for a pie tin, and tad-poles poured over my wet hand.

The Nutcracker came crunching through the brush. For a moment I held his bloodshot gaze. There was not so much as a flash of recogni-tion, let alone embarrassment or apology. I held his beer stein out to him. "Here," I said.

He took the few steps toward me and reached out for the stein, lean-ing far down from his giant's height. He jerked his head, I guess in some sort of gesture of appreciation. He cocked the lid with his thumb and drank, still looking at me. I saw them through the glass bottom of the stein: swimming small and unfinished, vulnerable, trapped, as he drank them down.

"*Prost,*" I said.

GERMAN PANCAKE

.·.

3 tablespoons unsalted butter
3 large eggs, at room temperature
Pinch of salt
½ cup whole milk
½ cup unbleached all-purpose flour
Generous pinch of freshly ground nutmeg
Zest and juice of 1 lemon
Confectioners' sugar

• Preheat the oven to 425°. Add butter to an 8-inch skillet or heat-proof pie pan and place in the oven. While the butter melts, whisk together the eggs and salt until the eggs are well beaten, then add the milk. Sift the flour and nutmeg over the bowl and whisk just until smooth. When the butter is melted and hot, add the batter. Bake for 15 minutes, until puffy and browning. Remove from the heat and sprinkle with lemon zest, juice, and confectioners' sugar, and serve immediately, cut into wedges.

Makes 2 to 4 servings.

We Think of the Key

THE WEEKEND THAT MY BROTHER JOHN'S FINGERS WERE CUT OFF during a Boy Scout camping trip was the same weekend that I expected my mother to change all the locks at our house and leave my father a suitcase out on the front porch. Though she no longer confided everything in me, I sensed there was a plan afoot, and I presumed I'd be the messenger waiting outside to deliver the bad news when my dad and brothers returned from their trip. That's not what happened.

At the last minute my father backed out of his commitment to chaperone the scouts. The assistant scoutmaster took the boys instead, and my father stayed in town. I was sure he knew. Through my bedroom curtains I watched him pull cautiously down the driveway and turn around in our cul-de-sac, looking back up at our house before heading downtown to his office on a Saturday morning.

I don't remember all of what happened after. The details came reluctantly. Nobody wanted to talk about it; talking about it made it more real. I still wish I couldn't remember any of it.

One of the scouts had been waving a hatchet around and chasing the other boys. My little brother tried to stop it, reaching one hand out for the hatchet.

There was a couple with a camper and a CB radio parked close to the scouts' campsite. The couple radioed to Anchorage so an ambulance could meet them halfway, and Billy ran back to the scouts' campsite to search through the leaves for John's fingers. He found everything but the tip of John's pinkie. The couple with the CB put John's fingers on dry ice and drove.

When John got out of the hospital, he moved into the spare bedroom, a room our mother always called "the studio" with wishful insistence, imagining it as the place where she would finally get to express her frustrated artistic longing. Instead it had become the family dumping ground, the place where everything useless got abandoned. My mother stayed in the studio with John so she could keep his hand clean and moistened with antibiotic salves to minimize scarring, as the surgeon had recommended. At John's request our mom kept the door closed and locked. Billy and I weren't allowed in; John didn't want us to see his hand. I stood outside the door by my father's dictionary stand, looking up words, listening. "Now no one will ever like me," I heard John whisper to our mother. When John finally let us inside, he sat on the sofa bed, his face pale, his bandaged hand hidden under a blanket.

By some miracle the surgeon had been able to reattach John's severed fingers, except for the end of his pinkie. It would take a long time, but eventually some of the nerves would grow back. The scar tissue would soften and his fingers would bend. He would look normal from a distance. Except for the tip of his pinkie, the small emblem of something big that was gone, most of the damage was internal.

MY MOTHER NEVER changed the locks at our house, though about a year after John's accident, when my father moved to a condominium across town, she installed a deadbolt on her bedroom door and a private phone line, which she used to call us from inside her locked room when he came over. "Is he still here?" she'd ask whichever one of us picked up the ringing phone somewhere else in the house. "Tell him to leave." "I'll do it," I'd tell my brothers. At fifteen, I figured it cost me nothing to further alienate my father and draw his anger. We were both used to it.

You disgust me. I'd heard these words so often, my father's voice acid with contempt, that I can't recall any particular time or place, the words unattached to anything except to me. For one of my independent studies with Ruby Evans, she'd given me a final exam with one question: What do you want from your life? All of her exams were like that, one thought-provoking question no matter what the subject of the class: What is the meaning of integrity? How will you change the world? *From my life,* I wrote on my final, *I want to be known.* At some point in my life, I wanted even just one other person to really know me, to understand what mattered to me and what I felt. It was perhaps a selfish desire, but it was an honest answer, and it was what I wanted to offer of myself, as well—the compassion of empathy. Ruby gave me an A. Why I showed my final exam to my father I don't know, unless it was an unremitting hope, despite all odds, to gain his approval. He read my answer, the *A* marked at the top in Ruby Evans's dramatic, calligraphic hand.

"If anyone really knew you," my father said, shaking his head with pity, "they would despise you."

MY FATHER CAME to our house every day. He came bringing pizzas for dinner or boxes of Dunkin' Donuts for breakfast, letting himself in with his key, looking around in stunned shock as if he'd never seen any of it before, our family's familiar artifacts.

There was nothing on the walls of my dad's condo, nothing on the shelves or in the refrigerator. His only furniture was a bed, a television, and a dresser on which he lined up old studio photographs of Billy, John, and me taken after we moved to Palo Alto. Our small open faces smiled out from the photos, our teeth tiny, our cowlicks identical. When our father muttered the invitation that we could go to his house, my brothers and I never wanted to. It was too depressing, that empty house.

My mother had studied for the real estate licensing exam and passed. She slept until noon or one o'clock most days, but then she'd get dressed in businesslike clothes and meticulously apply her makeup and go out to meet clients. She was never home when Billy and John and I got back from school. Since none of us ever seemed to remember to bring our keys, we were always locked out of the house, and we spent a lot of time waiting in the garage.

The garage was crammed, as all our garages had been, with moving boxes that were never unpacked, untouched stacks of *National Geographic,* tools and bicycles and retired appliances—our first microwave oven, eight-track players already obsolete. Our extra freezer was there, and there was a phone jack in the wall. One day Billy thought to take one of the phone extensions out to the garage, just in case. I made carrot cupcakes and put them in the freezer. And I moved the black-and-white television from my bedroom and left it in the garage, too.

We would meet there, the three of us, and though it happened day after day, we never discussed it. Walking up the hill from the school bus, I'd feel the bottom of my purse for keys, find nothing but the sticky broken remains of a bottle of lip gloss, and I wouldn't even bother to try the front door. When I walked into the garage, John would be there, one hand held gingerly in his pocket, the other placing a cupcake in the microwave. An hour later Billy would arrive, his hair wet from swim practice.

We watched reruns in silence, never reacting to the laugh tracks, and on days when it was very cold outside, so that Billy showed up with his hair stiff and frosted on his head, and we'd run out of cupcakes and frozen hamburgers, and it grew later and later, John would walk to the phone and with one pointed finger dial our father's number.

CARROT CUPCAKES
.·.

2 cups unbleached all-purpose flour
½ cup whole wheat flour
1 teaspoon cinnamon
1 teaspoon ground ginger
½ teaspoon nutmeg
½ teaspoon salt
3 teaspoons baking soda
4 large eggs, at room temperature
1½ cups vegetable oil
2 cups granulated sugar
1 cup chopped walnuts, lightly toasted and cooled
3 cups grated carrots

- Preheat the oven to 325°. Line 30 to 36 muffin cups with paper liners.
- Whisk together the flour, whole wheat flour, cinnamon, ginger, nutmeg, salt, and baking soda in a bowl and set aside. Beat the eggs on medium speed until uniform and frothy, then add the oil and sugar and beat until well mixed and light, about 3 to 5 minutes. Gradually add the flour mixture, a cup at a time, mixing until the flour completely disap-

pears and the batter is smooth. Add the nuts, then the carrots, mixing thoroughly. Spoon into muffin cups to two-thirds full. Bake for 20 to 25 minutes, until a toothpick inserted into the center of a cupcake comes out clean and the cakes spring back when lightly touched at the center. Allow to cool in the pans for about 10 minutes, then transfer to wire racks to cool completely before frosting.

CREAM CHEESE FROSTING

1 pound cream cheese, at room temperature
½ cup unsalted butter, at room temperature
¼ teaspoon salt
1 teaspoon vanilla
4 to 5 cups confectioners' sugar

• In the bowl of an electric mixer, starting at low speed and increasing to medium, beat the cream cheese and butter together until thoroughly mixed and light. Beat in the salt and vanilla. Add the confectioners' sugar a cup at a time, beating on low speed at first and increasing to medium, until the frosting is thick enough to spread and hold its shape. Don't overbeat.

Makes enough to frost 36 cupcakes or an 8- or 9-inch two- or three-layer cake.

FOR A TWO- OR THREE-LAYER CARROT CAKE:

• Butter and flour two or three 8- or 9-inch round cake pans. Divide batter evenly among the pans and bake for 45 to 60 minutes.

Brownies for Mr. Wilsey

FOR TWO YEARS I SAT ON THE COUCH IN THE WILSEYS' FAMILY ROOM watching my boyfriend, Greg, watch *Battlestar Gallactica* as he drank liter bottles of Sprite, a family-sized bag of chips between his knees. *This is so great,* I'd say to myself. *I have a boyfriend!*

Greg's father reclined in a reclining chair in the corner of the room. Greg's mother sat at one end of the couch doing needlepoint, Greg sat at the other end, and I sat in the middle between them.

"Gregory, don't you want to offer Kate something to drink? Maybe some of that enormous bottle of soda?" Becky Wilsey would ask, peering at Greg from over the top of the magnifying eyeglasses she wore on a chain around her neck, motioning that he should go to the kitchen and get me a glass.

"She doesn't want any," Greg would mumble, hardly moving his lips and not taking his eyes off the screen. Then he'd knock the Sprite back and drink, glug glug glug, straight out of the bottle.

"Greg, what about some of those chips? I bet Kate would like a snack, too."

"Nah," Greg would mumble to his mother, "she doesn't want any."

Mr. Wilsey would clap his hands over his eyes and sink down in his recliner, shaking his head.

I could hardly believe my luck. It was so great having a boyfriend, I had to concentrate to keep from grinning ear to ear as I watched television with his parents. Greg was six foot three and had the body of a young Apollo. He was a three-sport athlete at another high school across town, a fact that granted me, his girlfriend, a certain mysterious cachet in the vigilant cliquish fishbowl that was East Anchorage High. This was arguably as good as my becoming inexplicable best friends with the homecoming queen, which was maybe not altogether inexplicable since Elsa was so sweet she was best friends with everybody.

Greg was fifteen when we met, starting his junior year of high school like me, both of us cruising the Sears Mall with friends old enough to have driver's licenses and permission to use their parents' cars. Greg was shy. He didn't have much to say that night, and I'm not exactly sure how the whole thing came about, because he didn't have much to say most of the time. His friends called him Grunt. "My god, Becky, the boy lives!" Mr. Wilsey once exclaimed when Greg replied to a question with more than a mumble and a shrug.

My boring single days were over! No more driving out to the airport with Elsa to live vicariously through vacationers returning from Hawaii, puka shell necklaces blindingly white at their tan necks, their arms full of pineapples and boxes of chocolate-covered macadamia nuts. No more watching *Donny and Marie* by myself on Saturday nights when Elsa had a date, or making up the excuse that I had a babysitting job on the same night as the Sadie Hawkins dance, or eating batches of cookie dough alone in my locked bedroom. Now I could make cookies for Greg, and watch him eat them. What's more, I had a reason to get out of my parents' house every day: to watch my boyfriend eat the cookies I made for him while we sat around at *his* parents' house.

But that's not all we did. The Wilseys had a pool table, so I watched Greg play pool. Greg had a Pong game, so I sat on the couch next to him and watched while he thwacked little balls back and forth. We looked at his beer can collection, which he'd inherited from his older brother, who was away at college. We listened to REO Speedwagon and America and Journey, Greg's favorite bands. I stood on Greg's driveway while he rode his all-terrain cycle up and down his street, twisting violently into his turns so the huge bouncy tires would lift off the asphalt. I read his automotive magazines and we came up with clever phrases for the vanity license plates he wanted to get for his eventual car; his brother had IXLR8 on the license plate of his truck. Once Greg made me a metal engraving of the insignia for Alpha Romeo in his art class.

When he turned sixteen and got his driver's license, Greg was given access to his mother's Oldsmobile Toronado, which was our means for touring the fast-food establishments of greater Anchorage, where the tables were always crowded with teenage girls watching teenage boys

eat. On Friday and Saturday nights, we joined in the tedious but cultur-
ally unavoidable cruise of the Sears Mall. In that enormous boat of a
car, we looked like the grand marshals of a parade.

In the fall, during football season, I went to all of Greg's games and
sat in the stands with his parents. In the winter Greg played basketball,
and I went to all of his games and sat in the stands with his parents. In
the spring Greg ran track, and I went to all of his meets and sat in the
stands with his parents. One day as I was sitting with Mr. and Mrs.
Wilsey at a football game, everyone screaming in the bleachers, Mr.
Wilsey turned to me and shouted, "You know those brownies you
brought over? Those were the best fudge brownies I've ever had!"

That was all the encouragement I needed. Greg always ate the
cookies I baked for him, but he didn't offer much in the way of
feedback—about the cookies or anything else. I had two brownie
recipes I liked to make: one that was really chewy with a rougher
crumb, another that was dense and creamy textured, which I slathered
with chocolate frosting while the brownies were warm. When I arrived
at Greg's house with a Pyrex pan of brownies covered in foil, Mr.
Wilsey would rub his hands together gleefully and ask, "Which ones
did you bring today?"

A couple of times a year, Greg's parents would go to Hawaii,
Alaska's standard-issue holiday destination: It was closer by air than
anywhere else and, of course, it gave you a chance to warm up. The
Wilseys would leave an envelope of money on the kitchen counter for
Greg to buy gas and feed himself while they were gone. Though there
was a clear assumption that I'd be coming over in their absence—Becky
instructed me, not Greg, in the watering of the houseplants—it never
seemed to occur to anyone but me that there would be a teenage couple
alone and unsupervised in a house with two weeks' worth of cash.

While Mr. Wilsey and Becky were in Hawaii, I supplied Greg with
baked goods, and in the evenings he'd drive us to McDonald's or
Arby's and we'd order the meal deals so that Greg could save most of
the money his parents gave him toward the purchase of a car. Sometimes he'd splurge on Hamburger Haven, and we'd watch the moth-
eaten lion pace in its rusty cage outside while we ate our greasy but
superior burgers. Even on the weekends, after we'd watched a few
hours of prime-time television, Greg would stand up from the couch
and stretch, yawning conspicuously.

"Better drive you home, little missy," Greg would announce, pulling his mother's car keys out of the pocket of his Lee's corduroys.

"I think this is finally going to be it," I told Elsa during the winter of our senior year, when Greg and I had been going out for a year and a half. The Wilseys were in Hawaii again, and Greg's friends had talked him into having a party. Tim Colombo, one of Greg's teammates and the boy Elsa had a crush on, was going to be there, too. Tim was the most popular boy at their high school and that year's homecoming king. Elsa and Tim had the makings of a beautiful couple: Blond, adorable Elsa could have been the model for the girl on the Swiss Miss Hot Chocolate box. Tim was an honor student who looked like Bruce Jenner, and he'd called Elsa to see if she wanted to study for the SATs together.

"But it really wasn't a date," Elsa told me afterward, perplexed. "He just wanted to study."

It didn't matter, I assured her. The party would be different. Elsa helped me bake a massive quantity of M&M cookies and we shopped for new outfits. I told my mom I was spending the night at Elsa's, and Elsa told her parents she was spending the night at Tina Bannister's, since no one ever slept over at my house. On the night of the party, Greg gave all the money he hadn't spent on chips and soda to a friend, who bought beer with his fake ID. The Wilseys' huge gracious house was packed with teenagers—teenagers drinking beer, teenagers throwing cookies and chips at each other, teenagers dancing around shrieking to Greg's blaring stereo, "This ain't no party! This ain't no disco!" After a while Elsa pulled me aside in the kitchen.

"Notice anything?" she said.

"You mean, that we're the only girls at this party?"

Was that a good thing or a bad thing? By one a.m. it was starting to come clear. Tim Colombo had gone home citing church in the morning, saying a long, handsome goodbye to Elsa at the door. Greg was sitting upstairs on the couch playing Pong with the rest of the malingering male party guests. It was becoming evident to me that Greg would continue to play Pong indefinitely, and that his motivation to continue to play Pong was that I was still there. Elsa and I crawled into bed in our clothes in Becky Wilsey's pretty guest room, both of us keeping one foot on the floor against the whirling-down-tornadoes from all the beer we'd drunk. The next morning, Elsa and I cleaned the

Wilseys' house and watered the plants, and Greg had us hunch down on the seats of the Toronado so the neighbors wouldn't see us as he pulled out of the garage.

During a basketball game later that season, while I sat between Greg's parents and the crowd screamed all around us, Becky leaned toward me and shouted, "Today is our twenty-fifth wedding anniversary. Isn't it, Henry!"

Before I could say congratulations, Mr. Wilsey mumbled, "Twenty-five years of that woman is enough to choke a horse."

"What did he say?" Becky asked me.

"Never you mind, little missy," answered Mr. Wilsey, shooting his wife a big smile.

Becky elbowed me in the arm, beaming. "Ain't love grand?" she shouted in my ear.

FUDGE BROWNIES TWO (OR MORE) WAYS

∴

These two brownies have different textures: One is chewier with a coarser crumb, a perfect foil for the addition of walnuts. The other is creamy and dense, like a flourless chocolate cake, and is topped while warm with chocolate frosting. You can make the first version without walnuts and the second without the frosting—my daughter prefers them that way—but this is the way I like them.

CHEWY VERSION

Optional: 1½ cups walnut halves

1½ cups unsalted butter

9 ounces unsweetened chocolate

3 large eggs

1 teaspoon salt

2¾ cups granulated sugar

1 tablespoon vanilla

1½ cups unbleached all-purpose flour

• Heat oven to 350° and butter a 13-by-9-inch baking pan. If using walnuts, toast them on a baking sheet for 8 to 10 minutes, watching carefully and removing once they start to smell nutty and are lightly browned. Let cool.

• Meanwhile melt the butter over low heat in a medium-sized saucepan, then remove from heat. Add the chocolate, broken into pieces, and cover the pan for 5 to 10 minutes, until the chocolate is melted. In a mixing bowl, whisk the eggs, salt, sugar, and vanilla until beginning to get a little thick, creamy, and lightened in color. Whisk the butter and chocolate until smooth, then add to the sugar-egg mixture, mixing just until well combined. Add the flour and fold in with a spatula, using as few strokes as possible just until the flour disappears. Fold in the walnuts and turn into the prepared pan. Bake for 25 to 30 minutes, checking after 22 or 23 minutes: You do not want to overbake these brownies! The brownies will be ready to take out of the oven when the tip of a knife inserted in the center has moist crumbs attached (not liquid, but moist). When done, remove from the oven and let cool undisturbed in the pan for several hours or overnight before cutting.

Makes 24 brownies.

CREAMY VERSION

1½ cups unsalted butter
12 ounces unsweetened chocolate
1½ cups granulated sugar
1¼ cups brown sugar
5 large eggs, at room temperature
1 teaspoon salt
1 tablespoon vanilla
1½ cups unbleached all-purpose flour

• Heat oven to 350° and butter a 13-by-9-inch baking pan.
• Melt the butter over low heat in a medium-sized saucepan, then remove from heat. Add the chocolate, broken into pieces, and cover the pan for 5 to 10 minutes, until the chocolate is melted. Whisk the butter

and chocolate until smooth, then add the sugars, again whisking until smooth. Add 3 of the eggs and the salt and whisk in just until combined, then add the remaining 2 eggs and the vanilla and whisk just until combined. Fold in the flour with a spatula, using as few strokes as possible just until the flour disappears. Bake for 25 to 30 minutes, checking after 22 or 23 minutes: You do not want to overbake these brownies either! The brownies will be ready to take out of the oven when the tip of a knife inserted in the center has moist crumbs attached (not liquid, but moist). When done, remove from the oven and let cool. While the brownie is cooling in the pan but still warm, make the frosting.

CREAMY CHOCOLATE FROSTING:

3 ounces unsweetened chocolate, chopped
6 tablespoons unsalted butter, at room temperature
⅛ teaspoon salt
2½ cups confectioners' sugar
3 tablespoons milk
1 teaspoon vanilla

• Melt the chocolate in a double boiler over simmering water or in a bowl covered with a paper towel in the microwave for 1½ minutes. Allow to stand for a few minutes; if the chocolate is not completely melted, microwave for another 30 seconds and allow to stand, covered with the paper towel. When completely melted, let cool before proceeding.

• In the bowl of an electric mixer, beat the butter for a minute or two, then add the salt and confectioners' sugar. Beat until well combined—it will probably be too stiff to be "creamy"—then add the milk and vanilla and beat for several minutes, until creamy. Add the completely cooled chocolate and continue to beat for several minutes, until the frosting is very smooth, light, and creamy.

• Frost the brownie while still warm. The frosting will melt somewhat, getting darker and developing a shiny crust.

• Allow the brownie to cool completely in the pan on a wire rack before cutting into squares.

Makes 24 brownies.

CHAPTER

25

Bon Voyage

"HOLD OUT YOUR HANDS."

My dad was standing between the family room television and me, blocking my view of the screen. I did as I was told, and he dumped a stack of thick college admissions guidebooks onto my outstretched arms. It was the fall of my senior year of high school.

"I don't need these," I said. "I don't need to go to college," I announced, "I'm going to be a writer."

"No you're not," my dad said, screwing up his face as if I'd just said something so preposterous—*I'm going to orbit Mars in a lawn chair, I'm going to give birth to a litter of iguanas*—that the only reasonable response was to dismiss it with a derisive snort. "Now pick some colleges. Once you have a few, I'll write your applications."

It's all but inconceivable that a high school senior today could be as naïve as I was then. But I was. Somehow I had managed to get through seventeen years of life and more than three years of high school without once stumbling on even the most basic, practical mechanics of college—what it was, how long it took, what you'd do when you got there, or why you'd go in the first place. The year before, I'd watched from a skeptical distance as Billy went on a trip to visit colleges with our dad, coming back with brochures and application forms and exotic souvenirs. In the fall he'd flown away to Claremont Men's College in Southern California, but all I'd gleaned from my observations of Billy's experience was that in Los Angeles you could get a donut called a bagel.

As I thumbed through the college guidebooks, I soon found they divided institutions into two categories: "competitive" and "noncompetitive." After a lifetime of being locked with my brothers in a bitter struggle for our parents' elusive attention and unpredictable approval, the last thing I wanted was to find myself in a place that defined itself as competitive. I didn't know that the guidebooks were referring to academic standards, not how nice people were to each other. "Noncompetitive," I assumed, meant that there were schools where the people were known for being friendly and supportive. To go somewhere guaranteed to be noncompetitive: what a radical, comforting idea! Who knew that college could be therapeutic?

I'd been missing California ever since we left. Under the "Noncompetitive" headings in the guidebooks, I found just one college in California, in the Central Valley town of Stockton, about an hour east of San Francisco. The University of the Pacific—didn't "pacific" mean soothing and peaceful? After the University of the Pacific catalog arrived in the mail, I was sure it was the right place for me: an old-fashioned campus of red-brick buildings covered with ivy, a school with broad green lawns and marble columns under shade trees. It looked like the kind of place for someone who wanted to be a writer.

"I found a college," I told my dad. "I'm only going to apply to one."

He peered at UOP's application packet, nodding in a begrudging way. "Good thing it's noncompetitive, with your grades," he said.

There was one thing I knew for sure about college, something that my older brother's recent departure had made abundantly clear. It meant that you got to leave home.

BAM BAM BAM. "GET UP."

But it's Sunday, I thought blearily. I pulled the sheet tighter over my head, and, half-asleep, began sending telepathic curses in Billy's direction before I remembered he wouldn't be home from his freshman year of college for another week.

Bam bam bam. "Get up *right now.*"

It was my father. My parents' divorce was about to be finalized—for all I knew maybe it already had been, it was not a topic of discussion around the microwave—and still he came to our house every weeknight after work and every weekend morning to stand around in bleak despair. If my mother was home, she stayed in her deadbolted bedroom, asleep or making infinitesimal repairs to her Lee Press-On nails. Mostly she managed to anticipate his timing and flee to parts un-

known before he arrived, only returning after he'd exhausted his muttered excuses for waiting her out and had driven funereally home to his
empty condominium.

Bam bam bam bam.

I peeled back the covers and stumbled to my feet. "Hi, Dad, got the
donuts?" I said at my bedroom door. It was the last week of May, but
good weather arrived late to the Siberian lower level of our house, and
I wore socks and floor-length flannel nightgowns to bed all year round.

"Come get a load of this," my father said in greeting. He was
wearing his trademark look of patronizing contempt, the unmistakable smirk of schadenfreude that was reserved primarily for our family, but also indispensable for bank clerks, Republican politicians, and
inept waitresses. Nothing made my father so gleeful as someone else's
stupidity.

I'd been the recipient of this look so many times it didn't pierce me
anymore. I was feeling pretty invincible, anyway. My graduation was a
couple of weeks off, and I could already taste the flavor of California
air and escape. I was chafing to get out—out of our gloomy house, out
of Anchorage, away from my family's collapse. I was, strangely,
happy—strange because I thought I should be the opposite. My parents were getting divorced, I'd broken up with my boyfriend, and my
childhood was ending. Shouldn't I have been suffering, at the very
least sobered and contemplative? I wasn't. I was buoyant.

It had been so long since I'd felt anything at all, I didn't know what
to make of it myself. Greg would call me, distraught—sometimes
even his mother called me—to talk about my abrupt decision to
dump him. I listened, and I listened to myself make up limp, plausible
rationales off the top of my head, feeling like someone overhearing a
conversation in an elevator. I'd get off the phone and the whole
thing—his wretchedness and confusion, our two years of common
(if banal) history, my inability to come up with any genuine reason at
all for breaking his heart—would pop like a soap bubble and disappear. I couldn't tell Greg's mother any more than I could tell Greg
why I'd broken up with him. I didn't know. I'd get off the phone and
turn up the mixer for the angel food cake I was making, my conscience as light as a hummingbird, light as my airy cake, despite my
inscrutable heart.

There were other reasons for the weird elation I seemed to be

buffered by. Since my breakup from Greg, nice smart boys who had ignored me for years, boys who had always turned into mute statuary
when they saw me in McDonald's or at the mall, boys who were president of the student body or the honor society or captain of the debate
team, boys who I had long been sure had drawn the wrong conclusions about me, thinking I was empty-headed (we took the same AP
classes, but I still spent most of my time forging hall passes at Ruby
Evans's desk) or easy (I'd dated that hulking, hunky athlete from another high school for two years) were suddenly declaring admiration
for my oral report on *Wuthering Heights,* or asking what I thought of
To Kill a Mockingbird. They were calling me at home, shuffling ner-
vously through veiled admissions of long-standing crushes, and actually asking me out—not to meet by chance during a cruise of the Sears
Mall, or to watch them play some sport, but real dates, like taking a picnic to Big Lake, or escorting me to the graduation parties.

Escort me! I hung up the phone from their awkward nice-smart-
teenage-boy calls, feeling almost maternal toward their eggheaded
earnestness—Paul who buttoned his shirts to the top button, skinny
Sam in his mother's Pinto, Gus who didn't play any sports at all and
wore rainbow suspenders—and sometimes, for a split second, I'd have
a sharp hiccup of anxiety: What if they really did think I was stupid and
slutty? What if they were asking me out because they thought I'd been
banging the handsome athlete? Or worse—what if they'd figured out
that I'd broken up with Greg because I couldn't stand to live inside the
Potemkin village of my childhood for a single minute longer? That losing my virginity had seemed like the one sure way to burn that sucker
down, but Greg had been too terrified of getting caught to sleep with
me? What if they knew that I'd broken up with my boyfriend to escape
feeling ashamed of my stupid, slutty self, the bad, selfish girl who'd ruined my family?

But no—no one knew, not even me. And through the hole my sudden anxiety had punched in my defenses would rush back that elevat-
ing cushion of relief, which felt like carefree, untrammeled joy: I was,
really, a *nice* girl, a *smart* girl, a *good* girl, not some desperate wrecked
person trying to shed her skin like a snake.

I let myself wallow in the unexpected gluttony of feeling noticed,
feeling liked and appreciated; feeling weirdly weightless and free, like
an escaped balloon. I wasn't ready to commit to anything yet. My

grandmother was flying in from California for my graduation, which gave me a convenient excuse for not firming up any social plans. Her arrival also carried the guaranteed benefit that my dad, so humiliated by the divorce, wouldn't want to hang around much while she was staying at our house, and he'd give his sad, angry vigil a rest for a few days.

Now he was leading me up the stairs and into the living room, smiling meanly about something. The drapes were still pulled shut against the cathedral windows, but I could see through the uncovered panes at the pitch of the ceiling that it was a clear, sublime day outside, one of those rare exalted days of Alaskan springtime, the air blue and ice-cool but edged with a promise of solar warmth as the days lengthened, birch leaves semaphoring greenly in the breeze. My dad was spying on the street through a slit he was holding barely open between the drapes. I figured he was looking for my mother.

"Here, Dad, I'll do it," I said, stepping past him to pull on the drapery cords. As the drapes slipped apart I saw what he must have seen when he reached the top of our hill that morning. Two boys from my class—one of my new admirers and a friend—were in our front yard. They'd set up a bunch of old furniture and appliances from the dump to look like the rooms of a house—a bedroom set, a refrigerator and stove and kitchen table, a living room with a battered plaid couch and coffee table and a La-Z-Boy recliner. They'd even brought props to make it look more homey. There was a ruffled coverlet and matching pillows on the bed, and one of them was sitting back in the recliner reading a newspaper while the other one poured coffee for them both. They were wearing sport coats and ties, and after they'd grinned and waved at me, they resumed having their coffee and sharing the paper as if it were perfectly normal to play house in my front yard. My admirer pulled a pipe out of his pocket and chewed on the end of it while he read.

It was a silly, charming prank, one of several practical jokes that had been pulled on various people in our class in those last weeks before high school ended, and I was so flattered they'd picked me I could feel my face go hot as I blushed. I was still beaming down at them and waving back when my dad yanked my arm, pulling the sleeve of my nightgown so hard I thought he'd ripped it from the seam.

"Get away from there and put on something decent," he snarled at me, twisting my arm back and jerking me away from the window, his pale blue eyes almost colorless with disgust, "you look like a whore."

I CLOMPED UP the stairs of our house in my new Candies heels, the silky graduation gown billowing around my legs, adjusting my cap and its tassel for my official entrance. My mom and grandmother were sitting upstairs on the couch, waiting to see how I looked. My dad would be arriving any minute to drive my mother and my grandmother and me to my graduation. My brothers had already driven ahead to the high school, Billy to join his friends, last year's graduates, all just back from college, too, as they compared notes and walked the empty halls like superior, visiting ghosts; John, perpetually helpful, to finish the setup in the gym with the other student government kids.

We'd all been playing our roles for my grandmother's benefit, my father subdued and accommodating, offering to take everyone out to dinner one night and acting as chauffeur on a sightseeing trip to Portage Glacier, my brothers and me politely listening to the familiar family tales and curious about our California cousins, who were already making plans for Billy and me to join them at Thanksgiving. Even my grandmother played along, dressing up in my cap and gown for photographs, looking startled behind her eyeglasses but a good sport.

She seemed diminished since I'd seen her last, so much more addled and confused, though both she and my mother pretended nothing had changed—it was just more of my grandmother's classic dottiness, like the time she sent me a sexy lace negligee for Christmas when I was twelve. "Oh, I must have wrapped the wrong box!" she'd gasped over the phone, my mother laughing and rolling her eyes. Now my mother rolled her eyes and laughed, "Oh, Mother!" when my grandmother neatly folded her dirty laundry and left it in the trash compactor, or set the table with spoons on both sides of each plate—spoon for the fork, spoon for the knife, spoon for the spoon—or toddled out into the middle of our cul-de-sac with her ladylike pocketbook dangling at her elbow, telling me she was waiting for the bus when I found her. "Mother, there aren't any buses that stop on this street!" my mother had said, as if, had there been a bus, it would have been perfectly fine for her increasingly frail, bewildered, elderly mother to get on one and wander an unknown city by herself.

I had never doubted that my mother loved her parents. She had been raised to be a dutiful, obedient daughter, and she was. Her stories about them had always been tinged with pride and affection, respect and humor—except the one. "How could she have done it?" she'd asked me when I was twelve, thirteen, fourteen, repeating the story of the night before her wedding, telling me again and again, as if in its repetition she would finally be able to make sense of what had happened to her life. She'd posed the question to me as if I, her child, would somehow have the answer. Her green eyes enormous with disbelief, dark like a forest in shadow, tears streaking down her face: "How could she do it? I was so young—and she was my mother!" Despite herself, despite her romantic, unconventional, but not so farfetched dreams, my mother had been an obedient daughter, and it had cost her.

As much as she was clinging to a carefree show of normalcy during my grandmother's visit, it was taking its toll. I could see the brief moment of hesitation before she rose from a chair at the dinner table, as if she were struggling against a current that was sucking her down. Sometimes she'd leave the door open as she stood in front of the bathroom mirror putting on her makeup, and as I passed by, glancing at her as she smoothed foundation over her high cheekbones, over her delicate jaw, I saw her staring at herself almost frightened. Some part of me felt for her, even as I watched from a cool distance. I knew what it felt like to resent your mother, to feel she'd betrayed you, and to act, out of the loneliness of self-preservation, like everything was fine.

Which is why I thought they were still laughing about my grandmother posing in my cap and gown as I rounded the staircase landing. I stood at the top of the stairs, waiting for them to notice me, and I realized it wasn't laughter. My mother was weeping on the couch, keening, rocking back and forth with her arms tight across her thin ribs. My grandmother was sitting next to her, reaching her trembling, arthritic hands out as if toward something about to shatter.

"Twenty-two years," my mother sobbed brokenly, rocking back and forth. "Twenty-two years—"

"Oh no, oh no, oh no," my grandmother kept repeating, her shaking hands held inches away from my mother's side. "If I'd known—if I'd known you really meant it—"

My mother suddenly stopped moving, turning sharply toward her mother. I could see her now, her face sheeted with tears, her mascara, her careful makeup running down her cheeks. "What did you think?" she said, her voice high and accusing. "I was desperate, I was begging you to help me—"

"Oh no, oh no," my grandmother answered, touching my mother's shoulder, clutching at her hand. "I thought you were just nervous. Everyone gets wedding jitters. I was only trying to help you, I was trying to do what a mother should do. If I'd thought you really meant it, I would have never, I would have never—"

My mother buckled, collapsing into herself, weeping uncontrollably. "I was so young," she heaved, weeping for her lost self. "I wanted to be an artist. I wanted to go to Paris—"

"I am *so sorry*," my grandmother was saying, her demeanor suddenly cleared, clarified with a horrible understanding, not like a dithering old lady anymore, but a mother desperate to ease her child's pain. She had her hand on my mother's back, holding it there. "I am *so sorry*. I am *so sorry*. If I had understood, I would never have made you go through with it."

LATER THAT NIGHT, my diploma in its leatherette case handed over to my mother to take home, I'd slipped out of one of the graduation parties at someone's parents' house with a nice smart boy, a junior. We drove in his mother's car to the edge of Big Lake, turning off the engine and staring out at the gravel beach and the fireweed in the permanent dusk of an Alaskan summer night in June, talking for a while about his plans for his presidency of the student body before I wrestled him into the back seat. We made out there, his thin ropy runner's body hard against me, his mouth hot and strange and pulpy inside, until I clutched at his belt buckle and he said in a brave voice, "I bet they're missing you back at the party."

We drove back not talking, not holding hands, and Elsa—everyone's favorite, a nice, smart, good girl—found me in the bathroom, splashing water on my face. Her eyes were glittering from too much beer, her face raw and scraped and puffy from making out with someone, just like mine.

"Let's get out of here," I said, and she started looking for her shoes.

We took her mom's Fiat Spider to the deserted streets of downtown, past the lit-up shipyards and the strip bars and the Pioneer Cabin, to the Dunkin' Donuts drive-through window, where we bought boxes and boxes of donuts, baker's dozens, all different flavors. Then we drove up and down the empty streets for hours, fast past the houses of everyone we knew, past our own, all night long, in our high heels and our new high-school-graduate outfits, the convertible top down and our hair flying loose and tangling across our faces, eating just one bite out of each donut before flinging the rest out of the car. When there were no more donuts, we reached for our silky blue graduation gowns, pulling them out from where we'd tucked them behind our seats, and we threw them out, too, letting them catch in the wind we were speeding through, sailing them out into the bright lasting night, the northern lights spraying ribbons of color above us, waving like handkerchiefs as the ship leaves its anchorage.

ANGEL FOOD CAKE

.·.

1½ cups sifted confectioners' sugar

1 cup sifted cake flour (or unbleached all-purpose flour in
    a pinch)

1½ cups egg whites, at room temperature (about 12 large
    egg whites)

1½ teaspoons cream of tartar

¼ teaspoon salt

1 teaspoon vanilla

1 cup granulated sugar

• Move the oven rack to the lowest setting, and preheat the oven to 350°. Make sure to bring the egg whites to room temperature about an hour before baking.

- Combine the sifted confectioners' sugar and flour and sift three times. Set aside.
- In the bowl of an electric mixer, using the whip attachment, beat the egg whites on low until foamy, then add the cream of tartar, salt, and vanilla and increase speed to medium. Whip just until soft peaks form, then, still beating on medium speed, gradually add the granulated sugar a tablespoon at a time, beating until the whites form soft peaks but are not stiff.
- Sift one quarter of the flour mixture over the whites and fold in lightly by hand using a rubber spatula, and repeat with the remaining flour in quarters. Turn the batter gently into an ungreased 10-inch tube pan.
- Bake about 40 to 45 minutes, until a toothpick inserted at the center comes out clean and the top springs back when touched lightly. Invert the cake onto the neck of a wine bottle and allow to cool completely, 2 or 3 hours, before removing from the pan.
- To finish the cake, simply sift confectioners' sugar over the top, or it can be frosted or glazed as you please. See some of the suggestions below.

Makes one 10-inch cake.

VARIATIONS

For Citrus Angel Food Cake:
Grate the zest of 2 oranges, 3 lemons, or 3 or 4 limes. Fold 1 teaspoon of orange or lemon extract into the egg whites after they have been beaten with the granulated sugar. Right before adding the flour, toss the zest with 2 tablespoons of the flour mixture to prevent the zest from being too clumpy, then fold in the floured zest as the last step.

To finish the cake, dust it with confectioners' sugar, or frost with Simple Buttercream prepared with the same citrus flavor (see page 42), or make a glaze of the juice of the zested fruit used in the cake: Whisk together about ½ cup juice, 3 cups confectioners' sugar, and a pinch of salt, adding additional zest or citrus extract flavorings to taste. Pour over the top of the cooled cake and allow to drip down the sides.

For Coffee or Mocha Angel Food Cake:
For Coffee Angel Food Cake, sift 1 tablespoon instant espresso powder with the last of three siftings of flour and confectioners' sugar. To finish,

frost with Mocha Frosting (page 10), Chocolate Buttercream (page 43), or Brown Sugar Glaze (page 327).

For Mocha Angel Food Cake, sift 1 tablespoon instant espresso powder and ¼ cup sifted unsweetened cocoa powder with the last of three siftings of flour and confectioners' sugar. To finish, frost with Mocha Frosting (page 10) or Creamy Chocolate Frosting (page 210).

For Spiced Angel Food Cake:
To the last of three siftings of flour and confectioners' sugar, add 1 teaspoon of cinnamon, nutmeg, cardamom, five-spice blend, or quatre-epices. All of these flavors work well with Brown Sugar Glaze (page 327) or orange glaze (see above under "Citrus Angel Food Cake"); nutmeg is also good with lemon glaze (see above under "Citrus Angel Food Cake") or Lemon Buttercream (page 42), cinnamon with Mocha Frosting (page 10) or Light Chocolate Frosting (page 10).

Sweetheart of Archania

*B*AM BAM BAM.

Even three thousand miles away, I couldn't escape from the pounding on my bedroom door. Now it was my fellow college students, and I didn't want to open the door for most of them, either. On this particular day, in the spring of my freshman year, I was holed up in my dorm room with a quarter sheet cake covered in frosting roses, and a fork. With the window blinds pulled down, crouched on the floor in protective silence over my cake, I was hiding from people who looked like they'd just walked off a photo shoot for *The Preppy Handbook*.

In a display of gullibility I learned to regret, I'd gotten myself elected "sweetheart" of a fraternity at the beginning of my freshman year. The frat boys serenaded me under my dorm room window and flung roses they'd swiped from the off-limits garden in front of the university chapel. Shortly thereafter, based on the endorsement of a bunch of boys who thought I was an ideal potential sorority girl because I made them cookies and wrote their English lit papers, a sorority had pursued me as a pledge, taking me out to lunch off campus and leaving swag bags full of candy and girl-crush mash notes in my dormitory mailbox.

Almost every night of the summer before we left for college, Elsa and I had hung out at her house, watching her dad's new Betamax video player, one of the first to appear in Anchorage. Elsa's dad had only bought one movie, so by August we could recite *Animal House* line by line. How hilariously quaint, I thought: the olden days of college, when everyone was drunk, never went to class, and strolled lockstep through a treacherous social gauntlet wearing the same clothes and driving the same cars and doing all the same WASPy things. It never occurred to me that I was getting the best preparation available for what my introduction to college would actually be like.

Who would have guessed that there was still such a bastion of archaic conformity as the "Greek system" anywhere, let alone at a small California liberal arts college, and that my cultural life would be held captive by swaggering boys wearing luridly colored golf pants with turtles embroidered on them, and pearl-accessoried girls who kept their real underwear beneath their beds so that the frat boys on scheduled panty raids would take only the decoy panties that had been planted in the bureau drawers for that specific purpose?

By the time I learned my sweetheart duties, it was too late to back out, and at first, I didn't want to. After all my years of being misunderstood and underappreciated, it seemed like my time had arrived. The boys of Archania gave me a T-shirt with the fraternity's insignia and *Sweetheart Kate* embroidered across the back. They sang to me and flung more roses and took my picture, which they hung with those of all the other sweethearts on a wall in the fraternity house, right over their pledge paddles and the closet where they stored keg hoses. Among my official responsibilities, I had to make myself available for groundless compliments, serenades, and public admiration at every subsequent frat gathering. Also, I was expected to surprise the brotherhood by stealing their laundry and returning it clean, bartend in a Playboy bunny outfit for pledge-recruiting theme parties, be the getaway driver during hazing rituals, and act as on-call "study partner" (read tutor and ghostwriter). But my main job was to supply my big brothers with treats.

That last part sealed the deal for me. Before freshman orientation was over, I was baking sugar cookies in the shape of the fraternity's vintage fire truck, spending what little cash I had and using my emergency credit card like a savings account to keep the frat boys provisioned with junk food.

For the first few weeks of school, I was too busy ministering to the varied appetites and custodial needs of my big brothers to take anything but fleeting notice of how little college resembled what I thought it would be. I'd imagined it as collegial in the dictionary sense, a melting pot of people with different experiences united in cooperative pursuit, gathering as equals to argue philosophical tenets and explicate poetry. But except for the stacks of textbooks required by professors for their classes, the only poetry available in our school store was on cheesy greeting cards written by Susan Polis Schutz and a slim volume called *Touch Me* by Suzanne Somers from *Three's Company*.

I wondered why my roommate in the dorm was such a sourpuss, refusing to go to any parties and hunkering over her chemistry textbook in a disdainful huff as I tossed my nicest clothes around the room in a race to get dressed and make it to the sorority for dinner before the House Mother sat down. "Don't you like college?" I asked.

"This isn't college," she snorted. Her twin sister was at Stanford, but my roommate hadn't been admitted to any of the schools she'd wanted, none of which I'd heard of—Bennington, Bard, Brown. University of the Pacific had been her last choice. "Don't you know this is the school you go to if you didn't get in anywhere else? As soon as I can, I'm transferring out of here."

I wasn't sure how to process this information. I'd heard some of the frat boys gloat that our private college was "eleven dollars more expensive than Stanford"—a decidedly lame standard of superiority for an academic institution. But I was eager to learn, poring over my literature textbooks late at night after I'd performed my sweetheartly obligations, avidly underlining words and passages that struck me, preparing questions for my classes the next day. My professors took notice of my earnest attention, sometimes seeming to address their lectures on "The Rape of the Lock" or Blake's mysticism to me alone, since I was one of the few students I knew who showed up for every class. One morning I watched a professor dropkick *The Norton Anthology of Poetry* through an open window, terrifying a flock of pigeons that had been perched on the ivy-covered gable outside, because no one in the room besides me had read that week's assignments.

I'd declared myself an English major as soon as I was allowed to file the form, but I was far from publicly admitting I wanted to be a writer. To be a writer, I was discovering, you had to have something to write about. What did I have to write about? I was eighteen years old and nothing had ever happened to me. Nothing that I would want anyone to know about, anyway. Nonetheless, I lurked outside the English department office reading announcements for book prizes and newspaper clippings about authors, all the books and writers who'd ascended to lasting greatness despite my ignorance of them, and hoped the good fortune of strangers would rub off on me by osmosis.

It was the fall of 1980, the year of a presidential election. Instead of casting my first ballot as a citizen of legal voting age, on Election Day I made red-white-and-blue cupcakes in the dorm kitchen to take to the frat house. Later that afternoon, I stepped outside just as a siren started to crescendo to an ear-splitting whine, accompanied by clanging bells and whooping in the street. A professor I thought I recognized from the English department was unlocking his bicycle from one of the marble columns across from the library. We both looked up. Archania's fire truck rolled slowly toward us blaring its ruckus of sound down the main avenue of the campus, dozens of frat boys in their Greek insignia T-shirts crowded onto the bed and hanging from its sides. More fraternity brothers and sorority girls were running across the lawns toward the truck, shrieking with happy delirium as they were pulled up onto the runners.

"He's won! He's won! The Gipper's won!" they rejoiced.

Uh . . . wait a minute. Maybe there was more than one conceptual misunderstanding about college that I needed to get cleared up. I thought I was at a *liberal* arts college. Just when I thought the whole scene couldn't get any more bizarre, I saw that the assembled fraternal order of Archania had hoisted a flag over their heads and were waving it side to side as they drove their fire truck through campus. A Confederate flag.

I stared in disbelief.

The professor had wheeled his bicycle beside me. He gazed after the frat boys and their flag, squinting behind his wire-rimmed glasses. "Henry James. 'The Art of Fiction.' Great essay. You know it?" he asked me, scowling into the bowl of his pipe after tapping it on the handlebars. He must have seen me around the department; there weren't that many English majors. " 'Try to be one of the people on whom nothing is lost.' That's his advice to young writers," the professor continued, biting down on his pipe stem. "But it'll work for right now, too," he said, nodding at the screaming Greeks. "Nice shirt, Sweetheart Kate." He got on his bike and pedaled away, a cryptic smile on his face.

I waited behind a column until the fire truck was gone, and then I took cover in the library. One of the brothers had told me "archania" meant "first," as in the first fraternity at the university, its charter written just prior to the Civil War. In the reference department, I could find no such word. The closest I could find was "arcane": hidden or secret. I looked up the history of the fraternity and found a mealy-mouthed rationalization for using the Confederate flag as their symbol: It was to acknowledge their antebellum founders' "Southern sympathies" and heated support of "states' rights"—the political expedient used by the Confederate states to justify slavery. Whether or not the current membership of Archania knew what their brotherhood stood for, I now did. I felt like a jerk, beguiled by flattery and a few limp flowers.

Back at the dorm, I pulled the shirt over my head and threw it in the trash. The cupcakes I'd made for the frat boys were waiting on my desk, all ready to go. I sat alone in my room and ate them.

AT THE END OF the winter break, I found that my roommate had transferred to another university. I was supposed to move into the sorority house, but as I was carrying my boxes across the street to Fraternity Row, past the Mercedes convertibles and late-model BMWs lined up at the curb, I kept walking. At the college housing office, I told them I wanted to stay in the dormitory. They wouldn't let me occupy a double room alone, so I was reassigned to a different building across campus, a single room that looked out onto an interior courtyard. It took a while for my big brothers to find me there. After complaints, mostly from me, that frat boys were scaling the gate and singing in the courtyard on Sunday nights, leaving a mess of trampled flowers and beer bottles, the custodian installed a security camera. I didn't answer when the frat boys banged on my door. Eventually they stopped coming.

In the dorm where I now lived—the Greeks sneeringly called our minority coterie "independents" as if it were an insult—my dormmates met for study sessions in the lounge or foreign films at the student union; they were the people I'd sometimes seen searching through the otherwise deserted stacks in the library. They drove unremarkable cars if they had them at all, and they came from places like Nigeria, Peru, Illinois, and Burlingame. There was the guy whose family ran a

mortuary, a girl who worked at her family's flower farm during vacations, another who'd grown up in Stockton, students from the conser-
vatory of music whose rehearsal schedules were so intense we hardly
ever saw them. There were a couple of guys who privately admitted
they were gay. To my astonishment, the secret boyfriend of one of
them was a member of Archania, a water polo player with a vicious
serve.

Though I was no longer underwriting the carbo-loading of the frat
boys, I was still broke. I spent everything I had on twelve-packs of
Twinkies and bags of toffee-covered almonds, or on coconut cream
pies from Marie Callender's, or sheet cakes from the Snow White Bakery, where I had them write "Congratulations" or "Happy Birthday"
in frosting so if I ran into anyone I knew on my way back to the dorm,
it wouldn't look like I was going to eat the whole thing by myself.

One weekend I was invited home by a friend from the dorm. Carole had been raised by her mother since she was one year old; she'd
met her father only once that she remembered. I imagined their
house would feel diminished and lonely, though I should have known
better—Carole had been the one to suggest I paint my dorm walls
red. Their small home was both welcoming and self-sufficient, need-
ing nothing and no one else to complete it, though Carole's mother
greeted her, and me also, with easy warmth. Every room was a different color, the woodwork stained a pellucid leaf green, soft throws
draped invitingly over the furniture. There was a fire crackling in the
front room, the lamps turned low beneath their amber shades when
we arrived in a hard March rain. Carole's mom, Elaine, had made
soup and warm yeasty rolls and we sat together in front of the fire,
talking over dinner as raindrops trailed down the glass of the dark
windows.

"Mom, you made truffles!" Carole exclaimed when we carried our
plates back to the kitchen. I didn't know what a truffle was: small,
lumpy balls of chocolate rolled in cocoa.

"They're really easy," Elaine told me. "I'll give you the recipe. I
make them with my classes every year." She was a home ec teacher at a
high school south of San Francisco. "But for you, since you're adults
now," she said, sliding us a wry look, arranging the truffles on a plate
for us to eat in front of the fireplace, "I flavored them with liqueur."

Were we adults? Is this what it was supposed to feel like? That euphoric sensation of being an escaped balloon had shifted into feeling I was completely untethered to the world. I was an independent, all right, which I'd thought I wanted. I never heard from my mother at all. As soon as I left for college, she seemed to forget I existed. My father called occasionally with the excuse of making travel arrangements or to ask if I needed money. His checks came without notes, folded inside sheets of yellow legal paper, and I'd cash them at the student store and return to the dorm with a replenished hoard of candy and baked goods. No matter how much cake or candy I ate in secret, groaning and prostrate from a Twinkie overdose, I always felt empty.

Carole was one of the few people I could talk to. She was empathetic and levelheaded, confident enough to express her own anxieties and disenchantments, and meeting her mother, I could see where she got those qualities.

"This is something I do with my students," Elaine was telling us as she pleated a sheet of paper and carefully tore it into even strips. "I tell them to write down whatever it is that's troubling them. Use as many strips of paper as you need. And then you ball up the papers, one by one, and throw them away. Even better is to burn them, which is what we can do," she said, handing out the paper and pens. "It's not going to solve your problems, but it can make you feel a little less burdened by them."

"Chocolate helps, too," Carole joked, taking another truffle from the plate.

"Actually, that's true," Elaine said. "It's high in magnesium and triggers endorphins, so chocolate can actually reduce stress."

Carole and Elaine were busy jotting things down on their strips of paper, but I didn't know what to write. I couldn't articulate how centerless I felt, and how dumb, in every sense.

"That's okay," Elaine said. "Maybe the words will come to you later."

We balled up our troubles and took turns tossing them into the fire. Carole passed me a truffle and I took a bite of the soothing chocolate, watching as my scrap of paper sent off a little tail of smoke, then flared, then charred and curled and floated up, weightless, on the fire's draft, black as a densely packed page, though I'd written nothing on it but my name.

CHOCOLATE TRUFFLES
∴

12 ounces high-quality chocolate (I recommend 70% bittersweet or milk)

4 tablespoons unsalted butter, at room temperature and cut
into small chunks

¾ cup heavy cream

2 to 3 teaspoons liqueur or liquor: framboise, Grand
Marnier, amaretto, cognac, Kahlúa, bourbon, or Scotch

4 ounces high-quality dark chocolate

About ½ cup unsweetened cocoa or ground chocolate

• Finely chop the 12 ounces of bittersweet or milk chocolate and place in a heatproof mixing bowl with the butter. Heat the cream to just under boiling, then pour over the chocolate and let sit for a minute or two. Stir the chocolate with a rubber spatula in one direction until the chocolate and butter are completely melted and the truffle mixture is utterly smooth and glossy. Stir gently to avoid aerating the chocolate. Stir in the liqueur to taste. Chill until firm, at least 4 hours.

• When the truffle mixture is completely chilled and firm, line a baking sheet with parchment or waxed paper. Using a melon baller or two teaspoons, scoop out teaspoon-size amounts of truffle and shape into lumpy irregular balls between your hands and place on the baking sheet (I like my truffles to look like their namesakes, but if you like yours perfectly round, go ahead). If the truffle mixture softens during the shaping process, it can be rechilled; running your hands under cold water and drying them quickly but thoroughly will help keep the truffles cool as you work. When all the truffles are shaped, place the baking sheet in the freezer for half an hour.

• Finely chop the 4 ounces of dark chocolate and heat just until barely melted, either over a double boiler or by microwave for about 90 seconds, covering the bowl with a paper towel. Allow the melted chocolate to cool until it is just warm, and place the cocoa or ground chocolate in a small shallow bowl. To finish the truffles, remove them from the freezer. Spoon a small amount of melted chocolate into your palm and roll a truffle around in the chocolate to coat lightly, then return it to the lined baking sheet—the chocolate will freeze immediately. Repeat with all the truffles, then roll them one by one in the cocoa or ground chocolate and return to the baking sheet. Chill them in the refrigerator until about half an hour before serving. To serve, arrange on a pretty plate and allow to come to room temperature.

Makes about 3 dozen truffles.

Thunderbird Falls

Late in the summer before my sophomore year of college, my father insisted that I go for a walk with him at Thunderbird Falls, a hiking spot outside of Anchorage where a receding glacier had left behind a deep creekbed cut through a face of rock. I was still wary of my dad, despite how unexpectedly solicitous he'd been during my first year away at school, even buying me a used car so that I could drive down to visit him in Southern California, where he was now traveling frequently for his work.

I slapped at mosquitoes as I walked beside him under a canopy of birch and cottonwood trees, the forest on either side of the trail blanketed with primeval-looking ferns and weirdly fluorescent devil's club lit by bright spots of sun filtering through the trees. Neither of us had anything to say, and we could hear the river thundering over the falls ahead of us.

"Look at this, Cis," my father said, pointing. "Forget-me-nots."

Then I noticed what seemed an entire meadow of the tiny blue flowers growing close to the ground, all around us.

"They've always been my favorite flower," my dad said, his eyes scanning the forest floor as he continued walking.

My dad had a favorite flower? I didn't know he had a favorite anything. He said nothing more, and I thought about this chance revelation as we continued to walk the almost-deserted trail, only an occasional runner pounding past, breathing hard and lifting a hand in an acknowledging wave. When we got to the falls, I pulled my windbreaker closer around me against the mist spraying up over us from the water hurtling down the rock face to the creek below, a surging froth of white racing under the suspended boardwalk where we stood. My dad had his hands on the railing as he gazed at the falls, and as soon as he turned around I began to also, ready to get back to the parking lot and home and the relative safety of my bedroom with its locking door. He surprised me by reaching for my hand, his own hands shaking, and I realized his face was not misted from the falls. My father was crying.

"Cis," he began, kneading my hand between both of his, his voice hoarse and barely more than a whisper, "I'm sorry." Tears were pouring down his cheeks. "I've been a terrible father. I'm so sorry." His pale blue eyes were tortured. "I let you down. I let your brothers down. And you—" He took a deep, rattling breath. "—I don't know if I can bear what I did to you. I blamed you. I was wrong. It should have stayed between your mother and me. But you look so much like your mother, you were so close, I couldn't see—" He wept silently, slowly shaking his head as he clutched my hands. "Please forgive me for what I've done," he said. "I'm going to try to make it up to you and your brothers. I'm going to try to be the father I should have been."

I had never seen my father cry. When we got back to Anchorage, I didn't mention what had happened to anyone, though there wasn't really anyone to tell. I spent my days xeroxing files for lawyers or selling cheap clothing to teenage girls. My mother and I had lived through the summer like fellow residents in a boardinghouse, keeping our own hours and our thoughts to ourselves. Billy had already left for Europe, where he was spending his junior year abroad. John was working at a salmon cannery on the peninsula before he, too, would go to college. A few days before the fall semester started, I packed my suitcases and left for school, not yet aware of the deep channel my father's apology had cut through me.

WHEN I GOT BACK to college that fall, I couldn't concentrate, and I couldn't sleep. I could hardly drag myself out of bed to class in the morning, and then I just didn't go at all. I kept the sheet pulled over my face and ignored the soft knocking on my dorm room door when anyone came around to check on me. What frightened me most was that I couldn't do the two things that I had counted on to keep myself going for as long as I could remember: I couldn't eat, and I couldn't read. I had no appetite, and when I opened a book and tried to focus on a page, the words drifted off in a thousand directions, meaningless, my mind racing but blank.

University of the Pacific had a fully equipped infirmary with a permanent staff of nurses and on-call doctors on the far side of the campus, and that's where I ended up living for most of the fall semester of my sophomore year, spending the days waiting for my daily visit with a psychiatrist, avoiding the view out the windows and the stacks of magazines spread over a table in the common room. The nurses would sometimes coax me out of my room to sit with them during their breaks as they knitted and watched the breathless windup to Luke and Laura's soap opera wedding on *General Hospital*. Or they would bring me plates of food from home to try to entice me, pieces of cherry pie, their special meatloaf recipe. My friends stopped by every few days, sitting on the end of my bed, fingering the blanket, not knowing what to say.

On the day I moved into the infirmary, Carole and another friend had shown up at my dorm room and demanded I give them my parents' phone numbers. My father had been traveling for his work so frequently since the divorce, I had no sure way to reach him. I'd already called my mother several times, and I knew what she would say. Though I'd been stunned at first not just by her unwillingness to help me but by her denial, even anger at the suggestion that anything was wrong, now it seemed no more than an objective fact. As Carole talked to my mother on the phone, I listened from what I thought was an impenetrable distance, their conversation escalating into a shouting match.

"Mrs. Moses, she's *not* faking. There's something really wrong. Please, she's your *daughter*—"

When Carole hung up the phone and turned around, her face was drained of color. "You were right," she told me. "She thinks you're making this up. She kept telling me she's always been a great mother." She hesitated, not wanting to tell me the rest. I felt sorry for her, my friend; she was fighting back tears. "Your mom said you're just trying to get attention. . . . That you don't have the guts to try to kill yourself. But you wouldn't, would you?" she asked, her chin trembling. Our other friend began emptying the drawers of my dresser into a paper bag.

Students came and went with pneumonia or asthma attacks or broken limbs, but I never left the infirmary. I had a nightgown and a few changes of clothes and my toothbrush in the hospital-like room I had to myself, with various configurations of drapes on a sliding ceiling rail I could keep closed all day.

I'd never met a psychiatrist before, let alone talked to one. I wasn't sure what to do as Dr. B and I sat across from each other in my dim room, or what he was getting out of my answers to his questions, which seemed ordinary, even a little beside the point. I didn't think I'd told him anything different from what anyone else could have told him about themselves; weren't all childhoods and all families pretty much the same? And what did it have to do with the fact that I was a sham of a person? After a few days of nodding across from me, taking notes now and then, Dr. B leaned toward me and said, "Do you understand that nothing that happened in your family was your fault?" Maybe I still had trouble eating and reading after that because my body and my brain needed all the room they could spare to try to fit that untried idea inside myself.

I spent Thanksgiving in the infirmary, taking a tentative walk outside that morning with Dr. B and his two Belgian sheepdogs through a misty park in Stockton, then going back to my austere, quiet room, where the nurse on duty had brought me a plate of turkey dinner wrapped up in tinfoil. I tried, but I couldn't eat it.

The entire campus was going to close down for a month over the December holidays, and I was petrified at the idea of going back to Anchorage. In the common room I stared dumbly at Luke and Laura on the TV, knowing vaguely that other people were trying to figure out what to do with me, relieved that they were in charge, not me. Finally a decision was reached. My father would come to Stockton in early December to pick me up.

I wasn't going back to my mother's house. My father was taking me to the home of a new friend of his, Nancy—a woman he'd met while working in Southern California. He'd first introduced me to Nancy during spring break my freshman year, when he flew Billy and me to Laguna Beach for our vacation. One night we went out to dinner, and suddenly there was Nancy with her hazel-eyed toddler daughter, Goldie. Billy and I had no idea who they were or why they were sitting at our table. Or later, for the rest of our vacation, why we kept visiting Nancy and Goldie at their house to swim or have a barbecue, or why we all went to Disneyland together. A professional musician, a harpist, Nancy was droll and witty and generous, and Goldie was a quirky, funny little girl. My father seemed relaxed, as close to happy as I'd ever seen him, in their company. During my long empty days at the infirmary, I'd started to wonder if Nancy had somehow influenced my father's never-expected redress to me. Now she was offering to let me stay at her house for as long as I wanted.

When my father came to the infirmary for me, I packed the few belongings I had into a paper bag and he walked me to his car, holding the door open for me while I settled into the passenger seat.

"I got these in case you get hungry," he said when he'd buckled his seat belt, reaching toward the back seat to pull a crinkling sack of pink and white circus animal cookies out of a grocery bag.

It was a long drive to Nancy's, seven hours down Interstate 5 through California's fertile Central Valley. We didn't talk, but as my father drove I watched out the window as we passed acre after acre of harvested fields, shreds of picked cotton clinging to the fences along the highway in the whipping December air, orderly leafless orchards lined up to the horizon, man-made aqueducts carrying dark ribbons of water to places where water didn't flow, and for four hundred miles my father never let go of my hand.

Apprentice

"Back in the garb of the unwashed, eh?" he said, grinning and biting down on his pipe. "I almost didn't recognize you."

It was the professor with the bike, the one from Election Day. I'd returned to college just in time for the optional winter term, which meant that in four weeks I could make up the credit for one of the classes I'd missed during my semester in the infirmary. Registration was long past, so I took whatever class I could get. It turned out to be Arlen Hansen's.

Arlen's specialty was American fiction. He taught Mark Twain and Hawthorne and Melville, but his passion was the expatriates, the Lost Generation—the writers who responded to the brutality of World War I and a newly ambiguous world by flocking to Paris in the 1920s to reinvent art and themselves. Later that spring I would take his signature course, which wasn't only about fiction writers but also poets and painters and photographers and dancers and musicians and patrons and critics, Europeans as well as Americans: Gertrude Stein and Samuel Beckett and T. S. Eliot and Josephine Baker, Hemingway and Fitzgerald and Picasso and Copeland and Joyce and Anaïs Nin—all these ambitious, talented people who'd shrugged off the constraints of the past and come together in a place and time that was vibrant and accommodating and ripe with possibility; it was about being geniuses together—which was the title of one of the books he would later give me to read, and was also what it felt like to be Arlen Hansen's student.

Arlen liked to promote the idea of himself as an unforgiving, cynical curmudgeon, but when he stood in front of us talking about these people, his hands shoved in the pockets of his faded corduroys, his shoulders hunched in a fisherman's sweater, his pipe a prop he stared at and tamped as he walked back and forth at the front of the classroom, it was as if they were his intimates and ours, too, their pluck or foolishness or brilliance something he understood, not only their artistry but their humanity felt as deeply as if he'd been there.

My first class with Arlen focused on Hemingway's short stories, and it would culminate, he warned us, with his annual "write like Hemingway" contest instead of a final exam. I'd never thought about the possibility that a writer's style might be a conscious decision, not simply a function of the historical moment and serendipity—that writers might have an overarching philosophy or aesthetic worldview that shaped their relationship to language and how they expressed themselves.

At night in the dorm, I studied the condensed reportorial prose in Hemingway's Nick Adams stories, the terse description of the tortoise-shell cat in "Cat in the Rain," the girl fingering the beaded curtain in "Hills Like White Elephants," every word weighted and necessary. Seven-eighths of an iceberg, Hemingway had said, was below the surface; if a writer had done his job, if he was writing truly enough, it was there in the story. It would all be there, submerged but felt by the reader. Our assignment to write like Hemingway was not to set a story in Spain or during a big-game hunt, which I couldn't do anyway because I couldn't imagine it: I didn't know where the light would slant in or how the air would smell after the gun went off. To match Hemingway's tip-of-the-iceberg style, I had to write about something I knew truly enough to submerge. I thought about the story "Soldier's Home" as I described what happened when John persuaded me to leave Nancy's house after three weeks and come back to Anchorage for Christmas. Billy was in Europe, and John didn't want to be the only one at home.

I thought about Harold Krebs, Hemingway's soldier, who found that no one wanted to hear about the war when he was finally ready to talk about it, and to be listened to at all he had to lie. In Anchorage my mother had decked the halls, swags of greenery and ribbon up the staircase, a tree that reached to the cathedral ceiling. Andy Williams crooned from the stereo all day long, and our stockings were hung over the fireplace, CISSY in pink felt letters on mine. It was Christmas as always, as if everything were perfectly normal. On Christmas morning my mother gave me a doll as she had every year of my life. When I unwrapped it, it had a jointed cloth body, but its porcelain head was that of a pig.

Don't you love your mother, dear boy? Krebs's mother had asked him. *No,* he'd answered, and then he walked to the schoolyard to watch his sister play baseball.

"Isn't it cute?" my mother gushed, pleased with herself, as she watched me unwrap the pig doll.

"No," I said.

What I didn't put in my story, the seven-eighths of the iceberg under water, was what had happened that fall, and later, through the month of January in Anchorage, how I sat in my nightgown wrapped up in blankets in the bleak drafty family room downstairs. I didn't turn on the television. Sometimes I didn't even turn on the lights. When John came home from school with his friends to play Atari and eat bowls of Raisin Bran, he'd see me sitting in the dark and head back up the staircase. Somewhere in the distance my mother went about her business. I'd hear her upstairs, both of her phone lines ringing, the sound of the garage door rising as she prepared to leave for one of her appointments.

Finally John, kindhearted gentle John, lost it. "What's wrong with you?" he shouted at me, so furious his balled fists were shaking. "You were my smart, pretty sister. My friends all had crushes on you. Now I can't bring anyone here—I don't want them to see you like this. *I* don't want to see you like this! Don't you know I look up to you? You were the strongest of all of us, Billy and I always thought so. What's going to happen to me if you end up like this?"

Nothing that transpired in my family had ever surprised me more. If my brothers, after all we'd seen and done to each other, could hold such a high opinion of me, it was worth striving to live up to. I got dressed and called the airport to book my return flight to California.

At the beginning of class on the last day of the Hemingway course, Arlen returned our stories marked with our grades. I was only physically present for the rest of the class as he teased us about what we'd written, couching compliments in the sarcastic wisecracks and pungent retorts we relished. I was too mortified to enjoy Arlen's banter: At the top of my story there was no grade, only *See me during office hours* dashed off in his impatient script.

I couldn't believe how stupid I'd been, not just by writing about myself at all, but by laying myself bare. Arlen Hansen would think I was as shattered and damaged as the girl in my story, though through-out his class, in fact ever since John had yelled at me, I'd begun to feel more like the person he and Billy had imagined me to be, strong and smart and resilient.

"Easy now," Arlen said, leaning back in his chair with his feet up when I walked into his office. "This isn't about your grade. If I could give you something higher than an A, I would. Sit down." He eased his legs off the desk and unlatched the window to empty his pipe. "Eh, beat it," he muttered at the pigeons on the window ledge. "So," he said, pat-ting his shirt pockets for his tobacco. "You're serious, aren't you?"

He didn't look at me until he'd lit his pipe and tossed the spent match out the window. I knew right then that he wasn't interested in whether my story was factual. He was interested in whether, in Hem-ingway's terms, it was true.

"Yes," I said. "I want to be a writer."

"Okay. That's good," he said, small bursts of white smoke chug-ging out of his pipe as he spoke. "You're already a writer, my friend. But you're going to need all the humility you can stand and more if you're serious. Since you *are* serious, for whatever it's worth, which may not be much, considering the source—I'd like to help you."

He started to map out a plan for me. Reading was essential, and English literature was a solid foundation, but I needed to branch out. "Art history," Arlen said. "There's a new young professor, a woman, Merrill Schleier. I hear she's good. Take whatever she's offering. And talk to Sally Miller in the history department. Take some religion classes, some geology and astronomy and psychology. Look behind you on that shelf, that book with the blue spine, there—"

It was a copy of *The Autobiography of Alice B. Toklas* by Gertrude Stein.

"That's the first book we're reading in my class next semester. Go ahead, take it now and get started. Where's the other one—" He pulled out all of his desk drawers and finally found what he was looking for, *Being Geniuses Together,* a memoir of Paris in the twenties by Robert McAlmon and Kay Boyle. "You are going to love Kay Boyle," Arlen said, sliding the book across his desk to me. "She was fearless. She wanted to be a writer, and she just did it. She never waited for anyone to give her permission for anything. So here's what I want you to do:

Start with these, and every time you come across a name or a title or a work of art, look it up. Find out who's who. Read their books, look at the art, listen to the music. Take it all in."

Be, in other words, one of those people on whom nothing is lost.

"We'll meet outside of class so you can show me what you've found. Once a week, I'll meet you at the columns in front of the library. Bring whatever turns up," Arlen said. "That should get us going. I'll figure out the rest after I see how you do. We've got some time, you're what, a sophomore? But whatever you do, don't start thinking about going to a graduate writing program, the workshops. They're cutthroat. They'll eat you alive. I know, I was at Iowa. It'll ruin you. I mean, you already have what they can't teach you, and the rest of it you can get on your own. You get yourself out of here, get out into the world. Meet people, go places."

"Okay," I said. I'd been taking notes. "But tell me anyway. What's a workshop?"

Arlen raised his arms and leaned back in his creaking chair, knitting his fingers behind his head. He was smiling. "You're not so bad," he said.

I MAY HAVE FALLEN as much in love with Nell as I did with her youngest son. I first saw Peter that spring in the parking lot behind the freshman dorm, leaning into the open hatch of his Volkswagen squareback, checking his oil. There was a surfboard propped against the side of the car, a black neoprene wetsuit draped over the roof rack like a lost shadow waiting to be sewn back on. His long skinny legs ended in Birkenstocks, and when he stood up straight I saw an unruly mop of curly brown hair. He smiled and I realized I was staring.

"You'll like my mother," he told me a few days later, leading my fingers to the soft blond curls at his temples, which he said he'd gotten from her.

When Peter was in high school, his two older sisters and brother already away at college, his parents sold the house where they'd grown up across the bay from San Francisco and built a new house at the crest of a redwood-covered ridge in the Santa Cruz Mountains. The house was like a comfortable hunting lodge, with a huge stone fireplace and glass walls that overlooked the vista of mountains, cats curled asleep in armchairs on either side of a woodstove in the kitchen, and two black Labradors, "the girls," waiting at the screen door, their thick tails paddling. Peter's dad, Lee, called the hillside he'd planted with grapevines his chardonnay lawn, and below was Nell's orchard, where she grew heirloom apples and plums and berries and most of the vegetables they ate. Lee still drove the car he'd been given as a wedding present from his father-in-law twenty-five years before, and the four kids had collected a fleet of used squarebacks identical except for their sun-faded paint jobs. With the pale blue '68 Karmann Ghia my dad had found for me, a car that was like driving a mechanical robin's egg, I fit right in.

The first time Peter took me home to meet his family, we met up with his oldest sister, Molly, in downtown Santa Cruz. While Molly and her fiancé saved up for their wedding and spent weekends working on the Victorian farmhouse they were renovating in town, they were living in the bunkhouse down the hill from Nell and Lee's, where all the kids stayed when they were at home—hence its nickname, the Punk House.

"Nobody will mind if I'm there with you?" I asked Peter. I was less concerned about his siblings than what his parents thought about their eighteen-year-old son bringing his girlfriend home for a weekend. I couldn't begin to imagine a conversation about sleeping arrangements with either of my parents.

My question was so foreign to Peter's experience of his family that I'm not sure he understood. "That's why my parents built it," he said, "to house the punks. We'll sleep down there, but don't worry, we'll be up at the big house bothering Nell and Lee all day long."

We found Molly shopping at a flower stand. "What do you think of these alstroemeria?" she asked me, holding up an armful of speckled pink-and-orange blooms on long thin stems, delicately exotic.

"Astro . . . ?"

"Alstroemeria," Molly repeated. "Peruvian lilies. Or I could get tulips . . . but I think Nell will like these better, they're so tall and dramatic."

"Is it a special occasion?" I asked.

"Oh, no," Molly said lightly. "Well, you're here, but otherwise, no—Nell always has fresh flowers in the house. We better hurry and get back up the mountain, though, Nell and Lee are waiting for us."

Nell and Lee: something else that was new to me. Peter and his brother and sisters always called their parents by their first names. It didn't seem weird or distancing. It felt intimate and humanizing, an extension of how admired and loved they were by their children, their status beyond parental.

So this is what a family can be like, I thought to myself that night while I sat at the grand oval dining table at the center of the house, the vase of cascading flowers moved aside so we could see each other better as Peter and his siblings and his parents and a few friends passed platters and fought for the floor, arguing and laughing. What struck me most was the genuine pleasure they expressed in being in each other's company, their curiosity about each other hard to satisfy even after all of their years together, and how that curiosity extended to me, too.

It was impossible, though, to ignore the dinner. Peter had told me that Nell was an exceptional cook, but my experience was so limited on that front that it didn't mean much until we were standing around the kitchen sipping flutes of champagne and nibbling slices of warm Brie baked in puff pastry as Nell chopped Italian parsley to garnish our plates. My plate: It looked like something from a restaurant I wasn't old enough to patronize. Leg of lamb crusted with garlic and herbs from the garden—I'd been an avowed vegetarian for a few years, though that was a function of the tedium of a lifelong diet of hamburger. I took my first bite of roasted lamb, my first bite of crisp, buttery *pommes Anna,* my first bite of fresh steamed asparagus trickled with a creamy sauce of tarragon—asparagus, as far as I knew until then, only came from a can.

It was by far the best meal I'd ever had, and the most festive and fun, served on oversized plates glazed in assorted rich colors and eaten with lustrous old silver while Bix Beiderbecke played on the stereo in the background. Molly began to regale us with the tale of Nell meeting Hank Williams when she was young—a prized episode of family legend—and Peter and the rest of his siblings chimed in: how Nell had gone backstage after the concert, and Hank Williams had talked to her for hours. Maybe they'd even dated. Maybe even . . . At one end of the table, serene stately Nell declined to deny or affirm as the story became more and more embroidered. She sipped her wine, mysterious and regal as a sphinx, leaving the details to exuberant speculation.

I didn't know how dessert could possibly be better, but even Peter's family, who were used to this sort of thing, were wowed: Nell had baked aromatic Bosc pears with curls of lemon zest and dots of butter, then served them in a pool of warm butterscotch sauce. Everyone at the table scraped their plates clean, moaning with happiness.

The next morning, when we trooped up the terraced steps from the Punk House and slid open the glass door to the kitchen, there was a pound cake cooling on the butcher-block counter—just in case anyone needed a pick-me-up during the day, Nell said with a shrug, sitting by the woodstove with a glass of the tart orange juice Lee had squeezed, a cat and a cookbook in her lap. The shrill noise I heard was Lee grinding coffee beans. By midday I'd learned how to make real coffee and scramble eggs so they'd stay creamy—patiently, over low heat, adding nothing but salt and pepper to the whisked eggs until they were nearly set—and what pesto was, a rich herby flavor I instantly remembered having eaten when I was little at family-style Italian restaurants on the Sonoma coast during my summers at Camp Meeker, but never had a name for. Coffee beans, olive oil, fresh herbs and garlic: I was twenty years old and I'd never seen anyone use these things before.

Peter had wanted to drive me back down the mountain for a beach tour of Santa Cruz, but I couldn't tear myself away from Nell's kitchen, where a still life of freshly picked butter lettuce and long branches of rosemary, edible nasturtium blossoms and thin-skinned Meyer lemons was laid out on the counter in preparation for that night's dinner. I poked around her walk-in pantry, where she kept a freezer full of homemade chicken stock and tomato sauce, various nuts and flours and ripe persimmons from the trees in her courtyard.

"Would you mind if I just stay here and watch you cook?" I asked Nell, studying how she trussed up a whole salmon, tucking slices of lemon and rosemary sprigs inside before lacing it with kitchen twine and slathering the whole thing with olive oil. Nell was making a chocolate cake for dessert; before going to bed the evening before, she'd covered raisins in Scotch to soak overnight. Close to a full pound of chocolate for the cake was melting in a double boiler.

"Of course not," she answered. "In fact, you can help me. Peter told me you like to bake." She handed me an apron, and I became Nell's apprentice.

I suspect that some of my early lessons in her kitchen were trials for Nell, not to mention that I was the fifth wheel on her maternal car for several years, though she was too gracious to complain. Despite my overconfident pride in my baking abilities, I knew almost nothing about any but the most rudimentary equipment, procedures, and ingredients. What, you can't substitute equal measures of honey for sugar or whole wheat for cake flour? My maiden voyage with the food processor, used to mix a cheesecake—I'd seen Nell do it plenty of times—resulted in rubbery tumors of cream cheese suspended throughout the cake because I didn't bother to bring the ingredients to room temperature or blend them properly.

What I initially lacked in grace and experience I made up for in enthusiastic mimicry, which eventually, with practice and encouragement, became skill. Practice and encouragement I had in abundance. Nell and Lee were unreservedly welcoming, and like their children, there was no place in the world I would rather have been than in Santa Cruz with them. I'd tag along with a Jane Austen novel when Peter and his brother Dan got up early to surf; or we'd pile into a couple of the cars and dance at reggae concerts downtown with their sister Sue; or Nell, Molly, and I would go to movie matinees or the art openings of Molly and her friends. I'd stack firewood with Lee and join him at the sink for dishwashing duty so I could hear more tall tales about his friends, whose nicknames, like "Pear-Shape," were always as choice as the stories about them. Late on summer nights, all the kids swam in the pool in the dark to the sound of owls and plaintive coyotes. But when it was time to cook, I wanted to be in the kitchen with Nell.

I see myself standing next to her, both of us aproned, Nell tall, poised, her soft curls far blonder than those she passed on to either of her sons, her confident authority only underscored by her generosity: her good-humored self-effacement, the rueful tales of her own foibles, and the questions about my life and my dreams that she asked with such focused interest while we worked. We played Fats Waller or the Carter Family or the Grateful Dead on the stereo as we cooked for her family, people both of us loved, Nell's prickly Abyssinian cat, Nersy, who only tolerated the rest of us, weaving between her ankles.

Nell never treated me as a beginner, although that's what I was, in the kitchen and in almost every other way. "What do you think this needs?" she'd ask, or she'd deputize me to take over tasks she thought I'd enjoy or learn from. We pored over her cookbooks together, sitting in the blue armchairs by the woodstove discussing menus, planning the balance of flavors, textures, and colors. I felt I'd gained Nell's imprimatur when, on my first Christmas with the family, she gave me a copper double boiler, its rosy polished sides a mirror, its inset made of thick, sleek white porcelain—still a treat to use twenty-five years later.

When we weren't in the kitchen, Nell and I took long rambling walks with "the girls," listening to them crash around in the redwood underbrush. Or I helped with the gardening and read in the sun on the deck. Once, coming up from the Punk House, I found a dead hummingbird on one of the hillside steps, its wings flared and its ruby throat and metallic green body vividly iridescent, though a swarm of ants was trying to carry it away. I called Nell down to see, knowing she would think it as beautiful and sad and amazing as I did.

I MET ARLEN once a week at noon under the columns, bringing books and questions and my lunch: a wide slab of Nell's butterscotch layer cake, a stack of six persimmon cookies wrapped in foil.

"That's your lunch?" Arlen would ask me, his eyebrows raised behind his glasses, elbows on his knees.

"Yup," I'd answer, happy. "Aren't you eating?"

"Nah," he'd say. "But you go ahead. Knock yourself out."

It was delicious, all that I was discovering—my sense of the world building like a cathedral, stone by stone. I savored my conversations with Arlen, the hours I spent sitting on the floor between the library stacks, words piercing me; the unremitting astonishment I felt looking at a slide of *The Rokeby Venus*, knowing that a human hand had transmitted paint into flesh. The feel of a chunk of mineral on my palm, the technical terms for its properties ringing poetic in my ear: *adamantine, lithic, to cleave.* It wasn't Paris, but between my weekends at Nell's and sitting under the columns with Arlen, my life felt like a moveable feast.

"NOW, KATE, YOU ARE coming up for your birthday, aren't you?" Nell asked as she walked Peter and me out to our cars one Sunday shortly before I turned twenty-one. "You have to tell me what you'd like for dinner, but more important, what kind of cake do you want?"

What did I want? Just to be asked was almost too much. For a year Peter's family had included me in everything; now I would be part of this tradition, too, of birthday dinner and cake at the pleasure of the celebrant. I couldn't decide. As much as I loved cake, I really didn't have a favorite. I asked Nell to pick for me.

"All right," she said. "I'll bake something wonderful, just for you."

"Wait until you see what Nell's got going," Molly said, meeting me out in the courtyard as I arrived on my birthday. "But it's really a surprise, and you can't go inside yet," she said, taking me by the elbow and steering me back to my car. "Go downtown to Bookshop Santa Cruz. You'll see why when you get there."

Peter, who was now going to school in Santa Barbara, was waiting for me at the bookstore with a bouquet of heady tuberose and a biography of Virginia Woolf. He ushered me to the beach, where Sue and Dan and some of our friends were waiting for my arrival. When we got back to Nell and Lee's, our hair and clothes scented from our driftwood bonfire on the beach, more family and friends and neighbors had arrived. Lee, dapper in a forest green waistcoat, was pouring Kir Royales for everyone, and Nell had made a salad of duck confit and sour cherries, poached salmon with hollandaise, and potatoes dauphinoise for dinner. But the cake—the cake was over the top, even for Nell. Three layers and six inches high, it was light and white and spicy, studded with pecans roasted in cinnamon and nutmeg and vanilla and candied in brown sugar and butter, the tawny buttercream frosting thick with more spiced pecans. It was magnificent, that cake, utter transcendent bliss, as wonderful as Nell promised—the cake that became my lasting favorite the first time she baked it, just for me.

SPICED PECAN BIRTHDAY CAKE

∴

Nell's recipe came from Paul Prudhomme, and it was perfect. Nevertheless, over the years—I have never had a birthday since without this cake—I have gilded the lily, making modifications so that it is now even more completely outrageous.

The spiced pecans must be completely cool before adding them to the cake and the frosting. I usually roast them the night before making the cake.

FOR THE CAKE:

4 cups coarsely chopped pecans

½ cup firmly packed light brown sugar

4 tablespoons cinnamon

1 tablespoon firmly packed, freshly grated nutmeg

½ cup unsalted butter, melted

5 tablespoons vanilla, in all

3 cups unbleached all-purpose flour

2 tablespoons baking powder

½ teaspoon salt

¾ cup unsalted butter, at room temperature

2 cups granulated sugar, in all

3 large eggs, at room temperature

1 cup plus 2 tablespoons milk

•   Preheat the oven to 375° and spread the pecans evenly on a rimmed baking sheet. Roast for 10 minutes, stirring occasionally. Meanwhile, in a medium-sized bowl, combine the brown sugar, cinnamon, and nutmeg, then add the melted ½ cup of butter and mix. Add the roasted pecans to the butter mixture and mix thoroughly, then return to the pan, scraping out all the butter mixture with a spatula and mixing it in. Roast the pecans for 10 minutes more, stirring twice. Drizzle 4 tablespoons of the vanilla over the pecans, stir, and roast for 5 minutes more. Remove from the oven and set aside to cool completely.

•   To make the cake, preheat the oven to 350°. Butter and flour three 8-inch round cake pans. Sift the flour, baking powder, and salt together into a bowl.

•   In the bowl of an electric mixer, cream ¾ cup butter for 2 minutes, then add 1½ cups of the sugar and beat on medium speed until very light and fluffy, about 8 to 10 minutes, scraping down the bowl occasionally. Separate the eggs, placing the whites in a medium mixing bowl and adding the egg yolks one at a time to the creamed mixture, beating for 2 minutes after each addition and scraping the bowl often.

•   Divide the cooled pecans into two equal portions. Combine the milk with the remaining 1 tablespoon of vanilla. Add the flour mixture in three parts and the milk mixture in two parts alternately to the butter mixture, starting on low speed and increasing to high, beating until thoroughly mixed and scraping the bowl between additions. Fold in one portion of the pecans by hand (save the second portion of pecans for the frosting).

• With clean beaters in a separate bowl, beat the egg whites until frothy, about 30 seconds, then gradually add the remaining ½ cup granulated sugar and continue beating on medium-high speed until the egg whites are stiff, glossy, and hold firm peaks, about 2 to 3 minutes. Gently fold one-third of the egg white mixture into the batter with a spatula, then fold in the rest just until the mixture is combined. Divide the batter evenly among the three prepared pans, gently spreading with a spatula so it is slightly lower in the center, as the cakes will peak during baking. Bake the cakes for 20 to 30 minutes, checking after 20, until a toothpick inserted near the center comes out clean and the cake springs back when lightly touched. Let cool in the pans for 10 minutes, then turn out onto wire racks, using an additional rack to turn the cakes right side up. Cool thoroughly before glazing and frosting.

FOR THE GLAZE:

1 cup cool water
½ cup granulated sugar
1 teaspoon vanilla

• Combine the water and sugar in a small saucepan and bring to a boil over medium heat. Boil for 5 minutes, then remove from heat and stir in the vanilla. Immediately brush the glaze over the top of each cake layer with a pastry brush, a little at a time, using all the glaze.

FOR THE FROSTING:

1½ cups granulated sugar
¼ cup light corn syrup
¾ cup water
8 large egg yolks, at room temperature
½ teaspoon salt

1 pound unsalted butter

3 to 3½ cups sifted confectioners' sugar

1 tablespoon plus 1 teaspoon vanilla

2 cups spiced pecans, completely cool

• Combine the granulated sugar, corn syrup, and water in a small saucepan and bring to boil over medium heat. When it boils, clip on a candy thermometer and continue to cook, not stirring, until the sugar syrup reaches the soft-thread stage, 230°. This will take about 15 minutes.

• Meanwhile, place the egg yolks and salt in the bowl of an electric mixer and beat on high speed to combine, about 30 seconds. When the sugar syrup has reached the right temperature, remove it from the heat and, with the mixer running on low speed, begin to pour a thin stream of the syrup over the egg yolks until you have added all of the syrup, scraping out the sides of the saucepan with a heatproof spatula. Gradually increasing the mixer speed so the egg-sugar mixture won't splash, continue to beat until it is thoroughly cooled and thick, shiny, and very pale, about 10 minutes. If crystallized sugar builds up on the sides of the bowl, don't scrape it in: It will make the frosting lumpy.

• When the mixture is completely cool, lower the mixer speed to medium and gradually add the butter by the tablespoon, continuing to beat until the mixture is very smooth and thick, about 5 minutes—it will start to firm up significantly as the last quarter-pound of butter is added. Lower the speed to lowest and gradually add 3 cups of the confectioners' sugar and the vanilla, beating until the mixture is completely smooth, then add the pecans and beat on high speed until the frosting is very thick, about 3 minutes. If the frosting seems too soft to spread, add the remaining ½ cup of confectioners' sugar and/or place the bowl in the refrigerator for about 30 minutes, until firm enough to spread.

• To frost, place one cake layer on a cake plate and spread with a generous cup of frosting. Add the second layer and spread with another generous cup of frosting. Add the final layer and use the remaining frosting for the top and sides. If the frosting still seems very soft, refrigerate the cake for at least an hour as the frosting sets.

Makes one spectacular three-layer 8-inch cake.

A Gift

Louis leiter's face was as pink as a newborn piglet. He was bald and petite and crossed his hands on the seminar table when he wasn't tugging at the corners of his bow tie or tapping the tips of his fingers lightly at his temples. During class he smirked at us in a knowing, conspiratorial way from his perch on the backrest of an armchair, and he never took notes or even produced a pen, except to offer it, with gentlemanly discretion, to an unprepared student. There were brown dappled spots on the backs of his hands that matched a few more at the crown of his head. He was an elegant dresser and appeared at every class in natty wool worsted suits. I was intrigued by his remarkably miniature feet in their scuffless black wingtips, and by the way his yellow bow tie illuminated his shiny pink chin from below, like a buttercup. In all he looked rather troll-like, and cunning, as if he were about to ask us to solve a riddle in order to proceed further.

I came to Louis Leiter's classroom as much to observe him—his insinuating voice and the huge, spotless lenses of his black-rimmed spectacles, his quirky habit of tugging at his tie—as to get the credit for his course. He reminded me of something or someone else, although it didn't come to me right away. Then I recognized him: He was Peabody, the erudite little dog with the big glasses from the cartoon, who with his sidekick, a naïve kid named Sherman, traveled through time in a "way back" machine to alter the march of history. I guess that made me his Sherman.

Dr. Leiter's courses were among the most obscure electives offered at my college, often filled erroneously by students who'd mangled the registration procedure. I suspected that most of the seven people in our class were surprised to find themselves stranded in "Archetypes and Symbolism" when they thought they'd signed up for "Film Survey" or

"Intro to Communications"; most of the students at UOP looked like they belonged in "Intro to Communications."

I was one of the few who had taken the class on purpose, floored that a whole college course could be devoted to something that seemed so ineffable and subjective. But even the most random details made sense when illuminated by Dr. Leiter. His lectures were a handbook for the meaning of life's moments and disappointments. Did she drive through a swarm of bees in her boyfriend's car? That means love is dead. Twice a week I charged up the shallow steps of the old Gothic hall that housed the English department and its classes, lugging my books in a bulging bag, poised for explanations. It didn't matter that the questions in my life were not the ones being answered. What mattered was that someday, I felt sure, they could be.

Meanwhile, previously unassailable mysteries were unraveling. As the head of the department, Arlen had hired me to teach introductory literature courses as an assistant lecturer, and the more I tried to articulate what I knew for the benefit of other people, the more I understood myself. All around me the world seemed etched in high relief, like the fine lines in a Dürer print. I seemed to notice everything, the doors of my perception flung wide open: how the desks in the lecture hall were perpetually flocked with a dark velvet layer of peat dust, which blew in from the agricultural fields beyond the campus; that the air in my unambitious college town smelled faintly of pencil shavings; how I could tell time in the late afternoons not by looking at the clock but by listening to the ratcheting and shush of bicycles as professors rode by my house after their last classes. This must be how Galileo felt, I remember thinking, when he looked up at the night sky pulsing with stars and imagined a pattern to the ticking of the planets.

MY HOME THAT YEAR, my senior year, was a run-down stucco bungalow just off campus. Because of its proximity to the school, the owner had resigned himself to renting cheaply to students and left the house in blatant disrepair. Neither the exterior nor the interior of the house had been painted in years, and in my bedroom a previous occupant had pushed his or her bed into a corner, right against the walls, so that the dirty shadow of a sleeping body, rubbed over many nights into the faded paint, lived like a ghost in the room with me.

Despite what a dump the house was by any objective judgment, it was the first home I'd made for myself, the one I'd longed for when I was eleven, and I felt tender toward its details. There was hand-notched wainscoting in every room, and narrow five-panel wooden doors with elaborate, skeleton-keyed doorplates and porcelain door-knobs. I even found one of the original door keys in the back of a kitchen drawer, covered with breadcrumbs and lint. There was a tiled fireplace that worked, and my bedroom had a bay window with a seat, where I folded up a quilt and read on foggy afternoons with a pillow behind my head. When it was sunny, I sat in my yard under the green light of a lemon tree, surrounded on all sides by ivy and climbing trumpet vines, and watched the stooped campus gardener drive his tractor over the quad across the street and stab tumbling sheets of paper with a pointy stick.

What little furniture I had I'd gotten from salvage places or Camp Meeker, which had also been a salvage job. The previous summer Peter and I had made a weekend excursion to Camp Meeker and found the cottage a ruin. No one had stayed there or maintained it in years, and the house on its stilts had all but washed down the eroding hillside after many hard winters, the porch roof sagging under the weight of pine needles and dead leaves. The front door—lock-picked, battered—was creaking open when we arrived. Someone was in the process of emptying the rooms. All the carefully packed barrels of my family's stored belongings, everything my parents left behind when we moved from California, had been hauled away. The woodstove was gone. The heavy oak chairs where the grown-ups sat during their poker games were staggered around, salvageable though coming unglued from years of damp, but the matching table had disintegrated completely, nothing but a heap of moldy pieces on the floor. What I couldn't believe was that my grandmother's dishes—her mother's "Denmark Blue" dishes, with their delicate indigo filigree pattern—were still on the shelves in the kitchen, and so was the tall enamel measuring cup we'd used for our berry picking. There was no way to secure the house. Peter and I loaded everything we could fit into his squareback and drove it to Santa Cruz for safekeeping.

My grandmother had finally been moved into a convalescent home. When I visited, the nurses walked her to me in the common room, supporting her as she took her trembling, tentative steps. "Look who's come to see you, Marie," they'd say. My grandmother would smile, peering at me through her smeary eyeglasses, and announce, "My sister . . ." Except that my grandmother had never had a sister.

I didn't overtly dissuade her, but I tried to coax her toward me, telling her about myself and about my brothers. Away from our parents, we'd discovered that we actually liked each other, and I was proud of their accomplishments. Billy was now in South Africa on an academic fellowship, in his spare time teaching black children from the townships to swim; John was an honor student and a member of a traveling men's choir in his second year at Cornell. After my visit to Camp Meeker, I reminded my grandmother of her mother's dishes.

"Do you remember the eggcups?" I prompted her. "The covered cheese plate with the ventilation holes in the top?" I told her I'd rescued all of it, the whole set with all of its precise utilitarian pieces.

"You've always loved those dishes, ever since you were a little girl," my grandmother said. I didn't know if she was talking to me or her imaginary sister. "You should keep it," she urged. "Keep all of it and use it. That's what it's for."

"It's Cissy, Grandma," I said gently. "You really want me to keep it all?"

"I know who you are," she said sweetly, blinking behind her glasses.

THE DISHES, THE RICKETY CHAIRS, the paint-peeling wooden dresser with tassellated drawer pulls that my mother had slept in as an infant: I moved it all into my little house in Stockton. Graduating friends had willed me a mattress and a kitchen table, and at Goodwill I found bookcases and a tufted sofa, threadbare but with a few miles left on its dainty turned legs. Except for the dishes none of it was nice, but it was serviceable, and what really mattered to me was that all of it— the ramshackle house, its timeworn furnishings, and my life there— was mine. My father had married Nancy, and though I was always welcome when I visited, their house was not my home. I visited my mother only at Christmas, sometimes not even then, and I still rarely heard from her during the school year. I knew that my little bungalow was an eyesore, but it felt like a refuge to me, its stained walls lined with books, with a tattered screen door and a typewriter and a big window to look out of.

The Central Valley's late autumn rains had come, and through the misted afternoons and evenings I moved with my books from sofa to window seat to kitchen table, relishing the company of words, hearing nothing but the stippling of rain on leaves through the windows I left intentionally open to the clean washed air. I'd begun reading *To the Lighthouse* for Dr. Leiter's class, and I sat in my kitchen cross-referencing the novel against the Woolf biography that Peter had given me, seeing through the character of Mrs. Ramsay the author's yearning for the mother she lost as a girl, the book an elegy to memory and childhood and a summer home lost as well; and in Lily Briscoe I recognized a reflection of Woolf herself, the self-doubting young artist, as yet unsure of her vision. I'd begun to get carried out on the current washing back and forth between stories and lives, facts and fictions, when I heard my phone ringing in the front room.

"Hello?" I said into the receiver, a little irritated to have the siren song of my inner world interrupted.

"Cis?" my mother answered. "Honey, it's Mom. You sound wonderful! It's so good to hear your voice!"

"OH, NO!" MY MOTHER cried out three days later from the bedroom of my shabby bungalow. I knew that sound: It was the cry you make when you wake up and instantly know that your life is truly as ruined as you feared when you fell asleep.

The day after her phone call, my mother was on her way to Stockton. For a few hours I'd actually entertained the notion that she was coming to see me, but when she pulled up in her rented car it became abundantly clear that I was any port in a storm. I'd been feeding her and sitting up all night with her ever since, and I'd skipped some of my classes to babysit her. It was now the middle of the afternoon and she was still in bed, so I'd taken the opportunity to try to catch up on some of my reading assignments.

At my mother's yelp I left *To the Lighthouse* facedown on the sofa. I was back on duty. "Mom," I called at my closed bedroom door, knocking softly. "Can I come in?"

She was moaning on the bed, holding her arms rigidly at her sides. She seemed to have been flung deep into my mattress by a mighty force. "Why?" she asked. "Why has he done this to me?"

Oh God, she is freakish, I thought, newly aghast. Her mascara had crept into the crease of her eyelids, leaving thick black Egyptian smudges under her eyebrows. She wore her current favorite jewelry, a handful of gold chains, twenty-four hours a day, including to bed. Each tiny gold link had stuck and left a dent in her clammy skin while she slept, so she was covered with what looked like miniature tire tracks. The Lilliputians had tied her down, but she was too strong for them— some of the chains were burst and hung, hopelessly tangled, around her neck. Only her floridly enameled nails were perfect.

I sat down next to her. I had met Jim Thompson, my mother's fiancé, a few times at her house in the last couple of years, and I hadn't liked him. He seemed unctuous, arrogant, and untruthful. Since my mother had abdicated all but the shallowest semblance of parenthood years before, it was not my business to pass judgment on her boyfriends. It would have been unkind, at this traumatic juncture, to point out that Jim Thompson's betrayal came as a surprise to no one but her.

"Can I get you something?" I asked. "Would you like some tea? It might make you feel better, something warm."

Her face went wild. She was mashing at her wet eyes with one fist and feeling around on the floor for her glasses with the other hand. I picked up the glasses and handed them to her. She looked forlorn, like a neglected child, behind her glasses. Her mouth peeled back into a grimace.

"Oh, I can't stand it, Cis. This is so terrible! That silver-tongued devil!"

"I know, Mom. It really is terrible. But maybe if you take a shower while I fix you something to eat, at least you'll feel a little better."

Over forty-eight tearful hours I had pieced together what had happened from my mother's fractured narrative. She had married Jim Thompson, or was about to—this I could never get straight—when he went on some trip, a reunion of some sort. He'd acted strangely in the months following, taking many short "business trips" using my mother's charge cards. Her phone bills had become extreme, or maybe there were lots of calls to the same unfamiliar number. Somehow she had decided to call a number in California listed numerous times on her bill and heard a woman's voice. On a hunch, my mother asked for Jim Thompson.

"Jim's not home right now," the woman replied. "This is Mrs. Thompson. Can I help you?" My mother hung up the phone.

Jim and the newest Mrs. Thompson were holed up at that moment in a hotel in San Francisco, attending some kind of conference, according to my mom. Maybe a lying bigamists' conference? I wondered. Jim was driving my mother's car and spending money from her bank accounts.

"You have to be my spy, Cis," my mother begged. "He'll never recognize you," she told me in a tone that implied that she thought this was somehow a good thing. I didn't think it would help to tell her what I was now sure she didn't know: that Jim had called me a few weeks before from San Francisco, saying he was doing some business for my mother and she had asked him to take me out to dinner. I'd met him at the bar at John's Grill, where he gassed on and on about *The Maltese Falcon*. His hand, at first patting my shoulder in a fatherly way, had migrated lower and lower on my spine. I left before our steaks arrived, making the excuse that I had a class to teach in the morning, and wolfed a burrito over the steering wheel of my car somewhere around Livermore. Now my mother was sitting on my sofa, pulling papers out of her purse and weeping. She was looking for cigarettes and the name of the hotel where Jim Thompson and his most recent wife were staying. She'd been wearing my bathrobe for two days.

"Mom, I really don't think it's a good idea to approach him this way," I said, holding out a steaming plate of scrambled eggs and a slice of linzer torte, last night's dessert that I'd warmed in the oven. My mother didn't look up, but pulled a wad of ragged tissue out of my bathrobe pocket and wiped her nose. "I think you need to see a lawyer," I said.

"A lawyer!" she cried. "I can't see a lawyer! Then he'll stay with *her*!" She looked up and stared at the plate. I handed her a fork and sat down on the sofa, holding the plate for her.

"No, what he needs is a good scare," she mumbled, eating the eggs. "He needs to know I won't put up with these kinds of shenanigans."

"Mom," I said, keeping my voice level and speaking slowly. "Mom, he's a loser. He's a jerk. He's married to two women. It's illegal. You have protection."

"Well," she said, beginning to cry again and tugging on the front of my robe, "well, I don't know."

"What do you mean, you don't know, Mom?" I said, trying to keep the exasperation out of my voice. "You mean you don't know that bigamy is illegal? You understand that, right?"

She paused to chew or stall me, or both. "Wow, Cis, these are good eggs. I really taught you how to cook, didn't I? Do you have any apple butter?" She could tell from the look on my face that I didn't. "That's okay. I'll have this linzer torte. It's *so* good. Where'd you say you got the recipe from—Alice . . . ?"

"Alice B. Toklas. You know, *The Autobiography of Alice B. Toklas*? Gertrude Stein? 'A rose is a rose is a rose'? It's the oldest cake recipe on record, but I got this one from her cookbook."

"Oh. I thought you meant the movie about the waitress, *Alice Doesn't Live Here Anymore*. Or maybe I was thinking of 'Alice's Restaurant.' "

"Mom. Just tell me this: Do you have your marriage certificate, anything like that, something you can take to a lawyer?"

She didn't answer.

"Mom?"

She turned away and started to stuff the papers back into her bag. "I don't want to talk about it," she said.

"What do you mean? Did you marry this guy or not?"

"I'm not going to talk about this," she said, rising from the sofa and slipping her purse over her arm. "Why are you being mean to me?" she mumbled. "We're supposed to stick together—"

"Oh great," I said.

"This can't be happening to me," she muttered to herself as she stumbled down the hall back to my bedroom, where I found her lying on top of the blankets, staring at the ceiling.

"Really, Cis, if you would just do me this one very simple favor," she droned, eyes on the ceiling. All the air had gone out of her voice. "I need your help, Cis. If you would just go to the hotel. You don't have to talk to him. All you have to do is take my car key and steal my car back—"

"Mom, I can't steal your car—"

"—and then, very quietly, leave him a mark of Zorro. Something that will tell him, look here, you silver-tongued devil, you can't do that to me."

"What do you mean, a mark of Zorro?" I asked cautiously.

"Oh . . . I don't know. I'll have to come up with something."

I studied my mother, prone on my mattress on the rugless floor. She looked and smelled frightful. She'd put on lipstick when she got out of bed, God only knows why, but it was smeared all over from blowing her nose. She couldn't get through a day, even while having a mental breakdown, without her protective cloud of perfume. Her fine dark hair was flying in every direction, as if it, too, were desperate to get as far away as possible.

"Oh, I must look awful," she moaned, noticing me watching her.

"Nobody looks good when they're upset, Mom," I said.

She sighed. "You've always taken such good care of me, Cis. What would I do without you?"

I didn't say anything.

"You know, though," she said, perking up a little, "I really like this new short haircut you have. I think I like it almost as much as your long hair."

"I haven't had long hair for years, Mom," I said.

She looked shocked. "No!" she said. "Are you sure?"

"Yes," I said. "I haven't had long hair since tenth grade."

"No!" she said. "I'm sure you had long hair last summer."

"No, I didn't," I said. "I cut it years ago. And I didn't come home last summer."

She stared at me, her mouth dropped open in awe. "Well, that's simply amazing. I could have sworn you had long hair. Long, honey-colored hair. It was *so* beautiful."

"No," I said.

"Well, I just don't know," she said. "If you say so. I guess I must be thinking of someone else."

"I guess so."

"Hmm," she said. "Oh well." There was a pause. "You know, I almost forgot. I brought you a present," she said.

"You did?" I replied, not sure I wanted to know what it was.

She reached over the side of the bed. "It's in my purse . . . now let's see," she said, digging around through all of her junk—huge aerosol can of hairspray, scraps of paper, keys, pocketbook, cigarette lighters, bottle of Moon Drops, contact case. She went through everything, then went through it all again. Then she unzipped all the pockets. Finally she pulled out a little felt bag and turned it over in her fingers, a raccoon with a shiny bottlecap.

"Do you remember when I used to let you peek in my jewelry box when you were a little girl? Do you remember something special that I told you Grandma Moses gave me as a wedding present?" She upended the felt bag into her palm. Out fell a bauble smaller than a thumbprint. "Do you remember this?" she asked me.

I looked. It was a locket shaped like a wicker basket. On the top was an enameled scene. I knew what it was. I knew what was inside.

"It's Moses in the bulrushes," she said. "See the cloisonné? There he is, floating down the Nile in a basket. And do you remember what happens when you open it up?"

"Oh, yes," I said. It was enchanting: When she opened the clasp, the locket was lined with blue velvet. Resting there was a tiny gold baby Jesus the size of an ant. I'd been fascinated by it when I was little. She'd let me hold the tiny baby in my hand so I could examine his arms and face and his etched-on swaddling.

"Oh, look," I said. "There he is again."

"I always knew that someday I would give him to my little girl, just like my doll collection," my mother said. We both looked at the gold baby nestled in his blue bed. "Do you remember the story?" she asked.

"Sure I do," I said, not taking my eyes off the baby.

"His mother had to abandon him to save him," she said. "She sent him down the river in a basket. But he survived, and he became great."

I couldn't look at my mother. I could tell from the little clicks I heard that she'd started trying to untangle her chains. Then the bed shook.

"I've got it, Cis! The mark of Zorro!"

"What?" I said, looking up at her finally, blinking hard.

"Jim knows all about my Moses!"

"What?" I said again.

"Here's what you do. Just go to the hotel desk and find out what room he's in. Act nonchalant. Tell them you're Jim's daughter, that's right. Then when you find the room, take this lipstick"—she produced a lipstick from her bag—"and write 'bulrushes' on the door. Or 'Herod.' Just make sure no one's in the hallway."

"Oh, Mom," I groaned.

"It'll be perfect," she mumbled, drifting off into some satisfyingly retaliatory vision in her head. "He'll open the door and his little plan will all come to an end."

I didn't say anything. She was snapping the clasp on the little gold locket and poking it back into the felt bag.

"Oh, Cis, I'm so glad I can count on you," she said, shaking her head and dropping the felt bag back into her purse. "I'll just keep the little baby safe for you, for some time when your life is more settled." She zipped her purse closed and set it on the floor, then lay back on the bed again. "This is all so awful, Cis. I don't know why this is happening to me." She shut her eyes.

"I don't know, Mom," I said. "There must be some reason for all of this." *You are completely selfish,* my unforgiving twenty-one-year-old self thought, *and this is your punishment for not taking care of us.*

"I guess so," she said. After a pause, she opened her eyes and looked at me. "We're still good friends, aren't we, Cis," she said. "You'll always be my best friend."

"Sure, Mom," I answered.

LINZER TORTE

.·.

1 ¼ cups finely ground almonds or almond meal

2 ¼ cups unbleached all-purpose flour

1 teaspoon baking powder

½ teaspoon salt

2 teaspoons cinnamon

1 teaspoon ground cloves

1 teaspoon unsweetened cocoa powder

Zest of 1 orange

Zest of 1 lemon

1 cup granulated sugar

1 cup unsalted butter, at room temperature

2 egg yolks, at room temperature

1 teaspoon vanilla

1 ½ cups raspberry jam

- Whisk the ground almonds, flour, baking powder, salt, cinnamon, cloves, and cocoa in a bowl and set aside. In a small bowl, rub the orange and lemon zests into the sugar until the mixture is uniform.

- In the bowl of an electric mixer, beat the butter on medium speed for a couple of minutes. Add the sugar and beat for 3 to 5 minutes, until very light in color and creamy. Add the egg yolks, beating for a couple of minutes, until very light and fluffy. Add the vanilla and mix until well blended. Add the flour mixture and "pulse" the mixer cautiously on low speed a few times to keep the flour mixture from flying out of the bowl at first, then mix on low speed just until the flour disappears. Divide the dough into two portions, wrap in waxed paper or plastic wrap, and chill until firm, several hours or up to 2 days.

When ready to assemble and bake the torte, preheat the oven to 350°. On a generously floured work surface, knead one portion of dough just until pliable, then roll into a circle large enough to cover the bottom and sides of an 8- or 9-inch tart pan with a removable bottom; the dough should be about ⅜ inch thick. Fit the pastry into the tart pan, patching as needed so that the bottom has no cracks and the sides are a uniform thickness. Roll the rolling pin over the top edges of the pan to cut off any excess dough; save any excess to add to the second portion of dough. Chill the filled pan while you roll the dough for the lattice top.

- Briefly knead and roll the second portion of dough to the same thickness and diameter as the first. Using a ruler and a knife or pastry wheel, cut strips about ½ inch wide. Fill the chilled bottom crust with the raspberry preserves, smoothing the surface. To make the lattice, over the raspberry-filled bottom crust lay strips parallel to each other about ½ inch apart and overhanging the edges of the pan. Lay a second layer of strips either crosswise to the first layer or at a 45-degree angle, again ½ inch apart and overhanging the edges of the pan. To tidy the edges and seal the lattice to the bottom crust, use the pad of your thumb or finger to press each lattice strip end to the bottom crust, cutting off the overhanging dough.

- Leftover dough can be gathered and rerolled, then either used to make a second small torte with additional raspberry jam filling, or cut out with round or heart-shaped cookie cutters and sandwiched together with jam between. See instructions below.

• Bake the torte for 35 to 45 minutes, until the crust is browned and the filling is bubbly. Allow the torte to cool completely in its pan on a wire rack, then slip off the exterior of the tart pan before serving.

Makes one 8- or 9-inch torte and possibly more.

TO MAKE LINZER COOKIES OR TARTLETS:

• Prepare the dough as for the torte. For cookies, cut the rolled dough with cookie cutters: Every cookie will need a bottom and a top of the same size with a center cutout—two graduated circles, fluted circles, or a heart with a smaller heart or circle as the center cutout. Lay the cookie bottoms on baking sheets. Spoon raspberry jam onto the bottom, leaving a border of ½ inch all around, then top each with a cookie with a center cutout. Gently press the edges of the two cookies together to seal. Bake for 15 to 25 minutes, until the cookies are lightly browned and the filling at the center is bubbly. Allow to cool for 5 to 10 minutes on the baking sheet, then remove to a wire rack to cool completely. If desired, the cookies can be dusted with confectioners' sugar before serving.

• For tartlets, use individual miniature tart pans and cut the rolled dough just slightly larger than the pan indentations. Press the cut dough into the tartlet pans, fill with a spoonful of raspberry jam, then top with a lattice of a single cross of dough strips, trimming the rough edges of the lattice strips. Bake for 15 to 25 minutes, until the tartlets are lightly browned and the filling is bubbly. Allow to cool for about 10 to 15 minutes in the pans before gently turning the tartlets out and cooling completely on wire racks. If desired, dust with confectioners' sugar.

Make Believe

JULY, 1984. THAT SUMMER MORNING TWO MONTHS PAST MY COLLEGE GRADU-
ation, when I was on my knees in my frilly pink Anchorage bedroom
zipping up my suitcase to leave, it was hard to say who was crazier: my
mother, who less than a day after my arrival was kicking me out of her
house for cleaning her refrigerator, or me, for coming back at all.

I could hear my mom stamping around upstairs, raving about me to
Jim Thompson, her loathsome but evidently unvanquished bigamist.
Jim had been at our house in the middle of the night also, party to my
mother's sudden demand that I leave first thing in the morning. The
two of them had then marched to the bottom of our driveway to reclaim all the rotten food I'd thrown away, Jim holding a flashlight over
the heaps of garbage in the purpled near dark of Alaska at three a.m.

I stood and gazed around my room, unchanged after four years, the
top of the canopy sagging with dust. Dozens of dog books still lined the
shelves. China animal knickknacks filled a glass case on the dresser, next
to the stack of tiny notebooks I'd hoarded to safeguard my poems and
stories, all girlish innocence. My doll collection stared vacantly from the
hutch. Had I ever been innocent, or allowed to be? My twenty-two-
year-old face, haggard with too little sleep but awash in shocked clarity,
stared back at me from the mirror. This was it, I was done. As surely as
I'd ever known anything, I knew I would never come back. I would
never leave myself open to my mother again.

ON THE DAY of my graduation, I'd been launched into postcollegiate
adulthood with an honors degree, a brand-new Cuisinart from Nell,
my own copy of *Being Geniuses Together* from Arlen, and a sizable
check toward my first trip to Europe, an unexpected gift from my fa-

ther. The morning after the ceremony, I packed up my funky Stockton bungalow, loaded my grandmother's dishes into the Karmann Ghia, and followed Peter in a rented U-Haul truck to Santa Cruz.

There was absolutely no reason for me not to buy myself a plane ticket and go—go places, meet people, get out into the world, just as Arlen had told me to do—except for the sudden petrifying realization that I was wholly responsible for myself. Generous as my dad had been with his gift of cash, he was too hardwired for anxiety and pessimism to let me spend it without offloading his own bleak fears for my future as a bon voyage.

"And just how are you going to support yourself when you get back and you're broke?" he wanted to know, cross-examining me over the phone as I mooched temporarily off the largesse of Nell and Lee, all the Camp Meeker furniture bivouacked under plastic tarps outside the Punk House, their attic walls banked with my boxes of books, the Cuisinart pristine in its unopened carton. "Nobody gets paid for wanting to be a writer. What are you going to do about getting a job? Where are you going to live? How are you going to pay the rent?"

My brothers and I had all worked since high school. We financed our college educations with student loans. I never expected to be anything but self-supporting, and yet I honestly didn't know what I was going to do. I'd had no doubt that Arlen was right—I didn't have the stomach for a competitive graduate writing program, and I hadn't applied. I realized too late that I hadn't asked him the most obvious question: How do writers pay their rent? Paralyzed by how simpleminded, even magical, my plan for my life now seemed, I couldn't possibly squander my only asset—maybe the last ballast I'd ever receive from one of my parents—on wandering through Europe. I deposited my trip money in a savings account so that I could eke it out slowly to cover my living expenses while I looked for a secretarial position. The banality of my comeuppance might have plunged me into despair over my forfeited fantasy of a writer's life if not for the tiny kernel of relief I felt but wasn't ready to admit: If you risk nothing, there's scant room for failure.

Enter my mother, whom I had not seen and had only nominally communicated with since her mascara-stained breakdown at my house the previous autumn. That Christmas, when for the second year in a row I elected to stay in Santa Cruz, I wasn't surprised by the arrival of an enormous package from Anchorage that, I knew, would contain some kind of bizarre and totally undesirable present. My mother was notorious for indemnifying the meagerness of her maternal attention year-round by burdening my brothers and me with ever more random gifts on Christmas. She never asked us what we might want, she just piled on the indiscriminate flotsam, as if volume alone could make up for the promiscuity of her selections.

This time it was a fully furnished plastic dollhouse. I wanted to kick myself later for not opening the grandiose box in private, rather than under the tree on Christmas morning with Peter's family. It was painful enough to see that my mother still clung to the idea that I was her eight-year-old protégé, the willing lieutenant of her boundariless narcissism, charged with protecting her from the truth of how badly she'd failed me as a mother. It was worse to have anyone else witness her complete lack of interest in knowing who I had become.

Underscoring her indifference to any part of my life that didn't include her, my mother had not attended my graduation. She wasn't there to see me stride across the stage beside the marble columns to accept my diploma, or to hear my professors single me out for recognition; to witness Arlen, who received the university's highest award for distinguished teaching that year, calling out a mock warning to me in the crowd of polyester-gowned graduates: "You'll get yours, Moses!" My mother wasn't at my house for the party afterward, in preparation for which I'd baked for two days, my friends and professors and former students packed elbow to elbow into the little bungalow with my dad and Nancy and Goldie and Peter and his family, drinking champagne and chowing down on the dozens of cookies and cakes and tarts I'd made, their buoyant, celebratory conversations spilling out onto the sidewalk, their glasses raised to toast me and tease me and confirm their confidence in my promise.

But two months later, while I huddled in my squatter's encampment at the Punk House in Santa Cruz, forlornly scrutinizing the want ads, my mother was inexplicably on the phone urging me to come back to Anchorage.

"Come home!" she cajoled. "I miss you!"

It was surreal: as if my mother had no memory of the breaches of trust that had wrenched us apart. As if she—no, both of us—had been caught in a suspension of time and history for four—no, ten, a dozen, more—years, and I was still the little girl who skipped school in Pennsylvania to learn to waltz with her across the front room. She didn't sound like the frantic delusional mess she'd been when I last saw her. She sounded like the mother I'd idolized in another life: whimsical and fun, excited and joyful and bursting with plans for us.

"Come home, and we'll paint in the studio!" she promised. "We'll watch old movies on TV! We'll go out to lunch! It'll finally be *just us!*"

Just us. Skeptical, but not immune to her seduction and her now frequent calls, I pondered my mother's invitation while my self-doubt mounted. I racked up rejections for entry-level clerical positions all over the Bay Area, and worse, no response at all from a desperation round of blind applications and resumé-broadcasting that didn't net me so much as an interview for a minimum-wage job *selling* books. When I couldn't even land a job to once again peddle tacky clothing to teenage girls, spending a few weeks watching movies with my mom started to sound increasingly attractive.

I didn't need a mother anymore, I reassured myself—I was no longer the child who yearned for my mom to take care of me and not the other way around. *Wanting* a mother, my mother, was a different matter. That was the longing I'd never gotten over. But now that I was grown up and I didn't need anything from her that she wasn't able to give, I told myself, maybe my mother and I might have a chance for the real friendship she'd always claimed we had. If she could pretend that nothing ugly had ever happened between us, maybe I could, too.

IT WAS TWO O'CLOCK in the afternoon when I landed at the Anchorage airport, searching the eager faces at the arrival gate for my mother's. She wasn't there. I waited as the passengers on the next flight checked in and hovered around and finally boarded their plane. When my mother didn't show up, I headed downstairs to the baggage claim. After collecting my suitcase and standing outside for a while, expecting to see our station wagon come careening up the ramped drive and shudder to a stop in front of me, my mother burbling her usual emphatic apologies for being late but thrilled nonetheless to see me, I shuffled my suitcase back inside to call home from the bank of pay phones located in the shadow of a stuffed grizzly bear, seven feet tall on its back legs, its snout taxidermied into a vicious, yellow-fanged snarl and its hairy clawed forearms raised in flesh-shredding menace, harmless behind a wall of glass. The phone rang and rang but no one picked up.

So she was on her way. I waited outside for another half hour, an hour, resisting the knee-jerk reflex of feeling set up, left to fend for myself yet again, and the anger that was starting to burn in my chest. It was just like all the times I'd been sent home from school because of my chronic stomachaches: After the nurse called my house, I'd sit on the cot, bent over and hugging my gut, waiting for my mother to pick me up. When the station wagon finally squealed to a halt in front of the school, spraying gravel all over the sidewalk, my mother would burst into the building as if she'd rushed to get there in a panic of worry over me, though her flawlessly fresh makeup and her hair bouncing on her shoulders in perfect curls were dead giveaways that she'd taken a couple of hours to dress before she got in the car. She'd always rolled her eyes at the argument from my brothers and me that her chronic tardiness was infuriating and rude, since she thought it was one of her charms—there was that story of my birth that she loved to tell me, when she insisted that the labor nurse bring her a mirror so she could put on lipstick before she pushed me out. Once when I was in junior high, she didn't arrive to take me home until after school was over for the day, the buses and teachers all long gone, and the janitor had to ask me to sit outside at the flagpole to wait for her, humiliated, while he locked the building.

Remember, you're an adult, I told myself. *You don't need her to take care of you.* I lugged my suitcase inside to the pay phones once more. My dad now lived in Southern California with Nancy and Goldie, but he still traveled constantly for his work and he was often back in Anchorage, where he'd held on to his condominium. I was in luck—he was leaving the next day on a business trip, but he was in town, and he could pick me up right away. When he pulled up at the baggage claim, he told me he would lend me our ancient Volkswagen to drive while I was home, and we swung by the condo so that I could drop him off on the way to my mom's.

My mother's house came into view as I crested our hill, revving the Beetle's sputtering engine to make it to the bottom of the steep driveway. I parked alongside the embankment where my mother's strawberries were overrun by volunteer fireweed and dandelions gone to seed, a few valiant shriveled berries poking up red here and there under their leaves, refusing to give up entirely though they'd been forgotten for years.

Before I turned my key in the front door, the dogs were already barking on the other side, and I was picturing my mother in her bathroom upstairs in a cloud of hairspray and perfume, desperately slapping on makeup, ripping electric curlers out of her hair, late as usual but hurrying through her extensive toilette to come and collect me. I imagined her feeling guilty for keeping me waiting, which made me feel a bit less irritated, even a tiny bit sympathetic.

My mother, however, was not in the bathroom finishing her makeup, or hunting through kitchen drawers to find her house keys. Other than the barking dogs, the house was still.

"Mom?" I called, but there was no answer.

I left my suitcase in the entry and picked my way up the stairs, almost completely blocked by paper-stuffed grocery bags lining every step, their contents spilling over into sliding piles on the landing. My mother's bedroom door was closed and locked. I tried the studio door, which moved a few inches before whatever was jammed inside prevented it from opening further. I wedged my face to the edge of the door and saw that the whole room was buried in junk—real estate signs on the floor, the exercise bike squatting in the middle of the room, mounds of clothes thrown over the sofa bed arms.

There was only one lock in our house that couldn't be picked with a straightened bobby pin, and that was the deadbolt my mom had installed on her bedroom door. She hadn't turned it, though, and I poked a bobby pin into the doorknob and eased the door open. The curtains were drawn, and my mother was out cold on her back. She had a satin mask pulled over her eyes and her arms splayed out at her sides, each newly polished finger spread apart to dry, flexed like a hand model's even in sleep. There was a shoebox full of fake Lee nails and nail enamel beside her, cuticle pushers and emery boards sprinkled across the red velveteen coverlet; a flight of dreg-stained wineglasses on the bedside table; a couple of silver ashtrays overflowing with cigarette butts. Both of her phones were off the hook. Clothes and multiple pairs of knee-high black leather boots lay scattered over the carpet. She was still wearing the Lilliputian gold necklaces in a tangled mess at her throat. With the ostentatious wrought-iron lamp hanging by a chain from the ceiling next to the bed, the red bedspread, the red fingernails, the red telephones, the red velvet curtains, the overpowering scent of perfume and smoke, everything multiplied in the mirrored closet doors, she looked laid out in the dim room like a pharaoh's daughter surrounded by grave goods for the afterlife, or maybe a dead madame from a Wild West bordello.

"Mom, it's me. I'm home," I whispered.

She fought her way up from utter collapse, moving nothing but her lips. "What time is it?" she muttered.

It was about four. She mumbled something about being up *really* late the night before working on some *really big deal,* and fell back asleep.

I closed her door and surveyed the house. My mother had been living alone for two years, since John left for college. She'd always been a pack rat and none of us had been particularly tidy except under duress, but now the house looked like it had been ransacked by secret police. The grocery bags blocking the stairs were bursting with unopened mail, and there were more bags and containers sandbagged along the upstairs walls, some filled with ice cube trays or desultory office supplies, out-of-favor shoes corraled in laundry baskets, cases of Tab stacked on top of my dad's dictionary stand, shopping bags stuffed with dozens of new pairs of nylons or Coach leather purses with the tags still on. She had blazed a narrow trail through the squalid heaps from her bedroom to the bathroom and through the living room to the kitchen. There were months' if not years' worth of newspaper towers propping each other up in front of the fireplace. The top of the piano was covered with Christmas ornaments. My mother's bathroom counter was so crowded with hair-curling apparatus and perfume bottles that I had to ratchet my elbows up above all the precarious stuff to keep from knocking everything into the sink when I washed my hands. Downstairs, the bedrooms looked like in situ museum displays, preserved untouched beneath thick coats of dust, but the family room appeared to be a holding area for more real estate signage, and a Vesuvian eruption of unfolded laundry had flowed off the couch and spread over the shag carpet. The dogs had been nesting on it.

The poor dogs. My little Maltese, Barry, had probably not been brushed since the last time I was home, two years before. His whole body was felted in a continuous mat of filthy fur; I could see immediately there was no solution but to have him shaved down to the skin.

His face was so matted that he couldn't see, and when I found a pair of scissors to cut away the fur over his eyes I was horrified—both eyes were ulcerated and ghastly. Thor, now an eighteen-year-old arthritic rattle bag who could barely make it up the stairs, seemed to be blind as well, his eyes filmy with cataracts. What few teeth they had left were mushy in their bleeding gums, and Barry's lower jaw had been broken at some point and healed askew. Their nails were so overgrown they'd curled up into their footpads. There was no evidence of dog food anywhere, not even a water bowl.

Scrambled eggs, I thought, opening the refrigerator to make some emergency food for the wretched toothless dogs. I saw with relief that the refrigerator was staggeringly full, although it took a moment to register, as I dug for the egg carton, that it was like one of those seventeenth-century Dutch still lifes of a table opulent with gloriously ripe fruit and vegetables, which on closer examination you realize are oozing rot and maggots. I cracked the first egg into a bowl. Nothing came out. The inside of the shell was dry and empty. I tried a second egg. It, too, had evaporated inside the shell. I looked at the date on the carton: September. But was that September last year or the year before? I wondered, finding the rock-hard packets of sugar cookie dough wrapped in waxed paper that I'd made on my last visit.

All the produce in the bins had deliquesced, black and swampy at the bottom of the fridge. The mayonnaise was translucent in the jar, the milk clotted; I gagged as I screwed the lid back on. A pound of dessicated hamburger rattled like gravel under its cellophane. Every other container was unidentifiable or furred with mold. The freezer was just as overloaded, and everything in it ancient and frostbitten—chicken à la king packages I remembered from seventh grade, crystalized ice cream, grayed slabs of steak stuck together with ice.

"Mom," I called, opening her door just enough so she could hear me. She shuddered under the covers, groaning. "Mom, I'm going to the store. I'm going to buy us some healthy food. I'll be back soon."

Before I left, I called the vet and made an appointment for the next day. At the grocery store I loaded a cart with canned dog food, eggs and milk, yogurt and grapes and cheese and salad greens, and a box of lawn-and-leaf bags. When I got back to the house, I mashed dog food into a couple of bowls and watered it down into a soup. I brought the trashcans in from the end of the driveway and started loading them up, emptying the fridge, the freezer, the pantry, where moths fluttered out of the oatmeal when I opened the cabinet. When the cans were full, I used the trash bags I'd bought.

There were a few times during the afternoon—clearing the staircase of bags of mail so I could drag the heavy trashcans back down without killing myself, searching for toilet paper, realizing as I was defrosting the freezer with pots of hot water that it was almost seven o'clock and my mother still hadn't stirred—when I suddenly thought, *Who lives like this?* But I tamped those thoughts down. I went into Little Mommy automatic pilot, stacking the newspapers at the bottom of the driveway with the garbage, sorting through the toiletries and organizing my mother's bathroom after I'd finished cleaning the kitchen. Regardless of what I might have thought before I arrived—that I no longer needed a mother—my mother still needed me.

When it had gotten so late that it seemed my mom was asleep for the night, I left her a note outside her bedroom door, telling her I'd gone to see Elsa. Elsa, who'd dropped out of college after our freshman year and gotten married, had recently moved back in with her parents after her husband, a bouncer at a local bikers' bar, pulled a shotgun on her mom and dad. It wasn't until Elsa had already filed for divorce that she realized she was pregnant. For a couple of hours, I held Elsa's hair away from her face and rubbed her back while she vomited and cried. It was midnight by the time I returned to my mom's. The house was dark. I watched while the dogs bolted another helping of watery mush, then peeled off my clothes in my old room and crawled into bed, exhausted.

THERE WAS A SUDDEN flare of light and a violent bang as my bedroom door smashed open against the wall. My mother was yanking one of the full trashcans through my door. It was three in the morning.

"How *dare* you!" she snarled at me. "How dare you touch anything that belongs to me! I paid money for this food and it's mine!"

She kept raging, and I scrambled out of bed. Every light in the house was on. Jim Thompson's face appeared behind her, an evil courtier proffering a crumpled package of stained butcher paper.

"She got the steaks, too," he muttered into my mother's ear, cutting his accusing eyes at me. Hearing this, my mother raised her fists, shaking, her face a mask of fury directed at me.

"Mom, I was just trying to help—" I said. "The dogs were starving. Everything had gone bad—"

"Frozen food *never* goes bad!" she sneered. "Those steaks were fine!" She must have gotten a perm recently. Her normally wispy hair stood out from her head in a crimped triangle. Every time she moved her head, her hair levitated with static in the dry Alaskan air. "You have no respect for any boundaries," she spat at me, starting to weep vengeful tears, her hair crazed and witchy. She'd never taken off her mascara from whenever it was she had conducted her *really big deal*. It was running in black horror-show streaks down her face. "*I'm* the mother here, and this is *my* house! Everything in it is *mine!*"

"I was trying to do something nice," I defended myself. "I went to the store and bought fresh food for us. It's all put away in the refrigerator. I was cleaning things up. Everything I found was rotten. There was cookie dough in the fridge that I made two years ago."

"But you never made those cookies, did you? Just like you never wrote the letter. Your father was right—you're the one who's rotten! You think of nothing but yourself. You're heartless and selfish! You're a monster! You think you can do whatever you want and then just show up here and throw away everything I worked so hard for," she raved, black tears running down her long thin neck.

"Mom, you asked me to come. I bought the ticket out of my graduation money. I waited at the airport and you never came. It's a good thing I did come, because the dogs are suffering. You haven't taken care of them, there was no food or water."

Everything I said only made my mother more furious. "You're a liar! You're making this up!" she ranted. "You always lie!" Finally she glared at me, her eyes cold. "You have abused the privilege of staying in my house," she announced. "I want you to leave."

And she left the room, dragging the garbage can behind her and slamming the door.

IT WAS NO SACRIFICE to bid farewell to a house for which I had not an iota of affection or nostalgia. I felt nothing but bitterness for the years I'd spent within these walls. Here, my bedroom closet: For three years I hid boxes of tampons in my room to avoid telling my mother I'd gotten my period at twelve, not trusting her to keep from making an embarrassing scene. It was the first secret I ever kept from her. When my hand was forced by a ninth-grade gym teacher who insisted we bring notes from our mothers to verify our menstrual cycles, my mother's response was just as I expected: giddy, emotional, an exaggerated fountaining of tears. I begged her not to tell anyone, and she agreed to let me sit in the car while she raced us to the grocery store for "supplies." Even so, she outfoxed me. As I sat on the front seat twiddling the radio dial, she walked out of the market blubbering delicately, blowing her aristocratic nose—a beatific Madonna behind her Jackie O shades, escorting a shopping cart full of industrial-sized boxes of Kotex pads, which were pushed to our car by a senior boy I recognized from my new high school.

John's room, next to mine: A week before his accident, I found a lovingly detailed pencil sketch of an eagle on his desk. Sick with jealousy, afraid he would usurp me in our mother's eyes as the artist among her children, I ripped up his drawing and threw it away. I *threw it away*—my little brother's drawing. My little brother whose fingers would be cut off a few days later when he tried to stop some jerk from playing with a hatchet.

The landing at the top of the stairs, where my mother abandoned me at the crucial moment she'd coached me toward. I told Dad he had to leave. We all wanted him to leave. She hated him, we all did. My father was ferocious, no more willing to back down than I was. *Stop, Cissy! Dad, don't!* My brothers pleading, sobbing, trying to hold us apart. *You're the one who's ruining this family,* my father hissed in my face. *You're rotten to the core.* I turned to my mother for support, my mother cowering behind me, and saw the calculation in her eyes. It was me or her. She stepped back without a word, escaped behind her bedroom door. The deadbolt clicked into place.

The studio, the family room, the kitchen, the garage. There was not a room in our house untainted by shame and betrayal and neglect and loss, the brutal rupture of a family. My brother Billy's room, where he admitted to me, "I'm afraid of your memory." It was the last time we were together in that house, the only time we came close to talking about what had happened to us. "I'm scared you'll never forget," he said, "that you'll remember all of the bad things forever." "So am I," I answered.

Just before I left for college, while looking for a suitcase, I'd discovered a framed, hand-tinted photograph of an infant girl in the crawl space beneath the stairs.

"Who is this?" I asked my mother.

"It's you, of course," she said. "Look at how beautiful you were! My beautiful baby girl!"

"But, Mom," I said, "this can't be me. This baby has dark hair and green eyes."

"Oh, no, it's you," she argued. "I was so tickled to have a little girl I had this portrait made of you. See, I had them hand color all the details."

"It doesn't look like me, Mom," I said. "It looks like you. My eyes are brown, and you told me I was bald when I was a baby."

She shrugged her fine shoulders, bristling. "Have it your way, then. Maybe I'm wrong," she said, turning haughtily away. "Maybe it's me."

I'd turned the frame over. The stamped studio date was 1962, the year I was born.

I PULLED MY SUITCASE upright and cautiously opened my bedroom door. It sounded like my mother was in the kitchen now, still yammering on to Jim Thompson about how terrible I was. She wouldn't hear me leave, and I wasn't planning to say goodbye.

"Here, guys," I called quietly to the dogs. Barry tottered to his feet from the pile of laundry. Thor heaved himself slowly upright and limped painfully toward me on his stiff legs. I was taking them with me. I'd stay at my dad's, get the dogs to the vet, figure out what to do next. I maneuvered my suitcase out to the Volkswagen, the little dog under one arm, encouraging Thor behind me, his long toenails scraping against the driveway with every step. I shut them inside the car, and then I went back for my purse.

I will never come back, I vowed to myself, *never*. Opening the front door, descending the stairs, entering my bedroom for the last time, unmoved. I was already hardened against all of it. Against her. I wouldn't allow myself not to be. I took my house key off the ring and set it on my dresser. I slung my purse over my shoulder.

"Boys don't care about sentimental stuff," my mother had whispered to me over and over again through the years. "You're the girl.

You'll get it all." She'd long ago promised me her grandmothers' watches, the Count's emerald ring, her dishes and silver and wedding crystal, the velvet Victorian dresses and the prom gowns, the little Moses in the bulrushes. Camp Meeker—that, too, was supposed to have been mine, and even seeing it looted and destroyed, I hadn't been able to stop myself from envisioning my brothers and me there with our own families someday, in a future that would never come, picking warm berries in the lane, teaching our own children to swim. I could no longer desire any of it; the price was too high. I had to let it all go.

I glanced around my room. Was there anything, anything I could not live without? I asked myself to be sure. Was there anything I would miss? Would I wake up some day in my later life and be sorry I didn't take something, some relic of my childhood, if for no other reason than to prove to myself I survived it?

My dolls. They were all there: on their stands in the hutch, on the shelf behind my bed, wrapped in tissue in the closet.

I saved them for you, the little girl I knew would be mine, and someday you can give them to your little girl. Leaning over my mother's shoulder, holding my breath as she folded the tissues back to show me.

I could already feel the pang of regret; I'd felt it so many times in my life. I was as finished with regret as I was with everything else I was about to leave behind. I grabbed as many of the dolls as I could hold— Nancy and Susan, the Madame Alexanders, the porcelain ladies in pantaloons, the ancient Chinese dancer with the infinitely delicate fingers—and I headed for the open front door.

My mother was waiting for me. "What do you think you're doing?" she demanded.

"I'm leaving, like you told me to," I answered.

"Not with my dolls, you're not." She reached out and took hold of one as I stepped across the threshold.

"*Your* dolls?" I said, turning back to face her, incredulous, wrenching the delicate Chinese dancer away from her. "*Your* dolls? They're not your dolls, they're mine. You gave them to me."

"Well, I want them back," she announced. "You don't deserve them. You never take care of anything."

I stood on the front porch. I couldn't believe what I was hearing. "*I* don't take care of anything?" I said. Now I was the one shaking with rage. "What about you? You lure me here, but you can't get out of bed to pick me up at the airport. You've got thousand-year-old eggs in the refrigerator. You're living like a bag lady. There was no dog food, no toilet paper, no real food of any kind when I got here. But this is nothing—" I took a breath. I hardly knew where to start. "You're supposed to be my mother! I trusted you and you used me, and I was only a little girl. You knew I would do anything for you, but when the chips were down you didn't protect me, and what I needed protection from most was *you*. You told me it was my job to take care of you. You told me it was my job to help you get a divorce! You told me if I wrote a letter to McLean Stevenson, we would be rescued! How could you have done that to me—made me, a child, responsible for both of our lives? How could you tell me that your happiness depended on me? How could you let me believe that?"

My mother stood in the doorway, staring at me. Her face, which had been stony and unforgiving, began to crumple like a building under a wrecking ball, sliding off its extraordinary bones as I watched. "What do you mean," she asked, almost whispering, "let *you* believe it?"

I had told myself I would never go back, and I did not. Years have passed when I have not seen or spoken to my mother at all; other years have passed when we have found a tentative common ground at a distance. I have, a few times, visited the house where my mother lives now, on a lush hillside coaxed out of a desert. From the kitchen windows you can see a carefully tended garden.

Twenty-five years ago, as my mother stood alone in an open doorway, her arms hanging empty at her sides, there was nothing more to say. I stepped toward her and started handing her the dolls. I filled her arms, curling her fingers around the stiff bodies so they wouldn't fall. My mother stood there, hugging the dolls to her chest, as I turned and walked to the car. I started the engine and glanced up into the rearview mirror. For a moment my mother was still there, behind me, in reflection. In reflection—just as she had always seen me. And then I could see only that hillside of forgotten strawberries. The fruit hadn't been picked in years. It would never be picked. I saw them there as I drove away: small clotted hearts struggling to survive, dangling on their stems among the weeds.

STRAWBERRY SHORTCAKE FOR MY MOTHER

.·.

FOR THE SHORTCAKES:

2 cups unbleached all-purpose flour

Heaping, packed ¼ cup light brown sugar

1 tablespoon ground ginger

3 tablespoons candied ginger, finely chopped

¼ teaspoon salt

1 tablespoon baking powder

6 tablespoons unsalted butter, very cold or frozen, cut into
   chips

¾ to 1 cup heavy cream, cold, plus a little more for glazing

2 to 3 tablespoons turbinado sugar

These shortcakes are at their best when they're still warm from the oven. If you can't put them together at the last minute, you can bake them earlier in the day and rewarm them for a few minutes right before serving.

• Preheat the oven to 400° and line a baking sheet with parchment paper.

• Combine the flour, brown sugar, gingers, salt, and baking powder in a mixing bowl, stirring with a fork. Add the chips of butter, tossing with the flour to coat, then with your fingertips lightly and quickly work the butter in until it is in pieces ranging from pea-sized to flakes. Make a well in the center and pour in ¾ cup of cream. Toss and lightly stir with the fork just until the mixture begins to come together as a soft dough. If it seems too dry, add more cream a tablespoon at a time, but it's better to have a slightly streaky, drier dough than to overwork it, which will make the shortcakes tough.

• Turn the dough onto a floured surface and knead lightly to incorporate any remaining dry ingredients, then gently pat the dough into a 5-by-8-inch rectangle about 1 inch high. Cut the dough into 6 or 8 squares, and place them on the cookie sheet with several inches between each square (don't be alarmed if they look small; they will rise and expand quite a bit during baking). Brush the top of each shortcake with cream and sprinkle with turbinado sugar. Bake for 18 to 25 minutes, turning the baking sheet after 10 minutes for even baking. When the shortcakes are risen, golden and browning on the edges, springy when gently touched, and a toothpick inserted in the center comes out clean, they are ready to remove from the oven. Allow to cool for about 15 to 20 minutes before serving, or rewarm at 400° for about 5 minutes if necessary.

FOR THE BERRIES AND ASSEMBLY:

6 cups perfectly ripe, juicy organic strawberries, hulled
    and sliced
About ½ cup light brown sugar
Zest and juice of 1 orange
1 cup heavy cream
1 cup sour cream or crème fraîche

•   While the shortcakes are baking, hull and slice the berries and place in a bowl, mashing a few of the berries if they aren't very juicy. Add brown sugar to taste (I use about a teaspoon per cup of berries, more or less depending on how sweet the berries are), about a tablespoon's worth of orange zest, and a few tablespoons of the juice of the orange. Toss gently and macerate.

•   When ready to assemble the shortcakes, softly whip the heavy cream, then fold in the sour cream or crème fraîche. Stir in a few tablespoons of orange juice (and a little orange zest if you like). Split each warm shortcake by piercing it with the tines of a fork around the middle and gently prying the shortcake into halves as you would an English muffin. Lay the bottom half of a shortcake on a dessert plate, spoon berries and their juice over the bottom, then add a dollop of cream and a sprinkling of brown sugar. Rest the top half of the shortcake on the cream and berries, and serve immediately.

Makes 6 to 8 servings.

VARIATIONS

You can substitute other varieties of berries (mashing some if they are not
   particularly juicy), sliced peaches, nectarines or juicy plums, peeled kiwi,
   or chunks of fresh pineapple or papaya for the strawberries.

If you're an old-fashioned shortcake purist, omit the gingers from the
   shortcakes. For almond shortcakes, substitute ½ cup ground almonds or
   almond meal for ½ cup of the flour; you can also add 1 teaspoon of almond
   extract with the cream—these shortcakes go well with raspberries or
   peaches. Or you can substitute ½ cup finely ground cornmeal for ½ cup
   of flour, which is good with blueberries. An addition of orange zest can
   be made to the ginger flavoring of the shortcakes, or lemon or orange
   zest without ginger. Or substitute 1 teaspoon of cinnamon for the gingers
   and add 1 teaspoon vanilla to the cream in the shortcakes, and fill them
   with blackberries, or Santa Rosa or elephant heart plums.

An Alphabet for Would-Be Gourmets

I'D JUST CALLED MY FATHER WITH MY THRILLING NEWS, SO ECSTATIC I could hardly contain myself: I'd been offered a full-time job in the editorial department of a small publishing company in Berkeley, working with real authors and editors and books. They actually wanted to pay me for the privilege—an astounding nine thousand dollars a year! I waited for my father's reaction, listening to him breathing through his nose on the other end of the line.

"I know you're excited about this," he finally, cautiously began. "But if you take this job, you'll be poor for the rest of your life."

Ah, my dad. We'd both made progress in three years, but even Rome wasn't built in a day.

When I'd seen the listing for an opening at North Point Press, I'd recognized it as the ambitious young publishing company that had recently reissued *Being Geniuses Together* in the handsome edition that Arlen gave me as a graduation present, a jacketed paperback with a sewn binding, produced with care. Unlike most publishers, North Point was in California, not New York, and championed books that were considered financially risky: serious literary fiction, poetry, history and essays, translations and out-of-print classics. Why not go to Berkeley, I'd asked myself, and become a writer by learning, albeit surreptitiously, from people who were as devoted to books as I was?

The dedicated staff worked in a desanctified church. North Point's founders joked that it was a good thing we were there since we'd be praying a lot. In the nave where the congregation used to sit were raw pine shelves loaded to the ceiling with the press's inventory; when a new title was delivered from the printer, the entire company lined up to unload shrink-wrapped pallets of book cartons off the truck and relay them inside, fire-bucket-style. Hanging in the elevated chancel where the pulpit had been, now North Point's publicity and marketing department, was a painting left over from the building's former life, a depiction of Jesus stumbling up Mount Calvary with his cross. Someone had taped a thought balloon to Jesus's mouth that read, "No publicity is bad publicity."

I worked upstairs in what had been the sanctuary. A big part of my job was managing the manuscripts sent by hopeful would-be authors, five or six and sometimes a dozen a day arriving by mail. They were stacked on either side of the narrow staircase, and stacked on the shelves and the file cabinets and the big table in my office, and stacked in a solid block of listing paper under the table. Keeping ahead of the slush pile was an unending, monotonous task, every once in a while rewarded by something priceless popping up—sometimes good, though more often something so thrillingly bad it became the topic of our weekly Friday afternoon staff parties. My favorite was the epic novel about a nineteenth-century livestock drive across the western plains, a heroic tale of wanderlust and bravery and tragic consequences, of murderous rustlers and five-thousand-head stampedes and rugged male bonding that could have been another *Lonesome Dove* except that the earnest author's crusty, do-or-die protagonists were wrangling a flock of turkeys.

Tacked over the threshold of my office was a quote by W. H. Auden: "Critics are the people who ride in after the battle is over and shoot the wounded." Even when the manuscripts around my desk were truly terrible, I was still impressed that so many people had the vision and tenacity to write a whole book at all, let alone the courage to send it out into the world for strangers to assess. Though out of necessity we had boilerplate language for most of our rejections, in keeping with North Point's idealism and its loyalty to writers, I typed the letters individually and signed them, trying to soften the blow with an expression of appreciation for some aspect of the writer's work.

I probably spent too much time on a handwritten manuscript by a local guy named Amos Hanks, intrigued to read that he was distantly related to Abraham Lincoln's mother, Nancy Hanks, though his book was a memoir of banal blue-collar jobs and car camping with his kids—not the kind of book North Point published, which is what I explained in my rejection letter. Amos Hanks called me a few days later.

"Are you sure you can't publish my book?" he asked. "Listen. You seem like a nice girl. I could set you up with my son Tom. He can tell you about me. Maybe you've seen his movie, *Splash*?"

Splash was Tom Hanks's first hit movie, but at that point in his career he was better known for a TV sitcom in which his character disguised himself as a woman to live in a cheap all-female hotel. I was still nursing a broken heart over the breakup of my romance with Peter, haunted by the natural consequence of losing Nell and the rest of their family and by a letter, intended for his parents, that had been sent to me by mistake: *I'm afraid Kate will be lonely for the rest of her life*, Peter had written, words that scarred me for years, as did the enclosed snapshot of Peter sitting on a Greek beach with his arm around a tanned, topless companion. But I'd had a lifetime of putting up a solid front in public—at least I thought I did. I joked with my coworkers that I didn't want to go out with a guy who'd been on a show called *Bosom Buddies*.

Berkeley's reputation for revolution had been created by radical students at the university, but in recent years the town had been nurturing another kind of revolution centered on a neighborhood christened the Gourmet Ghetto. The citizens of the People's Republic of Berkeley turned out to be as passionate about food as they'd been about the Free Speech Movement and ending the Vietnam War. Fanning out from the corner where Alfred Peet opened his first coffee store and the Craftsman-style house where Alice Waters's Chez Panisse became a gastronomic mecca were numerous satellites of culinary specialization, including Cocolat, the shop that started the chocolate truffles craze, and Kermit Lynch's imported wine store, and Acme Bread—where people stood in line until the day's baking of crusty loaves sold out—and, in a former bowling alley, the Berkeley Bowl, the most remarkable produce market in the country, where you could find forty varieties of tomatoes in the summer and half a dozen kinds of fresh ginger.

You couldn't spit in Berkeley or anywhere else in the Bay Area without hitting a boutique bakery or a microbrewery or a restaurant opened by a Chez Panisse alum. Or a bookstore, for that matter. There seemed to be at least one good independent bookstore on every major street, and more the closer you got to the university. There was even a free monthly newspaper about nothing but poetry. I could stop by Cocolat for a chunk of chocolate-covered toffee and nibble it next door at Black Oak Books while sipping my latte from Peet's. It was my kind of town.

You didn't have to be rich to eat well in Berkeley, which was a good thing since my father's gloomy prediction was partially true. After I paid my rent, I barely had enough money to cover gas and groceries for the rest of the month. But as an employee I was entitled to a free copy of every book North Point published, and once or twice a week I was included in business lunches at the Chez Panisse café or one of its offshoots. I started working my way through North Point's backlist, reading Ovid and Gina Berriault and Jean Giono, and invested what little discretionary cash I had on used cookbooks at Moe's Books or Black Oak.

At night I attended the free readings listed in *Poetry Flash,* or I studied my cookbooks to try to identify what I'd been eating and how to recreate it with the dazzling cornucopia of ingredients I found at the Berkeley Bowl. Biscotti dunked in *vin santo*? They were twice-baked Italian cookies, usually flavored with anise and almonds. What if I tried them with walnuts and black pepper? What about elephant heart plums instead of pineapple in an upside-down cake?

My coworkers, all gastronomes and accomplished cooks, were a willing audience for my baking experiments. More than once North Point's publisher reminisced at our Friday parties about his first crème brûlée: a cool October night in nineteen-fifty-something Paris, the ocher leaves of chestnut trees blowing down the sidewalk in front of the café, and a chilled ceramic ramekin brought to the table wrapped in a white linen napkin. The caramelized crust of sugar on his crème brûlée, he told us, looked like a translucent layer of flawless amber, still giving off a heat shimmer above the cold custard it enclosed, and when he tapped the back of his silver spoon to its surface, it cracked like a sheet of ice. "It sounded like the calving of the fjords," he said, closing his eyes. The first time he told this story, I had no idea what crème brûlée was and had to look it up later in the *Larousse Gastronomique* that was shelved with the reference books in my office.

At my desk in the sanctuary, I had a Rolodex with addresses for Eudora Welty, Gore Vidal, and Joan Didion. I fielded phone calls from Kurt Vonnegut and Toni Morrison and filed letters written by W. S. Merwin. Gary Snyder and Wendell Berry trooped past my desk on their way to talk to my boss. In those precomputer days, I learned how to paginate an index by hand and retyped entire manuscripts, decoding the fretwork of revisions that Stephen Dixon glued onto his copyedited pages and noticing how James Salter could trim a single phrase from the last sentence of a short story and shift the weight of everything that came before. I'd have been mortified if anyone knew I wanted to be a writer, too. My first impulse was to shut up and pay attention.

I'd only been working at North Point for a few months when the press had its first really big success in Evan Connell's *Son of the Morning Star*, a meticulous, obsessive history of Custer's Battle of the Little Bighorn and the Plains Indian Wars, which in novelist Connell's hands became a compulsively readable story—of Cheyenne boys derailing a train so they could see what was inside the cars, later tying bolts of calico to their ponies' tails and watching the cloth stream out behind as they galloped over the grasslands; of Custer during the Civil War, when he lost more men than almost any other commander but brushed his teeth with salt after every meal and anointed his wavy blond hair with cinnamon oil. The Custer book hit the *New York Times* bestseller list, and suddenly we were scrambling back to press for multiple printings. Everyone from *The New Yorker* to *People* was calling, wanting to talk to *Son of the Morning Star*'s intensely private author.

At sixty, Evan Connell was a disciplined artist, a lifelong bachelor living by himself in an austere apartment. He was the author of a dozen acclaimed books, including *Mrs. Bridge*, considered a masterpiece of sly American realism, republished by North Point and one of my favorite novels. Evan didn't give readings or promote himself in any way. I'd met him a couple of times at North Point events, where he held back at the fringes of conversations, seeming aloof and offering little. I could not help but imagine him as Douglas, *Mrs. Bridge*'s mystifying son, who spends weeks building a tower in an empty lot from junk the neighbors have thrown away, nailing everything from tree limbs to old suitcases to a chicken coop onto a foundation of two-by-fours and cement until his monument looms eccentrically over the backyard fences. Conservative, repressed Mrs. Bridge finds her little boy's bewildering industry so unreckonable that she asks the fire department to tear the tower down, telling Douglas that "people were beginning to wonder."

One afternoon Evan called North Point to report that *Son of the Morning Star* had been chosen for the *Los Angeles Times* book prize, and he was expected to show up to accept the award, which he was loath to do alone. I guess all of the likely suspects were otherwise engaged for the weekend of the awards ceremony, because somehow I was elected to accompany Evan to Los Angeles, and he approved. Why would a worldly novelist who was notoriously solitary want to be stuck for a weekend with a stranger, especially a peon like me? What would we have to talk about for three days?

We met at the airport, me racking my brain to come up with something interesting to say. Despite his reputation for shyness, Evan was gracious from the start, asking if I'd join him in a drink on the plane and friendly enough that I worked up my nerve to ask him a lingering question about the Custer book: "Do you know what kind of cake Lieutenant Calhoun's wife sent him?"

The brother-in-law of General Custer, Calhoun received a large cake sent by ferryboat from his wife while on the Bighorn campaign, and carried it to the battlefield; a few days before the massacre he promised that every officer would get a slice once Sitting Bull had been subdued. In his book, Evan had imagined the scene as Sioux warriors discovered Calhoun's surprising cargo and ate it, the lieutenant's body lying nearby in the blood-matted grass.

I'd imagined the scene, too, wondering about the days, maybe weeks, it would have taken the cake to reach Calhoun. It occurred to me that any nineteenth-century wife who took the trouble to ship a cake to her soldier husband would have baked something sturdy enough to survive the journey, probably a dense loaf, most likely a pound cake or a fruitcake, which would have been further preserved by a healthy dousing of brandy and a crust of royal icing. In other words, the cake might have still been perfectly fresh, which made the story even more eerie and strange. As I rambled on about Calhoun's cake, I realized that Evan was listening intently, stirring the ice in his drink with the plastic airline pick. He was distractingly handsome, tall and solemn, with a majestic face like something carved out of bedrock, his trim salt-and-pepper goatee banded like a badger, his hooded eyes grave.

"I don't know," Evan answered simply. "I'm not much of a cook." Then he paused. "Too bad I didn't have you to consult when I was writing that chapter."

We talked about writers and books we both admired, and Evan confessed, "I can't just enjoy a book. If I read something that I like, I always ask myself, how did the writer do this, and how can I steal it? How can I make it my own?"

There it was, however unintentional, a direct deposit to my grow-ing account: the box of pirate's treasure creaking open.

A YEAR INTO MY job at North Point, another invitation arrived. It was typed on a three-by-five postcard, white and plain but for a tiny printed stick-figure girl in one corner and the message, which was addressed, to my surprise, to me. "Dear Kate," it began, the neat letters ghosting a little from a fading ribbon, "When can you come up to discuss our picnic plans? If dinner suits your schedule, that would be lovely." It was signed in ink with a series of precisely shaped unciform initials that looked more like the announcement of a Roman *annum* chipped onto a stone tablet than a signature: M.F.K.F.

M.F.K. Fisher, called the best prose writer in America by W. H. Auden and "poet of the appetites" by John Updike, a candid sensualist who found her lasting metaphor in food, had invited me to dinner.

Part of North Point's editorial mission was to resuscitate seminal out-of-print books and authors, and they'd embarked on a program of reissuing M.F.K. Fisher's classics on the art of eating—books, really, about hunger in all its forms, and about living with keen awareness, whether through pleasure or anguished loss.

Mary Frances, as she liked to be called, was far from neglected or forgotten. She'd had a cultlike following of select readers and food professionals since the 1940s, but the reappearance of her books in North Point's stylish jacketed paperbacks coincided with a shift in American attitudes toward food: a new interest in how it was grown, how it was prepared, and how it could satisfy both the body and the spirit. It wasn't an original idea, just an idea rediscovered, and it sharp-ened a newly voracious appetite for M.F.K. Fisher's oracular wisdom.

During our mutual North Point days, Mary Frances lived in a small house that had been built for her by a friend on his five-hundred-acre ranch a few miles north of Sonoma. Designed to Mary Frances's spec-ifications, her "last house" was nestled among groves of fragrant bay laurels and live oaks and eucalyptus at the top of a sloping knoll, with a view of a wildflower meadow and the valley's boundary of mountains framed by the arched balcony of the west-facing veranda in front. The house had just two main rooms, connected by a crimson entrance hall lined with thousands of books: a combined bedroom and study where she read late at night and wrote in the morning, and a "big room" warmed by a Franklin stove, with a kitchen along one wall and opposite that, comfortable furniture arranged for the conversational ease of her frequent guests. She'd moved to Last House in an attempt to retire from the relentless hostessing that had shaped much of her adult life, but the fact was that Mary Frances was incorrigibly social.

Though she was then in her seventies and plagued by Parkinson's disease as well as arthritis and a bad hip, an endless stream of visitors crunched up the gravel drive to her open door, real and welcome friends as well as culinary sycophants and others eager for an audience, plying their sacred offerings to the reigning goddess of American gastronomy. They'd lift their willow baskets of Araucana eggs and Torrey-pine honey out of their cars, the fallen bay and eucalyptus leaves they'd crushed under their tires sending out a vaporous scent not unlike that rumored at Delphi: the intoxicating aroma of the deity's presence in the shrine.

It wouldn't be completely true to say that Mary Frances welcomed everyone who came to see her. She was outwardly gracious and charming, and she couldn't seem to stop herself from issuing invitations regardless of her desire for visitors, but she also did not suffer gladly the kowtowing of fools or opportunists or those who misunderstood her interest in food and translated it into license for epicureal preciousness. I heard that she once deposited a dead mouse into some visiting reporter's book bag. One evening when I was setting the table at Last House for dinner and trying not to eavesdrop on the telephone conversation she was having with some foodie person or other, I heard her almost helplessly cast out the offer of a lunch visitation and then listen and nod and make noises of assent to the list of comestibles her caller gushingly suggested she would bring along. "Oh really, the size of your thumb?" Mary Frances said in her breathy, whispered doll's voice. "It will be like a picnic for pixies." When she hung up the phone, her warm smile instantaneously puckered into a sour knot of distaste. I couldn't help staring at her perfect red lips. She had the most exquisite, kissable mouth I'd ever seen on any human being.

"Yet more baby vegetables!" she grimaced, shaking her queenly head.

But I'm getting ahead of myself.

I don't know who made the initial suggestion—I suspect it was

Mary Frances—but once a year the staff of North Point and their families gathered at Last House for a picnic. For the dozen or so who went to Last House every year, Mary Frances's company was a luminescent treat; for her it meant a daylong invasion. The staff trod as lightly as possible, organizing the food to please our hostess, bringing the wine and linens and glassware, leaving the house neat and orderly at the end of the afternoon. Mary Frances held court out on the redwood-beamed veranda, enthroned on a wicker chair that fanned above her head like a peacock's tail. Beyond the balcony's balusters the occasional cow shuffled past, black and white, clanking its bell.

The first year I attended the picnic I was the newest and youngest employee on North Point's staff. I was still in my stealth phase—stealth writer, stealth grown-up—trying to pick up tips on appropriate behavior the way a child raised by wolves figures out how to hold a fork in its paw by watching the other diners at the table. I was too self-conscious to elbow into the knot of people leaning in to hear Mary Frances's stories, so I stayed inside, mostly in the kitchen, replenishing the platters of food set out on the linen-covered refectory table and picking up abandoned glasses.

I studied the bookshelves—titles in English, French, Italian; cookbooks, mystery novels, old children's books, books on the stars and ants and bullfighting—and the mythic personal totems Mary Frances arranged on walls and tabletops and shelves. Grainy photographs of children in high-buttoned boots, a bird's nest, loose type from a printing press, teacups lustrous as mother-of-pearl and so fine you could see the shadow of your finger through their delicate sides. So this was a real writer's house, memory seeping up out of every photograph, each object imbued with story.

And then I wandered into her bathroom. It was almost as big as the bedroom, with an enormous claw-foot tub at its center surrounded by stacks of books, one glass wall revealing a circle of oaks outside, their leaves seeming to fall in slow motion, one at a time, to the ground. The rest of the walls were cinnabar red, the color of a Pompeian villa, hung gallery-style with real art, just as in the rest of the house. There was an unmistakable Picasso. There was another painting of a sensual young woman, nude, beautiful, whose dramatic egg-shaped face I recognized as Mary Frances. Another of her from behind, the swanlike contours of her back and shoulders, a dark chignon twisted at the base of her fine long neck: It had been painted by her husband Dillwyn Parrish, the great passion of her life, who'd suffered a horrible death after they'd been married for just two years.

The paintings, the falling leaves, the stacks of books, the three green apples by the sink, the little bottle of 4711 with its blue and gold label, the theatrical red walls repeated back to me in the mirror, just as Mary Frances returned over and over again in her books to moments in her life, tableaux of memory that time had not made less vivid. She'd written of eating freshly picked peas on a European hillside to the sound of cowbells, of bathing with her sister in a six-foot enameled bathtub as her newspaper-editor father shaved, naked and unashamed, at the mirror. Of her bookish mother's incomparable applesauce, and of dousing a handkerchief with 4711 and placing it in her mother's limp hand when she was pregnant and ill. Last House didn't feel like a house. Being there was like standing inside Mary Frances's beating heart.

I doubt I said more to her than a bashful thank-you for her hospitality that first visit, and during the year that followed, her communication with North Point was always with other people. So I don't know how it happened, but somehow I was put in charge of organizing the next picnic at her house—which was the reason for the invitation I'd received. I was delighted by the idea of having an evening with Mary Frances, another chance to soak up the atmosphere at her soul house, and this time to talk to her, my confidence bolstered by daily contact with people whose belief in my abilities was quickly outstripping even my own most outrageous fantasies. I wanted to help with the picnic, and I was flattered to be asked. I remembered reading what Mary Frances had written about learning to cook as a child, the sense of self-esteem that came from mastery, and from feeding, literally and figuratively, the people you care about: ". . . I still think that one of the pleasantest of all emotions is to know that I, I with my brain and my hands, have nourished my beloved few, that I have concocted a stew or a story, a rarity or a plain dish, to sustain them truly against the hungers of the world."*

I knew that feeling of pride and connection, too, a little bit, and clung to it. It gave me a sense of exterior solidity even when what was inside was still nebulous. I was happy to think I could help bring suste-

---

*The Gastronomical Me by M.F.K. Fisher (San Francisco: North Point Press, 1989), p. 367.

nance and pleasure, even a fleeting afternoon's, to this group of people who made me feel that a place in the world was opening up for me.

SHE HAD A FACE like an elegant cat's: glamorous, shrewd, serenely inquisitive, her almond-shaped gray-green eyes set wide under her arched eyebrows. She seemed feline in her attention, also, self-possessed but avidly watching, and not above toying with her prey. I've already mentioned her mesmeric bow-shaped mouth, always carefully highlighted in dark red lipstick. There was something of the Imp of the Perverse in Mary Frances as well. She had the look of a woman who had been the kind of little girl who said outrageous things for her own amusement, just to see how people would react.

Like so many before me, I'd brought her a present: homemade jam. I'd felt the jolt of connection when I read that the first thing she tasted and wanted to taste again was the pink foam that her grandmother had skimmed from the surface of strawberry jam as it cooked. I told Mary Frances it had been blackberry in my case.

"I've always liked making jam better than eating it," I blurted as I handed her the jar, immediately regretting the weak endorsement I'd just made for my own gift. Mary Frances slid her eyes over me, her beautiful lips pursed.

"So have I," she said evenly, after a beat. "Let's try yours anyway."

My face still burning, I broke the vacuum seal of the lid and Mary Frances scooped out a spoonful of blackberry jam for me, then one for herself. We stood by the sink together, letting the jam melt on our tongues, dark and musky. It was early evening, and there were blue veils of mist snagged in the tonal folds of the hills outside the windows. I saw that Mary Frances had made cookies, and I tried not to stare. Cat's tongues, their centers pale but their thin crisp edges rimmed with brown.

"Are these wild berries?" Mary Frances asked, polite but as yet noncommital, her hand trembling a little as she held her spoon.

"I picked them in my yard—well, technically it's not my yard, I sort of stole them from the downstairs neighbors, they're the only ones allowed to use the garden but they never do, and I had to climb over the gate—"

There was an almost imperceptible dilation of catlike interest. I kept babbling.

"—the best thing about blackberries, I think, if you pick them yourself, is that they smell like roses when they're warm. They taste like a rose should taste."

"Yes, exactly, they're related, you know—" Mary Frances said, nodding.

"I think that's why I liked the foam when my grandmother made jam," I went on. "It filled your mouth with that scent. The finished jam was never as good."

"That's true, it's always a bit of a letdown, isn't it?" Mary Frances said thoughtfully.

"Unless it's warm," I added. "On a pretty plate. There's a scene in *Anna Karenina*—"

"Yes, I know that scene," Mary Frances murmured, nodding and sizing me up, and then she reached toward the counter and picked up the plate of cat's tongues. I held my breath: *a cookie made by M.F.K. Fisher!* But instead of offering her rare delicacies to me, she swung open the cabinet under the sink and tipped the cookies into the garbage bin. I think I gasped.

"Something went wrong with these," Mary Frances said. "We were going to have them after dinner, and I planned to keep a discreet silence, but I have something better in mind for us now."

I realized I'd passed some sort of test.

"I almost killed my mother and my infant sister with blackberries," Mary Frances began, an anticipatory *frisson* of storyteller's relish in her voice as she lifted the lid from an enamel cook pot on the stove, releasing delicate involutions of steam.

We never did talk about the picnic. Over hot bread and potato soup—I took note as she snipped chives with a pair of scissors right over our soup plates—we discovered our mutual love for the poignant rolling hills of Sonoma County, which reminded Mary Frances of her idyllic time with Parrish when they lived in a farmhouse in a valley of wildflowers and vineyards at the edge of Lake Geneva. Weirdly, we found we had brushes with Nixon in common. Mary Frances's sister had gone to school with him, "a dog-faced Quaker boy."

The something better for dessert that Mary Frances pulled together as we talked was a kind of parfait, ingeniously simple. While a pint of good vanilla ice cream softened on the counter, she gently mashed two Hachiya persimmons that had been ripening to a translucent glow on the windowsill over the sink, then folded the two together, marbling the clear orange flesh of the persimmons against the white ice cream. We ate it from champagne flutes, watching the hills purple in phases as the sun sank behind them.

"The cookies would have been perfect with this," I said to Mary Frances, emboldened by wine and her mordant sense of humor. "Maybe I could just dig one out of your trash. . . ."

"You wouldn't be the first," she said, leaning back in her chair.

I was invited back to Last House a few more times on my own, always to plan the picnic, which we invariably failed to do, and always by way of a brief typed postcard with a stick-figure girl on it. After the first one they came signed "Love, Mary Frances." We talked about books and cat behavior and fetishes for pens and odd grandparents, and only incidentally about food. I gathered that she was ambivalent about most desserts, though she liked fruit and the occasional nibble of a really good cookie or pastry. After hearing about the Count and the Romanov treasures buried at the San Francisco dump, she pretended shock that I'd never heard of Raspberries Romanov, a kind of *fin de siècle* cousin to her persimmon parfait but refined and classic: fresh ripe raspberries folded together with sweetened whipped cream lit with liqueur, and served chilled in tall glasses. She'd included the recipe in her book *An Alphabet for Gourmets,* soon to be republished by North Point.

"I fear that's as close as you'll ever get to your Romanov rubies," Mary Frances told me.

The annual picnics were always a triumph of convivial hedonism, though the first one for which I was responsible is the one that lasts. Actually it's what happened afterward that I remember. I'd wanted to make something that would tempt Mary Frances for dessert, but I thought it was better not to try too hard to impress and to just make something I knew would be good. Even so I was a little chagrined as I unwrapped my dependable, chewy walnut brownies at Last House—I suspected the frosted ones would've made Mary Frances shudder—and in a spasm of insecurity I left them stacked on their platter by the sink rather than force them to compete with the poached figs in honey and tarte Tatin that other people had brought. Everything arranged and the wine already flowing,

I hurried out to join the party on the veranda, where my boyfriend at the time, a handsome young banker with a philospher's soul, was falling hopelessly in love with the beguiling M.F.K. Fisher. As Mary Frances might have said, he wouldn't be the first.

I forgot so completely about my brownies that I didn't realize I'd left them behind at Last House until I was halfway home, my awe-struck boyfriend shaking his head in wonder beside me, the teeny back seat of the Karmann Ghia loaded with dirty tablecloths. For the rest of the weekend, I pondered whether to muscle up and claim responsibility directly and thereby get my grandmother's Denmark Blue platter back, or try to pass the brownies off as the homely contribution of some unrevealed colleague. I was still weighing my options when Mary Frances beat me to the punch. Her thank-you postcard was lavish with appreciation for the opulent luncheon and the glorious day and the scintillating company (including handsome young men), and it ended with a request.

"But you must find out for me," she began, "and beg the recipe: Who Made the Delicious Brownies? Love, Mary Frances."

PERSIMMON PARFAIT, AFTER M.F.K. FISHER, WITH WALNUT–BLACK PEPPER BISCOTTI

∴

FOR THE BISCOTTI:

2½ cups unbleached all-purpose flour

2½ teaspoons baking powder

1 teaspoon salt

2 rounded teaspoons finely ground black pepper

½ cup unsalted butter, chilled and cut into small pieces

½ cup plus 3 tablespoons granulated sugar

½ cup plus 3 tablespoons light brown sugar

2 eggs, chilled

2 tablespoons milk

2 teaspoons vanilla

2 cups walnut pieces

- Preheat the oven to 375°. Cut an 18-by-24-inch sheet of heavy-duty aluminum foil. Fold it to make an 8-by-18-inch rectangle; put this on a large cookie sheet.
- Blend the flour, baking powder, salt, and pepper together in a food processor or with a whisk in a medium-sized bowl. Add the butter in chips and mix in until grainy, either pulsing in a food processor or cutting in with a pastry blender. Mix in the sugars.
- Whisk the eggs, milk, and vanilla in a large bowl. Add the flour-sugar mixture to the egg mixture and stir until a thick, soft dough forms. Mix in the walnuts. The dough will be very sticky.
- Scrape the dough onto the aluminum foil and spread it into a 6-by-16-inch rectangle about ¾ inch high, leaving 1 inch of foil on each side. Bake for 10 minutes, reverse the pan, and bake for 10 more minutes or until golden. Cool the loaf for 20 minutes outside the oven.
- Holding the edges of the tinfoil form, lift the dough from the cookie sheet and remove to a work surface. Score the loaf into ¾-inch-wide slices, then cut through. Use a long, thin metal spatula to move the slices back to the cookie sheet; place one cut side of the cookies down on the cookie sheet.
- Bake for 7 minutes. Reverse the cookie sheet and bake for 5 to 7 minutes more or until golden: Watch for the last couple of minutes so the cookies don't burn on the bottom.
- Turn the cookies over and bake for 7 minutes. Reverse the sheet and bake another 5 to 7 minutes or until the second side is golden, again watching carefully to prevent burning. Let cool for 10 minutes on the cookie sheets and then move the cookies with a long, thin metal spatula to a wire rack to cool completely.

Makes 2 dozen cookies.

FOR THE PERSIMMON PARFAIT:

1 pint highest-quality vanilla ice cream (for homemade,
    see page 82)
2 completely ripe Hachiya persimmons

- This recipe requires brief but last-minute preparation. About 20 minutes before serving, remove the ice cream from the freezer to soften.

Remove the persimmons' stems and mash them with a fork in a small bowl, leaving some chunks of firmer fruit pulp, if there are any, and removing any seeds. Add the softened ice cream and fold together with a spatula in a few strokes, so that the ice cream is swirled with orange persimmon streaks. Spoon into glass flutes or compotes and serve immediately, passing the biscotti and a bottle of *vin santo*.

Makes 2 to 4 servings.

For the chewy walnut brownies deemed "delicious" by M.F.K. Fisher, see page 208.

Being Geniuses Together

Nᴏʀᴛʜ ᴘᴏɪɴᴛ's ᴍᴏsᴛ ᴘʀɪᴄᴋʟʏ ᴀᴜᴛʜᴏʀ ʜᴀᴅ ᴍᴏᴠᴇᴅ ᴛᴏ ᴛᴏᴡɴ, and she was not happy with us. In a career that spanned six decades, Kay Boyle had published nearly fifty books, three of them recently with North Point, and though she stopped short of labeling us as incompetent, she said we were the most difficult publisher she'd ever had to deal with. That gave us pause, since she was currently suing another small publisher for its own snafu, a predicament we were eager to avoid. My first meeting with Kay Boyle, whose memoir of Paris in the twenties had led me to North Point in the first place, was meant to be a mission of appeasement.

Just wait until Arlen hears about this, I thought, driving to my appointment at Kay's house, which turned out to be a few short blocks from my apartment. He'd predicted that I would love her work, and he'd been right. Reading *Being Geniuses Together* and then Kay's novels and stories and poetry and essays, I'd realized how few women writers or women artists of any kind had been part of my education. Fewer still were the ones who were also mothers. Kay had led me to Kate Chopin, Toni Morrison, Alice Munro, Grace Paley, Sylvia Plath. It was because of women like Kay, her tenacious loyalty to herself, her fervent refusal to compromise, to be delimited by her gender or her culture or by what anyone else thought, that I began to see more possibilities for how I could shape my own life. It was just short of unbelievable that I was going to meet her.

The book that introduced me to Kay had begun as a memoir by Robert McAlmon, a poet and influential publisher who'd befriended Kay during her early years in Paris. McAlmon had started *Contact*, one of the "little magazines" of the era that were the provocative mouthpieces of modern art and literature, and his Contact Editions brought out Hemingway's first book. Though he was an incisive critic and a generous, if acerbic, benefactor to other writers, McAlmon held himself to such an impossibly high standard of artistic integrity that he refused to promote his own work, and he died all but unknown. Years later, in a gesture of loyalty and as a refutation of injustice, Kay Boyle reapproached McAlmon's forgotten memoir, inserting alternating chapters of her own reminiscences, and for the first time gained a wide readership for McAlmon with the book he had cynically titled *Being Geniuses Together*. It remains one of the foremost chronicles of that formative decade in modern art and letters.

Even with the best of intentions, it's an audacious thing to take another writer's work and shape it with your own, but Kay had been primed for audacity since childhood. Born in 1902, she was the daughter of a liberal activist and would-be photographer who taught her daughter that there was no higher ambition than a life devoted to art and social justice. Kay listened to Gertrude Stein's *Tender Buttons* as a bedtime story, and to the conversations of her mother's friends—labor organizers, journalist Lincoln Steffens, Alfred Stieglitz—at the dinner table. In 1913, when she was eleven, Kay was taken to the notorious Armory Show, where she saw *Nude Descending a Staircase* by Marcel Duchamp. Thirty years later Duchamp would be the godfather to Kay's son, Ian.

Newly married to a French engineer at twenty and with a publication in *Poetry* magazine under her belt, Kay sailed to France to meet her in-laws. The couple's intention was to stay for the summer, but Kay didn't go back to the United States for two decades. Out of her experiences during her first five years of living in France, Kay created five of her first six brazenly autobiographical novels, three short-story collections, and, much later, *Being Geniuses Together*.

Kay was among the literary revolutionaries who burned T. S. Eliot and Henry James in effigy on the Boulevard Montparnasse. At her first Paris party, she was introduced to James Joyce and his wife, Nora; she was photographed by Man Ray and designed sculpture with Constantin Brancusi. She bore six children to three men, the first, while she was still married to her first husband, by a lover who died of tuberculosis five months before his daughter was born.

The Kay Boyle of *Being Geniuses Together* was young, beautiful, tall, and needle slim, with jet-black hair and "the haughty self possession of a Seminole maiden," as another of the Paris set described her. She was acknowledged as one of the most talented writers of her generation and praised in print by her peers, writers as diverse as Katherine Anne Porter and William Shirer. William Carlos Williams reviewed her first book and called her the heir to Emily Dickinson.

Kay was amazingly productive, especially considering that she sometimes wrote sitting on the toilet in a locked bathroom with a typewriter balanced on her knees while her children rode tricycles up and down the hall of her apartment. By the start of World War II, she'd published more than a dozen books and was one of the most famous American women writers, an inventive stylist credited with the oblique, unresolved short-story form that became synonymous with *The New Yorker.* After the war her writing and her life become more overtly political, and Kay was subjected to a loyalty hearing during the McCarthy witch hunts and was blacklisted through the fifties. During the sixties Kay became a fierce political activist, taking part in actions in support of civil rights, free speech, Native American rights, and farm-workers, her participation in protests against the Vietnam War resulting in her public firing from her faculty position at San Francisco State and two jail terms.

Now she was eighty-three, still writing and publishing, still accepting teaching jobs around the country when they came up, still as idealistically impassioned and intellectually vigorous as ever, but her body was starting to have trouble keeping up. Arthritis and vertigo were beginning to bother her. While living in rural Oregon to be near Ian, her youngest child, Kay had taken a fall and fractured her spine, precipitating their move back to California.

I arrived with peace offerings: homemade cookies, predictably. Ian, who had the noble face of the Shakespearean actor he was but the good-natured, informal temperament that made him the perfect conciliator for his adamantine mother, came to the door to greet me. Kay had only recently been given permission to sit up after an endless convalescence on her back.

"Kay's got diverticulitis," Ian said under his breath when I arrived. "She may not be able to have the cookies. You might want to leave them here, if you know what I mean . . . what's in them?"

"They're just oatmeal with chocolate," I whispered back.

"Perfect!" Ian said, putting his arm around me and leading me to

Kay. "She's supposed to eat oatmeal and she's got a thing for choco-late. A point on your side."

Reclining on a cot with a cat, her moving boxes still stacked against the walls, Kay looked like royalty in exile. Her famed black hair was now almost completely white, though immaculately coiffed; she was still long and lean, age making her high cheekbones and distinctive Roman nose even more aristocratic. The heavy-lidded eyes that devas-tated so many of her contemporaries remained a clear aquatic blue. In her neat black pantsuit and signature white earrings and luxuriant blue satin scarf, which set off her eyes' penetrating gaze and the elegant gray waves in her hair, she reminded me of a great blue heron, concen-trated and dramatic, poised for the flash of movement in the water at its feet.

Over Dubonnet on the rocks and a dish of goldfish crackers to go with the cookies, Kay told me of her relief to be back in "civilization" after small-town Oregon. In the Bay Area, she was surrounded by friends and reminders of her tumultuous but gratifying years at the forefront of her second cultural revolution, the sixties; Amnesty Inter-national's local chapter, founded by Kay, fêted her at an annual fundraiser on her birthday. She and Ian told me about the enormous house they'd owned in the Haight Ashbury, a rallying spot for Kay's various causes and a second home for many of her students, now her lasting friends and correspondents. As Kay reminisced one of her two elderly cats, Dopey, curled up in my lap and fell asleep.

"Look at that, Ma," Ian said.

"She knows, I told you," Kay answered him, nodding. My assign-ment had been to smooth Kay Boyle's feathers, but her frustration with my employer seemed no longer at issue. She turned her unflinching blue eyes on me. "I am convinced that cat is my mother," she said. "She always knows the right people."

KAY AND I LIVED so close to each other that it was easy to stop by just to say hello, visits that invariably led to long conversations over the Dubonnet and goldfish crackers she always offered, or, when she was feeling better, a slow gingerly walk up the street to one of our local cafés, Kay impeccable in white ruffled blouses and trim dark pantsuits, always wearing crimson lipstick and white earrings. "I try to remember to wear this one," she'd tell me, referring to the blue satin scarf tied in voluptuous folds at her long neck, "because I know how much you like it." That Kay would think to wear her blue scarf for me touched me as much as her insistence that when she had to travel, Dopey would only be happy if I took care of her.

A bachelor, Ian had a house across the Golden Gate Bridge in Marin County, but he drove to Kay's daily, and we developed our own friendship, confiding in each other over romantic disappointments and escaping for dinners or plays by ourselves in "Peggy Red," Ian's vintage convertible. Kay and Ian felt like family, their stories becoming as known to me as my own, mine becoming part of their vocabularies as well, the three of us laughing in Kay's kitchen over what happened when Ian appeared before the draft board at age eighteen to apply for conscientious objector status. Asked if he would ever be willing to carry a gun, Ian responded, "If my country or my mother were invaded."

At the conclusion of a summer party that lasted long into a balmy August night, a dozen of us in Ian's backyard listening to his phenomenal record collection—everything from the original 1947 recording of "I'm My Own Grandpa" to Erik Satie to rare outakes of Miles Davis to the Mozart Ian's father had loved—I slept in the "auxiliary guest suite," a canting garden shed with a dirt floor, just big enough for the small iron bedstead it contained and nothing else. "This bed was my godfather's," Ian told me, sweeping the door open with a theatrical bow, "what tales it could tell . . ." I woke in Marcel Duchamp's bed to slices of light projecting through the spaces between the plank walls. Intrepid morning glory vines and tiny pink Cecile Brunner roses had maneuvered their way between the boards, too, so that the inside of the shed, its pitched roof and all four mossy walls, was entirely banked in flowers. The scent of roses was paradisical. It was like waking to a garden turned inward, as if your heart might bloom in your chest.

KAY'S FRIEND SAM in Paris was having trouble with his feet. Old age and discomfort were making him morbid. Kay had been updating me episodically on her attempts to cheer him up and get him into a practical pair of comfortable shoes.

"They've bothered him for years," she'd told me. They'd known each other since the *Being Geniuses* years, and most of the other friends from that era of their lives were gone. "He complains all the time, and finally I told him, Rockports. You need a pair of Rockport shoes."

Since Sam couldn't buy a pair of Rockports in France, Kay instructed him to trace his feet on pieces of paper, then purchased a pair of Rockports based on the tracings and mailed them to Paris, but they were too small. As I was about to embark on my long-awaited first trip to Europe, I suggested that Kay send a second, larger pair of Rockports with me and spare the trouble and expense of mailing shoes back and forth; if Sam didn't like the shoes, I could simply bring them home. When I picked up the Rockports from Kay just before leaving on my trip, she had wrapped the shoebox in a plastic bag with handles so it would be easier for me to carry, and with maternal resourcefulness advised me to open the box and pack my own things inside, too. "That way you won't waste any space in your suitcase," she said. "You can roll up your underthings and put them right inside the shoes."

I spent three weeks traveling through Italy on my way to Paris. I relished the vast and glorious *stupor mundi* of Rome, eating my first gelato on the steps of the flamboyant Trevi Fountain at midnight, my bare legs stretched out on the cool stone as floodlit Neptune and his Tritons struggled with their rearing sea horses under a dangling platinum moon. I cracked the wooden shutters in *pensione* rooms at dawn to sit by the window and watch the gradual assembly of Italian mornings: men dressed like dentists carrying slopping buckets of plaster up the scaffolding on a church; a lady in a flowered housecoat sweeping candied almonds from a cobbled alleyway in Assisi after the day before's wedding procession; the violet light lifting and hundreds of pigeons, thousands, circling the black-and-white-banded campanile of Siena's Duomo. Because I was in Florence and his name, tantalizingly, was Gary, I rode on a motorcycle with a civil engineer from Auckland, wearing his helmet and clinging to his broad back, passing dim olive groves in the dark and hit with the fleeting musk of fig trees as we wound up through the hills to look at the view from Fiesole. For a whole day I let myself be lost in the passing pageant that is Venice, a ravishment of sensory excess bathed in gold-toned light, everything seen as if from inside a kaleidoscope—shards of color tumbling all around me.

It seemed only fitting that in a city of indulgences I would buy myself a cake. As soon as I saw it in the window of one of the *pasticcerias* on the Strada Nova, I had to have the whole thing. Called a Cavour, it looked a bit like the Ca' d'Oro, the fifteenth-century "Gold House" that had once been the most opulent residence in Venice. The cake was three layers of crisp meringue filled with espresso-quickened whipped cream into which nuggets of candied chestnuts and chopped chocolate had been folded, its entirety covered with more whipped cream and a Moorish tracery of crumbled meringue, with a final ostentation of edible gold leaf. I borrowed a fork from the proprietor of my cheap *pensione* and ate my cake right out of its bakery box, lying on my back on the marble floor of the crumbling old palazzo's otherwise empty dining room and gazing up at the original trompe l'oeil ceiling, its fresco of curious birds and grinning cherubs gazing back at me.

On my first morning in Paris, I took the Metro to Montparnasse and emerged from a station on the Boulevard St. Jacques, Kay's friend Sam's name and address written in her angular, backward-leaning hand on a note card that I'd tucked into my wallet. I walked down the street, swinging Kay's plastic bag with the shoes inside, feeling virtuous and helpful, but it wasn't until I was rising in the elevator of his nondescript modern apartment building that it registered that I was bringing a pair of Rockport shoes to Samuel Beckett.

I heard the doorbell ring inside with a singular, abrupt rasp, and I waited in the hall. A minute or two passed before someone answered.

"*Oui?*" a man's voice called from behind the door.

"It's Kay's friend Kate," I announced. "I've brought the shoes."

There was a metallic niggling of locks, and the door opened a crack. A slice of Samuel Beckett's face appeared in the opening, his eye a watery blue.

"It's Kate," I said again. "I've brought your Rockports from Kay." I held up the bag.

Samuel Beckett opened the door wider, nodding hello but saying nothing. He looked like an impending ice age. His white hair was cut brushlike and cropped close to his head, his face lithic and planed. He seemed to be wearing a startling number of layers of clothing for summer, all gray. Taking the bag, he nodded again as he began to close the door.

"Do you want me to wait?" I asked quickly. "To see if they fit?"

"Yes, thank you," he said, and the door clicked shut.

I waited. The door opened again.

"Would you like coffee?" Samuel Beckett asked me.

"Yes, that would be nice," I said, but then he shut the door.

I stood in the hall. After five minutes or so, the door opened once more and Samuel Beckett handed me a coffee mug. The water was steaming and there was an island of Nescafé crystals effervescing on the surface of the water, slowly melting and darkening at its edges.

"Sugar?" Samuel Beckett asked me, a sudden afterthought. I said yes, thanks, and leaving the door open this time, he went back to his kitchen. We both pondered strategy for a moment as he offered me the sugar bowl, because I was already holding the coffee mug and wouldn't have another hand to hold the spoon; finally he tilted a spoonful of sugar into my mug, sinking the island. After the door closed again, I sipped my unstirred Nescafé and waited for the verdict.

"They're fine," he said decisively when he returned, standing in the open doorway and staring down at his feet in their new shoes. His sharp profile reminded me of the prow of a ship—an ice cutter—and of Kay's. Their faces were so similar they could have been mistaken for brother and sister. Kay had already told me she thought so, too. "Tell Kay they're fine. Thank you."

Nescafé, I was thinking as the elevator descended. I stepped out into the street, green leaves as large as hands blowing by. I shook my head. No one, maybe not even Arlen, would ever believe this.

I'm not sure what prompted me to think just then of the underwear I'd packed in Samuel Beckett's shoes. I ransacked my memory, but I just couldn't decide whether I'd taken my panties out of the box, or if I so desperately hoped I'd removed them that I imagined I had. I spent the rest of my days in the City of Light electrified by the weird mortifying thrill of having possibly, unintentionally, left my unmentionables with the author of *Waiting for Godot*.

I had one more week before I returned home. Despite the satisfaction of my job and the tenacity of my singular dream, my occasional surges of confidence and glimpses of self-containment, I was still not entirely grounded. The archipelago of my sense of self was still evolving, its borders unmapped. My inner geography would never have the bluster and grandiosity of Rome, the measured poise of Florence, the symmetry and cool arrogance of Paris. I was more tenuously Venetian, I thought: spanned by little bridges, with unexpected detours and a few dead-end alleys, cobbled together by filled-in canals and the holding of breath against the possibility, unthinkable but not impossible, that the glassy mirrored waters would rise too high and the whole bejeweled dreamscape would sink from sight.

I STILL DON'T KNOW how I summoned the nerve to do it, but I must have, because the letter came telling me the short story I'd submitted was one of the winners of the contest, and it would be published. The judges said I wrote like a poet—the highest, most humbling of praise. It wasn't a particularly notable contest unless you lived within a forty-mile radius of San Francisco, but there was a small cash prize, and my story would appear in the newspaper. It was the first story I'd written since college that anyone besides me had read, the first time I'd submitted anything. My first published story.

When I opened the newspaper and saw my name and my sentences and the photograph they'd insisted on taking, me squinting into the sun, overdressed and awkward, not knowing what to do with my hands, I felt as removed from all of it as Musette had seemed up on the roof in Sonoma, gazing indifferently at the kittens she was done with. Not that I wasn't proud, stunned by a euphoric astonishment that I'd actually scratched the surface of the thing I wanted most; it's just that in the transference from my bloodstream to the page, my story had turned into something else. A molten and kinetic thing, urgent for a shape, had cooled into an objective permanence I was no longer part of. I stood back and marveled.

Kay and Ian were the first ones to call. "I didn't know you had it in you, kid!" Ian teased me, then handed the phone to an insistent Kay, who demanded to know why the other winners' stories were published, since they were, in her opinion, vastly inferior to mine. "Oh well, give them their little moment," she said loftily, then told me she was taking me to dinner to celebrate and discuss "my work," as if I had anything else to show for myself.

Kay treated me to the good French restaurant in our neighborhood, where the waiters were all artists and they always welcomed her like a visiting duchess. "Now, it is essential that you simply write, don't think about it," she instructed, fixing me with her cool blue eyes. "Don't dwell, just get on with the writing. Soul-searching will only be destructive to your creativity."

"But, Kay," I said, "if you're supposed to write honestly and deeply about what you know, how do you avoid thinking about it?"

"It's brutally hard work, but one can, as Camus says, alter reality by creative means," she answered.

In her own art Kay was keenly observant, almost preternaturally attuned to the fateful moment of truth for an individual or a relationship or for bodies of power. Her novels and stories were nothing so much as panoramas from her own eventful life, and yet she was obstinately, philosophically resistant to self-reflection—for Kay the only purpose of the subconscious was in service to art. "I urge you to stop now, before it hurts you," she advised me several times, knowing I was deep in therapy, trying to come to terms with what had happened in my family. "I beg you as a mother," she implored, "the cost is too high."

A few days later I was at the grocery store loading carrots into a plastic bag to make a cake for Kay. A woman standing on the other side of the bin kept looking at me. Finally she spoke.

"Excuse me," she said, "aren't you the one who wrote that story? The one in the *Bay Guardian*? Kate Moses, right? I recognize you from your picture."

I blushed, flattered that she'd taken note of my name, and she came around the bin and stood next to me.

"So where do you get your ideas?" she asked, leaning toward me and searching my face. "Did all of that really happen? I know that street—which shop sells the Indian puppets? Did you have the abortion after all?"

I was horrified. Everything that had been so fixedly discrete, the fiction I thought I had objectively shaped and was removed from, was suddenly edgeless and indistinguishable from *me*—not just to this stranger but to myself. She had poked her finger through the fragile caul, and there I was, standing naked in the crowded produce section of the Berkeley Bowl. All those years of longing to be known for myself—how could I not have anticipated how vulnerable I would feel, opening my inner life to scrutiny? *If anyone really knew you, they would despise you.* No matter that my father bitterly regretted his cruel words, no matter how hard I had worked to defuse their power, they were embedded deep in me, and when I least expected it I'd step into them, a minefield. It would be years before I found the courage to send out another short story.

NOT LONG AFTERWARD there was a trash fire in the basement of the old Victorian where Kay occupied the first floor. Damage had been minimal, but Kay and Ian and I were all a little unnerved, and Ian and I agreed to trade off spending nights with Kay for a little while.

Kay was pleased that I'd be staying over and called me at work to ask what I wanted for dinner and breakfast. Kay wasn't cooking much anymore—Ian and I and other friends cooked for her, or the French restaurant sent dinners over—and as I had to work late that first night, I told her not to worry about me. When I arrived, I found that Kay had walked up the street to our local market and bought chocolate croissants for my breakfast. Annoyed to discover only after she got home that the croissants were stale, she came up with a remedy.

"It's so close to Christmas, I thought you should have something festive," she told me. She'd baked the croissants into a bread pudding, and urged me to try some while it was at its best. Kay watched me eat her warm, luscious pudding—she didn't have any herself—and then she led me to her bedroom, insisting that I sleep there, and she would stay in the guest room next door, where the Duchamp bed had migrated.

"Now, when you sleep in a new house," she told me, "you must look to every corner of the room and make a wish. In the morning, remember which corner your eyes first turn to, and that will be the wish that comes true."

"What if I only have one wish?" I asked.

"Then you're upping your odds, just like me," she answered, kissing me goodnight, cheek to cheek, before she closed the door to her room.

In the morning I woke to a sense of presence. When I opened my eyes, I saw Kay standing beside me, a frail, white-haired guardian in a quilted dressing gown.

"I've been watching you," she said. "I didn't want you to forget that wish."

KAY BOYLE'S *PAIN AU CHOCOLAT* BREAD PUDDING

.·.

4 or 5 day-old chocolate croissants
4 cups whole milk or half-and-half
4 large eggs
Pinch of salt
¼ cup granulated sugar
1 teaspoon vanilla
1 tablespoon turbinado, pearl, or coarse sugar crystals

- Preheat the oven to 325°. Butter an 8-inch soufflé dish or other high-sided baking dish with a 2-quart capacity. Slice the croissants about 1 inch thick and arrange them in the dish without crowding; they will expand when the custard is added and baked.
- Warm the milk or half-and-half until just before boiling. Meanwhile whisk the eggs and salt, then add the granulated sugar. Gradually pour the hot milk over the egg mixture, whisking constantly, until completely smooth. Stir in the vanilla. Pour the custard mixture over the croissants and allow to sit for 1 hour before baking. (Or cover the dish with plastic wrap and refrigerate overnight.)
- Just before baking, sprinkle the top of the pudding with turbinado, pearl, or coarse sugar. Bake for 45 minutes to 1 hour, until the pudding appears set and a knife inserted in the center comes out just barely streaky—the pudding continues to cook after it comes out of the oven. Allow to cool for about 15 minutes before serving.

Makes 4 to 6 generous servings.

Chrysalis

EVERY YEAR, AS IT HAS FOR THOUSANDS OF YEARS, SOMETHING FLIPS a switch in the microscopic brains of monarch butterflies and drives them down the central coast of California to the Monterey pine and eucalyptus trees of Pacific Grove, a tiny town at the southern foot of Monterey Bay. There, in a place they've never been before, successive generations of butterflies rest, eat, mate, die, hatch, metamorphose, and emerge, clumped like scraps of orange and black paper high up in the branches of their favorite trees for a few weeks, until something else triggers them to move on, flying en masse, farther up the coast toward Oregon and Canada, through California's Great Central Valley and the Sierras and the Rockies, the next year back down again, as far as Baja, in an annual migration that no one has yet been able to fully explain.

My own appearance in Pacific Grove, where I lived for a year as a new mother, was equally inexplicable. At twenty-six, I surprised myself and everyone who knew me by committing to a marriage and having a baby; my husband moved me to Pacific Grove with our four-month-old son and our big dog and a washer and dryer. He himself never completely moved, driving south to Pacific Grove for a couple of days most weeks while continuing to work in Berkeley.

Maybe it was an aftereffect of my forty-two-hour labor with my son. Maybe it was the exhaustion and overwhelming responsibility of sudden parenthood. Or maybe it was the move, which, though there were stated rationales, I never understood until later. Maybe it was loneliness. Whatever it was, for a year, while I lived in a small damp stucco cottage a block away from the Pacific Ocean, I existed in a state of bafflement. The fog folded in on itself and filled the bay most mornings. I watched it through the ancient slumping glass of my front windows and tried to see beyond it, through it being almost impossible.

My life that year, however mystifying, had its routines. There was my little baby and his needs, there was the dog. On Friday nights as I nursed my baby and ate my solitary dinner and folded laundry, I listened to the choirs practice, seemingly in stereo, in the two churches directly across the street from my drafty, low-ceilinged house. Sometimes one of the churches was lit with what I assumed must be candlelight, the stained-glass rose window flickered so from within. Every Saturday morning I spied through my drawn blinds on the wedding parties assembling in their tuxedos and big pastel dresses on the sidewalk, feeling my face burning at the memory of myself seven months pregnant and still unmarried, dragging my feet for reasons I wasn't prepared to examine. I watched the churches' tandem deacons sweep their steps of rice and birdseed after the ceremonies, often in readiness for yet more weddings that afternoon. Most weekends, I talked to no one, with the possible exception of a clerk at the market or video store.

About a week after my arrival, still wearing maternity clothes and surrounded by boxes, jobless, far away from anyone I knew, I got out the yellow pages and made a phone call. I had begun to suspect that my marriage was failing, and I wanted someone to tell me I was wrong. I'm not sure that the person on the other end of the line at a family crisis center could understand me, since my voice was heaving with sobs and I was cupping my hand over the phone in a feeble attempt at needless discretion—there was no one in the house with me but my baby and the dog—but what I said was, "Help me. I want to leave my husband, and I need someone to stop me."

That got me a cheap weekly visit with a therapist. I made my appointments for Tuesdays or Wednesdays, days when my visiting husband would more likely be around to watch the baby for an hour. Within a couple of months, talking to a therapist gave me the confidence to get out of my house and meet some people. I signed up for a mommy-and-me aerobics class that met twice a week in a former elementary school. I was sure, at first, that I would have nothing, save motherhood, in common with any of the women I was likely to meet: military wives from the nearby army base that was slated for closure, and housewives. I might be home with a baby now, but I'd had a *career* in a *city*. They would be women, I was sure, who never went to bookstores except to sit on the floor in the children's section.

On the first day of the aerobics class, I showed up at the address given by the Parks and Rec department to find another mother slumped on a bench just outside the gymnasium door, one hand rocking her three-month-old's car seat, her gym bag dumped on the asphalt. She was weeping. "I'm sorry," she said, glancing up at me before dropping her chin back to her chest. Her cropped hair was brown at the tips, but the rest was gray to the roots. The bags under her eyes were gray, too. "I'm forty years old. The door's locked, and I don't know why I thought I could do this." With her other hand she made a sweeping gesture, taking in the gymnasium, its hillside view of the bay, the parking lot where our cars were, and her baby.

I'd spent the morning trying to find something to wear to the class, anything that would conceal the fact that five months after giving birth, I hadn't lost even half of the seventy-two pounds I'd gained during pregnancy. But here was someone arguably worse off than I was, at least at that minute. I offered her a silent nod and stepped away to try the locked door. I saw through the window that the rest of the class had gotten inside the gym through the kindergarten entrance on the other side of the building. I picked up the other mother's bag and we made our way around.

"IT'S NOT REALLY RELIGIOUS. It's just art," I explained to my new friends when they stopped by my place with their strollers. My house was crowded with sacred objects: a heavy wooden cross entirely covered with tiny metal *milagros,* a wall of the dining room decorated with *ex-votos*—crudely made pictures painted on battered tin of people lying sick in bed or holding crutches next to crumpled cars, storied offerings created in thanks for illnesses and accidents and disasters survived. On the mantelpiece was a tall thin bishop made of worm-eaten wood that had once lived inside a Mexican church. My husband was an artist, and all of these things were meaningful, but no more so than our books or the Mali cloth that covered my desk or the sheet of banged-up yellow metal my husband hung as a painting after he saw it, I think, fall off the side of a bus.

None of the women I met in Pacific Grove, all of them new mothers, had time to think about God. A few, like me, were lapsed Catholics—or Episcopalians, or Baptists. Some almost certainly went to church. But all of us were too consumed with being at the center of our children's existence to have room for anything bigger in our lives. We were apostles, but our faith was in our babies. Nothing in our experience had ever been so huge.

I was heavy with the faith of motherhood like my friends, but more so. What came with my tentatively budding confidence that I did, in fact, have the power to save my marriage and keep my little family together was the corollary that everything was now up to me. I felt the responsibility of my ragged little world on my shoulders. There was my marriage: I actually visualized myself gritting my teeth, digging my feet in, and refusing to leave, my little blond boy's creamy angelic face floating like an icon before me. There was our crazy enormous dog, who couldn't eat anything except the white rice and lean ground beef that I had been cooking for him every day since he lapped up a corrosive poison around the time the baby was born; I never did figure out where he got it. As fragile as I knew he was in a way, he was also the size of a goat and literally pushed me around the house, not to mention that he could sprint forty miles an hour and did whenever he had the chance. There was my nursing baby, to whom I was everything, I feared, but I wasn't sure I'd be able to remember to teach him how to use a napkin properly when the time came. There was also my life, whatever that was. I honestly couldn't remember who I had been before motherhood, a fact that came alarmingly home to me when I was listing off my son's various family members in a singsong ("your daddy is a painter, your grandpa is a lawyer, your nana plays the harp . . .") and when I got to "your mommy," I couldn't think of anything to say. Whatever accomplishment, talent, identity I'd finessed in the last few years had evaporated into thin air, leaving no trace.

One afternoon my phone rang while I was feeding mashed banana to my son. It was the editor of the literary magazine to which I'd submitted my second short story just a few weeks before learning I was pregnant. Preoccupation with that story's fate had been swept away by more pressing concerns, and by the time the editor tracked me down I was so demoralized by my collapsing marriage and the numbing exhaustion of taking care of a baby alone that I was convinced she had the wrong number and the wrong person, and I hung up the phone. I had to teach my baby to eat, I had to cook for the dog, I had to fold the laundry. Self-less, blank, I was the equivocal glue holding it all together.

Huge with responsibility, I also felt huge physically. Pregnant, I'd gone from slight to impressively, then dismayingly, large. I took up space and air. "Can't you stop that?" my husband once said to me, shaking me awake one night when I was eight months pregnant, so great with child that I felt like I had a baby growing in my lungs. "You're breathing *too much*," my husband said. Nothing I did postpartum seemed to help nudge my body back to normal size, certainly not the mommy-and-me aerobics workouts, regularly interrupted as they were by the doleful crying of my baby from where he slumped on a gymnastics mat with the other brokenhearted infants at the edge of the room. I galumphed gracelessly through my tiny cottage, turning sideways through the narrow doorways, straining buttons, afraid of dropping things. There was no one bigger or more powerful than me. I had the power to keep my baby alive, to keep the dog alive, to keep my marriage alive—or not. "You have so many problems," my husband said to me more than once, shaking his head, confirming all I feared.

By January, I'd lived in Pacific Grove for nearly a year. I was used to seeing my friends and their babies a few times a week, making stroller dates in the afternoons, eating zucchini bread on somebody's rented or government-issue living room carpet while piling up toys for our children to knock over. On the weekends, my friends settled in with their husbands and I watched videos while my baby slept, or I'd bake something, and then, because there was no one else to eat it, it would sit on the kitchen counter like an accusation. Zachary and I would take long aimless walks through the narrow alleys and along the oceanside path, the baby in his striped beret in his stroller, chimney smoke curling up and snagging in leafless tree branches in the yards we passed. We would stop at the deserted elementary school to throw a ball for the dog, and then we hunted the dog down, calling hopelessly after him as he galloped to the far end of the playing field and away.

My life in Pacific Grove, I had months before decided, was a test of faith. The religion I was born into, Catholicism, had washed away many years before. I'd eventually decided that God wasn't something that could be applied externally, and that the church stuff was overkill. My parents' mutual misery and torturous rending of each other and us had taught me that people were what mattered, and what mattered most was being good to people. Even if I doubted my ability to get it together and teach my son anything practical, this was something I knew I wanted him to learn by my example. In Pacific Grove, I was lonely and confused and stranded, sometimes even despairing. Marriage and parenthood weren't something you were supposed to enter into lightly. It took me years to face the fact that I'd done exactly that. But I had a baby. I had to find a way to make it work.

For a while I had tried to convince myself that my suspicions about my marriage were just figments of my imagination. What I didn't anticipate was discovering that the marriage itself was a figment of my imagination, as was the illusion that I, so weighed down by the enormity of my obligations, wielded control over anything. Even my size was not up to me, apparently; I would shrink to normal and smaller within a couple of months, once my husband's confessions—ordinary, really—and hasty, permanent exit killed my appetite. Over the next two years, I became a kind of Alice—not Toklas or the waitress on the TV show, but the one in the looking glass—tumbling down a rabbit hole of my own making, shrinking and growing and shrinking and growing depending not on the potions I drank and the biscuits I nibbled but on upheavals in the bizarre emotional wonderland I'd entered. It wouldn't stop until finally a kind priest, consulted during the darkest hour of my prolonged dark night of the soul, when I was grasping at straws and thought maybe only going back to church could help me, advised, "You don't need to go to church. You need a babysitter and dinner in a nice restaurant and someone to take you out to a movie and tell you you're beautiful."

BROKEN AND HUMILIATED as I felt, the end of my marriage was no shock to me, but it had spread a palpable chill among some of the mothers I knew. Seeing me walking up the street with my stroller or running into me unexpectedly in the aisles of the local market made their eyes dart away before they mumbled excuses and fled. I terrified them. I was the embodiment of their worst nightmare. They were afraid what I had might be catching. *You're* scared? I wanted to say.

The mothers I was closest to, however, hovered near, one or the other of them checking in daily, since they knew I was always alone now, calling me before each class or get-together to insist I come, fierce in their loyalty even as they were mercifully diplomatic on the subject of my failed marriage.

Alicia, one of the aerobics mothers, invited me to her place one Saturday. We'd been taking the same class twice a week for a year, and we'd talked briefly and skimmingly at impromptu picnics in the park. I didn't know her as well as some of my closer friends. I arrived at her house expecting a handful of our aerobics moms, but it was just the two of us and our babies. Her husband coaxed our boys into another room to play, and we sat in her kitchen and talked over tea, then wine, then more tea, as she baked a batch of blondies and popped up now and then to fill sippy cups for the kids and I just sat, grateful not to have to go home, grateful for the look on her face as she nodded and listened. I had hardly been able to choke down anything for weeks, but Alicia and her husband ordered pizza and we watched a real movie together, not a kiddie video, and talked about it afterward. They gave me diapers when I ran out of the supply I'd brought. As Zachary and I were leaving I realized Alicia was thrusting the blondie pan, covered with foil, into my free hand. "Don't bring this pan back until you've eaten them all," she said. "I want you to have something sweet in your life, every day."

Another of the regulars in our aerobics class was Cindy, one of the military moms. They tended to stick together. They had inside jokes and their own babysitting pools. It wasn't that they were unfriendly; it's just that they often seemed streamlined in their social interactions with the mothers who didn't live on the base. One morning as we were approaching the kindergarten door to class at the same time, Cindy stepped ahead, holding the door open for me. "Hey, how ya doin'?" she said, peering down into Zachary's goofily grinning face. Her husband, like several others, had been deployed to Panama right before Christmas. He was coming home, but there was a lot of talk over beer at the canteen that there'd be war in the Middle East. If that happened, she'd move back to Oklahoma with her daughter to be near her in-laws. She would be packing up for the second time in a year, like me. "One thing the army's taught me," she said, now looking me in the eye, "you can survive anything, and you will."

I hoped I would survive, but I wasn't sure how. I had no job, no money in the bank, no relatives anywhere close, nothing I could rely on from my son's father. I had no idea how I would make the rent on my new place in Oakland. The fellowships I'd built during my life in Berkeley had been turned upside down by my sudden marriage. I had no friends with children except for the women in this distant town, and I would probably never see any of them again.

THE BUTTERFLIES WERE late in their exit that year. It had been unusually cold and wet, and they lingered on, clustered in the tree branches to warm themselves and conserve their energy before their long flights north. I'd thought about bundling up Zachary and strolling one last time to their misty wintering groves, but I didn't have any energy to spare, either.

It was still cold on a Saturday afternoon that March, but the sun had finally broken consistently through winter's gray, and I was sitting on the carpet in the high elated light streaming through the bare windows of my dank empty house, trying to pull the cord of my vacuum cleaner out of the rusted electrical socket where it was stuck. My husband had just driven away in a truck loaded with our remaining furniture, our art and Mali cloths and wedding gifts and washing machine, everything except our baby and the dog and my grandmother's dishes. And the vacuum. Both Zachary and the dog were asleep on the carpet, the dishes still stacked on their shelves. There were empty cardboard boxes and a pile of newspapers on the kitchen counter, all the grimy window blinds soaking in the bathtub.

A week before, I'd driven my packed car to the industrial Oakland neighborhood where I would be living in an even tinier house than the one in Pacific Grove, next to a junkyard and the BART tracks, with no neighbors nearby, but with my baby and my dog. I'd have the dishes and a futon and Zachary's crib and toys, and five of the six chairs I'd rescued from Camp Meeker, which had fit, strategically stacked with boxes of books, in my car on the first load. But not the sixth, and not anything else that my husband had just taken away in the truck. I was never going to see any of those things again, but I didn't know that yet. My husband would call me a few hours later, not to tell me that he'd taken all of our things to a locked storage unit to which only he would ever have access, but to find out when I was going to finish cleaning the house in Pacific Grove, and to tell me that he'd had to slow the truck to a crawl and roll up the windows as he'd driven past Watsonville into the Salinas Valley, because he and every other vehicle on the road had been surrounded by monarch butterflies. Thousands of them, hundreds of thousands, passing across the highway in their spiraling, weightless flight. That was one of the last civil conversations we would have for years.

My little boy was napping, bottoms up, on his baby quilt in a corner of the living room, surrounded by a random topography of his favorite toys. The chill March breeze off the ocean was coming right under the front door, riffling his pale hair. I'd watched him change and grow daily in this room, this house. While he bounced in his Jolly Jumper or learned to stand by pulling himself up on the dog, I'd seen a man defy a line of tanks in Tiananmen Square. "Why are you here?" the tank man had asked the Chinese soldiers. I watched the Berlin Wall come down, chunk by chunk. I'd held my baby tight during the Loma Prieta earthquake as our cottage convulsed, staring as the worm-eaten Mexican bishop tipped from side to side on the mantel but never fell.

My stripped, lonely home in Pacific Grove made me so sad, and I needed to get beyond it and figure things out. First, I had to get out of it. I kept tugging on the vacuum cord, hoping it wouldn't ravel out of its stuck plug and electrocute me. There were the dishes to be wrapped one by one in newspaper, all the cleaning and scrubbing and sweeping and dusting. And still there would be the mess of my marriage to clean up for years to come.

My legs were falling asleep under me. I stood up, shaking my tingling feet. The sky over Monterey Bay was crisp, brilliant blue, the sun sparking flares of white light off the surface of the water, and through the slumping plate glass I saw them coming. Some were just locking their car doors out along the curb in front of my house, two sharing the weight of a portable playpen between them. One was carrying a soup pot, her hands in kitchen mitts; another had a tin of cupcakes. Most were walking up the sidewalk past the churches, pushing their strollers. Over the handles were plastic grocery bags bulging with spray bottles and rubber gloves, babies turning their hatted heads and reaching out their small wind-pinked hands to pat the brooms and mops and window squeegees threaded alongside them.

They were coming to clean my house. To help me go.

Kim, who'd been one of the first women I gravitated to when I saw her rolling her eyes as she bounced up and down during the first week of aerobics class, and Pam, who always told me to bring my dog to play dates at her house so he could run around her big fenced yard. Cindy and Teresa and the other military moms. Erlinda, my neighbor, who adopted a baby girl and gave birth to a son six months later. Charlotte from Louisiana, who traded me pralines for a lesson in making straw-berry jam. Alicia, who had sent me home with blondies.

"It's going to get better," they said, surrounding me as they came up my front steps and filled my house, closing the cold out behind us, putting their arms around me, wiping my face with their hands.

ALICIA'S BLONDIES
∴

2⅔ cups unbleached all-purpose flour
½ teaspoon salt
2½ teaspoons baking powder
1 cup unsalted butter
1 pound firmly packed light brown sugar
3 large eggs, at room temperature
1 teaspoon vanilla
2 cups chocolate chips or coarsely chopped chocolate (milk,
    semisweet, or dark)
Optional: 1 cup walnuts, pecans, or almonds, coarsely
    chopped

• Preheat the oven to 350° and generously butter a 13-by-9-by-2-inch pan. Whisk together the flour, salt, and baking powder in a small bowl and set aside.

• Melt the butter in a heavy-bottomed, medium saucepan over low heat, then remove from heat. Add the brown sugar and mix thoroughly. Add the eggs one at a time, beating well after each addition. Add the vanilla and mix well. Add the flour mixture, stirring with a wooden spoon just until the flour disappears. Stir in the chocolate (and the nuts, if using) and quickly pour the warm batter into the prepared pan before the chocolate melts. Bake for 25 to 30 minutes; don't overbake. A tooth-pick inserted in the center will still have slightly wet crumbs—not liquid—attached to it. Allow to cool thoroughly in the pan on a wire rack before cutting into squares.

Makes 24 to 30 blondies.

Intersections

M ore than a year had passed in the tiny oakland victorian where I'd moved with Zachary and our big unruly dog, the only
house left in a neighborhood of anonymous cinderblock warehouses
next to the shipyards. Forklifts beeped back and forth all day unloading
pallets of God knows what in that industrial wasteland, but at night the
streets were deserted. Successive litters of feral kittens wrestled under
the rusty car parts behind the chain-link fence of the junkyard next
door, too shrewd to approach the food bowls I set out until I was out of
sight. The BART tracks ran through what used to be our house's backyard, so I made a game of holding Zachary up to the kitchen window
to wave hello to the passengers, who sometimes noticed us and waved
back as the trains clattered past. The one night I was glad to be so
isolated was a few days after we moved in, when I found a set of mismatched dishes, forgotten by the last tenant, in the built-in china cabinet. I waited until Zachary was asleep in his crib, then I carried the
dishes outside to the warehouse across the street and flung them as hard
as I could, one by one, against the wall. No one could hear as I
screamed until my lungs ached, sailing the plates like Frisbees, watching them smash into bits. When I'd broken every plate, I went back inside for the broom, and I swept the sidewalk clean of shattered china.

During the sleepless months when all I could get was a series of
temporary jobs and the occasional freelance assignment from a newspaper or a magazine, my income was so precarious that every few
weeks I'd cull my closet and my shelves, selling off clothes and books
to make my car payment, the utility bill, my student loan, the rent.
When Zachary's father picked him up for the day, to save money I
didn't eat. I could no longer afford a therapist, but the wise woman
who'd counseled me in Pacific Grove had told me to find companion-

ship however I could. I took Zachary to playgrounds and made small talk with the other mothers in the sandbox even though there was no guarantee we'd ever see them again, or I drove to the waterfront dog park at the north end of Berkeley, where I could count on a friendly dog owner or two to strike up conversations about my gigantic hound, and maybe some chitchat with the people hunting up signatures for their political petitions. If Zachary was with his dad, I attended one of the many twelve-step program meetings I'd found out about—it didn't matter what it was for—and sat in a circle with people whose stories and humility made me feel less alone for an hour. Awake at night, lying on my futon on the floor in front of the windows I'd covered in thumbtacked butcher paper, wondering how I would manage to pay the overdue phone bill before they cut off my service, I asked myself, Could you die from this? Could you die from being this afraid and lonely and forsaken?

What kept me going was the trusting open face of a towheaded blue-eyed toddler with a lisp like Elmer Fudd. The renewed gratitude and delight I felt each day at the sight of my son, knowing that I had some claim on this extraordinary little person, that I'd won the lottery of watching him grow and change, left me breathless. That he needed me, he was counting on me, was my reason to get out of bed every morning. I could not imagine myself without him, or before him for that matter. Soon after Zachary's birth my memories had shifted to accommodate his enormity in my life, photoshopping him in throughout my past. He redeemed me with his wonder at the world. I could swear he reached out his hand for the tassel on my cap as I held him in my arms at my high school graduation; that he was there, crouching over every lizard darting among the toppled columns, as I walked through the Roman forum; that I'd never breathed in the clove scent of wisteria until I watched him press his tender face into the twisted vines hanging from the rafters of our front porch as I carried him down the stairs. "Bawoons!" Zachary announced one day as I pushed his stroller up a hill in Oakland, heading for our tiresome weekly campout at a laundromat. I had the dog's leash wrapped around one wrist to keep him from bolting into the street, a duffel the size of a body bag full of dirty clothes slung over my back. I turned to see where my little boy was pointing: a clump of California golden poppies cheerily nodding their bright orange heads in the breeze, sprung up through the cracked dirt at the base of an untended tree in the sidewalk. Balloons.

It seems impossible given that I was his mother, but by the time Zachary was eighteen months old not so much as a molecule of refined sugar had passed my baby's lips. One balmy May afternoon when the glorious weather was pushing summer up by the roots, I decided it was time. I loaded the three of us into the car and headed for an old-fashioned ice cream parlor at the edge of the Berkeley campus, where sprinklers were chattering over the green lawns in prismatic rainbow arcs.

"What'll you have, little guy?" asked the college student leaning out from behind the counter. My innocent son glanced up from where he sat unsuspecting in his stroller, his pacifier pulsating like Maggie Simpson's in his mouth.

"Just vanilla, a single scoop," I answered, handing a fistful of loose change to the ice cream clerk, the finished cone to Zachary in exchange for the binky.

Zachary held the cone at arm's length for a moment, looking up at me, not sure he'd made a fair trade.

"Try it, it's good," I said, nodding encouragement. "It's ice cream."

Zachary wrapped both hands around the base of the cone, studied it, eased it cautiously toward himself. He lowered his mouth onto the scoop of ice cream, like a barfly descending on an overfull pint. I watched for his reaction. After a pause Zachary raised his head and the ice cream cone together, his eyes wide. His face, fair as an angel's, flushed red with the shock of sweet and cold. Without taking his lips off the cone, he let out a long, earsplitting shriek, cramming the ice cream deeper into his open mouth with a cry of unalloyed pleasure and surprise.

"Now I know you're mine," I told him.

ZACHARY WAS TWO and a half when I finally found a full-time permanent job, a position as the literary director of a nonprofit arts center in San Francisco's Mission District. At my son's new preschool, the children spent their days kneading colored wax into animals, cooking soup and learning to finger-knit, splashing through mud puddles dressed in velvet capes. I tried to assuage my guilt over Zachary's long hours in day care by telling myself it was a perfect place for him, my dreamy little boy wandering through his childhood in a state of fairy-tale rapture, a kid who wore a fireman's helmet day and night for a year and told me that if I opened the little blue door on his leg, an owl would fly out.

I loved my new job, an extension of the midwifery to other writers that I'd done at North Point, though Intersection for the Arts was a nonprofit in the most hair-raising sense. Our staff of six produced a dozen plays and just as many art exhibits and about eighty literary events every year, but we were barely scraping by, always scrambling to work within our minuscule budget and attract an audience to our dicey neighborhood, where I found "POLICE LINE DO NOT CROSS" tape draped over my car more than once when I was locking up late at night.

None of us made more than poverty-level wages, but we all pitched in doing everything, from cleaning the bathroom to writing grants, from curating the programs to answering phones, from building the sets and introducing the guest artists to arguing with terse postal workers over our bulk mail permit. I decided to start hosting self-catered receptions for my visiting writers, trying to make up for our paltry reading fees and the perpetual threat that our audiences would be demoralizingly small. By living on cheap apple fritters from the donut place across the street from Intersection—one apple fritter the size of a pie plate was lunch for two or three days—I could afford to buy the ingredients for a couple of pound cakes or bake an array of cookies to serve with wine at my receptions.

"It's fritter time!" our office manager Marni sang out when she saw me bounding up the stairs with my greasy donut bag. "Mmm-mmm, looks like a big one today, Katy. How about some of my yogurt to wash that down?" The receptions were a ploy that worked, in a way. The writers were flattered that I'd baked in their honor, and the starving artsy types of the Mission started attending my readings with greater frequency. They might not have been any more interested in Intersection's avant-garde literary series than they were before, but the free wine and the all-you-can-eat dessert buffets made up for sitting through an hour of Icelandic metafiction.

I had friends again, lasting ones: the patrons and performers and die-hard staff of our threadbare artistic outpost, all of us committed to nourishing the world with words and pictures and ideas even if we could barely feed ourselves. We helped each other move, borrowed cars and clothes and money, shored each other up. Paul, our theater director, was on a first-name basis with all the lost souls who stumbled by as he swept our entrance of used needles and broken glass every morning. "My rule is, tread lightly with people," he told me once. "You never know what someone else is going through." Marni and Chris, our publicist, and Marni's sister, Arden—who never let me down when my nighttime babysitter punked out an hour before a reading—became like sisters to me. "The problem is, men always think there's someone better out there," Chris observed one evening when we were drinking the leftover wine after one of my receptions. "But women know there could be someone worse." When Chris married our friend Hal, Marni and I spent two days baking the cake for the wedding, which was held at Brainwash, a hipster laundromat with a bar. Somehow in the commotion of cleaning up after the wedding, we left the surplus cake behind. Hal rushed over to Brainwash in the morning to retrieve it and found Hell's Angels sitting at the bar forking up big chunks of his wedding cake while they waited for their dryer cycles to finish. "Good cake, man, congratulations," said a biker in leathers, hoisting his beer in toast as Hal reached over him for the cake box.

Despite Intersection, I continued to have to take part-time work to keep Zachary and myself afloat, most of the jobs miserable or just plain weird. For one I was the photo editor of a book on people who'd survived accidental impalement; at another where I wrote breezy propaganda for an evil corporation, my robotic boss insisted that we sign in and out on our time sheets every time we went to the bathroom. It was more pleasant, though required more effort, to supplement my small salary by writing freelance articles. Writing nonfiction never felt so hazardous as writing fiction; with nonfiction, you aren't at the mercy of anyone's willing suspension of disbelief, least of all your own.

A photographer friend with whom I'd traded freelance advice had tipped me off to a contact of hers, an editor at the weekly Sunday magazine of our local newspaper.

"I think you should pitch a story to Gary Kamiya," Sibylla told me. "You have the same quirky taste. Plus he's really fun to work with. I think you'd hit it off. Seriously, send him a pitch."

I'd barely pulled together a likely query and typed it up and stuck it in the mailbox when my phone rang. It was Gary Kamiya saying he liked my story idea, and could I come in to the *Examiner* to talk about it over lunch?

By this time I'd published multiple feature articles and book reviews in, oh, a dozen publications, and not once had an editor ever asked me to lunch to talk about my pitch. The most I'd ever gotten was a rushed phone call and a contract without a cover note. This guy, I thought, must not have enough to do. But I needed the assignment, and Sibylla said he was easy to work with, so I said yes.

I didn't know that Sibylla had called Gary to tell him that he was an idiot if he didn't ask me out. Word got around in the fishbowl of the *Image* magazine office, and by the time I cleared security and ascended in the *Examiner*'s elevator to meet Gary for our lunch appointment, the entire staff of the magazine was leaning out of their cubicles to say hello, grinning and calling me by name as I passed by.

"What a friendly bunch," I said to Gary.

"They're friendly all right," he said, shuffling me quickly back to the elevator.

At a downtown bistro I learned that, like me, Gary was a San Francisco native, and "Kamiya" was Japanese; at the same time that my father's Eurasian family fled Japan for Australia in 1941, Gary's dad and the rest of his Japanese American farming community were removed from their central California town and imprisoned in an internment camp for the duration of World War II. Somehow the coincidence of our common Japanese ancestry seemed no more noteworthy than the fact that when Gary made an offhand reference to Leonard Cohen's song "Famous Blue Raincoat" I could sing it back to him, because I'd been playing *Songs of Love and Hate* in my car on the drive across the bridge. Or our mutual agreement that certain foods, like hamburgers and french fries, were much more satisfying if you stuffed your mouth full rather than observing the niceties of table etiquette. Gary was affable and complex, an intellectual rogue with a hearty appreciation for kitsch; our conversation, supposedly intended to pin down the fine points of my story assignment about the California missions, ranged from Nietzsche's theory of the eternal return to 1960s commercial jingles to the L=A=N=G=U=A=G=E poets to which character from *Wind in the Willows* we thought we were most like.

When the waiter asked us about dessert, I hesitated. I was hoping the newspaper would pay for our lunch, but just in case, I'd only ordered a salad.

"I'm not big on dessert, but you go ahead, get something," Gary urged. "It's my treat."

I don't remember what I ordered or how it tasted, but the waiter brought two forks. Gary ate half of whatever it was, telling me that his mother never served anything but fruit for dessert when he was growing up. As we left the restaurant Gary was still claiming he didn't have much of a sweet tooth even as he told me he'd been given twenty cents once a week during the summer when he was a kid, and he'd rushed from the house on his bike to buy ice cream cones. He was walking me back toward the parking lot near the *Examiner* building, regaling me with the story of the extravagant pastry he'd bought near the Hospital of the Innocents on a trip to Florence, just about to take his first bite while gazing at della Robbia's sweet ceramic babies over the loggia when a flock of pigeons flew over, dropping their load onto his *sfogliatelle*.

I was listening to Gary's deep amused voice, picking my footing carefully over a slippery metal grate in the sidewalk, when something happened. It was a feeling as clear and untroubled and oddly familiar as Gary's sonorous voice beside me, a voice inside myself telling me *you are going to know this man for the rest of your life.*

THREE YEARS LATER we were married on a rainy May afternoon. It didn't start as a storybook courtship. For a year I was so terrified that I couldn't bring myself to return Gary's calls most of the time. I listened to his messages on my answering machine suggesting we have lunch or a walk on the beach or meet at a museum. "It's me again," I'd hear him say, his voice consistently gentle and appealing. "There's a concert at the Greek Theater I think you'd like. I've got tickets, and I could make us a picnic. It's Sunday afternoon, I don't think you work then, do you? You could bring Zachary, or not, it's up to you. Whatever makes you comfortable . . ." I remember slumping to the floor beside the phone, anguished. I was as afraid for my son's heart as for my own, and I threw every possible obstacle in Gary's path to keep him from knowing me. But he figured me out anyway.

And Zachary—Gary figured him out, too. I see them in the photo album of my mind in those years: pale Zachary freckled and white-blond with his arms around Gary's brown neck in a bucolic Sierra lake, metallic green dragonflies buzzing their wet shoulders. Gary playing his electric guitar with his feet planted between loops of toy train track, Zachary on the floor beneath him playing with a town of blocks and dinosaurs and Playmobil people. And the night I was making dinner and saw out of the corner of my eye Zachary throw himself at Gary's knees as he arrived from work; Zachary hanging on, balanced on Gary's shoes, just holding his legs, not letting go. A few minutes later when Zachary left the kitchen, Gary reached for me. "I can't believe it," he said, tears welling in his eyes. "I think he trusts me—" It was like a scene from the movie of my life that I'd hoped someday could be made, even if production had been delayed for thirty years: a movie about my family, and we were happy.

BROWN SUGAR POUND CAKE FOR
THE ARTISTICALLY DISCRIMINATING
.·.

3 cups unbleached all-purpose flour
1 teaspoon baking powder
½ teaspoon salt
1½ cups unsalted butter, at room temperature
3 cups firmly packed light brown sugar
5 large eggs, at room temperature
1 cup milk
1 teaspoon vanilla

• Preheat the oven to 325°. Butter and flour a 9- or 10-inch tube pan, or two loaf pans, knocking out the excess flour. Sift the flour with the baking powder and salt.
• Beat the butter in the bowl of an electric mixer on medium speed for a couple of minutes, then add the sugar and beat, increasing the speed to medium-high, until very light and fluffy, about 3 to 5 minutes. Add the

eggs one at a time, beating well on medium speed for 2 minutes each, until the mixture again becomes light and fluffy. Scrape the beater and bowl.

• Combine the milk and the vanilla. Add the flour in three portions alternately with the milk, beginning and ending with flour, folding in by hand just until combined. Turn the batter into the prepared pan. Bake 1 to 1½ hours, checking after 50 minutes and every 5 to 10 minutes thereafter until a toothpick or skewer inserted near the center of the cake comes out clean. If the cake is very brown after 50 minutes but not yet fully baked, cover the top with a sheet of aluminum foil. When done, the cake will be springy to the touch and pulling away from the sides of the pan. Let cool in the pan for 10 to 15 minutes, then turn out onto a wire rack to cool completely before glazing.

FOR THE BROWN SUGAR GLAZE:

½ cup unsalted butter
1 cup firmly packed light brown sugar
¼ cup milk
¼ teaspoon salt
½ teaspoon vanilla
1 to 1½ cups confectioners' sugar, possibly more

• Melt the butter in a heavy-bottomed saucepan over low heat, then add the brown sugar and raise the heat to medium. Boil, stirring constantly, for 2 minutes. Add the milk and return to a boil, stirring constantly. Remove from heat and stir in the salt and vanilla. Let cool for about 10 minutes.

• Sift 1 cup of confectioners' sugar over the mixture, stirring with a whisk until smooth. Add the remaining ½ cup of confectioners' sugar and combine thoroughly, adding more sugar if needed for a thick, pourable glaze consistency. Immediately pour over the top of the cooled cake and allow to drip down the sides, like an action painter. Allow the glaze to set completely before slicing and serving.

Makes one very rich 9- or 10-inch cake or two loaf cakes, enough to serve 24 if sliced thinly.

VARIATIONS

For a Vanilla Pound Cake:
Follow the recipe, substituting 3 cups granulated sugar for the 3 cups brown sugar, and omitting the Brown Sugar Glaze.

Butterscotch Frosting:
Brown Sugar Glaze also makes a foolproof penuche candy-like frosting, excellent with many cake flavors: For a two- or three-layer cake, double the ingredient amounts for the glaze. After boiling the butter, brown sugar, and milk and adding the salt and vanilla, allow to cool for about 30 minutes before whisking in 3 cups of confectioners' sugar. If too thin to hold its shape, add up to 1 additional cup of confectioners' sugar; if too thick, whisk in additional milk a teaspoon at a time. The frosting sets completely as it cools.

The Child Within You

"THERE HE IS AGAIN—NO, THERE, WITH THE TEENAGERS BUYING focaccia at the espresso bar. He's looking at his train tickets."

Gary and I were traveling through Italy on our honeymoon, and everywhere we went, my dad was following us. Not really my dad, but men who looked just like him: blue-eyed northern European tourists with trim white beards and thin legs, wire-rim-spectacled older guys wearing fanny packs and Bermuda shorts and long black socks with their sensible shoes. We saw my dad so often it became the running joke of our trip—he was checking up on me, alleviating his chronic fears about me by making sure I hadn't made another huge mistake with my life.

In the years since my parents' divorce, my father had become an attentive hands-on dad not just to my brothers and me, but to my little sisters, Goldie and Adele, Adele born just three years before Zachary. To Zachary he was a gentle and protective grandfather, the volunteer who'd always go in search of a missing toy or blanky. He displayed his old fierceness for the first time in many years when I told him my marriage to my son's father was breaking up. "I don't care what you two do with your lives," he'd growled at me, "but you *put that little boy first!*" I got a kick out of the phone calls from my dad when he'd announce, after a few minutes of catching up with me, "Really, I called to talk to Zachary. Could you put him on?"

Transformed as my father's life had been after meeting Nancy, they hadn't had an easy time. My dad left the government to work with a private group of companies planning a new Alaskan gas pipeline, but it meant he traveled more than ever; for years he spent more time in airplanes than at home. He found himself cutting his own salary repeatedly as the project got more complex and his employers were bought out by successive corporations. With his anxiety-prone personality, it was no surprise that he developed high blood pressure.

During her pregnancy with Adele, Nancy grew increasingly, mysteriously dizzy. By the time she went into labor she couldn't walk unassisted. She was diagnosed with a brain tumor, though it was expected to be benign and the surgery to be routine as brain surgeries go. Instead Nan woke from her surgery—a woman still in her thirties, with a six-year-old and a six-week-old—unable to see, hear, taste, or move on her left side, paralyzed from a surgically induced stroke that stopped her from hemorrhaging to death. She was never able to play the harp again, but her desire to smile at her daughters and take care of them gave her the incentive to spend years enduring more surgeries and relentless physical therapy to regain as much control of her body as she could. While Nancy was recovering from another brain surgery when Adele was three, Billy happened to read an article about an experimental drug therapy for brain tumors like Nan's. She was entered into the program, which has kept her tumor at bay ever since, allowing her to learn to drive again, lead Adele's Girl Scout troop, complete her Ph.D. in musicology, and take care of my dad when he fell down the stairs the day after his forced early retirement, resulting in a spiral fracture of his leg that rendered him housebound for months.

My dad had finally recuperated from his broken leg when he was diagnosed with adult-onset juvenile diabetes a few months before Gary and I got married. In the days before the wedding, awaiting the arrival of my family who, with Gary's, would witness our marriage at the top of the grand staircase in San Francisco's City Hall, more than once I was struck by the gratifying thought that my dad didn't need to worry about me anymore. I was finally settled: I was marrying a good, honest man who loved me and my son. We were "throwing in our lots together," as Gary said, already planning for a near future when I'd be able to cut back on my work so we could expand our family. Meanwhile I had a fulfilling job and a reputation in my field, and I'd been chosen for a three-year residency at another local arts center, where I would be able to work on the novel I'd begun writing. Motherhood had galvanized me in ways I could never have anticipated, and now I was going to be an equal partner in a real marriage. As a daughter, I was on a different plane now. My dad could cross me off his list of anxieties.

I thought about this as I shopped for a Father's Day gift for my newly diabetic dad—I was looking for cookbooks with sugar-free dessert recipes. I would see my father for only a few hours on the day of the wedding, as Gary and I were leaving the next morning for Rome, but when we got back we were taking Zachary to Southern California for "the kids' honeymoon," a Disneyland weekend and belated Father's Day celebration with my dad, Nancy, and the girls. I wanted to surprise my dad on that trip with the one dessert I made that I knew he loved, the only one he'd ever asked for: cheesecake of the New York delicatessen variety, high and light and densely creamy, with a thin tangy layer of sour cream topping. I wasn't sure how I'd pull that off for a diabetic with high blood pressure, but I was going to find a way.

Motherhood had more than galvanized me. It had taught me that no matter how flawed or inadequate your parents might otherwise be, if they kept you fed and clothed and alive through your first three years, they deserved a lot of credit and no little appreciation. My dad had made terrible errors as a parent, but he'd acknowledged them and asked for my forgiveness and struggled to correct them, and he'd become the father I could rely on when I stumbled. I knew that his failings as a parent had been a result, ironically, of his greatest fear—of not living up to his responsibilities to us. Maybe it would only be a cheesecake, only *my* happiness, but I wanted to repay my dad even a little bit for all those years of anxiety.

Seeing him waiting for us outside City Hall, checking his watch in the rain, I was startled to see how white my father's hair had become. It hadn't been so long since I'd seen him—had I not noticed? But he looked good nonetheless: distinguished in his tidy beard, healthily trim, pleased as he held five-year-old Zachary's hand and admired the bow tie and miniature gray suit my little boy was wearing to serve as Gary's best man. Gary's parents were there, his brothers and sisters and their families, some of his cousins. Goldie was a bubbly articulate fourteen, helping Nancy, laughing, up the steps; eight-year-old animal-lover Adele, blue-eyed like our dad and blond as Zachary, wore her long hair princess-style, just like me at her age. I was too proud of my brother Bill to be disappointed that he couldn't make it to my wedding; he was in South Africa, an official observer to the national elections marking the end of apartheid, which he'd been working toward for over a decade. Neither could I take it personally that my mom didn't come. We had been in contact again since around the time of Zachary's birth. She, too, had remarried happily and was returning in less than a month from South America, where her husband had been working. But John came from Washington, D.C., where he was beginning a career with the Environmental Protection Agency, and introduced us to Marina, who would become my sister-in-law at a wedding we all attended before the end of the year, just as we'd assemble again for Billy's marriage to his fiancée, Tish, shortly before my first wedding anniversary. My brothers and I were all loved, we were doing good work, we'd made it. My wedding felt to me like a turning point in my family, not just for my little family of three, but for the people who'd made me.

Maybe it's odd that someone so aware of the indelibility and power of words would have no idea what was said at her marriage, but I don't. Not a syllable. When Gary and I talked about writing our own vows, I couldn't do it. I couldn't find the words that would assemble and contain all I felt. The story was happening, ineffable, all around me: our families encircling us in the rotunda at the top of the dramatic staircase, the quickening rain beating down on the bronzed dome above our heads, the smiling judge in his robes, and Zachary between us, clutching my skirt, murmuring "Thanks, Mommy . . ." as I helped him with the knot on the ring bag, which I'd tied too tightly. Realizing I was trembling, I could see only Gary's eyes as his hands enfolded mine, his calm tenderness coaxing me into our story.

When the ceremony was over, I turned from my new husband, flushed with a stunning joy, and there was my father. I saw him as if from behind the lens of a camera—the individual frames of his approach to me, his arms opening, his pale blue eyes glistening with tears, the roughness of his beard against my cheek. Even as it was happening, I knew I would always remember it this way: hugging my father at my wedding, every moment framed.

"OKAY, THERE—ON THE beach right below us. It's your dad again. He's reading his pedometer."

I glanced up at Gary's call from across our hotel balcony at Positano, forcing myself to look away from the pages of the absorbing, beautiful, heartbreaking book I'd brought on our trip, a book I'd picked because I wanted something memorable to read on my honeymoon: *A Death in the Family,* James Agee's autobiographical novel about his childhood, published posthumously after the author's untimely death, too young, from a heart attack. Before the trip I'd read only the novel's prologue, "Knoxville: Summer 1915," the few exquisite pages of which had been printed in a fine letterpress edition, the first gift I ever gave to Gary. It told of summer evenings when Agee had been, as he put it, "so successfully disguised to myself as a child," of fathers coming home from work to early suppers and coiling the garden hose, of mothers retracing their household steps and measuring out the cocoa for the next day's breakfast, of children playing until they are called from the gathering dark; and of his own family lying on quilts in the damp grass, talking quietly, listening to locusts, the stars close above them: people who know him and love him but "will not, not now, not ever; but will not ever tell me who I am."

In Rome, Pompeii, on the Amalfi coast, touring Sicily, I climbed through ruins and napped on beaches and whispered in churches and enjoyed my ebullient husband and ate, and when I wasn't doing any of those things I read my book, and everywhere, there was my dad. He was studying the CAVE CANEM mosaic in Pompeii, his hands clasped characteristically behind his back. He stood at the railing of our ferry from Naples, facing into the gigantic heaving waves we were crashing through, his windbreaker blown up like a sail at his back. We shared a funicular with him at Taormina, and he was watching the same Aristophanes play we attended in a Greek theater on a blistering day in Siracusa; he'd brought his own stadium cushion and battery-operated fan. And when Gary and I finally staggered out of an olive grove at dawn after hiking for hours in the dark, coming down from the summit of the island Stromboli's live volcano—our flashlight had died, we'd lost our picnic dinner, we were coated head to toe with gritty dust from wading through an ash field, punch-drunk with exhaustion, lava erupting fiery and sparking every fifteen minutes out of the mouth of the volcano behind us—there, on his way *up* the volcano, was my dad, belting out marching songs in German, Swiss, Danish, whatever language he was speaking this time, equipped with walkie-talkie and trekking poles and a miner's light, blindingly bright, strapped to his forehead.

I caught a last glimpse of him in Erice, a fortified village perched on a mountaintop overlooking the west coast of Sicily, famous for centuries before Virgil wrote about it in the *Aeneid,* the site of one of the ancient world's most revered shrines to a syncretic succession of fertility goddesses: Isis, Astarte, Aphrodite, Venus. A Norman castle had eventually been built over the shrine, and all that was left of the marble temple was a rocky promontory at the edge of a plunging cliffside with panoramic views, on a clear day, all the way to Tunisia. Local tradition held that if you brought an offering to the ruins, your prayer for a baby would be answered. That possibility and the town's more recent reputation for having the best *pasticceria* in Sicily was enough to put Erice at the summit of my personal itinerary.

After a couple of days exploring Erice's twisting cobbled alleyways and secretive limestone staircases, breathing in the pine-scented air from the forested slopes below and gathering the wildflowers and blush-pale roses blooming everywhere, sipping Campari in tilting piazzas with Gary crowing at the mind-blowing vistas, we carried my flowers and an assortment of *dolci* from Maria Grammatico's renowned shop up to the castle to make our chthonic petition. My arms were full of delicately fragrant petals and hand-painted marzipan fruit and *sospiri e désirs,* "sighs and desires," decorative little almond cookies flavored with honey and lemon, and Erice's specialty cinnamon biscuits embossed with a honeycomb pattern, after the golden honeycomb Daedalus was said to have dedicated at the temple's shrine. For me, tossing my cookies over the side of a mountain was going to be a real sacrifice.

As Gary and I climbed along the Punic walls, there was my dad sitting in the public garden, gazing out at the sapphire Mediterranean. He was alone this time, without his various wives or children or tour groups.

"Aww, there's my dad," I whispered to Gary as we passed by with our roses and pastries. Joke or not, I couldn't help feeling touched by my dad's intrepid pursuit of me.

"Eh, maybe not," Gary answered, squinting behind his glasses, "that guy looks a little like Berlusconi."

After we'd thrown our offerings off the cliff, making our request for a baby girl and promising to name her Erice in thanks, Gary and I turned back toward the village and promptly forgot our pledge. Neither of us thought about it again for years, until our daughter, Celeste, was in first grade and asked how she got her name. Maybe the benevolent goddesses decided to forgive us for the slight, granting us their favor anyway as a consolation for what happened next.

THE PHONE RANG at three in the morning. Gary and I had been back in San Francisco long enough to recover from jet lag and distribute all the presents we'd brought home for Zachary, and for me to hurry up and finish reading James Agee's moving novel, which had turned from its innocent beginnings into the story of a father's unexpected death and its impact on the young family he leaves behind. What a strange coincidence, I'd thought vaguely, the heart attack that sets the plot in motion, and James Agee's death from the same cause as he was completing his novel, almost as if he'd predicted it. But I had other things to think about, other things to do. The next weekend, we were driving to Southern California for our Disneyland assignation. My dad and Nancy would have just returned, also, from Alaska, a summer vacation with the girls that had been postponed by my dad's broken leg the previous year.

It was Nancy on the phone, calling from a hospital in Anchorage. My dad had suffered a massive heart attack in their hotel room. She and Goldie and Adele had been with him. He died instantly.

IN THE DAYS AFTER I met Nan and the girls at the Los Angeles airport, while we waited for the rest of the family to arrive from New York, Washington, D.C., Sydney, San Francisco, we did what had to be done, mimicking the actions of people who were in control of a crisis, not hurtling down an abyss of anguished disbelief. We even looked fairly normal, or so I thought when I saw Nancy and my little sisters walking toward me at the baggage claim from their long flight from Anchorage. Nothing made sense—they still looked like themselves. Except for the red eyes, the pallor of sleeplessness, the slow heavy steps, Adele's almost inaudible whisper, they were physically unmarked by the horrific trauma of the night before. How could it be that they did not look like a wife whose husband had turned blue as he napped on the bed during *The Sound of Music*? Or like a fourteen-year-old who ran screaming through a hotel, pounding on doors that didn't open, begging for help because her dad was dying? Like an eight-year-old who'd been taken to the zoo by her dad that afternoon, but a few hours later watched paramedics burst in and flip him to the floor like a rag doll?

Why didn't I look like the station signals from my brain had shorted out, and all I could see was my young dad cross-legged on the floor shining his shoes; my dad monitoring his watch and fuming with impatience in front of the Mad Hatter's Tea Party ride; my dad turning toward me in the mist of an Alaskan waterfall, his face sheeted with unexpected tears. My dad with the string of a pink donut box taut under his fingers; my dad insisting on slowly, methodically, maddeningly changing the oil in the Karmann Ghia he bought for me, wiping the dipstick on his handkerchief before he'd let me drive back to Stockton; my dad approaching to hug me at my wedding, each moment clicking forward like the shutter of a camera; my father's heart erupting in his chest like a chrysanthemum blooming in time-lapse photography. Why didn't I look like a wailing inconsolable orphan, which is how I felt? Maybe that is how I looked. I wouldn't know. I never checked.

No one was ready to contemplate having my father's body cremated. Nancy, my little sisters, my brothers, and I were all too haunted by what we'd seen or couldn't stop ourselves from imagining. My dad never liked the fakery and excess of Southern California, but it didn't seem that we had any choice but to bury him there. Nancy and I had a list of cemeteries, and we had to pick one, and then we had to bring my father's clothes to the mortuary. We had to plan a funeral and find someone to officiate at a service for a converted lapsed Catholic married to a Jew; we had to figure out what to do for my dad's relatives coming from Australia. There's something obscene about people sucker-punched from a death trying to organize what amounts to a party.

At the mortuary Nancy and I sat side by side, grocery bags of my dad's things in our laps as the funeral director described our various options with a respectful calm that was simultaneously soothing and unnerving, inadvertently reminding you that what you were doing was unthinkable. We didn't want a "viewing," private or otherwise. We didn't want to know about the special seals on the various gradations of coffin or why they were there. We didn't want one of those things that lowered the coffin into the hole as everyone sat watching in rented chairs. When the funeral director asked for the clothing my father was to be buried in, Nancy handed him my dad's best suit and a bag full of the rest—shirt, tie, underwear, handkerchief, socks.

I had the shoes. I reached into my bag and could get no farther. My muscles froze. I had my hand slipped under the tongues to lift them out but nothing happened. My body, my heart, no part of me, voluntary or not, wanted to give up my father's shoes. I'd polished them myself that morning with his shoeshine kit, buffed them to as high a shine as the old leather would take, but now I could not let them go. I looked up at the funeral director, helpless, new tears stinging my sore eyes. Under my fingers the inner leather was worn smooth, shaped to my dad's feet, surprisingly small. There was nothing left; this was the last I had. The funeral director waited, patient.

"Do you want me to?" Nancy asked, her hand resting on my knee.

"No," I said, embarrassed, angry with myself. The sound of my own voice broke the spell. I was thirty-two, not five. They were just shoes. I forced my arm upward, pulling the bag away with my other hand. This time, the last time of handing over my father's shined shoes, I saw only my own reflection.

BILLY AND JOHN arrived with Tish and Marina, looking as shattered and stuck in a nightmare as I felt. Together with Nancy we continued to sort through my dad's orderly papers, looking for insurance documents, deeds and car registrations, orthodontist bills, the details Nan would need to carry on. Knowing how constantly my father traveled, one of the first things Nancy and I did was to find his frequent-flier cards and call the airlines to see if there might be enough mileage credit to help us get the rest of the family to the funeral. My dad turned out to be the number one frequent flier on two airlines, one of them with over half a million miles saved up, altogether the equivalent of twenty first-class round trips and fifty coach fares.

Going through his things, we'd begun to discover more about my father than any of us, even Nancy, had known. In the last ten years, I'd come to understand his inability to share information about himself as not simply repressive or ingenerous, but, again, as a function of fear—of seeming immodest, of asking too much for himself. In an expansive mood during one of my recent visits with Zachary, my dad had admitted that there were three things he wanted in his life: an Old English sheepdog, a Citroën Deux Chevaux, and to go back to Sonoma. It crushed me to think he would never have these things, this humble list of desires—the closest he got was living vicariously through the little blue car he gave me in college. At his death he had no more material belongings than he'd owned when I was a child. In one of his bureau drawers I found the pair of Levi's I bought for his birthday one year, teasing him that it was time he joined the modern age and owned a pair of jeans. They were still folded inside the box I'd wrapped them in, the card slipped under the tissue paper.

In his desk I found a file of clippings from various newspapers around the country, all of them reviews of North Point Press books or features about the press's authors—he'd saved every mention of a North Point book he'd ever seen, whether I'd worked on them or not. We knew he'd attended Georgetown on an academic scholarship at seventeen, but not that he'd been awarded several other scholarships as well, including a full athletic scholarship to Princeton—we were dumbfounded to learn that our completely nonathletic father had been an exceptional golfer as a teenager, with a five handicap. He'd completed both his undergraduate degree and his Doctor of Law degree in five years, a full year ahead of his class, but he was not a U.S. citizen and so not permitted to take the bar exam. He petitioned the California state and federal supreme courts for the right to take the bar, becoming the first person in California history to pass the bar as a noncitizen, and one of the youngest practicing attorneys in the state.

I knew that my dad's area of legal expertise was mineral law, but I didn't realize it evolved out of an abiding environmental interest. Yes, I knew my parents went camping on their honeymoon (an immediate red flag, if you'd asked me), and my dad liked to stand around in national parks with his hands, as always, clasped behind his back, just like at the dump. I didn't know that his principal client was the National Park Service when we moved to Pennsylvania, and that against the backdrop of those monotonous Sunday drives, my dad was fulfilling a federal mandate to clean up the Schuylkill River, which had become so polluted it wouldn't freeze in the winter. Starting with the crisis over Native American rights at Wounded Knee, my dad negotiated agreements between the government and the tribal communities for protection and fair recompense of natural resources on Native lands. He worked on the Endangered Species Act and later on its enforcement, prosecuting illegal importations of endangered animals and drafting all the governmental stipulations for protecting nesting and breeding grounds during construction of Alaska's oil pipeline.

My careful attorney father, the government's counsel on the most expensive, disputed, and sweeping environmental project ever undertaken in this country, a man who faithfully logged his gas mileage for decades as if he were going to be tested on it, who lived by the letter of the law, who after his conversion to Catholicism not only thought divorce was a sin but wouldn't eat a tuna casserole on Friday because there was beef flavoring in the cream of mushroom soup my mom used as a sauce—he may not have talked about it, but my dad had everything carefully filed, documented, accounted for. Except for one thing. He died intestate, without a will.

We couldn't believe it. We looked everywhere, called his colleagues and old attorney friends. It was unimaginable. Or maybe, I have wondered in the years since, what was unimaginable to us was unimaginable to my father in a different way. Maybe not making a will had been my dad's underhand toss to fate, his one stab at optimism. For my father, who believed his life's duty was to provide, it was unimaginable that he would die at fifty-seven, with five kids and a little grandson and a disabled wife.

My brothers and Nancy and I were still staggering around, processing this news, when my mother called. I had been talking to her every day since my dad died. She was as shocked and devastated as the rest of us.

"I know it's hard to believe, but your dad and I became good friends in the last few years," my mother repeated with every call. She didn't need to. I knew it was true. Free of the bonds of their disappointment in each other, content in their second marriages, they had been able to find an accord I never would have predicted, a relationship that had very little to do with my brothers and me. Nancy's illness in particular had drawn them together. They had spent holidays together. My mom was something of a playful long-distance auntie to Goldie and Adele.

We, too, had reconciled since I became a mother, though initially my mom had been distressed to become a grandmother at—well, how old was she, anyway? I never knew until her seventieth birthday. She carefully guarded her age through my entire childhood, and for a while she had a driver's license that would have made her eleven when she had me. At my first wedding reception, when I was so monstrously swollen with maternal hypertension I looked like Jabba the Hutt, my svelte youthful mother had shown up in a red silk minidress. For a couple of years after Zachary's birth, she struggled to come up with a nickname that fit her image of herself: "How about if Zachary calls me Marmee? You know, like the mother in *Little Women?* I think that's perfect for me!"

Having a grandson also took some getting used to. During my son's first months, my mother sent me packages of lovely beribboned dresses for baby girls. "But, Mom," I reminded her, "he's a boy." "Oh, that's all right," she'd say. "They're so cute I couldn't resist. Don't you want to keep them anyway?"

We had both adjusted with time, and she came to visit and meet Zachary shortly after I'd moved back to Oakland, a reeling single mother. She wanted to offer her moral support; if anything, she may have been more distraught than I was. "That silver-tongued devil!" she cried at night, weeping next to me on the futon, my plight dredging up her own old ghosts of loneliness and the terror of contemplating leaving a bad marriage with small children. While I was out one day at a job interview, in her fervor to be helpful she managed to scrub off all the numbers on the dials of my rented stove.

"I've been thinking, Cis, and I need to talk to all of you about your dad's funeral," she said now. Her voice was thick. She'd been crying again, too. "I need to tell Nancy and Billy and John. This is *really* important."

"Okay, Mom," I said, bracing myself, thinking, *Oh God no, not something else that's really important.* I knew from experience that "*really* important" often signaled that it was not important, or time sensitive, or necessary; at the very least that familiar maternal phrase usually meant whatever it was would be massively inconvenient. This was the day before the funeral and there was a lot of stuff that *was* really important to do. Really. Such as coping, and comforting minor children who'd seen their father die.

"Cis, your dad and I really did learn to respect each other, we really were friends. But other people might not understand."

I listened, waiting for the inconvenient other shoe to drop.

"Nancy understands, I know that," my mom continued, her voice starting to catch. "But other people—" I could hear the pain in her voice. "Oh, *Bill*—" She called out, almost as if she thought she could talk him out of it. "Oh, poor Nancy, those little girls—they need all the support they can get, and I don't want to take any attention away from them. From Nancy, or Goldie and Adele, or you kids. Do you see what I'm saying? I don't think I should come to your father's funeral after all." She was sobbing openly now.

I was ashamed of myself. What was it I'd learned from my friend Paul? *Tread lightly with other people, you never know . . .*

"I do understand, Mom," I told her. It was so generous, to step aside when she was mourning, too.

"Your dad—I can't believe it—" she gasped, losing herself for a moment. "It's really shaken me," she said. "It's made me think about things. Maybe I wasn't such a perfect mother as I thought I was." She wasn't asking for a confirmation or a denial. She was letting me know.

To be known, to know myself: It was always what I wanted, what I'd longed for. To be meaningful, it meant finding the generosity to let other people come to know themselves as well, as best they could, however long it took.

"I understand, Mom," I told her as she cried. "What a selfless, kind thing you're doing."

The Australian relatives would be arriving from their hotel at any time, and the compassionate rabbi I'd found was stopping by to meet with us and finalize the service. Gary was flying in and bringing the flowers, a camping cooler full of forget-me-nots that my helpful neighborhood florist in San Francisco had been uncertain she'd be able to locate in early July. "It was a stroke of luck," she told me when she called back. "I found a source in Alaska, of all places." Everyone would be coming to the house after the funeral; a caterer friend had told us not to worry, he'd handle everything. I'd told him there was one thing I'd do myself.

I handed the phone to Nancy. My older brother Bill stood beside her, his arm around our stepmother, waiting his turn to speak to our mom. Tish and Marina were sitting with Goldie between them on the couch, wrapped in quilts, drinking tea and letting her talk and sob and talk. John was on the carpet with Adele, the two of them setting up "the guys," her collection of stuffed animals. I was with my family: We knew each other, we loved each other. We were letting each other be whoever we needed to be. From the kitchen I listened to their quiet conversations. I was making cheesecake for my dad.

MY FATHER'S FAVORITE CHEESECAKE
.·.

FOR THE CRUST:

1⅓ cups fine graham cracker or gingersnap crumbs
2 tablespoons granulated sugar
2 tablespoons unsalted butter, melted

• Preheat the oven to 350°. Mix the crumbs and sugar in a small bowl, then add the melted butter, mixing thoroughly. Turn the mixture into a lightly oiled, 8- or 9-inch springform pan with high sides, pressing evenly over the bottom and about 1 inch up the sides of the pan. Bake for 10 minutes, then let cool while you prepare the filling, leaving the oven on.

FOR THE FILLING:

2½ pounds cream cheese, at room temperature
1½ cups granulated sugar
Pinch of salt
1 tablespoon vanilla
4 large eggs, at room temperature

• In the bowl of an electric mixer, beat the cream cheese on medium speed until thoroughly smooth, about 5 minutes. Add the granulated sugar and salt and beat again until thoroughly smooth. Add the vanilla and mix. Add the eggs one at a time, beating for a full minute after each addition and scraping down the sides of the bowl, making sure to reach the bottom. When all the eggs have been added and the mixture is smooth, again scrape down the bowl all the way to the bottom; beat again until the filling mixture is completely silky smooth. Shape a sheet of heavy-duty aluminum foil over the outside of the cooled prepared pan, then pour the filling over the cooled crust (the foil will slow the cooling of the cheesecake after it is baked, which will help prevent cracks, and it will also catch any drips from the bottom of the pan during baking). Bake at 350° for 30 minutes, then turn down the oven to 325°

and bake for another 20 to 30 minutes, until the cake is risen, starting to brown, and firm to the touch on the edges but still somewhat soft in the center. While the cake is baking, prepare the topping.

FOR THE TOPPING:

2 cups sour cream
5 tablespoons granulated sugar
½ teaspoon vanilla

• Whisk the sour cream, sugar, and vanilla together in a small bowl. When the cake is done, remove it from the oven and pour the topping gently and evenly over the top. (If the cake has risen so high that it has cracked significantly at the edges, allow it to cool and the cracks to subside for a few minutes before adding the topping.) Return the cake to the oven and bake for an additional 5 to 8 minutes, until the edge of the topping is set. Remove the cake from the oven and allow to cool completely in the pan on a wire rack, away from drafts. When the cake is room temperature, remove the foil, cover the surface of the cake with plastic wrap, and allow to cool completely before refrigerating until thoroughly chilled, at least 4 hours or overnight. Do not refrigerate the cake until it is cooled to room temperature, or it will weep.
• To remove the cake from the pan prior to serving, warm the blade of an offset spatula or kitchen knife under hot water, wipe it dry, and run the knife carefully around the inside edge of the pan before opening the spring lock to release the cake.

Makes one 8- or 9-inch cake, about 16 servings.

Cakewalk

I WAS IN A CAKEWALK ONCE. IT WAS PART OF A SCHOOL'S ANNUAL PIC-
nic held in a meadow at Golden Gate Park, on a cloudless, faultless
spring afternoon—tulips bobbing in a sandy field by the beach, Stow
Lake sifted yellow with the pollen of cypress trees, crab apples and
fuchsia in bloom, the swaying crowns of eucalyptus clacking in the
faint breeze. The occasional disembodied trumpet note of a nuthatch
sounded from the trees. We sat on blankets spread over the grass and
watched as one by one each class assembled before a patient, admiring
crowd of families and teachers and performed a song or a skit or recited
poetry. The eighth graders, wearing circlets of wildflowers in their hair,
wove wide satin ribbons around a maypole as a last communal ritual before they'd scatter in the fall to different high schools and the rest of life.

After the potluck lunch, the games were set up: sack races and egg-
and-spoon races and a water balloon toss, a pet parade, a messy and ecstatic canned whipped cream fight. There was only one game I wanted
to play. I stood in line for the cakewalk, clutching my ticket to my heart
like all the other contestants, turning my head now and then to eye the
banquet table loaded with cakes and cupcakes and cookie baskets and
freshly baked pies as I waited for my turn.

When I got to the front of the line, I held out my ticket. "May I play,
too?" I asked shyly.

The ticket taker squinted at me from under her straw hat. "Sure!"
she said, smiling. "Just stand on one of the flowers in the circle and listen for the music."

I took my place on a big laminated paper cutout of a flower, drawn
in a loopy childish hand. Standing around me in the circle on each of a
dozen numbered flowers were six- and seven- and eight- and nine-
year-olds, a preschooler or two. I was forty-five.

The ticket taker pressed "play" on her tape recorder, and as I marched from flower to flower with the other contestants, I recognized the song: It was a song from my sixties childhood that I hadn't heard since I was six or seven years old myself. It was a song about childhood and its sweetness—about floating on the innocence of ordinary delight, of the joyous freedom that comes from knowing you are safe and loved. *Bicycles, tricycles, ice cream, candy . . . don't be afraid to be young and free.* My life as a child, that indelible time of fear and confusion, its bitterness and compensations so far removed from the childhood I ached for even as I was living it, came rushing back at me with such force I had to hug myself. I almost didn't hear the music stop.

The ticket taker had called the winning number. The children were pointing at my flower, jumping up and down.

"You won! You won!"

I can never get over the altruism of little children. Their swift forgiveness, even in the face of their own disappointment. The ease of their pleasure for anyone who wins.

I stumbled out of the circle, wondering how—how, with my life, my wounded and haunted past—did I manage to win? This is a question I've been asking myself throughout adulthood, at every triumph, however mean or profound: the parking place opening up right in front, love returned, a baby's toothless gaping grin.

> *Undo the locks and throw away the keys*
> *and take off your shoes and socks, and run you.*

The by-product of suffering, if you're lucky, is appreciation—the savor of chance windfalls. My windfall has always been a sweet tooth, the gold watch that deflected the bullet aimed straight at my heart. It wasn't only wounded and haunted, my past. The words of the song reminded me. Bicycles, tricycles, ice cream, candy . . . every phrase was a memory, a story, a moment I could still taste. Fluffernutter, Sugar Pops. Running through meadows, scaring up milking cows. Running down a beach kicking clouds of sand. Waltzing Matilda, Tweedledum and Tweedledee.

Cowboys and Indians, puppy dogs and sand pails . . .

Lolly pops, popsicles, licorice sticks . . .

Give a little time to the child within you, the song says. Remember the forget-me-nots, the joyous shout at the end of the game: *home free.*

At the cake table, there were more children crowded around. "You won—you can have anything you want—what are you going to choose?"

I scanned the possibilities, the table all but overflowing. There were some packaged delicacies from the city's chic bakeries, gâteaux and tortes and tartlets garnished with sprigs of lavender or whole hazelnuts or *fleur de sel*. There were cupcakes shoulder to shoulder, ten different renditions of chocolate chip cookies, brownies iced and plain, Bundt cakes, pound cakes, angel food cakes, cakes frosted pink and chocolate and lemon, crumbled with streusel, dripping with glaze. The music had started up again behind me, another round of players waiting for their turn to bask in the glow of random good luck, and there was more than enough—of optimism and generosity, of blue sky, of sweetness—for everyone. Even me.

A kindergartner was jabbing her finger toward a homemade chocolate cake, three layers high. It was listing a little to one side, its tilted surface thickly smeared with soft dark frosting, multicolored sprinkles showered with impetuous, unrestrained abandon over the whole thing: the unmistakable handiwork of someone's cherished child, the proof of love's indulgence.

"That one's mine," the kindergartner crowed.

I leaned down to her, lowering my voice. "Is it okay if I take it? It's beautiful, and it looks delicious."

She beamed.

"I choose chocolate cake," I said to the kids at the table, my entourage, my well-wishers. "Chocolate cake has never let me down." I fit my fingers under the cake's cardboard plate as a fourth grader lifted it from the table, handing it to me with a dignified bow, with the solemnity of a Nobel Prize judge.

Holding my cake, I watched the kindergartner bolt across the meadow, shouting for her mother. From a distance I saw the exchange: the mother crouching down to listen to her daughter's news, the little girl pointing at me, her face flushed with pride. My hands were full of cake, I couldn't wave. Instead I held the cake up high, the prize it was, and the mother pumped her daughter's fist into the air like a champion athlete's, both of them beaming.

And then I saw my family heading toward me. There they were, my redemption: my effusive husband limping from a bum knee with his shirt buttoned askew, flailing his arms to get my attention. My tall eighteen-year-old son, still a dreamer, floating on the euphoria of his recent college acceptance. My songbird ten-year-old daughter— Celeste *Erice* Kamiya, she tells people—shellacked head to toe with whipped cream. Even our sweet-faced shambling dog was there, beating his stub of tail.

"Hey, you won," said my family.

"I did," I answered, gazing at them, still surprised, my fingers covered with chocolate frosting. "I did win. I can't believe it—it was so easy."

ACKNOWLEDGMENTS

THOUGH THE MAJORITY OF THE RECIPES IN THIS BOOK ARE MY OWN, or passed down from family and friends, or so tinkered with over time that they little resemble their origins, I'd like to thank and acknowledge the following sources:

I bow to my cake ally and friend Sylvia Thompson for her Chocolate Cake Warm from the Oven (published in *Feasts and Friends: Recipes from a Lifetime,* North Point Press, 1988)—the moving spirit behind Plenty of Chocolate Cake with Mocha Frosting, for which I nudged Sylvia's ladylike restraint toward my own gluttonous tastes.

The versatile recipes for crostatas, in particular the Apple-Crisp Crostata, in *Cucina Simpatica* (HarperCollins, 1991) by Johanne Killeen and George Germon, owners of Al Forno restaurant in Providence, Rhode Island, form the basis for my own Free-form Crostatas with Crumble Topping. My family's favorite recipe for fresh fruit pies since our first visit to Al Forno when my children were small, this adaptation reflects my refinements over the years.

Paul Prudhomme's spectacular Spiced Pecan Cake with Pecan Frosting, which over twenty-five years I have altered, with, I hope, the delicacy of a jeweler, to create a version I can call my own Spiced Pecan Birthday Cake, was published in *Chef Paul Prudhomme's Louisiana Kitchen* (William Morrow, 1984).

I would also like to thank Jay Zynczak and his family for permission to include the lyrics of the Free Design's "Love You" in this book, and Russell Hoban and his agent and publisher, David Higham Associates and HarperCollins, for permission to quote Frances's "Lorna Doone, Last Cookie Song" as well as lines from *Bread and Jam for Frances,* *A Baby Sister for Frances,* and *A Birthday for Frances.*

Thanks are due to the following publications, where earlier versions of some of the material included in the chapters named below first appeared: *Bad Girls: 26 Writers Misbehave,* edited by Ellen Sussman ("The German Club Picnic"); *Ladies' Home Journal* ("Make Believe"); *Readerville Journal* ("Anna Karenina"); *Salon* ("Let Them Eat Cake," "Centrifugal Force," "Strawberry Milkshake"); and *San Francisco Chronicle Sunday Magazine* ("Treats and Threats").

I extend my gratitude to my cake allies and tasters past and continuing, with a whispered apology to those who sampled recipes that, for good reason, did not make it into this book: Marni Corbett and Andrew Davis, Arden Corbett, Chris Myers and Hal Pollard, Drew Beattie, the entire Kamiya and Alford families, Susan Faludi and Russ Rymer, Daphne de Marneffe, Ruth Lopez, Susan Straight, Beth Kephart, Emma King, Tom Centolella, Ed Lopez, Christina Koenig, Kelly Campbell-Hinshaw, Camille Peri, Tacy Gaede, the Cliff family, the Nelsons, Tobias Keller, and Ian von Franckenstein.

Thank you to Sylvia Brownrigg and Mary Pols, my Kitchen Cabinet—first and second and third readers, and stalwart friends. And again to Katherine Whitney and Farhad Farzaneh, Leyla and Kian, for their loving sustenance, both corporeal and spiritual.

Thank you to LuAnn Walther, for your compassionate ear and for urging me on from the start. And to Ellen Levine, for too much to list but more than anything for your unwavering faith in me. And to Beth Rashbaum, the joy of an editor every writer—and editor!—dreams of working with.

Heartfelt appreciation goes out to all the people, named and not, who appear in this book.

I offer loving thanks to my family for their generosity: Bill Moses and Tish Lee, John and Marina Moses, Nancy Moses and Goldie and Adele, and my mother, Kathleen Wagner. And to Gary, Zachary, and Celeste, no amount of thanks will ever suffice.

Though she does not appear elsewhere in these pages, this book was inspired by my dear friend Diane, the late biographer Diane Middlebrook, whose appetite for life, genius for friendship, and radiant mind and spirit continue to sweeten the memories and days of everyone who knew her. Thank you, Diane. Smooches.

ABOUT THE AUTHOR

KATE MOSES is the author of the internationally acclaimed *Wintering: A Novel of Sylvia Plath,* translated into a dozen languages and recipient of the Janet Heidinger Kafka Prize. She is also the coeditor of two popular anthologies of essays on motherhood, *Because I Said So: 33 Mothers Write About Children, Sex, Men, Aging, Faith, Race & Themselves* and the nationally bestselling *Mothers Who Think: Tales of Real-Life Parenthood,* which won an American Book Award. She lives in San Francisco.

For more of Kate's stories, recipes, and baking tips,
visit the *Cakewalk* blog at www.katemoses.com.

ABOUT THE TYPE

This book was set in Fournier, a typeface named for Pierre Simon Fournier,
the youngest son of a French printing family. He started out engraving woodblocks
and large capitals, then moved on to fonts of type. In 1736 he began his own foundry
and made several important contributions in the field of type design; he is said to
have cut 147 alphabets of his own creation. Fournier is probably best remembered
as the designer of St. Augustine Ordinaire, a face that served as the model for
Monotype's Fournier, which was released in 1925.